I0191839

GHOSTS OF WAR

GHOSTS OF WAR

NAZI OCCUPATION AND ITS AFTERMATH IN SOVIET BELARUS

FRANZISKA EXELER

CORNELL UNIVERSITY PRESS
Ithaca and London

First published 2022 by Cornell University Press

Printed in the United States of America

Library of Congress Cataloging-in-Publication Data

Names: Exeler, Franziska, author.
Title: Ghosts of war : Nazi occupation and its aftermath in Soviet Belarus / Franziska Exeler.
Description: Ithaca, [New York] : Cornell University Press, 2022. | Includes bibliographical references and index.
Identifiers: LCCN 2021026033 (print) | LCCN 2021026034 (ebook) | ISBN 9781501762734 (hardcover) | ISBN 9781501762741 (pdf) | ISBN 9781501762758 (epub)
Subjects: LCSH: World War, 1939–1945—Social aspects—Belarus. | World War, 1939–1945—Influence. | Belarus—History—German occupation, 1941–1944. | Belarus—Social conditions—20th century. | Belarus—Politics and government—20th century.
Classification: LCC D802.B38 E94 2022 (print) | LCC D802.B38 (ebook) | DDC 940.53/478—dc23
LC record available at https://lccn.loc.gov/2021026033
LC ebook record available at https://lccn.loc.gov/2021026034

Contents

Figures

Maps

Figures

Acknowledgments

This book has benefited tremendously from the intellectual guidance, conversations, and support that I was fortunate to receive over the course of my research and writing. The years at Princeton University were incredibly formative. I am very grateful for the mentorship of Stephen Kotkin, who always encouraged me to think more broadly about my manuscript. His incisive commentary and unrelenting support of the book have been invaluable along the way. I am also very grateful for the helpful input that I received from the other members of my dissertation committee, Jan T. Gross, Ekaterina Pravilova, and Amir Weiner.

I could not have imagined a better place than the International Center for the History and Sociology of World War II and Its Consequences at the Higher School of Economics in Moscow to further develop this book, and I thank Oleg Budnitskii, Liudmila Novikova, and my other colleagues at the center for providing such an exceptional, intellectually stimulating place. A Max Weber fellowship at the European University Institute provided the perfect place to exchange ideas with colleagues.

For the last several years, the Center for History and Economics at Magdalene College and King's College at the University of Cambridge has been the most wonderful intellectual home and an incredibly supportive environment to think broadly across the fields about questions of law and society. I am deeply thankful to Emma Rothschild for her trust, her insightful commentary on my work, and her inspiring mentorship. I am also very grateful to Sunil Amrith, Tim Harper, Gareth Stedman Jones, Inga Huld Markan, and David Todd. Curating the *Invisible Histories* project with Diana Kim continues to be a tremendous pleasure. At Free University Berlin, where I have taught since 2016, the Global History team constitutes a big source of inspiration. I thank my colleagues, especially Samuël Coghe, Sebastian Conrad, Valeska Huber, Christoph Kalter, Timothy Nunan, Ulrike Schaper, Thuc Linh Nguyen Vu, and Minu Haschemi Yekani, for long discussions, helpful comments, and in general for being such great colleagues.

I am very grateful for discussions with colleagues and fellow historians who at different stages of writing provided comments and help: Felix Ackermann, Tarik Cyril Amar, Seth Bernstein, Jeffrey Burds, Pey-Yi Chu, Michael David-Fox, Martin Dean, Sofia Dyak, Cristina Florea, Mayhill C. Fowler, Michael Gordin, Yoram Gorlizki, Jochen Hellbeck, Ulrike Huhn, Kristy Ironside, Ilya Kukulin, Elidor Mëhilli, Dirk Moses, Iryna Ramanava, Per Anders Rudling, David Shearer, Iryna Sklokina, Leonid Smilovitsky, Timothy Snyder, and Lynne Viola, with special thanks to Rachel Applebaum and Jared McBride. Aleksei Martiniuk made it possible for me to be affiliated with the Republican Institute of Higher Education in Minsk, which in turn enabled me to spend a year in Belarus. In Minsk, I thank Anatol' Vialiki and Siarhei Novikaŭ for helping me locate archival materials and for so generously sharing their knowledge of Belarusian history with me. Ales' Smalianchuk offered incisive comments at a critical juncture, for which I am very grateful. Our conversations in Grodno and Slonim were among the highlights for me that year. Aleksandr Litin introduced me to the Jewish community and history of Mogilev, and the wonderful Raisa Krival'tsevich opened her home for me both in Minsk and Novogrudok. I am deeply grateful to my interview partners who shared their experiences of the war and postwar years with me, and I thank Farid Berrashed, Elena Dokunova, Dina Fainberg, Raisa Krival'tsevich, Aleksandr Litin, Aleksei Martiniuk, Vadim Shmygov, Vladimir Sidortsov, Ales' Smalianchuk, Leonid Smilovitsky, and Aleks Solod for their help in establishing contact with them. I am grateful to Racheli Yahav and her family for granting me permission to reproduce an image of her mother, Chasia Bornstein-Bielicka, in this book. At Free University Berlin, I would like to thank Marjory Ruiz for her editing skills. I am very grateful to my colleague Siarhei Bohdan for so generously sharing with me his expertise in Belarusian history and helping me with transliterations from Belarusian.

One of the best things about Princeton is its international community, and I treasure the friendships I made on campus. The weekly German-Russian conversations with Michael Meerson are much missed. To Catherine Abou-Nemeh, Nimisha Barton, Rohit De, Rotem Geva, Rohit Lamba, Arijeet Pal, Ronny Regev, Margaret Schotte, and Mareike Stoll—thank you so much for your friendship! I am very thankful to my friends in Berlin and elsewhere, Phillip Ayoub, Oren Bar-Tal, Ursula Gießmann, Wolfram Knäbich, Karsten Krauskopf, and Caroline Marburger, for keeping me sane.

This book is based on many months of research in more than a dozen archives, and I was fortunate to be able to draw on the kind and knowledgeable assistance of numerous historians, archivists, and librarians. I thank the staff at the different archives and libraries in Belarus, Russia, Israel, Germany,

Poland, Ukraine, and the United States. I also thank the organizers of the many workshops, conferences, and panels at which I had the privilege to present my work over the years. The research for this book was supported by grants and fellowships from Princeton University; the Princeton Institute for International and Regional Studies; the Social Science Research Council (International Dissertation Research Fellowship, with funds from the Andrew W. Mellon Foundation); the Max Weber Program at the European University Institute; the International Center for the History and Sociology of World War II and Its Consequences at the Higher School of Economics in Moscow; the Programme on Exchanges of Economic, Legal, and Political Ideas, supported by the Andrew W. Mellon Foundation, at the Centre for History and Economics, Magdalene College and King's College at the University of Cambridge; and Free University Berlin.

At Cornell University Press, I had the privilege to work with Roger Haydon, for whose insightful comments and support of the book I am very grateful. I would also very much like to thank Emily Andrew, Allegra Martschenko, Mary Kate Murphy, and Carolyn J. Pouncy for their editorial expertise and support of the book. I am incredibly grateful to the two reviewers (of whom Lynne Viola later revealed herself to have been one) for their very helpful comments. Mike Bechthold expertly drew the maps. Parts of the fourth chapter have been published as "The Ambivalent State: Determining Guilt in the Post-World War II Soviet Union," *Slavic Review* 75, no. 3 (2016): 606–29. Parts of the fifth chapter have been published as "What Did You Do during the War? Personal Responses to the Aftermath of Nazi Occupation," *Kritika: Explorations in Russian and Eurasian History* 17, no. 4 (2016): 805–35. Parts of the afterword have been published as "Nazi Atrocities, International Criminal Law, and Soviet War Crimes Trials: The Soviet Union and the Global Moment of Post-Second World War Justice," in *The New Histories of International Criminal Law: Retrials*, ed. Immi Tallgren and Thomas Skouteris (Oxford: Oxford University Press, 2019), 189–219.

And finally, to my family—my sister Dorothea and Steve with Rona and Johan; Barbara and Michael; Kristen; Friederike and Jonas with Jurek—thank you so much for your support! I am deeply grateful to my parents, Ingrid and Ulrich, who always encouraged me to follow my interests and to do what I love to do. Lotte and Paul's arrival into this world brought a new perspective to the book; accompanying them on their journey fills my heart with so much joy. The biggest thanks of all, however, goes to Jasper for his support, love, and unrelenting encouragement over the years—as questions turned into an idea and, eventually, into a book.

Note on Language, Transliteration, and Terms

In this multilingual region, where every town's name existed in several versions depending on which language one spoke, the spelling of places and names is always a difficult question. With the exception of names familiar in English (such as Moscow, Kiev, or Białystok), I usually use the official name that a town or province had at the particular time that I am referring to, for example Vil'na province (instead of Vilnius province) when it was part of the Russian empire, or Nowogródek province when it was part of interwar Poland. For Soviet Belarus itself, the situation is a bit trickier. Formally, the interwar republic had four state languages (Belarusian, Russian, Yiddish, and Polish), but the main languages in which residents of the republic interacted with the state were Belarusian and Russian. In the late 1930s, Moscow began to put a stronger emphasis on Russian as the *lingua franca* of the Soviet empire. By the time of the Second World War, Russian had become the primary language of internal party-state documents; in the postwar decades, its predominance in official and private communication further increased.

Today's Belarus has two state languages, Belarusian and Russian. For a variety of different reasons, including a lack of state support for the Belarusian language, Russian has come to be almost the sole language of communication, at least in the cities. Still, for many people, it is no contradiction to self-define as Belarusian but to speak Russian most or all of the time, whether in private or in public. For these reasons (and because readers outside of Belarus will be more familiar with Russian than Belarusian town names, with, say, Mogilev instead of Mahilioŭ), I have chosen a pragmatic and yet hybrid approach, not quite unlike lingual reality in both Soviet Belarus and present-day Belarus. I speak of the Belarusian Soviet Socialist Republic (BSSR) or, in short, of Soviet Belarus (*Savetskaia Belarus'* in Belarusian) and not of Soviet Belorussia (*Sovetskaia Belorussiia* in Russian). I also translate the Russian *belorusski* into English as "Belarusian." Otherwise, though, I use the

Russian names for towns and other geographical places. In the case of villages, I provide either the Belarusian or the Russian name, depending on the original source. The second map provides the Belarusian and Russian names of the republic's largest towns.

In the case of personal names, I either use the one that is given in the source (which means that many Belarusian names will have been Russianized in party-state documents) or the one that the author self-identifies with. To give an example: in the case of the well-known writer Vasil' Bykaŭ, I use his Belarusian name, as he clearly self-identified as a Belarusian who spoke and wrote in his first language. (In Soviet-era Russian-language publications, Bykaŭ's name was often rendered as Vasil' Bykov, in a Belarusian-Russian hybrid close to the original.) In other cases—for example, Vladimir Khartanovich, who grew up in a Belarusian-speaking village west of Minsk but published his memoirs in Russian—I decided not to Belarusianize his name, as that would have gone against his own linguistic choice and lead to confusion with the sources. For transliterations from Belarusian and Russian, I have used the Library of Congress system. All translations are my own.

A note on Soviet terms: In postwar Soviet Belarus, the oblast (*voblasts'* in Belarusian, *oblast'* in Russian) was the largest administrative unit below the level of the republic. It can best be translated as region. The next level down was the district (*raion* in both Belarusian and Russian). The Politburo (*politbiuro*) of the Central Committee of the All-Union Communist Party (since 1952 called the Communist Party of the Soviet Union) in Moscow represented the leadership of the Soviet Union. Its corresponding version at the level of the republic was the Buro (*biuro*) of the Central Committee of the Communist Party of Belarus, headed by a first secretary. Subordinated to the Buro were the regional party committee (*oblastnoi komitet*, abbreviated *obkom*), the district party committee (*raionnyi komitet*, abbreviated *raikom*), and the city party committee (*gorodskoi komitet*, abbreviated *gorkom*). The Sovnarkom of the USSR (*Sovet narodnykh komissarov SSSR*, the Council of People's Commissars), renamed the Council of Ministers in 1946, headed the executive branch of the Soviet party-state. Its corresponding version at the level of the republic was the Sovnarkom (since 1946, the Council of Ministers) of the Belarusian Soviet Socialist Republic. Subordinated to the republic Sovnarkom were the regional executive committee (*oblastnoi ispolnitel'nyi komitet*, abbreviated *oblispolkom*), the district executive committee (*raionnyi ispolnitel'nyi komitet*, abbreviated *raiispolkom*), and the city executive committee (*gorodskoi ispolnitel'nyi komitet*, abbreviated *gorispolkom*).

Over the years, the Soviet Union's state security organs underwent many complex organizational changes and shifting divisions of tasks. In 1934, the political police, the GPU-OGPU, was abolished and its functions transferred to the NKVD, the All-Union People's Commissariat for Internal Affairs. The NKVD was briefly divided into NKVD and NKGB in 1941, subsequently reunited, and separated again in 1943. In 1946, when the people's commissariats were renamed ministries, the two agencies were renamed MVD and MGB. In the book, I usually specify which agency I am speaking of, but I also use the shorthand "state security organs" to refer to both NKVD / MVD and NKGB / MGB, as their tasks overlapped in practice. Following further organizational changes after Stalin's death, from 1954 on most of their responsibilities were taken over by the newly formed Committee for State Security, best known as the KGB.

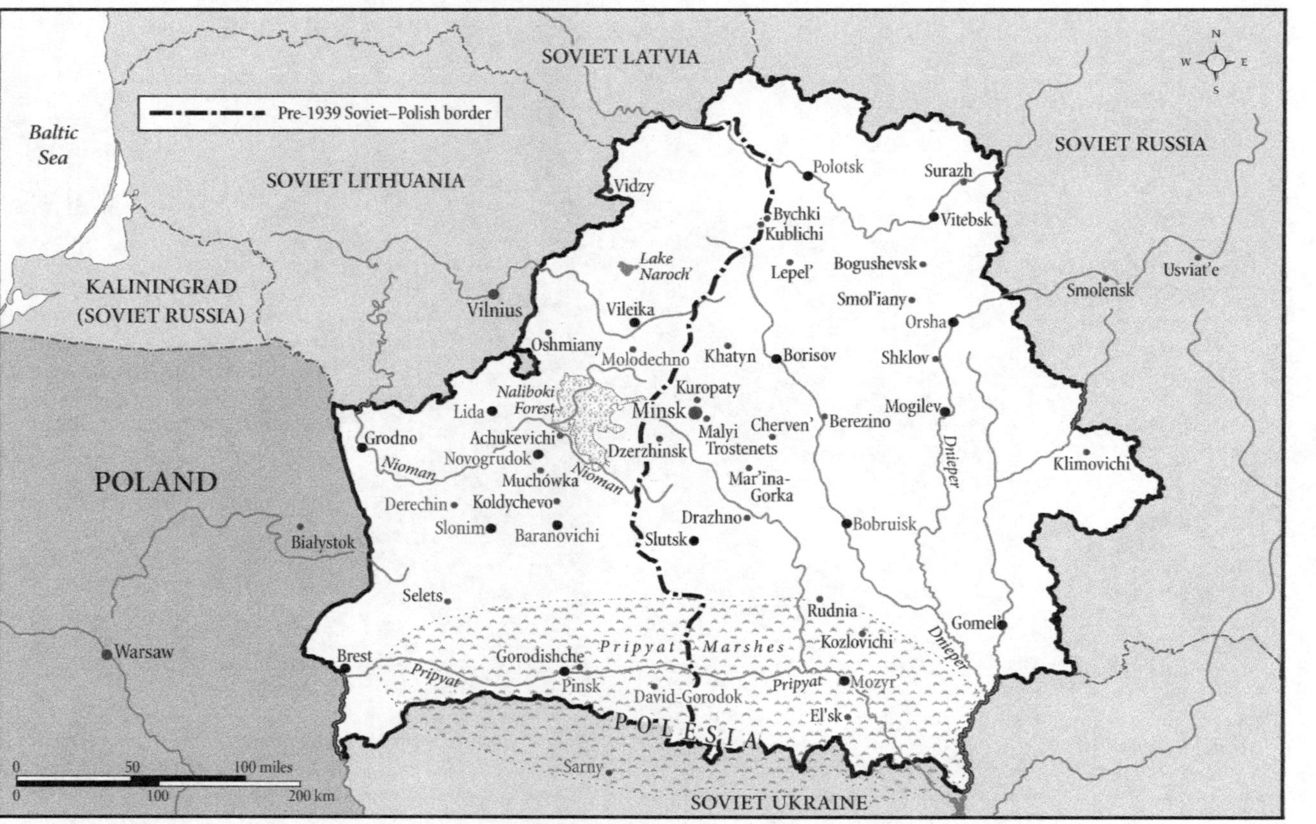

Map 1. Soviet Belarus in its post-1945 borders with some of the towns, villages, and other places that are important for this book. To this day, much of Belarus is covered in forests and marshes, but except for the Pripyat marshes and the Naliboki forest, these are not shown on the map. Map by Mike Bechthold.

Introduction

Truth, Guilt, and Justice in an Illiberal State

On June 22, 1941, Ol'ga Bembel'-Dedok woke up late. The previous evening, she had attended a theater performance in Minsk, where she lived with her husband, Andrei, and two children, Klara and Oleg. As she stood in the kitchen, preparing porridge for her young son, a neighbor came running over: "What are you doing? Don't you know? Turn on the radio! It's war!" At first, Bembel'-Dedok could not believe it: "War, that seemed too abstract." On the radio, they were playing military marches. Bembel'-Dedok continued to listen to the radio: "Like a machine, I was feeding little Oleg and listening to the story about the invasion at night, about Molotov's speech. Slowly, the truth was beginning to dawn on me."[1]

Earlier that day, the Germans and their allies had launched Operation Barbarossa. Roughly three million soldiers—most of them German but also Austrian, Romanian, Hungarian, Italian, Slovak, and Finnish troops—crossed the border into the Soviet Union. Their advance was accompanied by the Luftwaffe's aerial bombardment of cities and towns. The invasion caught the Soviet leadership by surprise, and in the first weeks, the Axis troops made large territorial gains. Within days, Army Group North pushed through the three Baltic countries, heading toward northwestern Russia. In early September 1941, it laid siege to Leningrad. Army Group South aimed to bring Ukraine, the southern parts of Russia, and the oil-rich Caucasus under its control. Its troops moved more slowly than those to the north, but by early

September, they had reached Kiev. On September 19, the largest Ukrainian city came under German rule.[2]

Meanwhile, Army Group Center marched through Belarus and western Russia, its eyes set on Moscow, the Soviet capital. Western Belarusian cities like Brest and Grodno fell within the first days of war, Minsk itself was conquered on June 28, and eastern Belarusian towns like Bobruisk and Borisov soon followed within days.[3] As German planes dropped bombs on cities and towns, fires spread, and panic and chaos broke out. In Grodno, Chasia Bornstein-Bielicka and her family awoke in the middle of the night to a city on fire. The noise was deafening: "Tanks fleeing, motors roaring and steel treads clattering over cobblestones. Shutters slamming against the walls with each bomb that fell. Windowpanes shattering against eardrums for hours on end."[4] Zofia Brzozowska, who lived with her family on a small estate not far from Novogrudok, hid in the basement for several days. When the family reemerged, they saw clouds of smoke over the town. "German troops appeared on the street."[5] By the end of the month, the German army already occupied more than half of Belarus. Among the places that the Wehrmacht conquered at the beginning of July was Litman Mor's hometown, David-Gorodok, in southwestern Belarus and Vasil' Bykaŭ's home village, Bychki, in the northeastern part of the republic.[6] For a while, the German advance slowed down, making it possible for some civilians to flee to the safety of the Soviet rear. Soon, however, Army Group Center continued its march east. By the end of August, all of Belarus found itself under German occupation.

Germany's attack on the Soviet Union marked the beginning of the single most destructive military campaign in history. During the years of war and occupation, some worlds were completely eradicated, foremost the world of East European Jewry, while others underwent fundamental change. The mass murder of the Jews—alongside the enslavement of the Slavic population, the economic exploitation of the occupied territories, and the destruction of communism as a political system—lay at the core of Nazi ideology. The German occupation regime was a regime of death and destruction, and millions of Soviet civilians and prisoners of war suffered, and died, under Nazi rule. It was also, however, a regime that depended on the limited involvement of some. In the occupied territories, the German authorities pursued different strategies toward different population groups. While Jews were singled out for destruction, the Slavic population was treated with a mix of brutality and co-optation. For civilians in occupied territory, in turn, it was impossible not to come in contact with the occupation regime, and willingly or unwillingly, some people became complicit or entangled in Nazi crimes. In regions where Soviet partisan warfare developed, individuals were also increasingly faced with demands not just from the German but from the partisan side, too, neither of which could they fulfill without fearing punishment at the hands of the other. As the Red Army began to reconquer the territory and push German troops from the western regions of the Soviet Union, one question hovered over encounters between the returning Soviet authorities and those who had lived under Nazi rule, between soldiers and family members, reevacuees and colleagues, Holocaust survivors and their neighbors: what did you do during the war?

This is a book about the ghosts of war: about the choices that people made under German occupation, the choices they were forced to make, and their political, social, legal, and personal repercussions.[7] It is a book about extreme moral circumstances, about the intense pressures and constraints within which individuals had to act, and the many reasons why they came to be associated with the German or the Soviet side (or both or trapped in between). It is also a book about different understandings of what constituted guilt and complicity, about the search for truth and justice in the aftermath of Nazi occupation, and the ways in which this process affected the rebuilding of Soviet state authority, personal lives, and the creation of war narratives. The literature on the Eastern Front, with its heavy emphasis on German-language sources only, fills many bookshelves. In comparison, studies that explore the aftermath of the monumental Nazi-Soviet war are still few. *Ghosts of War* traces the fate of local communities torn apart by occupation; shows how individuals sought retribution, justice, revenge, or assistance from their neighbors and courts; and assesses the role of Soviet party-state officials in the processes of retribution and reconstruction. It uncovers the many absences, silences, and conflicts that were never resolved, the truths that could only be spoken in private, yet it also investigates the extent to which individuals at once accommodated, contested, and reshaped official war memory. It is often assumed that in societies that experienced war, occupation, or violent conflict, the act of seeking justice and accountability contributes to the development of free public spheres and democratic societies (a process also known as transitional justice).[8] In contrast, this book shows how efforts at "confronting the past" played out within, and at times through, a dictatorship like the Soviet Union.

Geographically, the focus is on the Belarusian Soviet Socialist Republic (BSSR)—in short, Soviet Belarus—an East European borderland that was particularly affected by the Second World War. With its multiethnic and multilingual population, Belarus was one of the more than a dozen Soviet republics that, taken together, constituted the Soviet Union.[9] Like the other Soviet republics, it was not an independent state but subordinated to the larger Union structure and ultimately the Politburo, the Soviet leadership in Moscow. Catholics, Orthodox Christians, and Jews; speakers of Belarusian, Yiddish, Polish, and Russian; those who identified with one nationality or ethnicity and those who considered themselves primarily locals—all called this region their home.

Soviet Belarus is often thought of as a remote place, a forgotten backwater overshadowed by its bigger neighbors Ukraine and Russia. Yet what happened here during and in the aftermath of the Second World War transformed Belarusian, Jewish, Polish, and Russian history as much as it shaped Soviet and German history. Like few other places, the republic encapsulated the extremes of twentieth-century Europe. Created in 1919 out of the turmoil of war and revolution (and reestablished a year later), during the interwar years the Bolsheviks subjected the population of Belarus, like the rest of the Soviet Union, to violent transformations of its social fabric, political structure, and economic ways of life.[10] In the fall of 1939, following the Hitler-Stalin Pact, the Soviet Union invaded and then annexed eastern Poland. As a result, Soviet Belarus doubled its territory and population. During the war, this westward shift of the Soviet Union's borders was confirmed at the 1943 Tehran Conference. With the exception of most of the Białystok region and a small part of the Brest region, which were handed back to Poland in 1945, postwar Soviet Belarus now consisted of two almost equally large halves: eastern Belarus, the older Soviet part with the capital Minsk, and western Belarus, formerly northeastern Poland.[11]

In June 1941, Berlin broke the pact with Moscow and attacked the Soviet Union. By the end of August 1941, all of Soviet Belarus found itself under German rule. During the ensuing three years of Nazi occupation, the republic became a main site of the Holocaust. It was also at the center of Soviet partisan warfare against the Germans, and thus at the center of Nazi-Soviet total war. Historically, the Eastern Front is often (mis)remembered as a war between Germany and Russia—but the brunt of fighting and occupation was actually borne by the non-Russian western regions of the Soviet Union. Of all the Soviet republics, indeed of all European countries, Belarus suffered proportionally the highest human losses: About 1.7–2.1 million people, or 19–22 percent of the population that by June 1941 lived in the territories that would constitute post-1945 Soviet Belarus, were killed or died as a result of the war.[12] This included at least 700,000 Red Army soldiers from Belarus who died at the front or in German captivity, and almost the entire Jewish population of the republic, an estimated 500,000–671,000 people. As part of so-called antipartisan campaigns, the Germans also razed approximately 9,200 villages to the ground, more than elsewhere in Nazi-occupied Europe, and killed up to 345,000 civilians—some of them Jews, but the overwhelming majority non-Jewish rural residents. The Soviet partisans in Belarus lost at least 37,378 people, but probably many more, and killed at least 17,431 people, but probably many more, in their own retributive measures.[13]

While German rule over Soviet Belarus ended in the summer of 1944, and ultimately the war in May 1945, those who survived were not able to settle down soon. Nazi occupation brought tremendous death and destruction throughout the western regions of the Soviet Union, and Belarus was among the hardest-hit places. Most cities lay in ruins, entire rural districts had been burned down, and large parts of the population were uprooted or displaced. Massive war-induced migration and displacement, combined with a Polish-Soviet population exchange from 1944 to 1946, meant that hundreds of thousands of people were moving into, out of, within, and through the republic, trying to get home or trying to avoid just that. Many of the early confrontations with people's wartime choices thus took place at a time when the Soviet state was trying to reestablish its power amid a population in flux—and over a republic that was in many respects still divided into two parts: eastern Belarus, which had been Soviet for two decades before the war, and western Belarus (formerly northeastern Poland), which had by 1944 been longer under German than under Soviet rule. What this means is that it is impossible to understand the repercussions of people's wartime choices without recognizing how prewar Soviet legacies affected individual choices under Nazi rule, and how people's experiences with the Germans in turn affected how individuals related to the returning Soviets. Consequently, the book begins at the turn of the twentieth century and extends from the war years into the postwar years. With its focus on individual choices in the most extreme moral circumstances, *Ghosts of War* conceives of Soviet Belarus as both a historical place and a lens onto larger questions of universal humanity. The comparison between Belarus and the other western republics of the Soviet Union that were under Nazi occupation, and the comparison between the republic's eastern and western parts, is woven into the main narrative. The book ends in the 1960s, yet questions of memory take it all the way to the present day.

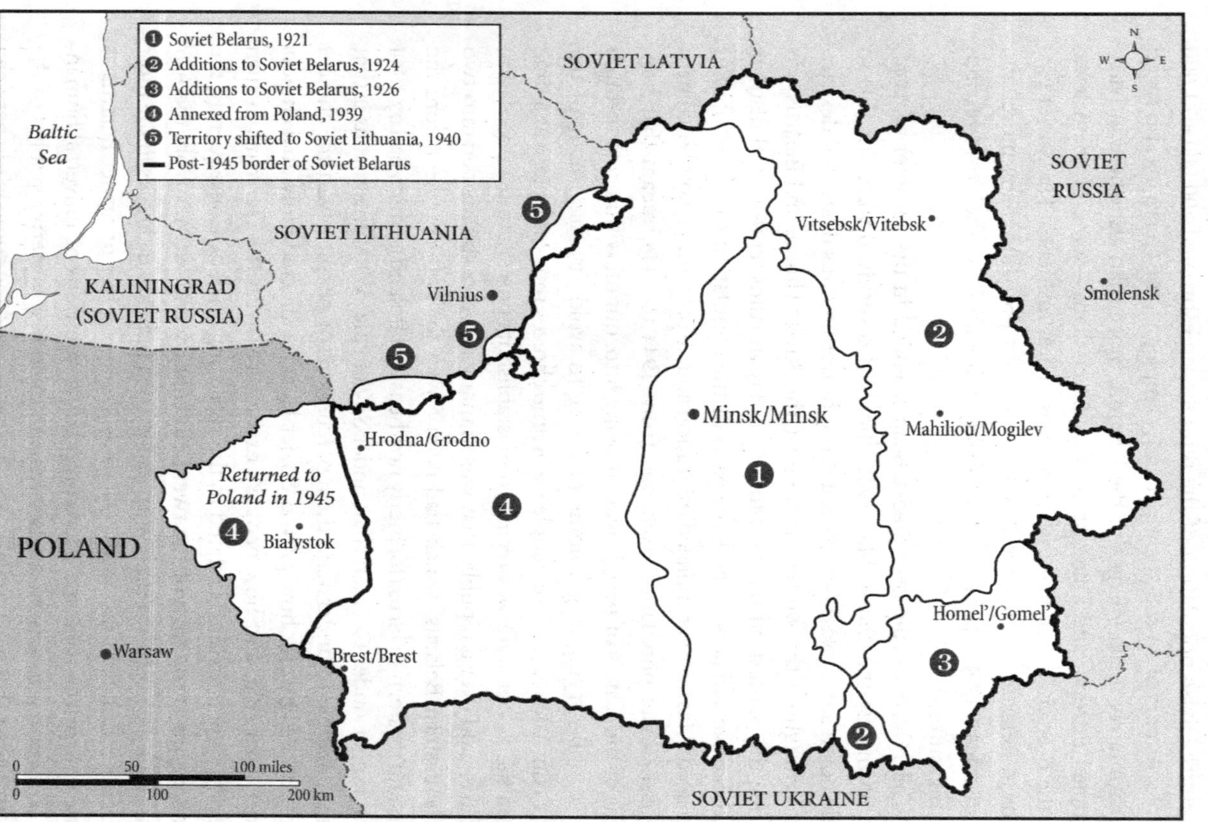

MAP 2. Territorial changes of Soviet Belarus, 1921–1945. Map by Mike Bechthold.

Wartime Choices

In all societies that find themselves under foreign occupation or in the midst of civil war, everyday acts can suddenly acquire immense moral significance. Seemingly simple choices—whether to continue working at a particular job or to provide strangers with food—can have far-reaching consequences. Office clerks, who literally remain at the same desk, now find their position incorporated into the occupation regime's administration, thereby becoming entangled in crimes. The strangers asking for food turn out to be partisans who can interpret the denial of their request as an act of disloyalty.[14] In Nazi-occupied Soviet territory, the situation for locals was such that contact with the occupation regime, whatever form it took and whatever choices it triggered, was unavoidable; carving out a niche in which one could hope to keep one's prewar life intact was impossible. In regions under both military and civilian rule, the German administration depended heavily on the employment of Soviet citizens, and in each district, Soviet citizens were appointed as town and district mayors. The Germans also created local police forces, which were staffed with Soviet citizens and subordinated to higher German police or military organs. In particular, in the countryside—where the German presence was, apart from large-scale punitive campaigns, scarce—the local police did much of the everyday legwork, effectively representing the Nazi regime in the localities. As the German authorities kept the organizational structure of the Soviet administration's lower levels (cities and rural districts) intact, many who had worked as, for example, office clerks in a Soviet city administration continued to work in the same positions under the Germans.[15]

It is impossible to write about the choices that individuals make under foreign occupation without writing about "collaboration." The meaning of that term, though, continues to spark much debate. Attempts at defining collaboration are often met with the concern that the notion fails to adequately capture the complexities of wartime reality. Local contact and involvement with the Germans occurred in a multitude of different forms, of which some carried much graver consequences than others. A town mayor or policeman who held power over life and death was both physically and morally in a very different position from someone who worked as a journalist for a German-sponsored newspaper. Some individuals—in particular, town mayors and policemen—were in direct contact with their German superiors, but in many other cases, contact was much more mediated and indirect, as was the case with teachers and factory managers. The motivations underlying people's actions were similarly diverse, covering a wide range of different, even conflicting reasons. And what to make of coerced engagement, such as when someone who had been forcefully recruited into police service became complicit in German crimes?[16] In my understanding of how local involvement with the occupiers came about, I follow Jan T. Gross in his description of it as an "occupier-driven phenomenon"—that is to say, one that depended on the roles that the occupiers assigned to the occupied (with or without local political autonomy, as active participants in murder and expropriation or not), and on the corresponding offers that they made. People's engagement with the Germans—its logic, appeal, self-justification, and social base—thus emerged in each country "at the intersection between the occupier's intent and the occupied's perception about the range of options at their disposal." This means that in each particular case, the meaning and character of involvement with the occupiers have to be carefully circumscribed in time, or else the terms on which it occurred cannot be properly understood.[17] For these reasons, this book is not concerned with determining whether certain behavior would merit the label "collaboration" (contingent, of course, on one's definition thereof). Rather, I am interested in tracing the reasons and motivations behind people's actions, and how these in turn were perceived and assessed by others after the war.

What choices the population in the western regions of the Soviet Union made during the war, however, was not only a question of how they responded to the options offered by the Germans. It was also a question of how they related to Soviet power. In the literature, the impact that Soviet rule had on people's wartime choices is discussed primarily with respect to relations between local non-Jews and Jews. In the summer of 1941, during the transition from Soviet to German authority, a wave of violence against Jews swept through the regions that the Soviets had annexed in 1939 and 1940. The perpetrators were usually local civilians or a mix of civilians and German-appointed local policemen. Some violence was committed before German troops arrived in a particular region or district, while other violence was committed with their direct participation or presence. Yet other pogroms took place after the Germans had already shown themselves in a given locality but then left shortly thereafter, leaving the town without clear authority for a few days. Just as German participation varied from town to town, so did the level of local anti-Jewish violence. In terms of intensity, scope, and brutality, it was highest in western Ukraine (eastern Galicia and Volhynia), in the Białystok region (from 1939 to 1945 the westernmost part of western Belarus), and in the Romanian-administered regions of northern Bukovina and Bessarabia. Mass killings of Jews with local participation also took place in Lithuania.

In Latvia and western Belarus, excluding the Białystok region, the level of local violence toward Jews was much lower. In Estonia, anti-Jewish local violence seems to have hardly taken place, probably because the republic's Jewish community (which was numerically much smaller compared to Ukraine, Belarus, Poland, or Lithuania) had mostly managed to flee before the arrival of the Wehrmacht. In the old Soviet territories that came under German occupation (eastern Belarus, eastern Ukraine, and parts of Russia), local pogroms against Jews during the summer of 1941 appear to have been almost nonexistent.[18]

The outburst of such personal, communal violence continues to puzzle historians and has led to much heated public debate in Poland and, to a lesser extent, elsewhere. One explanation for the regional variation in violence that is given in the scholarly literature is the impact that "double occupation" (first Soviet, then German) had on relations between Jews and non-Jews—namely, that the Soviet occupation and subsequent annexation of northeastern Poland in 1939 and of the Baltic countries, Bessarabia, and northern Bukovina in 1940 perpetuated the stereotypical image of Jews as supporters of communism. The pogroms in these regions during the summer of 1941 were thus motivated by a desire for revenge against those who supposedly sided with the Soviets.[19] Another explanation offered is that pogroms were most likely to break out in places with large Jewish communities that sought national equality with non-Jews. Local non-Jews perceived this as a threat to their political dominance and seized on the opportunity that the transition from Soviet to German power offered to rid themselves of their political enemies.[20] Others have argued that local violence was most intense in regions where the radical political Right had a strong base of support (as the radical Polish Right did in the Białystok region) or where radical anti-Soviet nationalist groups like the Organization of Ukrainian Nationalists were active. Correspondingly, violence was lower in regions where such radical nationalist groups were few or not organized in paramilitary formations.[21] Yet others have suggested that the absence of pogroms in the old Soviet regions attested to the success of the Soviet Union's interwar campaigns against antisemitism, and the government's efforts to achieve interethnic cooperation and societal integration.[22]

In these debates, it is conventional wisdom to assert that Soviet Belarus was different from the other western regions of the Soviet Union that were under German rule. According to this view, antisemitism was not widespread in Belarus, and the republic's non-Jewish population (implicitly understood in the debate as ethnically Belarusian) was more willing to help Jews than the population in neighboring Ukraine and Lithuania (or Poland).[23] Such claims to Belarus's exceptionalism, though, are too general to be of analytical value. Neither do they take into account variations across time and place, nor can they explain the broad spectrum of local behavior under Nazi rule.[24] As this book shows, there were indeed important regional differences between wartime Belarus and the other western republics of the Soviet Union, most notably in terms of the existence of radical nationalist groups, which were less prominent and much smaller in western Belarus (in its post-1945 borders) than in Lithuania and western Ukraine. There also existed, however, significant similarities between Belarus and the neighboring republics, above all in terms of the microdynamics of violence and the relevance of situational factors for individual behavior. Wartime Soviet Belarus was not the complete outlier, the exception from the norm. Yes, Belarus differed from Ukraine and the Baltic countries in some ways, just as western Belarus differed from eastern Belarus in some ways but not in others—and not in the ways it is commonly thought to have been different.

When the German army invaded the Soviet Union, the decisions that people in eastern and western Belarus made were initially often influenced by their prior experiences with Soviet rule, or else their relationship to the Bolsheviks. Party members or individuals who held important positions within the Soviet party-state were more likely to flee east, while many who had previously suffered under the Soviets were among those who joined the German-organized police forces. Once partisan warfare picked up in mid-1942 and civilians found themselves confronted with demands from both sides, though, people's wartime choices came to be much more determined by situational factors, including the will to survive, coercion, violence, patriotism (which was not identical with belief in communism)—or simply the proximity of one's village to either a German garrison or a Soviet partisan zone. In other words, people's decisions and their consequences varied over time, and complicity and entanglement were questions of degree. Moreover, since the partisans were by 1943 mostly people from Belarus, and since the lower organs of the German occupation regime remained overwhelmingly staffed with people from Belarus, locals found themselves fighting against other locals. In parts of western Belarus, this situation was exacerbated by the presence of the Polish Armia Krajowa (AK), and in southern Belarus, by the presence of Ukrainian nationalist formations. While members of these groups at times cooperated with the Germans (and some Polish units initially also with the Soviet partisans), in the end, the war behind the front erupted into a bloody, multidimensional conflict in which the Soviet partisans, the different nationalist partisans, and the Germans and their local representatives all fought each other—and civilians suffered greatly amid the violence.[25]

Consequently, and adapting a term coined by Lawrence L. Langer, many choices that people in occupied territory made were "choiceless choices."[26] By that I mean that when people were confronted with decisions, all options entailed a destructive effect on their personal lives, families, and local communities: for example, when a village head had to decide whether to hand over villagers as forced laborers to the German authorities and fear reprisals from the partisans, or refuse to do so and fear German collective punishment.

Saying that many choices under Nazi occupation were "choiceless choices," however, does not mean that everybody had the same choices to begin with. Although all civilians found the space within which they could act circumscribed, that space was much smaller, almost nonexistent, for Jews compared to non-Jews. Within the constraints of occupation, non-Jews had a range of options at their disposal. Some of these were far-reaching, such as volunteering to work in the German-overseen police forces or giving shelter to Jews, Red Army soldiers, and partisans and risking one's life in the process. Yet choices also included smaller, seemingly insignificant acts, such as taking furniture from a murdered Jewish neighbor's apartment or refraining from doing so. Those who were hiding others obviously tried to keep their actions secret, but many people made choices that were publicly visible and known around the neighborhood or village. As political circumstances, and thus the terms of involvement with both German authorities and partisans, changed over time, individuals reevaluated their previous choices. War, as Stathis Kalyvas has argued, is a "transformative phenomenon." The advent of war and the experience of violence transform individual preferences, choices, behavior, and identities, which are then continuously shaped and reshaped in the course of the conflict.[27]

In their behavior under Nazi occupation, the civilian population in eastern Belarus—the part that had been Soviet for more than two decades before the war—did not differ fundamentally from the civilian population in western Belarus, the part that had been annexed from Poland only in 1939. The one exception to this was the extent of local anti-Jewish violence in the summer of 1941. The level of violence was high in the Białystok region (then the westernmost part of western Belarus; from 1945 on, again part of Poland), much lower in the other regions of western Belarus, and possibly nonexistent in eastern Belarus, for which local pogroms against Jews have not been recorded. However, once the Germans began to establish their occupation regime, they could depend in both western and eastern Belarus, just like in the other western republics of the Soviet Union, on the participation of a small group of people who, primarily in their capacity as local policemen and town mayors, actively took part in the Holocaust. Similarly, in their treatment of their

Jewish neighbors, the non-Jewish civilian population in western Belarus displayed the same behavioral spectrum as in eastern Belarus, ranging from acts of rescue and providing shelter to expropriating Jewish property, blackmailing or denouncing neighbors in hiding, or even taking part in the killings.

The existence of a spectrum of human behavior, of course, does not preclude the existence of quantitative differences within it. In her comparison of the two neighboring regions Bessarabia and Transnistria (which correspond roughly to the territories of modern-day Moldova and southwestern Ukraine), Diana Dumitru found substantial differences in how the non-Jewish populations treated the regions' Jewish populations during the war. Until the Russian Revolution, Bessarabia and Transnistria were provinces of the Russian empire. During the interwar years, Bessarabia belonged to Romania, and Transnistria was part of the Soviet Union. In the summer of 1940, the Soviet Union annexed Bessarabia, but following the German invasion of the Soviet Union a year later, Romanian troops, with the help of their German ally, brought both Bessarabia and Transnistria under their control. As Dumitru has shown, in the subsequent years until the Red Army reconquered the two regions in the summer of 1944, the "civilian population in Bessarabia had a more antagonistic attitude, and the civilian population in Transnistria a more cooperative attitude toward the Jews during the Holocaust."[28] However, in the case of German-occupied Belarus—with the exception of the summer of 1941—such clear regional differences did not exist, at least not for the regions that constituted post-1945 Belarus. Where western and eastern Belarus did differ was in the type of support network that individuals could draw on. As a result of two decades of Sovietization, intercommunal relations among certain urban groups in eastern Belarus—younger people, those who no longer practiced a religion, and people who closely identified with the Soviet project—were less defined by traditional social and religious markers of identity than in western Belarus. During the war, this increased the chances that Jews in the urban centers of eastern Belarus would be able to depend on the help of non-Jewish friends or colleagues, especially if they were fellow Komsomol or Communist Party members. In this respect, higher prewar levels of interethnic integration in eastern Belarus shaped the makeup of support networks there during the war—thus reflecting a difference in how legacies of prewar Soviet rule bore on the choices that individuals in western and eastern Belarus made under Nazi occupation. It is possible that the different nature of people's support networks also translated into a numerical difference, meaning that overall, more non-Jewish urban residents in eastern Belarus were willing to help Jews than in western Belarus. However, the primary sources do not provide a conclusive picture.

If quantitative differences existed, then they would have been subtler than in the case of Transnistria and Bessarabia, where the contrast was more evident and thus probably methodologically easier to detect.[29]

The Soviet Politics of Retribution

Beginning in late 1943, the Red Army advanced into Belarusian territory; by July 1944, the republic had been reconquered in its entirety. As three years of Nazi occupation came to an end, party-state officials and refugees, demobilized soldiers and partisans, forced laborers and Holocaust survivors returned home. Among them was the prewar leadership of the republic, headed by First Secretary Panteleimon Ponomarenko (who also headed the Soviet partisan movement during the war). For the Soviet authorities, the task that lay ahead was enormous: to rebuild the Soviet state in an utterly destroyed region and a time of great flux and population movement. Especially on the lower levels of the party-state, the party leaders were faced with a dire shortage of qualified personnel. Many of those who had occupied these positions prior to the war had been killed or were unavailable in 1944, be it because they were still fighting with the Red Army or had been assigned to different jobs elsewhere in the Soviet Union. Rebuilding the Soviet state, though, was not just about the reconstruction of institutions and cadres. It was also a question of making sure that any resistance, real or imagined, would be destroyed—and it meant reclaiming authority over a region where the population was overjoyed to see Nazi occupation end, yet where many people in both western and eastern Belarus were apprehensive about the return of Soviet power as such. In turn, party leaders and state security officers were ambivalent about the local population, given its long exposure to German rule. One task therefore lay at the heart of Soviet state rebuilding, in Belarus as in the other western regions of the Soviet Union: determining what people in Nazi-occupied territory had done during the war—and punishing those the authorities considered traitors.

But who were the traitors? On July 3, 1941, Stalin addressed the Soviet people. In his speech, broadcast on the radio, he stressed that the war with Germany was no ordinary war between two armies but rather a war of the entire Soviet people against the Nazis. In the battle between good and evil, there were no gray zones. The fight against Soviet citizens in occupied territory who were said to support the Germans, Stalin warned, would be ruthless. Those deemed traitors only deserved one fate: death.[30]

That punishment would be harsh was repeated over and over again by Soviet wartime leaders. In a leaflet that was distributed by partisans in occupied Belarusian territory, Ponomarenko warned village heads, policemen, and those employed in the administration and commandant offices: "We tell you openly and frankly: your crime toward the motherland is immense, and if you continue to help the Germans, you will not escape strict punishment."[31]

During the war, the Soviet partisans dealt in their own ways with individuals considered traitors, which usually meant shooting them, sometimes including their families, thus inflicting collective punishment. Once Soviet power returned in full force, the state reclaimed its monopoly on violence, and the punishment of suspected wartime traitors was channeled into the military justice system. In absolute numbers, no country that was occupied during the Second World War prosecuted as many of its own nationals for what they had done under foreign rule as the Soviet Union.[32] From 1943 (the earliest date for which data are available) until the death of Stalin in 1953 (the latest date for which data are available), almost 260,000 of those Soviet citizens who were charged with treason were specifically accused of "treason and aiding and abetting the German occupiers" (*predatel'stvo i posobnichestvo nemetskim okkupantam*). The numbers, however, are incomplete, as the figures for 1944 are unknown. Assuming that these were as high as those for 1945, one would arrive at 308,000 individuals who, charged with treason, were specifically accused of "treason and aiding and abetting the German occupiers." The total number of prosecuted individuals was probably higher by at least a few tens of thousands, given that the Red Army began to reconquer parts of Soviet territory as early as late 1941.[33]

Unfortunately, the available statistics are incomplete; due to restricted archival access, they have to remain estimates. Still, these numbers provide a sense of the scale of the Soviet politics of retribution and allow for cross-regional comparisons. Conviction rates in the Soviet Union were higher than in other European countries, and the Soviet judiciary overwhelmingly upheld these convictions, which further distinguishes the Soviet case from most countries that participated in the war.[34] The majority of Soviet citizens who were charged with treason were convicted in secret, in quick trials that lacked fundamental standards of rule-of-law-based legal systems such as an independent judiciary, independent defense attorneys, and the assumption of "innocent until proven guilty" that form the precondition for any trial to be considered as impartial as possible. Although a variety of different actors (state security officers, military prosecutors, judges, and party-state leaders) were involved in the punitive process, the general course was always set by the leading Bolsheviks in Moscow, and as such was to be applied uniformly across the western regions of the Soviet Union.

The Soviet punishment of suspected wartime traitors was swift, harsh, and sweeping. At the same time—and contrary to official wartime proclamations—punitive practices were not static but rather varied over time, alternating throughout the postwar years between more lenient and stricter, less active and more expansive phases. The historical literature remains divided on how to explain these shifts. One argument is that the returning Soviet authorities considered those accused of having served the Germans not as by-products of the war but as eternal enemies that war and occupation had helped to uncover. The passing of time had no effect on the state's punishment policies.[35] In contrast, others have argued that the Soviet regime did not always live up to the harsh image that it projected. For pragmatic reasons, mostly resulting from a lack of qualified personnel, the authorities were willing to make compromises.[36] As this book shows, while both positions raise crucial points, framing the issue solely as one of ideology versus pragmatism does not fully capture the nature of Moscow's politics of retribution—and the kind of Soviet state that emerged after the war.

The prosecution of Soviet citizens accused of wartime treason began in late 1941, after the Red Army, in its first counteroffensive, regained territories in western Russia. In this early reconquest phase, punishment was particularly strict and indiscriminate, and the death sentence common. Soon, however, the Politburo grew alarmed by military tribunal reports that stressed the state security organs's improper qualification of crimes. Aiming to clarify the legal basis of punishment, several political and judicial central bodies in Moscow issued a series of instructions in 1943 that introduced a legal distinction between traitors and accomplices, specified the corresponding acts, and set different sentences ranging from imprisonment to the death penalty. The real turning point in the state's politics of retribution, however, occurred during the first half of 1944. By the late spring, the Red Army had pushed the Germans from western Russia, eastern and central Ukraine, including Kiev, and parts of eastern Belarus around Gomel'. During the first months of 1944, a noticeable change took place: overall, punishment became less strict. As reports by NKVD military tribunals operating in eastern Belarus show, during the first post-occupation weeks and months, the death penalty was less common than one might have expected.[37] The ratio of death penalty to prison sentence dropped further in the next two years. A similar trend—that labor camp sentences were much more common than the death penalty—was also observed in Ukraine between 1943 and 1945.[38]

The moderation of punitive practices should not be mistaken for an increase in due process of law: the Soviet legal system remained illiberal. Rather, shifting political circumstances led to a recalibration of state priorities. As the Red Army was reconquering more and more territory from the Germans, retribution evolved into a process in which different objectives and interests had to be weighed against each other: reclaiming authority by way of punishment yet portraying the Soviet state as a liberator and guarantor of justice, while facing a shortage of experienced personnel. A similar mechanism informed the proceedings of Soviet citizens accused of wartime treason that the authorities decided to open to the public. At the trials that took place while the International Military Tribunal (IMT) convened in Nuremberg from 1945 to 1946, the Soviet state took great care to draw a discursive connection between the respective local treason trials (or what today would be called collaboration trials), its ongoing domestic trials of Axis soldiers for war crimes, and the Soviet Union's participation at Nuremberg. At the same time, the authorities were determined to keep public media references about the involvement of Soviet citizens with the Germans to an absolute minimum in the first ten to fifteen years after the war. After Stalin's death, as part of limited de-Stalinization efforts, the Soviet state moderated its punitive policies and in 1955 issued a partial amnesty. In the 1960s, domestic and international changes spurred a second wave of public trials. Because a statute of limitations did not exist for treason, the prosecution of Soviet citizens accused of wartime collaboration continued until the late 1980s.

This balancing act, however, was not free of tensions and contradictions. The Soviet leaders were determined to punish local participation in German atrocities. Military tribunals sentenced numerous individuals who, usually in their capacity as local policemen, had abused, killed, or helped to kill Jewish and non-Jewish Soviet citizens during the war. Yet at its core, the search for those deemed traitors was about defining political loyalty. Correspondingly, despite the relative moderation of punishment that began in 1944, the Soviet leadership continued to regard the war as a test that revealed people's true loyalties—and thus showed no understanding for the moral gray zones of occupation. In their rulings, the military tribunals did not take external pressures or constraints into account as mitigating factors. "Choiceless choices"—that some individuals in occupied territory were forced to choose between two options that had an equally destructive effect on their communities—did not exist for the Soviet authorities. All the while, they were willing to accommodate their own pragmatic wartime choices—and did not hold everyone accused of treason accountable by the same standard. During the war, Moscow actively encouraged Soviet citizens who served in the German-organized police forces to join the Soviet partisans. This was a deliberate policy, promoted by none other than Panteleimon Ponomarenko and approved by Stalin. "Traitors-turned-partisans" were later also the only group in whose cases Soviet military courts systematically allowed for mitigating circumstances, thus lowering their sentences significantly.

Such contradictory practices resulted from tensions between ideological imperatives and pragmatic concerns, but they also resulted from tensions within ideology. On one hand, the state maintained that the civilian population in occupied territory, with the exception of a few people who were deemed traitors, had fully supported the Soviet partisans. In the official Soviet narrative of the war as an "all people's war" (*vsenarodnaia voina*), Belarus occupied a special place as the center of the "all people's partisan war" (*vsenarodnaia partizanskaia voina*) against the Germans.[39] On the other hand, Ponomarenko and other high-ranking Bolsheviks believed that the war had helped to uncover mass enemies in hiding, eternal enemies who had gone into hiding in the interwar years yet had resurfaced and joined the Germans in 1941. Ultimately, the authorities—from party leaders to low-level officials, state security officers to members of the judiciary—were unable to establish a consensus on just what exactly "working for the Germans" (*rabotali u nemtsev*), as internal state documents put it, had entailed. While the case of policemen and village heads seemed easy to judge, more confusion continued to exist with regard to teachers, agricultural specialists, or office clerks who had worked in the German-overseen administration. Given the dire lack of cadres, the Soviet state continued to employ many of them. Still, the authorities' suspicion, palpable in the denial of higher education or professional advancement, did not diminish over the years. Indeed, anyone who had lived under Nazi rule could be suspect—as best expressed in one line on the bibliographical questionnaires that Soviet citizens had to fill out before beginning a new job or entering university: "Did you live in occupied territory?" The Soviet state that emerged from the Second World War, then, was able to quickly reassert its authority in the formerly German-occupied territories—yet at the same time ambivalent about its politics of retribution.

Searching for Truth, Guilt, and Justice

For private individuals, the moment of return was first and foremost about the much hoped-for reunion with family members. Returning home, however, also led to encounters with former neighbors and friends, fellow villagers, and colleagues. These encounters not only threw into sharp relief that some, in particular Jews, had lost more than others during the war. They also, and inevitably, raised questions about people's wartime behavior.

One would probably assume that in a secret police state like Stalin's Soviet Union, where fear of informers was widespread and people were highly cautious about what they said in public, individuals would shy away altogether from talking about the war in ways that might deviate from the official line. That, however, was not the case. When Vasil' Bykaŭ returned to his village Bychki in northeastern Belarus after the war, fellow villagers came over at night and recounted how much they had had to suffer during the war: "From the Germans, from the partisans, from the *narodniki* [people associated with the administration] . . . Among others also from some people who came from the same villages, in particular from those who up to the war had been Soviet activists and during the war tried hard to serve the Germans."[40] As neighbors and acquaintances met in social settings, they did talk frankly about the war, including sensitive topics such as violence committed by Soviet partisans. Yet if people spoke about taking furniture from Jewish apartments, stealing food from villagers, or serving in the German-organized police forces, they usually always referred to *other* locals as having done such things, not themselves—and it needed a lot of personal determination and insistence to overcome people's reluctance to respond to uncomfortable questions, in particular ones that might have brought to light their own entanglement in wrongdoing or crimes.

When individuals found out or surmised that members of their prewar social communities had become complicit or entangled in Nazi crimes, or that their neighbors had taken advantage of other people's plight, they responded in different ways. Some sought comfort in the social relations that had survived, the friendships and solidarities that had not been destroyed by what people had done or not done during the war. Often, people cut all ties with those whom they suspected of wrongdoing, as Ol'ga Bembel'-Dedok did with her nephew Igor', a former Red Army soldier who had fallen into captivity and subsequently worked as a translator for the Germans.[41] Yet others like Litman Mor, a Holocaust survivor and former Soviet partisan, decided to altogether sever the bond to their local community, whether this entailed leaving one's hometown, region, or Belarus—or, if possible, even the Soviet Union itself. On his return home to David-Gorodok in 1944, Mor discovered that some of the town's inhabitants had participated in the murder and expropriation of his family. All social ties that he had once held to non-Jewish acquaintances shattered. As he explained: "My hatred of the Germans was common, not aimed at a specific German. But my hatred of the locals, who murdered my family, was personal."[42] Hoping against hope that some members of his extended family might have survived, Mor returned once more to David-Gorodok in early 1945: "This time, I walked around like in a cemetery.

I was completely indifferent. . . . I only knew—I will never return here."[43] Under the conditions of the Polish-Soviet population exchange, he was able to leave the Soviet Union and subsequently settled in Palestine.

As varied as people's responses to the ghosts of war were, one sentiment was widely shared by inhabitants of Belarus: the urge to seek justice and retribution—that is, punishment that people believed to be morally right. In its most extreme form, retribution meant revenge violence, such as beating up a fellow villager accused of having worked for the Germans. Yet individuals also pursued many other, less physical means of retribution. Some did so privately—for example, by confronting neighbors directly, demanding the restitution of property that these had acquired during the war. Many more, though, found themselves brought into contact with the Soviet state. In their efforts to determine what Soviet citizens had done under Nazi rule, the authorities relied heavily on local information, on an assortment of names, clues, and stories. Some of these were supplied unwillingly, as when torture during interrogations made people provide or fabricate incriminating material about friends or neighbors, or when people were blackmailed into becoming informers. Others agreed to become informers for the state security organs because they saw this as a chance to punish locals they believed guilty of crimes committed in the name of German power. While some consented to pass on information to the state after they were approached by its representatives, many more acted on their own initiative and wrote letters to the central authorities. Testifying to the state—whether to the members of the Extraordinary State Commission (Chrezvychainaia gosudarstvennaia komissiia, ChGK) or, if possible, as a witness at a public trial—was another means through which individuals could seek retribution. In doing so, some people found that their individual notions of what constituted morally right punishment overlapped or were congruent with those of the regime. When the authorities acted on their tip and arrested a neighbor they believed to have committed crimes in the name of German power, even someone who otherwise was not sympathetic to Soviet rule could see the state as a guarantor of justice. The same could apply to individuals who served as witnesses in court. The widespread desire for punishment made it possible for some inhabitants of postwar Belarus to find moral justice (*spraviadlivasts'* in Belarusian, *spravedlivost'* in Russian) within a state whose legal system was, and remained, profoundly illiberal.

At the same time, interaction with the authorities carried its own risk. People who engaged with the state could, of course, do so only on the terms set by the authorities.[44] There were boundaries to what could be said and done, and investigations could backfire on those who initially set them in motion.

Nowhere did this become more visible than in the ubiquitous property conflicts. What belonged to whom was an immensely contentious question in the immediate postwar years, a deeply personal and at the same time highly political question. The death and displacement of hundreds of thousands of people—in particular, the region's Jews—and the destruction of houses as a result of military operations or German punitive actions meant that a lot of property—be it apartments, furniture, or clothes—had passed through many different hands during the war. Just how did you manage to move into a new apartment during the war—because the Germans had burned down your house as punishment for ties to the partisans, or because the partisans had burned down your house as punishment for ties to the Germans? Or because a bomb had destroyed your house and you simply needed a new place to stay?

These questions inevitably arose when trying to solve the ubiquitous property conflicts, which is why we can read them as one of the ways in which people in Belarus grappled with the ghosts of war. Sorting them out was an inherently difficult task, both practically as well as morally. Red Army soldiers, Holocaust survivors, or former partisans often turned to the state, asking the authorities to settle the question of ownership or occupancy rights in their favor. In doing so, they had no choice but to work with Soviet normative categories, with the authorities' notions of right and wrong wartime behavior. In consequence, it was, of course, impossible to seek justice for wartime wrongdoing believed to have been committed in the name of the Soviet state. A peasant could not complain to Minsk, for instance, that Soviet partisans had stolen his cow during the war. The partisans were unambiguous heroes, people's avengers, and defenders of the socialist motherland. According to the official narrative of Belarus as the republic where the "all people's partisan war" had taken place, the local population in both the republic's eastern and western part had, with the exception of a few traitors, stood firmly behind Soviet power. In this respect, narrating the years of war and occupation was also about the creation of a new linear story of Soviet Belarusian statehood—one that firmly united eastern and western Belarus under the banner of the "Partisan Republic," as the postwar republic came to be known. After Stalin's death in 1953, the general Soviet war narrative and its specific Belarusian version became more inclusive, and within limits, some of its aspects could be contested. Still, because of the centrality of the "all people's partisan war" to postwar Soviet Belarusian statehood, there was no space to acknowledge that the relationship between Soviet partisans and civilians in German-occupied territory had been fragile, unequal, fraught with conflict, and at times antagonistic.[45] This book thus joins studies that have investigated the intricate processes of social and individual remembering, forgetting, and silencing, and that have demonstrated the complex and dynamic interplay within and between official and private memories—yet that have also shown the limits of individual agency in the face of state power.[46] The exclusively positive depiction of the partisan-civilian relationship was, and remains to this day, nonnegotiable in Belarus (and for that matter, in Russia, too). Violence committed by Soviet partisans against civilians continues to be a political taboo; challenging it comes with high professional and social costs.[47] Privately, individuals in postwar Belarus tried to make sense of the discrepancy between official and private memory by distinguishing between "real partisans" (who could be honored) and "bandits," thereby attempting to rationalize the abuse they had encountered from the latter—yet this reframing of their wartime experiences could publicly only be articulated at the cost of exclusion from the larger political community.

Those who felt that Soviet power had done them an injustice—either during the war at the hands of the partisans or after the war at the hands of Soviet officials—therefore resorted to particular strategies in order to be able to mobilize the state on their behalf: they wrote letters to party leaders in which they accused others of being German accomplices. While their efforts often turned out to be unsuccessful, the authorities usually benefited from them: on a more abstract level, complaint letters to the regime acknowledged that the Soviet state alone had the means to settle the conflicts brought forward by the authors. The importance that this affirmation of Soviet state authority had should not be underestimated, in particular considering how rapidly institutions in the western Soviet regions had collapsed in the summer of 1941. In that sense, and regardless of the author's intentions, each letter to the state contributed to the rebuilding of Soviet power in the aftermath of Nazi occupation. Unintentionally, "confronting the past" had a regime-stabilizing effect, not leading to the creation of more liberal, open public spheres but instead strengthening the mechanisms of power in an authoritarian regime like the Soviet Union.

The search for truth, guilt, and justice in the aftermath of Nazi occupation, then, was a multidimensional process located at myriad levels of state and society, one that was about defining political loyalty but also about establishing crimes; about finding moral justice in its different forms and meanings but also about revenge; one of tremendous personal grief, trauma, and enduring silences but also about the rebuilding of lives, belonging, and defining one's place in the postwar community of resisters. Yet precisely because confronting the ghosts of war was such a highly individualized and multidimensional process—contingent on a multitude of interacting factors, circumstances, and personal experiences—it is difficult to identify a clear contrast between western and eastern Belarus, between the new, formerly Polish and the old Soviet part of the republic. As several scholars have shown, the Sovietization of the regions that were annexed in 1939 and 1940 could be thoroughly carried out only after 1944. In consequence, differences between old and new Soviet regions manifested themselves in state policies and practices.[48] One might assume that these were also reflected in the personal ways in which inhabitants of Belarus responded to the aftermath of Nazi occupation: for example, that people from eastern Belarus were more likely to turn to the state than inhabitants of western Belarus or more likely to agree with the authorities' categories of right and wrong wartime behavior—and thus more likely to find moral justice through the Soviet state. Given the lack of comprehensive empirical data, this is, of course, impossible to rule out entirely. Still, I could not detect any obvious east/west differences in the available source material. What is noteworthy here is not the existence but rather the absence of a pattern that one would have expected to see.

If there was a line dividing the population not just in Belarus but in the Soviet Union at large, however, then it ran between those who had lived under German rule and those who had not. After the war, many civilians who returned from the Soviet rear or front shared with the authorities their distrust toward those who had lived in occupied territory. Like elsewhere in Europe, women faced a gendered stigma and were accused of "horizontal collaboration." The mistrust extended to those who had been taken to Germany as forced laborers and to Red Army soldiers who had survived German captivity. Even former Soviet partisans were not always exempt, depending on when and under what circumstances they had joined the movement.[49] Although people's prejudices toward those who had lived under Nazi rule did not always have to be articulated fully, biases nevertheless lingered on for decades after the war, with the potential to appear at any moment, often during small, everyday social conflicts. Social interactions and encounters, both in public and in private, therefore also showed that for many people, actual, alleged, or surmised wartime behavior and postwar belonging were intertwined issues—whether that meant belonging to a family, a local community, or the Soviet nation.

Private and Public Lives

Ghosts of War is based on a broad range of archival sources from sixteen archives in Belarus, Russia, Germany, Israel, Poland, Ukraine, and the United States. A large part consists of Soviet state documents that were for internal use only (such as Communist Party reports, reports from the people's commissariats/ministries, cadre statistics, or procuracy reports) and Soviet state documents like newspapers and speeches that were produced for the public. Unlike in neighboring Ukraine or Lithuania, the archives of the Soviet state security organs in Belarus are closed to researchers (as are the central archives of the Soviet state security organs in Moscow). However, reports from the state security organs, including on the work of the NKVD/MVD military tribunals, are available through the archives of the Communist Party of Belarus (although much material remains classified, too). Other archival sources include reports from the Nazi occupation regime and court files from postwar Germany. Together, these documents attest to regime policies and practices and the ways in which they changed over time.

As an exploration of both private and public lives, with its equal emphasis on state and nonstate actors, the book also draws on published and unpublished personal and autobiographical material written or recorded in Russian, German, Polish, English, and Belarusian. This includes memoirs and shorter recollections, interview transcripts, and Jewish memorial books, as well as diaries, complaint letters to the Soviet authorities, and oral history interviews that I conducted in Belarus, Israel, and Germany. With the exception of complaint letters that people sent to the Soviet authorities and the interviews conducted by the Commission on the History of the Great Patriotic War, an oral history project run by Isaak Mints of the USSR Academy of Sciences, most personal and autobiographical material was created decades after the war.[50] The delay may be attributed to personal considerations, such as the need for temporal distance or an urge only later in life to pass on memories to a younger generation. Audience reception probably also mattered. In the United States, it took at least twenty years for a larger public to become interested in personal Holocaust histories; in Europe, it took even longer.[51] Until the onset of perestroika in the Soviet Union, state censorship prevented the publication of memoirs, including on the Holocaust, that offered an alternative to highly state-regulated ways of narrating the war. Finally, the civilian side of war and the experiences of "ordinary people" only began to attract public and scholarly interest relatively recently, whether in the East or the West. This, in turn, is both reflected in and has shaped the ways in which the memoir literature on the Second World War has developed over time.

Knowing, as cognitive psychology and neuroscience studies have shown, that every act of remembering entails the reconfiguration of what is being remembered, some historians might caution against using such temporally removed sources as memoirs and strongly favor more immediate ones.[52] However, I do not entirely share these reservations. At the time of its creation, interpretations of events are always (and unavoidably so) already being written into a source. While authors of personal or autobiographical sources necessarily position themselves in relation to the larger political and social force field surrounding them, so, too, do the authors of state documents: for example, reports written by local officials or state security officers to Minsk or Moscow. This book draws on a wide range of different sources, of which each comes with its own specific set of methodological problems. At their core, however, the analytical challenge remains the same for all sources: to reconstruct how humans experienced and interpreted an event, to understand who speaks, from what position, and in relation to whom and what, and to identify the limits of what could have been said—and what was left unsaid. In what follows, I therefore juxtapose different sources relating to one particular process or phenomenon. At times, however, this is not possible, and all I can work with is one source, even just a fragment pertaining to a single event. The reason for that lies in an imbalance in the source base, and more specifically, within the available personal and autobiographical material. While members of all social strata wrote complaint letters to the state, urban residents overall left more detailed written traces than rural residents, and men more than women. Memoirs by Holocaust survivors—in particular. those from western Belarus who left the Soviet Union immediately after the war and later settled in the United States or Israel—are also more numerous than memoirs by other population groups. To compensate for this, I drew as much as possible on complaint letters and conducted oral history interviews myself. Although the imbalance is impossible to even out entirely, the available primary source material can nevertheless provide evidence of similarities and differences in human perception and behavior, reveal discrepancies and concurrences between institutional and personal responses to the aftermath of Nazi occupation, and, if interpreted cautiously, provide a sense of scale.

Ghosts of War

The first chapter introduces the tumultuous early twentieth-century history of the region that came to form post-1945 Soviet Belarus. It does so through the lives of some of its inhabitants from different religious, ethnic, and social backgrounds who, alongside others, will appear repeatedly throughout the book. Since individual choices under Nazi rule can only be fully understood if the prewar Soviet years are adequately explored, the chapter traces how larger political shifts and ruptures—in particular, the different ways in which Soviet power came to eastern and western Belarus—transformed personal lives and interethnic relations before 1941.

The second chapter examines the heart of darkness, the years of war and occupation. It focuses on three developments: the transition from Soviet to German rule in the summer of 1941, the murder of Belarus's Jewish community, and the growth of the partisan movement. Taken together, these three developments reveal particularly well individual preferences and motivations, local dynamics of violence, and the multicausal situational factors that increasingly accounted for the choices that individuals made and the choices that they were forced to make under Nazi rule.

The third chapter looks at the moment of return in 1944 and the worlds destroyed, worlds in flux, and worlds apart that it revealed. It examines the first encounters between those who had lived in occupied territory and those who had experienced the war elsewhere, and assesses how the returning Soviet authorities destroyed any resistance, real and imagined. It also explores the state's investigatory process and details the different strategies and sources that the Soviet state security organs drew on, including the help of partisan units, informer networks, captured German documents, witness statements collected by the Extraordinary State Commission (ChGK), and prewar surveillance and policing tools.

The fourth chapter traces the evolution of Soviet punishment of those deemed wartime traitors from the first reconquest phase to the early 1960s, when a second wave of trials took place. Analyzing secret and public prosecutions, the chapter shows that punitive practices were not static but rather varied over time, alternating between more lenient and stricter, less active and more expansive phases in response to shifting domestic and international constellations. At the same time, the state's politics of retribution remained both ideologically inflected and profoundly conflicted, attesting to the powerful yet ambivalent nature of the postwar Soviet state.

The fifth chapter shifts the focus from the state to the perspective of individual lives and local communities. It reveals the destructive impact that people's wartime choices had on personal ties and solidarities in a region that had already experienced much destruction of its social fabric under Soviet rule. The chapter analyzes how individuals sought accountability or revenge with the help of the postwar Soviet state, through nonstate channels, or by a combination of the two, and assesses the different meanings that justice, truth, and guilt held for people.

The sixth chapter reconstructs how different actors shaped the official image of Belarus as the "Partisan Republic," outlining its evolution from the war years into the first postwar decades. As acts of public remembrance contributed to public silencing and forgetting, party leaders increasingly ethnicized the war narrative in terms of both heroes and victims (with Jewish and Polish inhabitants of Belarus subsequently excluded from the narrative). By presenting the Soviet partisan movement in Belarus as a mostly male, ethnic Belarusian or at best an East Slavic undertaking, the authorities also marginalized the contribution of female partisans, who had, after all, constituted 16 percent of the movement's forces in Belarus.[53] At the same time, even many ethnic Belarusians found that their actual experiences with the partisans were not reflected in the state's narrative. The chapter identifies the many discrepancies that existed between official image and personal experiences and reveals the mechanisms of inclusion and exclusion that were underlying the memory-making process—but it also shows how individuals at once accommodated, contested, and reshaped official war memory.

The afterword locates the Soviet Union within the global moment of post–Second World War justice, a moment that saw hundreds of thousands of individuals prosecuted for their wartime activities in almost all former belligerent countries, that led to the emergence of international criminal law, and that witnessed public and official discourses on collaboration transcend national boundaries. Tracing their different postwar trajectories both within and outside Belarus, the book ends with the lives of Ol'ga Bembel'-Dedok, Chasia Bornstein-Bielicka, Zofia Brzozowska, Vasil' Bykaŭ, Vladimir Khartanovich, Litman Mor, Lev Ovsishcher, and Zinaida Suvorova. For these eight individuals, as for countless others, the war never became history but remained ever present.

Chapter 1

Contested Space

An East European Borderland before 1941

Ol'ga Bembel'-Dedok and Vladimir Khartanovich, Chasia Bornstein-Bielicka, Litman Mor and Zofia Brzozowska, Vasil' Bykaŭ, Lev Ovsishcher and Zinaida Suvorova were strangers to one another. Their personal lives did not intersect, at least not in any way that they were aware of. They spoke and wrote in different languages—Belarusian, Polish, Yiddish, and Russian—and they held different religions: Russian Orthodoxy, Roman Catholicism, and Judaism. Ol'ga Bembel'-Dedok was a Russian-speaking artist who lived in Minsk, Chasia Bornstein-Bielicka a Socialist Zionist from Grodno, Vladimir Khartanovich a Belarusian nationalist and communist sympathizer from a small village near the Naliboki forest, and Zinaida Suvorova a Komsomol activist from a religious Jewish family from Orsha. While Zofia Brzozowska's family was part of the landed Polish gentry in the Novogrudok region, Litman Mor came from a Yiddish-speaking family from Polesia, Vasil' Bykaŭ from a Belarusian-speaking peasant family, and Lev Ovsishcher from a Jewish family from Vitebsk oblast.

As different as these eight individuals were, what they had in common was that they called the same place their home: a predominately rural region that stretched from Grodno and Brest in the west to Vitebsk and Gomel' in the east, encompassing larger towns like Minsk and Mogilev and smaller ones like Novogrudok and Bobruisk, with dense forests and swamps, hot summers and snowy winters, isolated villages and few major roads. Located on the edge of Eastern Europe, this multilingual and multireligious region was a true borderland all the way into the mid-twentieth century: a contested space where imperial and national rivalries met, a construct of the political imaginary and simultaneously object of competing civilizing missions, and a place where different political actors, locals and nonlocals, could test out their national and social engineering projects.[1] Over the course of the centuries, it formed part of Kievan Rus', the Grand Duchy of Lithuania, the Polish-Lithuanian Commonwealth, and the Russian empire. During the First World War and the wars that subsequently followed, these lands were repeatedly turned into battlefields, with armies moving back and forth across the region. The 1921 Polish-Soviet peace treaty, also known as the Treaty of Riga, finally brought peace, but it also redrew boundaries across Eastern Europe. The western half of the region—with towns like Grodno, Brest, and Baranovichi—became part of the newly created Second Republic of Poland, while the eastern half of the region—with towns like Minsk and subsequently Vitebsk, Mogilev, and Gomel'—became part of Soviet Belarus. In September 1939, after the Red Army invaded eastern Poland and the region was annexed to the Soviet Union, northeastern Poland became western Belarus, and what until then had been Soviet Belarus alone became the eastern part of the expanded republic. Just two years later, on June 22, 1941, Berlin broke the pact with Moscow and attacked the Soviet Union. Within weeks, all of Belarus found itself under Nazi occupation, where it remained until the Red Army reconquered the republic in the summer of 1944.

This chapter introduces the tumultuous early twentieth-century history of the lands that would come to form post-1945 Soviet Belarus, from the beginning of the century until the eve of German invasion in June 1941. It does so through the lives of the eight individuals introduced earlier, who, alongside others, will resurface repeatedly throughout the book. In their native region, the "Age of Extremes" culminated in the German occupation from 1941 to 1944, yet as this chapter shows, the region had already experienced much violence before 1941.[2] By examining how personal lives were affected by the larger shifting political force field, the chapter pays particular attention to the radical transformations that the Bolsheviks enacted in this East European borderland. It also discusses how the different ways in which Soviet rule came to eastern and western Belarus—to the former as a revolution from within, to the latter as a revolution from abroad—altered interethnic relations before 1941. In turn, these different Soviet legacies would, to varying degrees, influence the choices that inhabitants of Belarus subsequently made under Nazi rule.

War, Revolution, and Civil War

At the beginning of the twentieth century, the region that Ol'ga Bembel'-Dedok and Vladimir Khartanovich, Zofia Brzozowska, Lev Ovsishcher and Chasia Bornstein-Bielicka, Vasil' Bykaŭ, Litman Mor and Zinaida Suvorova called their home overlapped in large part with five Russian imperial provinces (*gubernii*): Vil'na, Grodno, Minsk, Vitebsk, and Mogilev. It was in the last province that Ol'ga Bembel'-Dedok, the oldest of these eight individuals, was born in 1906. She was a native of the city of Gomel'. Her parents had moved there from the countryside, but ties to the village remained strong: Ol'ga Bembel'-Dedok usually spent her childhood summers with her grandparents.[3] The first European wave of industrialization had mostly bypassed this poor and overwhelmingly agricultural region, with its dense forests and extensive marshes and swamps. Most of the rural population belonged to the Russian Orthodox Church, yet others also adhered to Roman Catholicism or smaller Christian groups.[4] Many peasants spoke a Belarusian vernacular, commonly referred to as the local language, the simple language, or the "language from here" (*pa tuteishamu*). Overall, according to the first Russian imperial census of 1897, speakers of Belarusian as their native or first language (*rodnoi iazyk*) constituted, to varying extents, the largest language group in the five northwestern provinces—Vil'na, Grodno, Minsk, Vitebsk, and Mogilev. Depending on one's geographical location, whether further to the west or the east, Polish or Russian vernaculars were also frequently spoken. In everyday interaction, people often mixed these Slavic languages, making it difficult to draw neat linguistic boundaries. Further to the north, Lithuanian and Latvian vernaculars were spoken as well, whereas further to the south, Ukrainian vernacular was common, too.[5]

Census taking is, of course, one of the classical tools whereby modern states govern their populations, and as such, censuses reflect aims and biases particular to each state. Since the 1863 Polish Uprising, Russian imperial officials had viewed anything Polish as a threat to imperial power, and thus sought to make it less visible in public life. It is therefore quite likely that census takers deliberately increased the number of Belarusian-speakers in Vil'na, Grodno, Vitebsk, Minsk, and Mogilev provinces at the expense of Polish-speakers—just as the interwar Polish state would, in turn, use census taking as a way to increase the number of Polish-speakers at the expense of Belarusian-speakers.[6] Regardless of the exact numbers, though, the 1897 census clearly attests to the multilinguality and multireligiosity of the region. It also shows that in contrast to the overwhelmingly Christian and Slavic-speaking rural population, the urban population was mostly Jewish.[7] This settlement pattern can in large part be traced back to the residency restrictions that the Russian imperial government, in the wake of the annexation of Polish-Lithuanian territories, had imposed on the empire's Jewish population in 1791. Jews were only allowed to reside within the borders of the so-called Pale of Settlement, which included the five northwestern imperial provinces. They could settle outside the Pale only under exceptional circumstances and with government permission. After 1882, the government also prohibited Jews from purchase or lease of land in rural areas.[8]

By the turn of the twentieth century, half of the population of Minsk spoke Yiddish as its first language. In smaller towns, the percentage of the Jewish population was usually higher. These were the East European shtetls, also called *mestechki* in Russian, where traditional Jewish religious life shaped most social interaction. In Pinsk, a town to the east of Brest, 90 percent of the residents were Jewish.[9] Other languages spoken in towns and cities were Polish, which had been used by the aristocracy and royal administration in the Polish-Lithuanian Commonwealth, and Russian, the administrative *lingua franca* of the tsarist empire. Vil'na (today's Vilnius), the historical heart of this region, was predominantly a Yiddish and Polish-speaking town, with Russian as the language that people used in encounters with the state.[10] In towns, the region's multilinguality was even more pronounced. Many urban residents grew up speaking more than one language. This did not necessarily mean that they were fluent in most of the region's main languages, but many knew them well enough to be able to engage in basic interaction—for example, at the market.[11] At the same time, this was a region with a stark difference between towns and villages. The majority language—Belarusian dialect in its different variations—was primarily a rural language, seldom spoken by urban residents. Yiddish and Jewish culture, in contrast, were largely absent from the countryside. Like elsewhere in rural Europe, nationality mattered little, if at all, to people. The main marker of identity—and thus the main factor that set communities apart—was religion. Whereas boundaries between the different Christian denominations could be blurry, they were quite visible between Christians and Jews, which further contributed to the divide between the rural and the urban landscapes.[12]

The First World War marked the first big political rupture in the region's twentieth-century history, setting in motion a series of mostly violent political and social transformations over the course of the next years. Trying to seek advantage of the volatile situation, various political actors—locals and nonlocals, foreign governments and armies, socialists and nationalists—laid claim to this space-in-between, turning it into political laboratories where they could test out different national and social engineering projects.[13] As fields and villages became battlefields, hundreds of thousands of people fled to the Russian interior. Among them was Vladimir Khartanovich's family from the village of Achukevichi, not far from the town of Novogrudok in Grodno province. The Khartanoviches found refuge to the east in Mogilev province, where Vladimir was born in 1919.[14] Refugees from the Polish-speaking parts of the Russian empire also arrived in the village not far from Gomel' where Ol'ga Bembel'-Dedok's grandparents lived.[15] The Russian army deported from the border regions ethnic minorities that it deemed unreliable and potential German spies, a practice that affected primarily Jews and ethnic Germans. The situation grew worse when Russian defeats began to mount toward the end of 1914, and military authorities ordered the expulsion of Jews from the northwestern provinces, which also affected Jewish communities in Grodno and Vil'na provinces.[16] In the early fall of 1915, the Central Powers made deep advances into imperial Russian territory, leading to the flight of even more people from the battle zones.[17] The governments in Berlin and Vienna divided the newly conquered territories according to their spheres of interest and set up different civilian and military occupation regimes. For the remainder of the war, Mogilev and Vitebsk provinces, including the city of Orsha, where Zinaida Suvorova was born in 1914 into a religious Jewish family, would remain east of the frontline.[18] Parts of Minsk province would be occupied by the Germans only in February 1918, after peace talks with the Bolsheviks failed and the German army extended its control eastward. Grodno and Vil'na provinces, however, had already come under German occupation in the fall of 1915, where they remained as part of the German military state Ober Ost until the end of the war in November 1918.

Ober Ost was a colonial project, a self-proclaimed civilizing mission through which the German military sought to bring culture, hygiene, and order to the East. It was also a nationalizing project, which included promoting the region's non-Russian languages (instead of curtailing them, as tsarist Russia had done) through the creation of educational and cultural institutions. By supporting non-Russian nationalist projects and trying to foster the development of distinct national identities, Berlin hoped to destabilize the Russian empire. And indeed, this strategy opened up limited possibilities for local political activists, who sought to build nation-states under German tutelage.[19] Among the inhabitants of the region, the German occupation of the First World War left a mixed legacy. Because the Ober Ost administration did not discriminate against specific ethnic or religious groups, it offered the Jewish population relief from the deportations and forced expulsions that they had endured in the first year of war at the hands of the Russian military.

German occupation also brought relief from a wave of pogroms and violence, carried out mostly by Cossack units and directed against Jews, which had accompanied the imperial army's retreat from April to October 1915.[20] Local memories of the Germans as strict but overall relatively mild occupiers (especially compared to the violence inflicted by the Russian imperial army and after 1919 by the Polish army), had terrible consequences in the summer of 1941, when within hours or days, people had to make up their mind whether to flee east or not. The mother of Sulia Wolozhinski Rubin from Novogrudok "remembered the Germans from the First World War . . . She could not believe any harm would come to us."[21] Like Wolozhinski Rubin's mother, many Jews who had lived through the German occupation of the First World War decided against fleeing in the summer of 1941, thinking that they knew what to expect from German rule.[22]

In 1917, the Russian empire crumbled as a result of war and revolution, followed a year later by the demise of the German empire. After the First World War ended in November 1918 and the German army retreated, the region remained heavily contested. By the time Lev Ovsishcher was born in 1919 in Bogushevsk, a shtetl not far from Vitebsk, the former Russian imperial provinces of Vil'na, Grodno, Minsk, Vitebsk, and Mogilev were in the midst of violent upheaval.[23] As armies moved back and forth over the region, various political actors each proclaimed nation-states or socialist republics, one as fragile and short-lived as the other. Between 1918 and 1920, Belarusian statehood—whether in an exclusively national, socialist, or cosmopolitan form—was announced no less than six times.[24] Two forces in particular were struggling with each other: the newly (re)created Polish state and the still small group of Bolsheviks. Minsk, until then under the control of the Bolsheviks, fell to the Polish army in August 1919, only to be recaptured by the Bolsheviks a little less than a year later, in July 1920. All the while, across the lands of the former Russian empire, the Bolsheviks were engaged in civil war battles with the White Army, which fought for the reinstatement of the Russian tsar; the short-lived Belarusian Insurgent Army under the command of Stanisław Bułak-Bałachowicz; the Revolutionary Insurrectionary Army of Ukraine under the command of Nestor Makhno; and other anarchist peasant bands, including the so-called Greens. The local civilian population, and above all Jewish communities, repeatedly suffered from violence—looting, rape, killings—that these different groups inflicted on them. Most of the anti-Jewish violence took place on the territory of today's Ukraine, but members of the Polish army, the Belarusian Insurgent Army, and some Red Army soldiers also committed pogroms on the territory of today's Belarus, for example in Minsk, Mozyr', and Pinsk. From the summer of 1920 to the fall of 1921 alone, this left almost two thousand Jews dead, and many more wounded, raped, or orphaned.[25]

Redrawing Borders, Reinventing Space

In 1921, the wars finally came to an end. The Treaty of Riga, signed in March that year, ended the Polish-Bolshevik War. It also established new borders across the former imperial borderlands. As a result, the five imperial Russian provinces Vil'na, Grodno, Minsk, Mogilev, and Vitebsk were divided among different powers. Vil'na and Grodno provinces as well as the western part of Minsk province became part of the newly independent state of Poland, where they were reorganized into the four voivodships (*województwa*, provinces) Białystok, Wilno, Nowogródek, and Polesie. Taken together, these constituted northeastern Poland. The eastern part of Minsk province, Mogilev province, and most of Vitebsk province came under Bolshevik control.[26]

The first modern state by the name of Belarus, the Belarusian People's Republic (Belaruskaia Narodnaia Respublika, BNR) was declared by a small group of nationalist activists in Minsk, then under German authority, in March 1918. The first socialist Belarusian state, the Soviet Socialist Republic of Belarus (Savetskaia Satsyialistychnaia Respublika Belarus', SSRB) was proclaimed by the Bolsheviks in January 1919, yet it only lasted fifty-eight days. It was subsequently reestablished under the same name in July 1920, after the Bolsheviks drove the Polish army from the former imperial Russian provinces. The Treaty of Riga effectively confirmed the existence of Soviet Belarus. It also meant that modern Belarusian statehood from then on came to be tied to the Soviet project, as only with the Bolsheviks did a lasting Belarusian state emerge. For Lenin and other leading Bolsheviks who believed in the existence of a distinct Belarusian nation, the republic fulfilled several political purposes at once: as proof of their commitment to non-Russian nationalities, as a buffer between capitalist Poland and socialist Russia, and as a counterbalance to Soviet Ukraine with its supposedly nationalist tendencies.[27]

In December 1922, Belarus joined Russia, Ukraine, and the Transcaucasian Socialist Federative Soviet Republic in creating the Soviet Union, and in that process was renamed the Belarusian Soviet Socialist Republic (Belaruskaia Savetskaia Satsyialistychnaia Respublika, BSSR). Like the other Soviet republics, Belarus was subordinated to the larger all-Union structure and ultimately the Politburo in Moscow, the Soviet leadership, which from 1922 on was headed by Joseph Stalin. Following the Treaty of Riga, Belarus initially only encompassed the former imperial province of Minsk, but in 1924, the republic's size increased when the Bolsheviks separated territories around Vitebsk and

Mogilev from Russia and added them to Belarus.[28] This was also the year that Vasil' Bykaŭ was born into a Belarusian-speaking family who lived in Bychki, a small village between Minsk and Vitebsk. The new state borders cut directly through his family: while his father's village found itself on the Bolshevik side, his mother's native village was now part of Poland.[29] Two years after Bykaŭ's birth, Belarus further increased in size when the Bolsheviks added parts of the Gomel' region to the republic, again on the basis of economic and ethnographic considerations, and again at the expense of Russia.[30] Belarus, whose borders would remain stable until its expansion in 1939, was now organized into five administrative units: Minsk, Vitebsk, Mogilev, Gomel', and Poles'e oblasts.

As the region began to settle down in the early 1920s, many people who had fled from war and revolution returned to their native villages and towns. Much of this movement happened from east to west, to the territories that had been under imperial Russian rule before the war but now formed northeastern Poland. Among them were the Khartanoviches, a Belarusian-speaking peasant family, who came home to what had remained of their native village Achukevichi, now in Nowogródek voivodship in Poland. The family had deep ties to the village: Vladimir Khartanovich's grandfather had already lived there. During the First World War, most residents fled the village, which soon found itself on the front line and subsequently burned down. On their return, the villagers rebuilt their houses with wood from the small birch tree forest that had already begun to grow over the destroyed village.[31] Located in the same voivodship, but further to the south, just outside the town of Nowogródek, was the Czombrów estate. It was home to the Karpowicz family, who had inherited the estate in the early twentieth century. Their house, a wooden classicist manor with a large portico, probably served the writer Adam Mickiewicz, himself a son of the region, as a model for the Soplicowo manor in his 1834 poem *Pan Tadeusz*. During the interwar years, the estate was run by Karol Karpowicz and Maria Karpowiczowa. Their granddaughter Zofia Brzozowska, who was born in the early 1920s and lived with her parents and younger brothers on the small estate Muchówka, close to Czombrów, later recalled how every Sunday after church, the extended family would gather for lunch at the Czombrów manor.[32] About the same age as Zofia Brzozowska was Chasia Bornstein-Bielicka, who lived further to the west in Grodno. Her family likewise had deep roots in the region. Chasia Bornstein-Bielicka's maternal grandparents lived in a suburb of Grodno, across the Nioman river. Her paternal grandparents originally lived in a village not far from Grodno, but later moved to the city, and bought property on Podolna Street, also called Rebbe Eliyahu Street, where Chasia Bornstein-Bielicka grew up.[33]

FIGURE 1. The Muchówka estate close to Novogrudok where Zofia Brzozowska grew up. Courtesy of Ośrodek Karta, Archiwum Wschodnie.

As landowners, the Karpowicz family belonged to the local elite. Compared to their West European counterparts, though, the gentry in northeastern Poland lived in rather modest circumstances. As Zofia Brzozowska recalled, her family and the other Polish families who owned small estates in the Nowogródek region were constantly short of money.[34] To the other inhabitants of Białystok, Wilno, Nowogródek, and Polesie voivodships, however, their lives must have seemed comfortable. The vast majority of the population, about four-fifths, were peasants with small individual landholdings who barely managed to get by. Many urban residents (of whom in turn many were Jews) were mostly artisans or engaged in trade. Throughout the interwar years, the Polish state tried to foster economic development and aimed to improve the region's infrastructure, which had sustained significant damage during the war, but the results were limited, especially in the historic Polesia region, one of the largest wetland areas of Europe that stretches along today's border between Belarus and Ukraine. Litman Mor, who was born there in 1917 into a Jewish textile-trading family that lived in the small town David-Gorodok (from 1921 on officially called Dawidgoródek), recalled that at the time, there were no paved roads in Polesia. The main means of transportation was by boat along the Pripyat river and its tributaries, but with the new border between Poland and the Soviet Union in place, the trade routes along the river east were cut off.[35] Throughout interwar northeastern Poland, the towns retained their shtetl economy, and the low productivity of individual farming did not improve significantly; most peasant households continued to operate at subsistence level.[36] That is also how Vladimir Khartanovich remembered the situation in Achukevichi and neighboring villages in the Nowogródek region, where large families, who worked their lands individually, lived in crowded huts, usually did not own horses, and often had to go without bread.[37]

Some people in interwar Poland referred to this region as Poland B or Poland C, thereby implying that it was the country's poor and backward corner.[38] Although Polish now succeeded Russian as the official language of the state, it nevertheless remained a minority language. Most inhabitants of northeastern Poland spoke Belarusian as their first language, while others, about 10 percent, spoke Yiddish as their first language.[39] The situation was similar in southeastern Poland, where the majority of the population spoke Ukrainian and a significant number spoke Yiddish. In contrast, the overwhelming majority of civil servants, including judges and policemen, identified as Polish by nationality, at least according to official data collected by the Polish state in 1923. In these *kresy wschodnie* (the eastern borderlands, as interwar eastern Poland was called), the Polish state tried to increase the presence of ethnic Poles by encouraging retired Polish army servicemen and civilian colonists to buy land and settle there. The colonists (*osadnicy*) received government loans and subsidies, which were usually not accessible to peasants.[40] As public discourse became increasingly nationalistic during the interwar years and the antisemitic Polish Right gained in power, the Polish state also implemented discriminatory measures against Jews. This included entry quotas for Jewish students in universities, as a result of which the proportion of Jews in the entire university body was reduced by half from the late 1920s to the late 1930s. As Litman Mor recalled from his student days in the second half of the 1930s, at Vilnius University, as elsewhere in many Polish institutions of higher education, Jewish students were required to sit on benches on the left-hand side of the lecture halls, segregated from the non-Jewish students. Some high schools that taught in Polish also used *numerus clausus* policies to limit enrollment by Jewish students: for example, in Grodno, where Chasia Bornstein-Bielicka grew up.[41]

Despite significant discrimination, though, the different minority groups continued to be able to organize themselves in a variety of different political and cultural organizations and had political representation in the Polish parliament. Moreover, not all state measures that appeared to privilege ethnic Poles at the expense of non-Poles or aimed to curtail the influence of the latter necessarily had this as their sole objective. The closure of many Belarusian-language schools and cultural institutions throughout the interwar years—a violation of the 1919 Polish Minority Treaty signed at Versailles—was in some part also a response to the infiltration of these institutions by local communists, who sought to unite northeastern Poland, which they considered western Belarus, with Soviet Belarus.[42] Ultimately, what defined Polish policy in the *kresy wschodnie* was one idea, shared by many Polish elites both in Warsaw and in eastern Poland and across the political spectrum: to simultaneously transform and incorporate the *kresy* into a civilized, modern, and Polish state and to alleviate the multilingual population, under Polish guidance, of its supposed backwardness.[43]

In practice, that civilizing mission, with its emphasis on Polish cultural superiority, had little appeal to a Belarusian-speaker like Vladimir Khartanovich. Growing up in Nowogródek voivodship, Vladimir Khartanovich developed strong communist sympathies. Before the First World War, his father, Naum Khartanovich, had taught in Achukevichi's village school, but after 1921, a lack of knowledge of Polish made it impossible for him to continue teaching. In 1934, the Polish authorities closed down the private Belarusian-language high school in Nowogródek that Vladimir attended. Due to a family dispute and resulting financial hardships, he had to discontinue his education and help his mother run their small rural household.[44]

Looking back on his childhood, Khartanovich held the Polish state responsible for the peasants' poverty. In his opinion, Warsaw privileged Polish settlers and more generally adherents of Catholicism over the Russian Orthodox population. His criticism of capitalism was also infused with strong antisemitic sentiments: apart from blaming the Polish government, he also accused the Jewish shopkeepers and merchants in the nearby town, Liubcha, of living at the expense of the laboring peasants.[45] In Achukevichi and its neighboring villages, members of the communist underground spread propaganda, telling locals that just a couple of miles further east, in the Belarusian Soviet Socialist Republic, "under the leadership of the Soviet authorities, people live happily. Education free of cost and medical care is available to young people; all have work and can realize their own potential."[46] At the end of the 1920s and in the early 1930s, a few young people from Achukevichi decided to cross illegally into Soviet Belarus. In the letters that they wrote back home, they described their new life: "They all had work, families; some continued their education. They had everything that we were dreaming about." It did not matter that a Soviet censor might have kept an eye on such correspondence: according to Khartanovich, their descriptions left a big imprint on him and his fellow villagers.[47] At least Khartanovich never experienced disillusionment. On the contrary: the 1939 Soviet annexation of northeastern Poland to Belarus, in Soviet rhetoric presented as a liberation, and service in the Red Army during the Second World War further solidified his belief in the Soviet project. After the war, Khartanovich returned to Achukevichi, was assigned a post in the district executive committee, and helped to transform his home village into a collective farm.[48]

Sovietization from Within

As an alternative to capitalist modernity, Soviet communists sought to build an egalitarian, modern, and industrialized society. To workers and peasants, the Bolsheviks promised liberation from capitalist exploitation at the hands of factory owners and landowners; to ethnic minorities, the end of political, economic, and cultural discrimination; to all, except the members of the old elites and the "bourgeois classes," education and upward mobility, a social welfare state, and equal rights. This promise, whether in part or in whole, resonated with many in the Soviet Union and beyond.[49] During the 1930s, with the rise of the Nazi Party and the systematic persecution of Jews in Germany, and popular manifestations of antisemitism in neighboring Poland, visible in three waves of anti-Jewish riots, the Soviet Union appeared as the only country in Europe that considered antisemitism a crime.[50] Lev Ovsishcher from Bogushevsk in northeastern Belarus remembered his childhood in the 1930s as imbued with a strong sense of living in the best possible society, liberated from the tsarist "prison of nations"—where local authorities reprimanded or disciplined those who made antisemitic remarks in public.[51] The particular Soviet mix of national liberation and radical social reform was also enticing to someone like Vladimir Khartanovich. Throughout the 1920s, under the slogan of "nationalist in form, socialist in content," the Soviet government massively promoted the languages and cultures of its diverse population, a process that was known in Russian as *korenizatsiia* (indigenization). This led to the creation of sizable bodies of literature in languages that, like Belarusian, had until very recently mostly existed in spoken form. As in the other republics, the educational system in Belarus was expanded to include native-language instruction for non-Russian speakers (that is, the creation of Belarusian, Yiddish, and Polish schools) and the establishment of institutes of higher learning. The rationale behind *korenizatsiia* was state building. Promoting literacy and education in the Soviet Union's many languages would not only enable the Bolsheviks to reach the non-Russian speaking parts and ultimately contribute to the creation of Soviet nations. It would also help to produce qualified cadres and facilitate centralized control, thereby increasing the state's capacity.[52]

The radical political, social, and economic transformation of the regions that made up the Soviet Union was, however, achieved only through a tremendous amount of coercion. Violence was an intrinsic part of the

Bolshevik project of building a socialist modernity.[53] During the civil war, the Bolsheviks used military force to expropriate landowners, nationalize almost all industry, and requisition grain from peasants. They also dismantled many religious institutions. In Minsk, most synagogues and Jewish religious schools were closed down, and their buildings were municipalized.[54] Those who were branded members of the former bourgeoisie were turned into social outcasts. Deprived of their Soviet citizenship rights, they lost any right to housing, employment, education, medical care, and a ration card for essential food items.[55]

Throughout the 1920s, the Bolshevik hold over the countryside was still tenuous, which is why the Soviet leaders decided to make some concessions. For the time being, the peasants were allowed to keep their land and small private businesses were tolerated, if grudgingly. Spurred by a grain procurement crisis and a war scare, strategic compromise came to an end in 1928, when Stalin announced the beginning of a massive state-led industrialization drive. It was accompanied with the closure of all private shops and the collectivization of agriculture, which was supposed to finance industrialization.[56] In Belarus, as in the other Soviet republics, the authorities took livestock and land away from the peasants and required them to work for collective farms. Among those affected were Vasil' Bykaŭ's parents, whose village Bychki in northeastern Belarus was collectivized in 1932. A few days after a decisive village meeting, the authorities came and took the family's seeds away. Bykaŭ's mother "was sobbing, choking with tears and screaming. . . . It was the month of March, time to sow. And what could they do now? How would they feed the children?" His parents had to start working for the collective farm. As Bykaŭ recalled: "Like others, they got nothing for their hard labour, only promises of full payment, in cash and produce, by the fall. And late one autumn day my father came home, carrying a very light sack. The content of this sack was only farm produce. No money. And with this little sack my parents were supposed to feed the family for a whole year."[57] What saved the Bykaŭ family from death was a small plot of land they had been allowed to keep, a meager basis for self-subsistence. In addition to taxes and the government bonds they were forced to buy, Bykaŭ's parents had to hand over a substantial portion of their private harvest to the state. Hunger and poverty, Bykaŭ recalled, were a constant presence in their lives, lasting from the beginning of collectivization until well after the Second World War.[58]

With the peasantry, the collectivization of agriculture was a tremendously unpopular project. A mass-scale social engineering project, it was a violent, brutal, and messy endeavor.[59] At public gatherings, officials forced village members to identify who the "kulaks," allegedly rich peasants, were.

This destroyed social solidarities and altered relations not just between state actors and individual peasants but also between neighbors, friends, and families.[60] Seeking to prevent peasants from fleeing the countryside, the Soviet government introduced an internal passport system in 1932, which effectively tied peasants to their workplace and residence.[61] In the Soviet Union's main grain-producing areas in Ukraine, Kazakhstan, and the northern Caucasus, collectivization led to mass famine, claiming the lives of an estimated four to five million peasants.[62] Belarus was spared widespread famine, but collectivization nevertheless meant that an already poor region became even poorer. The economic situation was probably worst in Polesia, the southern region bordering Ukraine, where several villages reported in 1933 that people were dying of hunger.[63] Any resistance to collectivization, real or imagined, was met harshly by the authorities. Overall, the Soviet state security organs deported 1.7 million "kulaks" to the Gulag. Of these, an estimated 261,000 people were deported from Belarus during the years 1931–1934, at the height of collectivization. Many of them, especially children, died.[64] Among those who vanished were acquaintances of Lev Ovsishcher's family, the Madriks, who lived in the village Zaborov'e not far from Bogushevsk in northeastern Belarus. Branded "kulaks," their property was confiscated, and they were deported east. Like many others, the Madrik family vanished in the vast network of forced labor camps and special settlements: "What happened to them in faraway Siberia? That we did not know."[65]

State violence, though, did not end with collectivization. From the very beginning, the Bolsheviks perceived themselves as under threat from internal enemies and foreign agents, traitors and fifth columns who were infiltrating the country. Throughout the interwar years, the Soviet authorities forcibly resettled from its border zones—whether in Belarus, Tajikistan, or the Far East—those social or ethnic population groups that they deemed unreliable and replaced them with those they considered more trustworthy. In Belarus, the cleansing of districts that bordered Poland first started in 1930 and disproportionally affected ethnic Poles.[66] The notion of betrayal (*izmena* or *predatel'stvo* in Russian) was also central to the series of public trials of alleged political opponents that the authorities conducted in the interwar Soviet Union. These were mass legal spectacles, conceived by the regime as educative trials (*pokazatel'nye protsessy*), which served to define the Soviet body politic by excluding and eliminating those deemed political enemies.[67] The defendants at the trials were usually accused of counterrevolutionary crimes, which in the Soviet Russian penal code were broadly defined as "any acts directed at the overthrow, subversion, or weakening" of Soviet power.[68] In 1934, the legal category of counterrevolutionary crimes was expanded to include treason (*izmena rodine* in Russian, literally "betrayal of the motherland"), defined under article 58-1a as "acts committed by citizens of the Soviet Union to the detriment of the military might of the Soviet Union, to the independence of her state or the integrity of her territory."[69] The interwar series of mass legal spectacles culminated in the three Moscow trials of 1936–1938, which saw several prominent party members prosecuted for alleged treacherous activity.[70] They reverberated out from the center to the Soviet republics, where numerous public trials of "traitors" and "enemies of the people" were conducted in front of local audiences. In Belarus, the first of these local public show trials was held in March 1937 in the Lepel' district to the northeast of Minsk; more than a dozen followed within months. In general, though, the Soviet government sought to keep arrests out of the public eye. The NKVD usually carried out its arrests at night; and most people were sentenced to death or forced labor camp without trial.[71]

During the years of the Great Terror (1936–1938), the NKVD arrested more than 1.5 million Soviet citizens whom it accused of treason, spying for foreign powers, or economic sabotage. About 700,000 of them were executed, and the rest were sent to the Gulag, where many of them died.[72] In Belarus, as in other parts of the Soviet Union, the Great Terror began with purges within the Communist Party, the regional NKVD, and the Red Army, which led to a significant loss in experienced personnel. This included Nikolai Gikalo, first secretary of the Communist Party of Belarus from January 1932 to January 1937; his successor Danila Volkovich, who held the post for two months until March 1937; and Vasilii Sharangovich, who succeeded Volkovich. On orders from Moscow, these men had orchestrated Soviet state violence in Belarus before they themselves fell victim to it. They were arrested and subsequently killed.[73] In July 1937, Sharangovich was replaced by Iakov Iakovlev, who held the post of first secretary for fifteen days before he was replaced in August 1937 by Aleksei Volkov, who prior to that had occupied different party posts in Turkmenistan, Ukraine, and Moscow. Together with Boris Berman, then head of the NKVD in Belarus, Volkov oversaw the arrests of many regional and local party-state representatives. Within a few months, though, the two most powerful men of the republic were already demoted from power.[74] In May 1938, Boris Berman was arrested and replaced by Aleksei Nasedkin, who in turn was arrested in December 1938 and replaced by Lavrentii Tsanava, now head of the NKVD in Belarus, a protégé of Lavrentii Beriia, the head of the central NKVD (who like him hailed from the Caucasus). In June 1938, First Secretary Aleksei Volkov was replaced by Panteleimon Ponomarenko, a communist with Ukrainian-Russian roots who had only recently taken up a mid-level administrative position in the party apparatus in Moscow. Suddenly propelled into a leadership position as one of the beneficiaries of the Great Terror, he would occupy the post of first secretary of the Communist Party of Belarus until 1947.[75] Just as Ponomarenko's career benefited from the Great Terror, so did the careers of many lower-level party-state representatives who now ascended into local leadership positions.[76] Ponomarenko was a protégée of Georgii Malenkov, a leading Bolshevik in Moscow who himself saw his star rising during the Great Terror when he became a member of Stalin's inner circle. It was also Malenkov who, on Stalin's order, was sent to Minsk in the late spring of 1937 to personally oversee the repressions.[77]

The Great Terror in Belarus is commonly associated with purges of the political and cultural elites, and indeed, these two groups were greatly affected. Accused of counterrevolutionary activity, the NKVD imprisoned or killed many journalists, writers, and university lecturers, most of them Belarusian and Yiddish speakers who had benefited from the *korenizatsiia* program of the 1920s.[78] Just as in the Soviet Union at large, though, the majority of victims in Belarus did not come from elite groups. The largest group of victims, most of them probably peasants, were arrested as part of the so-called Kulak Operation, which, according to NKVD Order no. 00447 of July 30, 1937, was to target "former kulaks, criminals, and other anti-Soviet elements" who were accused of anti-Soviet activity. From August 1937 to the fall of 1938, the Kulak Operation was carried out throughout the Soviet Union. In Belarus, the NKVD took 25,414 individuals into confinement. An unknown number of them were executed.[79]

Two weeks after the start of the Kulak Operation, the so-called Polish Operation began. Conducted under NKVD Order no. 00485 of August 11, 1937, it was carried out parallel to the Kulak Operation. Although likewise an all-Union operation, it hit the western regions hardest, as its victims were mostly Soviet Poles accused of spying for the Polish state or other individuals associated with Poland, Polish culture, or Roman Catholicism. In Koren'shchina, for example, a heavily Roman-Catholic region around the village of Koren' about thirty miles to the north of Minsk, most of the arrested locals were accused of being agents of the Polish secret service or members of a Polish military organization.[80] In total, the NKVD arrested 19,931 individuals in Belarus as part of the Polish Operation, of whom almost 90 percent (17,772 people) were shot to death. Some of the victims were probably considered ethnic Belarusians or Jews by the authorities, but most of them would have been local ethnic Poles. Others were deemed German or Lithuanian "spies."[81] Before the Kulak Operation and the Polish Operation went into effect, Stalin and the Politburo set quotas specifying how many people were to be sentenced to forced labor and how many were to be executed. Operating in secret, local troikas—composed of a regional NKVD chief, a regional party leader, and a regional prosecutor—were responsible for transforming these quotas into arrests, executions, and deportations. Sensing that the center wanted them to exceed the quotas, regional party leaders sent requests to Moscow, asking to be allowed to raise the number of people who were to be shot or sentenced.[82] One of them was Panteleimon Ponomarenko, who in July 1938, just a month after having assumed the post of first secretary, appealed to Stalin to be allowed to raise the number of executions and arrests in Belarus.[83]

Adding up the numbers, the Great Terror claimed about sixty thousand victims in Belarus, of whom at least thirty thousand people were probably killed.[84] It is possible that Vladimir Khartanovich's fellow villagers, who had illegally crossed the border into Soviet Belarus in the 1920s, were among them. At some point during the 1930s, most of them were arrested as Polish spies. At least six of them did not return from the forced labor camps.[85] One of the NKVD's main execution sites in Belarus was located in the Kuropaty forest to the north of Minsk. Residents of the nearby village Tsna later recalled that they saw black cars driving through the village and at night heard shots from the forest.[86] In Kublichi, the small northeastern Belarusian town where Vasil' Bykaŭ went to school, the local doctor, the principal of his school and some of the teachers, some of the town's officials and all of the Catholic and Orthodox priests were arrested. Two of Lev Ovsishcher's teachers also vanished, arrested as spies and enemies of the people, their fates unknown. In Bykaŭ's home village of Bychki, the state security organs arrested all Catholic families. Just as people knew the victims, so at times were they familiar with the perpetrators: in Bychki, it was the local NKVD representative, a man by the name of Peretiat'kin, who usually carried out the arrests.[87] Rumors of arrests circulated around neighborhoods and villages. By the second half of the 1930s, Ol'ga Bembel'-Dedok, who had previously studied art in Leningrad, lived with her family on Grushevskii Lane in Minsk. When two of her neighbors disappeared, she did not question their guilt. And neither did her other neighbors: "Everybody simply wondered: There now, people lived side-by-side, we kept company with them, and they turned out to be enemies." Reflecting on the events many years later, Ol'ga Bembel'-Dedok wondered why it did not occur to her that these people might have been innocent. Back then, she was quite certain that the arrests were justified: "The talk about how someone was making a career now at the expense of these people's lives seemed to me like an attempt to exonerate the guilty."[88]

Taking all the numbers into account, at least 321,000 people in pre-1939 Soviet Belarus suffered from state violence during the 1930s, whether as a result of collectivization (about 210,000 people in 1931–1934, not considering the years from 1934 onward) or as a result of the Great Terror (about 60,000, of whom at least half were executed). For some, this meant deportation to "special settlements" in Siberia—in reality, a form of forced labor camp. Others faced deportation to the vast network of camps that constituted the Gulag, and still others suffered death by execution. If one adds to that the estimated 10,000 people who fell victim to Bolshevik violence in the 1920s (mostly old elites, religious authority figures, and political opponents, real or imagined), one arrives at the number of 331,000 inhabitants of Belarus who fell victim to Bolshevik violence between 1917 and 1939.[89] This is a conservative estimate, yet even then a significant number in a republic that by 1939 had reached a population of 5.19 million.[90] At the time, the full extent of the regime's violence against its own citizens was hidden from the population; indeed, its scale only became known with the opening of state archives after the fall of the Soviet Union. Still, everyone probably knew at least one of the victims personally or had a relative or friend, colleague or neighbor who was arrested or deported—or in any case would have heard about the many more who simply disappeared overnight, never to be seen again.

Sovietization from Abroad

In the fall of 1939, the communist revolution was exported west—and so were Soviet utopias of social engineering, inextricably tied to the duality of state violence and state promises. That August, Hitler and Stalin had found common ground in their desire to enlarge their countries at the expense of the independent states located between Berlin and Moscow. In the secret protocol that was part of the nonaggression treaty known as the Molotov-Ribbentrop Pact, the two leaders agreed to divide Eastern Europe between them. On September 1, 1939, the Wehrmacht invaded western Poland, and on September 17, 1939, the Red Army invaded eastern Poland. After a brief military campaign, the region was annexed to the Soviet Union. Southeastern Poland became western Ukraine, and northeastern Poland, including the Białystok region, became western Belarus. The inhabitants of these lands automatically received Soviet citizenship.[91] With that, Chasia Bornstein-Bielicka, Zofia Brzozowska, Vladimir Khartanovich, and Litman Mor found themselves living within the same Soviet republic as Ol'ga Bembel'-Dedok, Vasil' Bykaŭ, Lev Ovsishcher, and Zinaida Suvorova. As a result of the annexation, Belarus doubled its territory and population, which now stood at approximately 10.4 million people.[92]

To the Soviet government, northeastern Poland rightfully belonged to Belarus, given its high percentage of Belarusian-speakers, and southeastern

Poland rightfully to Ukraine, given its high percentage of Ukrainian-speakers. The Bolsheviks justified the annexation by claiming that the Red Army came to liberate the region's minorities from oppressive Polish rule and the peasants from Polish landowners and settlers.[93] *Sovetskaia Belorussiia*, the main Russian-language newspaper of Belarus, celebrated it as a moment of "friendship and brotherhood of the Soviet nations" and claimed that "socialism had annihilated parasite-exploiters."[94] In the fall of 1939, Ol'ga Bembel'-Dedok helped her husband Andrei Bembel' to create a relief for the Belarusian pavilion at the All-Union Agricultural Exhibition in Moscow. Titled *Western Belarus Joins One Unified Soviet Belarus*, it depicted peasants and workers who were joyfully greeting Soviet soldiers.[95]

And indeed, such scenes did take place. In villages and towns throughout western Ukraine and western Belarus, people came together to welcome Red Army soldiers. In Liubcha and vicinity—which included Achukevichi, Vladimir Khartanovich's village—local communist sympathizers set up a temporary committee that took over the administration. By the time the first Red Army units arrived in Liubcha, red flags were hanging from buildings and on the main street, a large banner had been raised that read "Welcome to the Red Army."[96] Yet the reasons why some locals other than communist sympathizers welcomed the arrival of the Red Army varied greatly, ranging from sheer curiosity to hope for land redistribution or joy over the demise of the Polish state. Local information about life in the Soviet Union was also mostly limited to the propaganda that the communist underground had spread in interwar Poland, and people's expectations of what Bolshevik rule meant usually did not correspond to later reality. Indeed, only a year into Soviet rule, a saying circulated among the local Belarusian-speaking population that "the Poles tried to polonize us for twenty years but did not manage to do so, and now the Soviets polonized us in one year."[97] For others—like Chasia Bornstein-Bielicka's family from Grodno, who had heard from Jewish refugees about the Germans' brutal treatment of Jews in western Poland—the Bolsheviks seemed by far like the lesser of two evils. In the first two weeks of September 1939, in the period between the German invasion of Poland from the west and the Soviet invasion of Poland from the east, the city of Grodno was more or less without any authority, at best under loose German control. Local gangs, in Bornstein-Bielicka's eyes Poles, took advantage of the power vacuum and broke into Jewish homes, looting and brutalizing their inhabitants.[98] Other sources describe the turmoil in town as originating from an uprising mostly staged by local Jewish and Belarusian communists and the ensuing battles as fighting between them and Polish soldiers.[99] When the Red Army took over the city on September 17, 1939, the Bielicki family welcomed their arrival, hoping that the Soviets would put an end to anti-Jewish violence at the hands of other locals, which is also what happened.[100]

Within weeks after the invasion, the Soviet authorities managed to extend their one-party dictatorship, with its planned economy and strong state security organs, to the new territories. The first to be targeted were the old elites, above all large landowners, Polish army officers, state officials, and Catholic clergy. In some cases, violence (killings, torture, beatings) was committed by locals in the interregnum before the arrival of the Red Army in a given region. The attackers were usually peasants, and their victims were Polish settlers, soldiers, or other representatives of the Polish state. After the Soviet forces arrived, their officers further encouraged such actions, allowing locals to seek revenge for perceived wrongdoing under Polish rule.[101] Among those who were killed in the fall of 1939 was Zofia Brzozowska's uncle Wacław Haciski. Her grandparents, who owned the Czombrów estate in what was now called the Novogrudok region, and her parents, who owned the neighboring estate Muchówka, were spared violent encounters with Red Army soldiers or local peasants. Within the first days of the Soviet invasion, "the new authorities, a committee composed of local peasants from the nearby village Nieznanowo," appeared in Muchówka. "They catalogued and confiscated the entire inventory and left only a cow and a piglet behind."[102] The seizure of the Czombrów estate proceeded similarly, although it is unclear from Brzozowska's recollections if this was again done by a committee composed of local peasants or by Red Army soldiers or officials who had arrived from the eastern regions of the Soviet Union. Furniture, paintings, the library, even her grandfather's collection of bugs was taken away. According to Brzozowska, "the village was happy about the arrival of the Soviets," but its inhabitants did not display any hostility toward her family, and people still felt bound by social customs.[103]

Polish landowners and settlers were the first but not the only ones who had their property seized. Once the first administrative structures were set up, Soviet officials expropriated factory owners, nationalized enterprises, and shut down private stores. State-run factories, grocery stores, and artels (cooperative associations of artisans) were put in the place of privately owned businesses; as a result, commodity and food shortages soon became part of daily life.[104] Despite official unification, the borders between the new and the old Soviet territories and between western and eastern Belarus remained closed; permits were needed to cross.[105] Party members from the old Soviet territories exclusively occupied the upper echelons of the Soviet administration, the executive committees, which existed on the regional, city, and district levels. These so-called Easterners (*uskhodniki* in Belarusian, *vostochniki* in Russian) also held many of the leadership posts in factories and schools. The center considered them more reliable than local cadres, including those who had been active in the communist underground in interwar Poland. As in the old parts of the Soviet Union, the NKVD set up a surveillance and informant network, and people were encouraged to report on one another. With the exception of the Communist Party and the Komsomol, all political parties and youth organizations were forbidden. Privately owned shops were closed down, as were many churches and synagogues, and private schools, including the Hebrew educational system with its schools of religious learning, were abolished. Polish and Hebrew, associated by the Soviets with Jewish nationalism, were banned from the school system.[106]

For Chasia Bornstein-Bielicka, the two years of Soviet rule over Grodno were mostly associated with a general atmosphere of fear and suspicion. Jewish communal life was severely restricted, and the Socialist-Zionist youth organization Hashomer Hatzair, in which she was active, was no longer allowed to exist. One night, her older brother Avraham Bielicki, who headed the local Hashomer Hatzair branch, was arrested by the NKVD. Held for several days in confinement, he was tortured during the interrogations and then released. Yet Soviet rule also opened up limited opportunities for Bornstein-Bielicka. The authorities removed the tuition that had made it impossible for poorer students to attend high school and abolished the entry quotas that had limited the enrollment of Jewish students in universities. Bornstein-Bielicka was now able to attend high school and receive an education previously not available to her.[107] Moreover, in May 1935, Grodno had been the site of a pogrom, carried out by local non-Jews and orchestrated by the extreme Polish Right, which had left several Jews dead and many stores destroyed. Similar anti-Jewish riots erupted elsewhere in Poland in 1935–1937.[108] Back then, Chasia Bornstein-Bielicka and her sister had asked their mother why people shouted "dirty Jews" or "lousy Jews" at them as they passed on the street. The Soviet authorities, however, took a strong stance against antisemitism. According to Bornstein-Bielicka, during the two years of Soviet rule over Grodno, no antisemitic incidents, whether taunting or outright attacks, took place.[109]

During the first weeks of Soviet rule, the authorities engaged in limited land redistribution from estates to small peasant households and created a few collective farms. These acts, however, served mostly propagandistic purposes. In reality, private farming continued to exist in both western Belarus and western Ukraine. The Soviet state introduced the collectivization of agriculture only after the war, in the late 1940s.[110] The reasons for that are unclear, but it seems plausible to assume that even though the Soviet authorities quickly managed to bring the region under their control, the center did not yet consider the situation stable enough to begin the radical transformation of the countryside.

Perhaps Stalin and his circle of leading Bolsheviks did not yet wish to alienate the Belarusian- and Ukrainian-speaking peasantry, in whose name they had "liberated" the region from Polish rule—or perhaps they wanted to wait until the state security organs had cleansed the newly annexed territories of people deemed unreliable or hostile to Soviet power. That process was carried out in two ways: first, through individual arrests, which took place continuously from September 1939 to May 1941 and affected about 110,000 people (of which about 43,000 arrests took place in western Belarus); and second, through large-scale deportations that targeted specific population groups.[111] The victims of these deportations were forester and settler families (*osadnicy* in Polish, *osadniki* in Russian), the families of repressed persons, refugees from western and central Poland, and others considered "anti-Soviet" and "nationalist elements." Their deportation to forced labor camps and special settlements in Siberia and Kazakhstan occurred in four waves: in February 1940, then in April as well as May and June of the same year, and finally in May and June 1941. In his capacity as first secretary of the Communist Party of Belarus, Ponomarenko kept Stalin informed about the NKVD's progress with the deportations.[112] All in all, at least 315,000 former Polish citizens were deported from the territories that had been annexed in 1939. Of these, the Soviet authorities considered 57.5 percent to be ethnic Poles, followed by Jews (21.9 percent), ethnic Ukrainians (10.44 percent), and ethnic Belarusians (7.62 percent). Of the 315,000 deportees, about one-third, 125,000 people, came from western Belarus, the other two-thirds from western Ukraine.[113]

Among the victims of arrest or deportation were relatives and friends of Zofia Brzozowska's family, including her aunt Maria Czechowiczowa, who was deported to the Arkhangel'sk region in February 1940. One of their employees, a Belarusian-speaking forester, was also deported, as was his elderly mother. In May 1940, the NKVD appeared at the Muchówka estate and arrested Zofia Brzozowska's father and her grandfather, Karol Karpowicz. They took them away in horse-drawn carriages; the children ran after them until they could no longer keep up and the carriages disappeared into the direction of Novogrudok. The moment remained etched into Zofia's memory. As she recalled many decades after the war, "Until this day I can hear the carriages disappear into the direction of Novogrudok."[114] Just three months later, in July 1940, Brzozowska's uncle Wojciech Karpowicz was also arrested and taken to the prison in Novogrudok. Two months after that, the authorities evicted the family's remaining women and children from the Muchówka estate and dismantled the house. Zofia Brzozowska's father was sentenced to eight years of forced labor. The family last heard of him in June 1941, when a short note, written on the back of a cigarette pack and probably thrown out of the train that took him east, reached her mother. "This was the only and last note from my father." Like her grandfather and her uncle, her father disappeared; the family never found out how the three men died.[115]

Adding up the numbers of arrested and deported people, including the number of Polish soldiers who were not released from Soviet confinement during the first months of the war but either killed or held in forced labor camps, one finds that overall, between 462,000 and 490,000 individuals who came from the formerly eastern Polish territories fell victim to Soviet state violence from September 1939 to June 1941. Of these, 33,100 people were killed and at least 25,300 died, mostly in exile as a result of harsh living conditions, hunger, or disease.[116] Of the total number of victims, about 178,000 people—125,000 deportees, about 10,000 soldiers of the Polish army who were still in Soviet confinement in December 1939, and 43,000 individuals who were arrested—came from western Belarus (which at that time included the Białystok region).[117] In proportion to the overall population of western Belarus, which by the fall of 1939 amounted to 4.73 million people (including the Białystok region), this translated into 3.7 percent of the region's inhabitants who from 1939 to 1941 were either deported, arrested, or (a smaller part) killed.[118] As in eastern Belarus, where about 6 percent of the overall population fell victim to Soviet state violence during the 1930s, this meant that every person in western Belarus was likely to have known at least one of the victims personally and had certainly heard of many more who suddenly disappeared.

Numbers alone, of course, cannot reflect the extent to which individual lives were shaped, altered, and transformed by the Soviet project, nor can they reflect the depth of individual suffering, including the impact that the loss of a family member had on those who did not personally fall victim to state violence. Neither can numbers give a sense of individual agency and its daily limitations, the negotiations and compromises that people had to make when engaging with the state, or the room for maneuver that they were able to carve out—in some cases more, in others much less.[119] In the East European borderland that Ol'ga Bembel'-Dedok and Vladimir Khartanovich, Chasia Bornstein-Bielicka, Litman Mor and Zofia Brzozowska, Vasil' Bykaŭ, Lev Ovsishcher and Zinaida Suvorova called their home, the years of Nazi occupation marked the height of the "Age of Extremes." At the same time, the region and its inhabitants had already been subjected to different waves of political upheaval, rapidly changing configurations of power, and state violence prior to 1941. War, revolution, and civil war deeply affected these lands, disrupting and destroying individual lives and ultimately leading to the redrawing of state boundaries.

The region also witnessed the coming and going of civilizing missions, which, although espoused by a range of very different political actors, had in common the belief that these lands and their populations needed to be "modernized." The Bolshevik approach was by far the most radical. Employing violence and coercion, the communists turned the borderland into a site of massive social engineering. In eastern Belarus, the collectivization of agriculture in the 1930s fundamentally changed the economic and social structures of village communities, punctuated by another period of state violence during the Great Terror. In western Belarus, formerly northeastern Poland, the social, political, and to some extent economic order was radically transformed during the years of Soviet rule over these lands from 1939 to 1941.

On the eve of Nazi occupation, then, the two parts that made up Soviet Belarus were in some ways quite similar; in other ways, however, they were quite different. Economically, this was still a poor region—the western part less so because of the continued existence of individual farming—and one that continued to be largely agricultural. In eastern Belarus, the first five-year plan had brought about limited industrialization, and urbanization had also increased, but the effect was, overall, modest compared to developments that would set in only after the war. Many villages, particularly in densely forested or swamp regions, were in their day-to-day lives quite isolated from the outside world.[120] Moreover, despite the radicalism with which the Soviet authorities turned traditional ways of life upside down, alternative values, beliefs, and identities continued to exist even in eastern Belarus. While some of these were in conflict with state-sponsored identities, others existed in parallel and could even be reconciled in seemingly harmonious ways. Despite prolonged antireligious campaigns and the closure of many churches and synagogues, religious traditions, whether Christian or Jewish, endured in private, even among some party members.[121] Lev Ovsishcher, for example, hardly knew Yiddish and already spoke Russian or Belarusian with his family at home. At the same time, his family celebrated Jewish holidays, even after the Soviet state authorities had closed down the town's synagogues in the early 1930s.[122] Older forms of social and economic organization survived as well. Although the collectivization of agriculture fundamentally altered the world of the village, smaller peasant markets continued to operate—officially undesired yet unofficially of crucial importance to the rural economy and peasant survival. Throughout most of the interwar years, the small towns, where Jews still constituted a sizable and often majority population group, by and large maintained their role as commercial intermediaries between the city and the countryside—probably less so than in interwar eastern Poland, but they did not cede that function altogether.[123]

At the same time, there were also important differences. To eastern Belarus, Sovietization had come as a revolution from within, over the course of two decades and with much local agency. Many of the lower-level Soviet officials but also some among the leadership—whether ethnic Belarusians, Jews, or Russians—were born or else had grown up in what became Soviet Belarus after the 1921 Treaty of Riga. This stood in stark contrast to western Belarus, to which Sovietization came as a revolution from abroad, as an express Sovietization over the course of only two years, with limited local agency and imported cadres from the old Soviet regions. Consequently, a generation grew up in eastern Belarus that knew no political system other than the Soviet one, one that constantly emphasized its superiority over the capitalist world and sought to instill in its young citizens a strong sense of patriotism for the Soviet nation. As Lev Ovsishcher recalled from his youth in the 1930s, he firmly believed what he was taught in school: that his parents' generation had saved them "from a terrible past" and that the Soviet Union, the "first nation of workers," was "building a bright future—a socialist society."[124] Similarly, for most of her adulthood, Ol'ga Bembel'-Dedok, like her husband Andrei Bembel', identified with the Soviet project, the building of socialism. For her, Soviet power was "dear, familiar, native" (*rodnaia mne sovetskaia vlast'*), the system that she was brought up with, the state that had enabled her, a woman from the provinces, to study in 1920s Leningrad—and it was likely also to have been the only form of political organization (and not just for lack of alternatives) that she could imagine living in.[125] By the summer of 1941, a sizable Soviet constituency existed in eastern Belarus, much more so than in western Belarus—although the extent to which socialist values had taken hold among the population of the republic's eastern half is impossible to quantify. In the countryside, which had just suffered a violent transformation of its traditional forms of organization and ways of life, Soviet power was generally widely disliked. Identification with the Soviet project in eastern Belarus, it seems, was primarily an urban phenomenon, and more prevalent among the younger generations, among people like Lev Ovsishcher and Ol'ga Bembel'-Dedok.

Another difference between eastern and western Belarus concerned the nature of intercommunal relations. At the beginning of the Second World War, local communities in western Belarus were still largely determined by religion and class. Zofia Brzozowska's world, for example, was distinctly Polish and Catholic: her family's social circle, both relatives and friends, consisted primarily of other Polish-speaking families from the landed gentry, whom they met every Sunday at church. As Brzozowska recalled, relations with the peasants were friendly yet did not extend beyond work and were limited by social barriers.[126] Vladimir Khartanovich's social community was mostly composed of family and friends from his small Belarusian-speaking village in western Belarus.[127] Although Brzozowska and Khartanovich must have attended high school in Nowogródek at around the same time, the former went to a Polish-language school and the latter to a Belarusian-language school; they thus remained within their separate, parallel communities. In a similar vein, although Chasia Bornstein-Bielicka attended a vocational school where Polish was the main language of instruction, her social life revolved exclusively around her Socialist-Zionist youth organization. Among her siblings, she was the only one who spoke Polish without an accent, a skill acquired at her vocational school that would later help her survive the war years. The Bielicki family was on friendly relations with their neighbors, among them the Mikhailoviches, a Christian-Orthodox family. Their houses shared a courtyard and the children often played together. However, as Chasia Bornstein-Bielicka recalled, encounters with other Polish neighbors were limited to the public street. Even if the families were on cordial terms, they did not really befriend each other but rather lived side by side, in close proximity yet at the same time apart.[128]

In contrast, among particular individuals and social groups in eastern Belarus, intercommunal relations did transcend previous religious and social boundaries to a greater degree than in western Belarus. This, however, was primarily the case with urban residents, usually belonging to the younger generations, who led largely nonreligious lives or, to varying degrees, identified with communism.[129] As a result of labor migration of Jews from smaller to bigger towns and cities within and outside of the republic, and of non-Jewish migration from the countryside to the cities and towns, the distinction between the overwhelmingly Jewish cities and the Slavic countryside was overall less pronounced than at the turn of the century. Although the countryside remained primarily Slavic, the population structure in cities and towns changed significantly during the interwar years: as towns grew, the percentage of Slavs increased and, consequently, the percentage of Jews decreased. By 1897, for example, the Jewish population of Vitebsk had constituted a bit more than half of the town's population; by 1939, its share had decreased to one-fifth.[130] In the January 1939 census, 55 percent of Jews in Belarus still named Yiddish as their native (or first) language (*rodnoi iazyk*), but 38 percent of them already declared Russian their first language. Although many of the latter remained fluent in Yiddish as well, since that was often the language spoken at home, the 1939 census indicates a lingual shift that was taking place among younger Jews: Russian was the language of choice in the urban public sphere and the language of social mobility and opportunity. A similar trend took place among ethnic Belarusians, who by the end of the 1930s constituted a larger share of the urban population than ever before.[131]

Moreover, with religious institutions closed down, religious practice mostly limited to the family home, and only communist political organizations permitted, there were few to no options available for young people to develop alternative ways of expressing political and cultural diversity. For teenagers, the Komsomol became the primary organization through which they were inducted into a communist way of life. This, for example, was the case with Zinaida Suvorova. Although she came from a religious Jewish family, she gave up her adherence to Judaism by the time she became a teenager. Her father was a teacher of Hebrew and Yiddish and because of that had been deprived by the authorities of his right to vote. Although he found himself at the margins of society, discriminated against by the Soviet state, he did not object when his daughter sought inclusion in the secular, communist world. Instead, he told her that "you take the road in which you want to believe—if you don't want to, don't believe."[132] Although she spoke Yiddish with her religious parents, Russian became her primary language in social interactions outside the family. Through her involvement with the Komsomol, but also through her attendance at a Russian-language high school in Orsha, her social circle included many non-Jews. On the eve of the war, she was married to a Russian, spoke only Russian with her two small children, and was a candidate for membership in the Communist Party.[133]

Although Zinaida Suvorova was only one individual among many, her example is representative of a larger trend: on the eve of the German attack on the Soviet Union, intercommunal relations among certain urban groups in eastern Belarus—younger people, those who no longer adhered to a religion, and people who closely identified with the Soviet project—were less defined by traditional social and religious markers of identity than in western Belarus. As a result, these groups were more integrated, bound together by experiences of shared (Soviet) sociability. This situation, however, pertained primarily to urban residents, in both larger and smaller towns. Even in eastern Belarus, the life worlds of the rural Slavic population and the Jewish urban population remained separate in many ways, with little to no contact beyond the economic exchanges at what had survived of the town's markets. In eastern Belarus, sociocultural change affected the towns and cities more than in western Belarus, but this did not significantly decrease the cultural distance between Slavic peasants and Jewish urban residents. By and large, each group continued to lead separate lives.[134] These similar yet also different legacies of Soviet governance in eastern and western Belarus had repercussions for the coming years of Nazi rule, affecting the choices that individuals would make, and the choices that they would be forced to make, under German occupation.

Chapter 2

At the Heart of Darkness

Wartime Choices, 1941–1944

On June 22, 1941, Zinaida Suvorova went about her work as usual. An administrator at the main theater in Orsha, a city close to the Russian border, it was her job to look after the artists, run errands, and take orders. Suddenly, bombs started dropping on the town. Suvorova, who was in charge of the theater building that day, left her children with her sister Fania and her mother. As she reached the building, she could no longer get inside: bombs were hitting the building, someone was shooting, and fires broke out. She ran back to her sister's house, where she met her brother-in-law Il'ia. "I looked at him, he stood there and cried: 'Oh, Zina, dear, what are we going to do?'" Feeling that she needed to take the lead, Suvorova decided that the family should head to the shoe cooperative where she had previously worked. In its cellar, they could seek shelter. But when they got there, "there was no longer any space, it was full with children, with elderly people—everyone was there." The family, it seems, somehow managed to squeeze into the shelter. Just then, one of her sister's little daughters had an asthma attack. Zinaida Suvorova took her niece, who was gasping for air, and stood with her close to the exit. Bombs continued to fall.[1]

The Luftwaffe bombed Orsha again on the night of June 24–25, leaving the city center severely damaged. During those first days of the war, Zinaida Suvorova's husband, Ivan, was drafted into the Red Army; as she later found out, he died shortly thereafter. Suvorova tried to persuade her mother, Sara Dribinskaia, to flee east, but her mother declined: she remembered the German soldiers who had occupied the city during the First World War as decent people who did not hurt the Jewish population, and she did not think that the war would last longer than a few weeks.[2] After heavy fighting, the Wehrmacht arrived in Orsha in mid-July 1941. Located in the rear of Army Group Center, the town subsequently came under the control of Ortskommandantur I/842 headed by Baron von Ascheberg and his deputy, Paul Karl Eick, who would play a key role in the murder of Orsha's Jewish community. Immediately, the commander's office imposed forced labor on the Jewish population, which consisted mainly of clearing the city of the ruins left after the bombings and forcing Jews to wear a black armband with a yellow star on it.[3] The Germans also organized police forces that were staffed with Soviet citizens. Some of these policemen took over the house of Zinaida Suvorova's mother. As Suvorova herself had lost her apartment in the bombings, the family moved in with a friend. In early September, the German authorities established a ghetto in Orsha, where about two thousand people were to be concentrated. Among those who were forced into the ghetto were Suvorova's mother, aunt, and brother with his wife and children. Suvorova, however, did not move into the ghetto. Instead, she decided to try to survive by passing herself off as non-Jewish. Alone, with two little children aged four and six to care for, she first left for the nearby town Smol'iany, where the ghetto was not enclosed, and then for the countryside.[4]

This chapter investigates the years of war and occupation and the choices that individuals made under the extreme constraints of Nazi rule. For civilians, the situation in occupied territory was such that contact with the occupation regime, whatever form it took and whatever choices it triggered, was unavoidable; carving out a niche in which one could hope to keep one's prewar life intact was impossible. Telling the story of victims and perpetrators and victim-perpetrators, the chapter details how people in Belarus acted under the constraints of Nazi occupation and how they related to the options offered by the Germans—but it also investigates to what extent different personal experiences with prior Soviet rule affected individual wartime choices. The focus is on three time periods and developments: the transition from Soviet to German authority in the summer of 1941; the murder of Belarus's Jewish community, which began in the fall of 1941, reached its height in 1942, and came to an end in the fall of 1943 with the destruction of the Minsk ghetto; and the growth of the Soviet partisan movement, which slowly began in mid-1942, accelerated throughout 1943, and continued until its disbandment in the summer of 1944. Taken together, these three developments reveal particularly well individual preferences and motivations, local dynamics of violence, and multicausal situational factors that increasingly accounted for the choices that individuals made, and the choices that they were forced to make, in German-occupied Belarus.

From Soviet to German Rule

As German troops and their allies crossed the border into the Soviet Union and Red Army units disintegrated under the onslaught, the Luftwaffe dropped bombs over cities and towns in the western regions of the Soviet Union. Multiple raids left the old center of Novogrudok, where Sulia Wolozhinski Rubin lived with her family, severely destroyed. When Zofia Brzozowska emerged from the basement in which she had sought shelter with her family, she could see the clouds of smoke over Novogrudok in the distance. Like other towns, Minsk was bombed repeatedly over the course of several days.[5] As fires engulfed towns and buildings went up in flames, panic started to spread, and people fled from the towns. Some of them sought refuge with relatives in the countryside, in villages off the major roads that were still largely left untouched by the attack. Others tried to head east to an unknown destination, hoping to reach the safety of the Soviet interior. With train stations overcrowded and roads clogged by military vehicles, they often simply set out on foot. Among Jewish communities, in particular, fears of impending German rule ran high. Hundreds of thousands of Soviet soldiers also ended up trapped behind the front line. Some managed to hide in the forests or seek shelter in villages, pretending to be civilians, but many were captured by the Germans and confined in prisoner-of-war camps.[6]

Among the first to flee from the advancing Germans were Soviet officials, party members, and state security officers. Their flight took on large proportions. On July 21, 1941, Regina Kaplan, a Polish communist, wrote a letter to the Central Committee of the Communist Party in Moscow. Writing about her experiences during the first days of the war, Kaplan provided details of the widespread flight of Soviet officials. In Białystok, then the westernmost part of Belarus, the regional party leaders and NKVD officers were concerned only with "sending their children, wives, and piles of personal property" in cars to the east. No announcement of official evacuation was made, leading some people to remark to Soviet officials that "you yourself are running away, but you are leaving us behind."[7] Several heads of children's orphanages in Białystok also fled, leaving the children unattended. As reported to Kaplan from other party members, all officials, including the party secretaries, and the complete staff of the regional party committee of Pinsk left before the German arrival. As a result, the inhabitants of Pinsk started to panic, "fleeing the town in total chaos." In Bobruisk, the "panic took on fantastical dimensions," with party and state officials leaving the city at a time when the enemy was still far away.[8]

The flight of Soviet officials resulted from a combination of circumstances: the overall chaos and confusion, absence of clear directives from the center, lack of prior evacuation plans, and fear for one's life and family, especially if one was Jewish.[9] The decision to leave or stay was taken on an ad hoc basis sometimes with, sometimes without consulting other comrades. In Lida, a small town in Baranovichi oblast, the local leadership had just gathered in the building of the district executive committee when German airplanes began to bomb the town. When fires broke out and communication lines stopped working, people started to panic. The head of the district executive committee, a man by the name of Zaitsev, and another official left Lida to try to reach their superiors in Baranovichi. In the meantime, all party secretaries of the district fled, and some NKVD and NKGB officers as well. As Zaitsev explained in his subsequent report to the Central Committee of Belarus, this was "less out of fear and fright and more out of [a feeling of] helplessness and lack of knowledge of what to do." Above all, he remarked, it was the Easterners (*vostochniki*) who left, individuals from the old parts of the Soviet Union who accounted for the vast majority of Soviet officials and NKVD officers in western Belarus.[10]

The more elite an official was, the higher were his chances of reaching the Soviet rear. Among those who were able to flee was the leadership of Belarus. On the night of June 24–25, three days before the Wehrmacht conquered Minsk, First Secretary Panteleimon Ponomarenko and other members of the Central Committee secretly left the capital. They were joined by members of the Belarusian Sovnarkom, the council that headed the executive branch of the party-state, and the Presidium of the Belarusian Supreme Soviet, formally the highest legislative body of the republic. Together with their families, these high-ranking party officials traveled to Mogilev, where the military command of the Red Army's Western Front had already retreated.[11] As the Wehrmacht closed in on Mogilev, the republic's leadership continued to flee, first to Gomel' and eventually to Moscow. After a short stay further east in Kazan', the core of the republic's leadership, including First Secretary Ponomarenko, returned to the Soviet capital in January 1942, where the Central Committee of Belarus would be based for the remainder of the war years.[12]

Contrary to what the Soviet authorities would later proclaim, from most of the republic—including all of western Belarus (Białystok/Belostok,

Vileika, Brest, Pinsk, and Baranovichi oblasts) and the western parts of eastern Belarus—state-organized evacuation effectively did not take place. The quick German advance simply made this impossible, in particular in regions where the Wehrmacht arrived within a day or two. Yet in a place like Minsk, which the Wehrmacht entered only on June 28, the question of what to take along and what to leave behind made visible that the Soviet authorities prioritized some resources over others. In the days prior to the leadership's departure from Minsk, Soviet officials and NKVD officers, afraid that sensitive material would fall into German hands, began to destroy internal documents and prepared others to be shipped off to the east.[13] In the little time that they had, the authorities managed to evacuate the NKVD and NKGB archives from Minsk. At the same time, in an attempt to maintain public order and control, the leadership tried to prevent individuals from fleeing of their own accord. On June 23, as the NKVD was preparing to evacuate its archives, the Central Committee instructed local authorities to make sure that people would not be able to leave their workplaces, factories, and collective farms.[14]

When the German advance temporarily slowed toward the end of June, the Soviet authorities were able to organize the evacuation from some of the eastern parts of Belarus—in particular, larger towns with good railway connections. By mid-August 1941, two weeks before the Wehrmacht would bring the entire republic under its control, a few dozen industrial enterprises and several hundred thousands of animals had already been evacuated from Gomel', Vitebsk, and Mogilev oblasts. Also sent to the Soviet rear was the central party archive, which until that time had been located in Mogilev.[15] As a rule, civilians were evacuated only as part of the necessary work force attached to a particular factory, enterprise, or academic institute that the authorities wanted to transfer to the Soviet interior. Given that most of these were located in towns, official evacuation privileged urban over rural residents.

What made individuals eligible for evacuation was not vulnerability or need but membership in a particular work collective.[16] Still, those eligible for evacuation could usually take family members along. In other cases, some workers were able to obtain evacuation permits for their family even if they themselves had to stay behind.[17] The stalled German offensive also provided individuals with more time to leave without official authorization (what Soviet officials called "self-evacuation") and increased the chances that they would reach the safety of the Soviet rear.[18] The majority of the Jewish population of Rechitsa, a town in Gomel' oblast, was able to flee or be evacuated before the Wehrmacht entered the town on August 23.[19] From memoirs, it is not always clear just how individuals managed to obtain a spot on a train that carried them east, but it often appears to have been a combination of luck and circumstance. Among those who were able to escape were Lev Ovsishcher's mother and two sisters, who fled from Vitebsk oblast to central Russia, where they worked on a collective farm during the war.[20] In August 1942, the deputy to the head of the Belarusian Sovnarkom estimated that 700,000 people had been evacuated from Belarus, but it is unclear if this number also included those who had left of their own accord.[21] Given the constraints on time and resources, almost all evacuees as well as the majority of refugees would have come from the eastern parts of the republic. Correspondingly, most of the Jewish inhabitants of Belarus who would survive the war would do so in evacuation and were therefore primarily from parts of eastern Belarus.

State-organized evacuation, then, made visible the priorities of the Soviet leaders: to protect the party's secrets, held in its archives, and to preserve economic resources—factories, research institutes, workers, and livestock. Prisoners were another priority. As the Wehrmacht advanced, the NKVD used the little time that it had to clear out the prisons and corrective labor colonies that it operated in the western regions of the Soviet Union.[22] Apparently, the NKVD deemed it too dangerous for the inmates to fall into German hands, perhaps expecting that they would join the German side. The main prison in Minsk was emptied during the night of June 22–23. Members of the NKVD marched the inmates southeast toward the small town of Cherven'. Along the route, inmates from other regional prisons and from Kaunas, Lithuania, joined the march. In total, the group must have comprised up to ten thousand people. On the way, NKVD officers executed a few thousand of them. The remaining 2,200 inmates who reached Cherven' on June 26 were either shot or assigned to the Red Army's penal battalions.[23] In Grodno, a local communist leader by the name of Poziiakov gave the order on June 23 to "shoot all counterrevolutionary elements that were confined in the prison" (*vsekh kontrrevoliutsionnykh elementov, nakhodiashchikhsia v tiur'me, rasstreliat'*), as he later reported to Moscow. A few hours later, the prison was hit by bombs, and the remaining inmates managed to flee.[24] Overall, of at least 36,000 people held in prisons and corrective labor colonies on Belarusian territory, up to 11,161 inmates were evacuated to prisons further east. A few people, mostly women with children and minor offenders, were released from confinement. Of the remaining twenty-five thousand or so inmates, an unspecified number, but certainly amounting to several thousand people, were shot by the NKVD.[25] The rest managed to escape, were left behind in the cells, or were killed as a result of German aerial bombardment.

As the Red Army retreated and Soviet officials fled east, some locals took advantage of the ensuing power vacuum and ransacked shops and private apartments. The NKVD officer Khmelevtsev reported from Mozyr' in Poles'e oblast that before German troops arrived in town, the "population from the nearby villages looted all shops, warehouses, and some of the apartments" whose inhabitants had fled east.[26] In Kublichi, a small town in Vitebsk oblast, peasants from the vicinity rushed to rob abandoned shops and warehouses, whereas in the village of Antonovo in Baranovichi oblast, it was the deputies of the village council themselves who distributed the goods held at the local store.[27] In Minsk, as Regina Bakunovich, who would live through the German occupation, later recalled: "people plundered food warehouses and bases as well as stores that were not destroyed by bombs. The plundering started already before the Germans arrived, not paying any attention to the noise of the airplanes above. . . . People didn't even pay attention to the dead. . . . One has to say, though, that the great plunder saved many from dying of hunger during the months of the occupation."[28] Some of the lootings also appear to have been directed specifically against Jews, or else overlapped with the general looting. Shortly before German troops arrived in the small town of Iv'e in Vileika oblast, peasants "invaded Jewish homes and looted property—goods, furniture, and other articles, loaded them onto wagons and brought it to their homes."[29]

Apart from the plundering of stores and private homes, Jewish and non-Jewish, some people also committed violence against Soviet officials, Communist Party members, and Red Army soldiers. Such initial violent incidents were, it seems, limited to western Belarus, although later denunciations of communists to the Germans would also occur in eastern and not just in western Belarus. In Brest, for example, the lecturer of the Brest regional party committee, a man by the name of Ioffe, witnessed how on the first day of the war, unknown individuals opened fire from some houses along Belostok street, aiming at retreating Soviet soldiers. In Grodno, unidentified individuals fired shots at NKVD officers and army personnel.[30] In Luninetskii district in Pinsk oblast, the NKVD reported that "kulak-hostile elements" (*kulatsko-vrazhdebnye elementy*) who were said to be opposed to Soviet power had organized a partisan unit, killed the district state prosecutor, a man by the name of Panteleev, and wounded another comrade.[31] And according to Major Dychovich, deputy to the head of the NKGB in Belarus, refugees from the western regions reported that around Białystok, Brest, Volkovysk, and other towns where the Germans arrived within days, at times even hours, "gangs composed of local residents, primarily Poles, were organized." These gangs, Dychovich wrote, were "fighting against those who are loyal to Soviet power," killing "refugees and retreating Red Army soldiers."[32]

The Occupation Regime

Once German troops and their allies arrived at a given locality, they assumed authority and began to establish their occupation regime. This entailed creating different military and civilian administrations throughout the western regions of the Soviet Union. By the late summer of 1941, Belarus itself was divided into five administrative units that cut across the republic's pre-1941 borders.

Most of eastern Belarus, including Vitebsk, Mogilev, and Gomel' oblasts, fell under the administration of Army Group Center Rear Area, an area of military jurisdiction behind Army Group Center that was under the command of General Max von Schenckendorff.[33] Large parts of western Belarus as well as a small part of eastern Belarus came under the civilian administration regime General Commissariat Weissruthenien. Headed until 1943 by Wilhelm Kube, and from 1943 on by Curt von Gottberg, General Commissariat Weissruthenien comprised towns like Minsk, Baranovichi, Vileika, and Novogrudok. It constituted a subunit of the larger Reich Commissariat Ostland that also included Lithuania, Latvia, and Estonia. In 1942, a small strip of land to the northwest of Minsk, until then part of the General Commissariat Weissruthenien, was incorporated into the General Commissariat Lithuania. The southwestern region of Belarus—which included towns like Brest, Pinsk, and David-Gorodok—became part of General Commissariat Volhynia and Podolia, whereas the southeastern region—which included towns like Mozyr', El'sk, and Rechitsa—became part of the General Commissariat Zhytomyr. Both General Commissariats, in turn, were subunits of the larger Reich Commissariat Ukraine, the civilian administration of Ukraine. The westernmost part of Belarus, Białystok/Belostok oblast—as well as small parts of Grodno, Baranovichi, and Brest oblasts—were merged into District Białystok (*Bezirk Białystok*), which came under its own German civilian administration.[34]

Like elsewhere in Nazi-occupied Europe, the SS and the German police active on Soviet territory were under the command of different higher SS and police leaders. These men, in turn, reported to Heinrich Himmler, chief of the SS and police. The higher SS and police leader for the terrain behind Army Group Center—and thus for large parts of Belarus—was Erich von

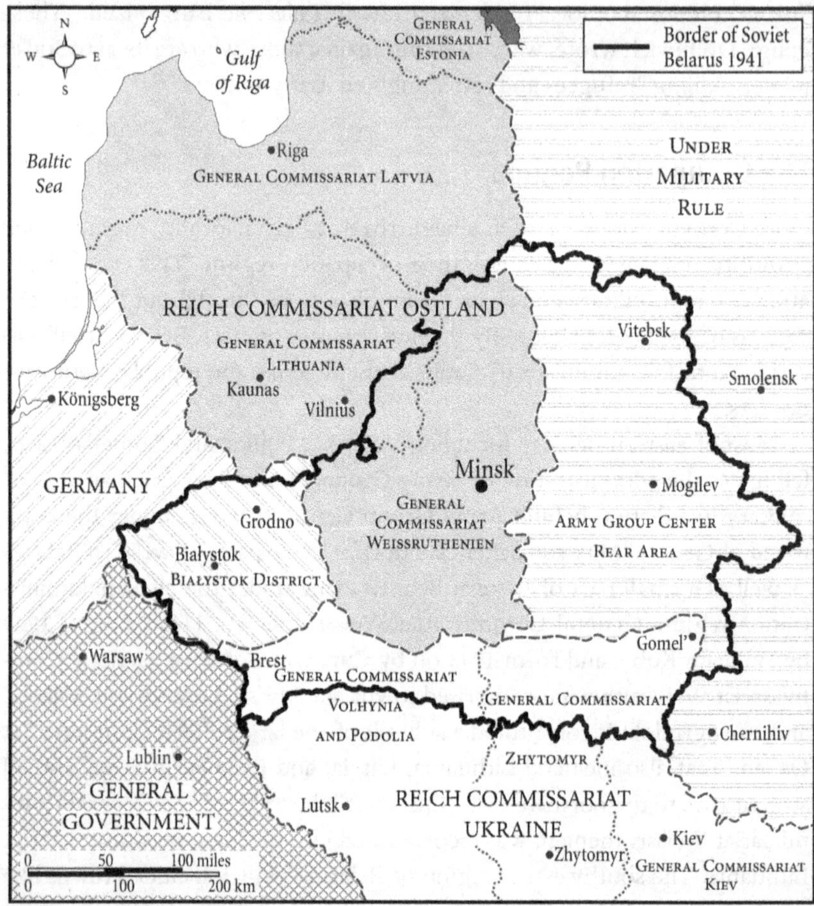

Map 3. The administrative division of Soviet Belarus under Nazi occupation, 1941–1944. Map by Mike Bechthold.

dem Bach-Zelewski. Bach-Zelewski joined the SS in 1931 and soon rose through its ranks. Hitler is said to have regarded him as a "man who could wade through a sea of blood." From 1942 on, Bach-Zelewski was also in charge of German antipartisan operations in the occupied Soviet regions. In 1944, he led the brutal suppression of the Warsaw Uprising.[35]

Regardless of whether a region was under the civilian administration of Reich Commissariat Ostland or Reich Commissariat Ukraine, or under the military administration of Army Group Center Rear Area, the essence of occupation policy was the same. The mass murder of the Jews, alongside the enslavement of the Slavic population, the economic exploitation of the occupied territories, and the destruction of communism as a political system lay at the core of Nazi rule.[36] In the long run, parts of Ukraine, the Baltic states, and District Białystok were to be settled with German farmers. Although most of Belarus and western Russia was not included in this Nazi quest for settlement, all Soviet regions were designated as food-producing colonies. To fulfill German demands, the government in Berlin planned to get rid of thirty to forty-five million people deemed useless eaters. In the case of Belarus, the most radical prewar plan envisioned the death through starvation of the whole urban population and half of the rural population, about six million people.[37]

When the Wehrmacht invaded the Soviet Union, however, Berlin soon realized that it could not easily starve millions of people to death. To extract as many resources as possible from the occupied regions, more local labor, in both industry and agriculture, was needed than originally thought.[38] The German administration therefore required urban residents to register with newly created labor offices, which allocated them jobs and imposed taxes on the population. Not unlike prewar Soviet practices, they also set grain delivery quotas for the villages. By 1943, labor concerns began to trump food concerns, resulting in the deportations of hundreds of thousands of Soviet civilians as forced laborers into the Reich. From the territory of post-1945 Belarus alone, an estimated 380,000 civilians, most of them women, were forcibly taken to Germany.[39]

In the occupied regions, the Nazis pursued different strategies toward different population groups. Shortly before the invasion, the Wehrmacht command issued two orders that called on German soldiers to fight ruthlessly and to show no restraint, in particular against Asian Red Army soldiers, communists, and the Jewish population.[40] At the front, German officers often executed captured Red Army commissars, Jewish soldiers, and anyone deemed superfluous on the spot. Meanwhile in the rear, the Einsatzgruppen, special SS death squads, were in charge of killing civilians. Active on Belarusian territory was Einsatzgruppe B, a unit of about 665 men that was headed in 1941 by Arthur Nebe, the former head of Germany's criminal police. The task of the Einsatzgruppen was to kill members of the Soviet elite, communists, Jews, partisans, "radical elements" such as "saboteurs" and "propagandists," and anyone else deemed undesirable, such as people with disabilities, Roma, and psychiatric hospital patients.[41] Beginning in the summer of 1941, the Einsatzgruppen combed through the rapidly expanding prisoner-of-war as well as civilian camps for men of military draft age, murdering those considered members of the Soviet elite, communists, or Jews.[42] Soon, prisoner-of-war camps also became the site of another kind of murder: by making no provisions for food, shelter, or medical care, the Wehrmacht deliberately starved Red Army soldiers to death. One of the deadliest camps, Stalag 352, was located close to Minsk. Here, prisoners were packed together so tightly that they could hardly move. By late November 1941, death rates had reached 2 percent per day. Overall, 3.1 million Red Army soldiers did not survive German captivity; most of them were systematically starved to death. On Belarusian territory alone (within the republic's post-1945 borders), the Germans killed about 700,000–800,000 Soviet prisoners of war.[43]

In the east, even Wehrmacht soldiers who would not have thought of themselves as supporters of Nazism brought with them a sense of German cultural superiority and racial arrogance. Just as the government in Berlin incorrectly spoke of the war as a war against Russia, so did German soldiers usually not distinguish between the different Slavic groups that they encountered. To them, most local peasants were simply Russians. In letters home, Wehrmacht soldiers repeatedly described the population as "simple," "dirty," "infectious," "backward," and "uncivilized." It was the duty of the German soldier to "clean up" the east.[44] The rural population was required to deliver grain and taxed heavily; their property plundered at will by soldiers. Any resistance, alleged or real, was met harshly. Many local women, Jewish and non-Jewish, became victims of sexual assault and exploitation. In Glusk, Poles'e oblast, for example, intoxicated German soldiers forced women to drink and dance with them. At night, they entered houses, stole everything they could, and raped the women. One of the victims, a woman by the last name of Mints, was brutally assaulted and then shot in a nearby forest. In Piatenka and other villages in the district around Glusk, soldiers entered peasant huts and raped the female inhabitants.[45] Women and girls were also forced into military brothels, where the victims suffered multiple rapes each day. Such brothels existed in Gomel', Mogilev, and Baranovichi, but likely in other larger towns as well.[46] In Minsk, as the physician Iurii Taits recalled, the Germans opened up several bars for officers and soldiers. Officially, local girls and women were recruited to work in these bars as waitresses, but unofficially, they were coerced into prostitution.[47]

According to Berlin's plans, the Soviet Union was supposed to become a vast agrarian colony that could provide the Reich with the necessary resources that it needed to build, sustain and feed its empire. Soon, however, the German authorities realized that they would have to depend heavily on the employment of non-Jewish locals to be able to rule over the conquered territories. Throughout the western parts of the Soviet Union, they kept the organizational structure of the Soviet administration's lower levels (district and below) by and large intact. In each district (*raion*), Wehrmacht leaders appointed local residents to serve as town and district mayors, and in

FIGURE 2. German infantry and motorized troops on their way through a village not far from Minsk, August 1941. Courtesy of the Bundesarchiv.

each village, a local was designated to serve as head of the village or village elder (*starosta*). The town and district mayors oversaw an administration that included departments from housing to health, finances to education and the like. The administrative staff had usually been employed in similar jobs under the Soviets.[48] In each district, the Germans also created police forces that were under the command of a German police officer but otherwise staffed with local residents or else Soviet citizens. In regions under German civilian control, these police forces were called Schutzmannschaften (Hilfspolizei in District Białystok); in regions under military control, they were called Ordnungsdienst. Depending on the specific regional context, they differed in terms of ethnic composition, proportion of German superiors to local policemen, and mobility. As their responsibilities in the Belarusian territories (in their post-1945 borders) resembled each other, though, I simply refer to them as the local police; inhabitants of the occupied territories who spoke an East Slavic language usually called them *politsai*, from the German word *Polizei*, police.[49]

It is difficult to estimate how many locals held these low-level representative posts, by which I mean policemen, mayors, and village heads. On the territory that would constitute post-1945 Belarus, 50,000–60,000 people served as policemen, 20,000 as village heads, and an unknown number as town and district mayors. In other words, 80,000–100,000 individuals represented the German occupation regime in the localities, about 1 percent of the pre-1941 population of that territory.[50] If the Białystok region is included, the number must have been higher by several thousand. Applying this ratio to the estimated 60 million Soviet citizens who lived under German rule, one arrives at a number of 600,000 locals who, throughout the western territories of the Soviet Union, represented the Nazi regime in the localities. However, considering that an estimated 300,000 Soviet citizens alone served in the local police forces in the Ukrainian and Belarusian regions under civilian control (thus excluding the Baltics and the Belarusian, Ukrainian, and Russian regions under military control), the total number must have been higher, probably more than one million.[51] Even this number does not include Soviet citizens who fought as military auxiliaries in the Wehrmacht or SS or served as armed village home guards in the occupied territories. It also does not include the many more individuals who worked in the local city or district administrations as head of the individual departments, clerks and translators, or as agricultural specialists. In Belarus alone (in its post-1945 borders), it is estimated that overall, the German authorities could depend on more than 150,000 Soviet citizens who worked in the police, the general administration, and the agricultural administration.[52]

The Holocaust

The occupiers employed a mixture of brutality and limited co-optation toward the Slavic civilian population, with violence becoming more systematic and widespread once German antipartisan operations increased in mid-1942 and the campaigns for forced labor intensified. Jewish communities, however, were immediately subject to systematic discrimination and abuse, restriction of movement, marking, and forced labor. In contrast to Slavs, they were also singled out for destruction as a group.

Most Jewish communities were shot to death over ditches and pits that were often located on the outskirts of the towns where they lived. The killings were usually joint operations carried out by the Einsatzgruppen and German police formations (Security Police, Order Police, and Reserve Police Battalions), supported by native-staffed SS or police formations, of which more will be said later. Often, the men raped Jewish women prior to their execution. Wehrmacht units were involved in all stages of the killing process, as soldiers helped to round up the victims, led them to the killing site, and cordoned off the area, shooting anyone who tried to escape. In many cases—for example, in the small town of Krupki northeast of Minsk—

Wehrmacht soldiers also participated directly in the killings.[53] The German authorities established several concentration camps on Belarusian territory, most notably in Malyi Trostenets, south of Minsk, and in Koldychevo, close to Baranovichi.[54] Some of the Jewish populations in District Białystok were also killed in death camps farther west in German-occupied Poland. Among those who died at Treblinka was Chasia Bornstein-Bielicka's father, who was deported from the ghetto in Grodno.[55]

For a variety of different reasons—including frontline developments, institutional rivalries, and the need of local authorities to balance the demand for food, housing, and Jewish labor—the timeline of the Holocaust differed slightly in the occupied Soviet regions. At first, primarily male Jews, often those considered part of the local elites, were killed, but some women and children were already among the victims, too.[56] On the territory of pre-1941 Belarus, German violence against Jews most massively and rapidly accelerated in and around Białystok. On June 27, 1941, a day after German forces had entered the city, Police Battalion 309 murdered 2,000–2,200 Jews in Białystok, including some 800 people who were burned alive in the Great Synagogue. In the following days, three hundred members of the Jewish intelligentsia were killed. The violence further escalated with a July 7 visit by Heinrich Himmler, after which another four thousand Jewish men were murdered. About two weeks later, the remaining Jewish population was forced into a ghetto.[57]

In the bulk of the Belarusian territories that were under the control of the Reich Commissariat Ostland and the Reich Commissariat Ukraine, the ghettoization of the Jewish communities followed a similar pattern. From July 1941 on, Jewish residents were forced into specially designated, heavily guarded neighborhoods, where overcrowding, hunger, and disease alone led to high mortality rates. In the regions farther east that were under military control, ghettoization usually took place a bit later. In some cases, mass executions occurred without prior ghettoization.[58] One reason for the difference was that the shift from the selective killings of male Jews to the destruction of entire Jewish communities occurred here sooner than in the regions under civilian control. In eastern Belarus, the Einsatzgruppen began their work in August 1941. Within weeks, the mass killing of the Jewish population of Bogushevsk, Lev Ovsishcher's hometown in Vitebsk oblast, took place. Of Ovsishcher's relatives who stayed behind in Bogushevsk, all perished.[59] By the fall of 1942, all ghettos in the Belarusian regions under military rule had been liquidated, their inhabitants killed. In the Belarusian regions that were under civilian administration, the destruction of entire Jewish communities began later and was usually carried out in several steps, with ghetto liquidations reaching their peak in 1942.[60] Those deemed useless laborers were killed first and those deemed temporarily useful, last. In Novogrudok, for example, the first mass killing took place in early December 1941. As SS units arrived, Wehrmacht officers and men from the Seventh Company, Infantry Regiment 727, surrounded the town to prevent anyone from escaping. The killing was combined with the ghettoization of those selected for labor.[61] Among those temporarily allowed to live were Sulia Wolozhinski Rubin's parents, who were dentists by profession, and their two daughters. Confined in the building of the former courthouse where the selection took place, they watched other family members being forced onto trucks. As Sulia Wolozhinski Rubin recalled: "We rushed to the windows boarded with wooden planks. Through the spaces we saw loaded trucks with screaming people and children. Blood and corpses were all over the yard as some had refused to go on a truck or had tried to run."[62] Their relatives were taken to pits that had been prepared in advance, near the village of Skrydlevo, where they were murdered: "People were shot behind the barracks outside of town, buried not too deeply and sprayed with chlorine. Many were only wounded and buried alive. We were told the earth shook for three days until all had died."[63]

That day, more than 5,000 Jews of Novogrudok were murdered, and about 1,300 people forced into the ghetto. A few weeks later, Sulia Wolozhinski Rubin managed to escape to the nearby forests, where she joined a Jewish partisan unit. Wolozhinski Rubin's parents survived two more rounds of selections but were murdered during the fourth mass killing in May 1943. In September 1943, most of the remaining 250 Jews escaped from the courthouse, which served as their place of confinement after the liquidation of the Novogrudok ghetto, through a tunnel that they had dug. Some of them made it to the partisans in the nearby forests, but others, among them Sulia Wolozhinski Rubin's sister Ruth, died in the attempt to flee.[64] That same month, following a Jewish uprising, the Germans liquidated the ghetto in Białystok and, in October 1943, the ghetto in Minsk, the largest one in the occupied Soviet regions.[65] By the early winter of 1943, all ghettos had been destroyed. Of the roughly 755,000–855,000 Jews who, prior to 1941, lived in the regions that would constitute Belarus after the war (thus excluding the Białystok region), an estimated 500,000–671,000 people were murdered.[66]

Local Complicity and Entanglement

During the war, the situation in Nazi-occupied territory was such that it was impossible for civilians not to come into contact with the occupation regime. That contact—whether directly with Germans or mediated through their local representatives—took on multiple forms. For some, it meant the occasional encounter with German soldiers who came to their village to request grain or search for partisans; for others—in particular, for people who worked in city administrations or factories that were overseen by Germans—it entailed more sustained, regular contact. For many, these encounters were incredibly violent, yet for others, they could also come in the form of pragmatic interactions, cordial exchanges, even romantic relationships. Many tried to avoid contact with the occupation regime as much as possible, but others, with their own interests in mind, sought it actively. Consequently, some individuals became entangled or complicit in German crimes—some reluctantly and unintentionally, yet others much more willingly, on their own initiative.

Above all, it was the local policemen (Schutzmannschaften, Ordnungsdienst, or Hilfspolizei) who actively participated in the abuse, mistreatment, and murder of other locals. Prior to a mass execution, local policemen usually went from house to house, delivering German orders. During the killings, they rounded up the victims and cordoned off the execution sites, and they participated directly in the shootings. On the territory that would constitute post-1945 Soviet Belarus, the Germans also employed Lithuanian, Latvian, and Ukrainian police forces during the killings: for example, in December 1941 in Minsk.[67] Following a mass execution, local policemen searched the ghettos for people in hiding and combed through the forests for Jewish fugitives. When Sulia Wolozhinski Rubin's sister, Ruth, escaped from the ghetto in Novogrudok, it was local policemen who caught her along the way. They raped and tortured her to death.[68]

Due to ever-pressing demands at the front, the German presence in the countryside was scarce, and many smaller police outposts were left with only one German in charge or even no German supervision. Whenever a mass killing of Jews was scheduled to take place in a given town, the German presence increased temporarily. Yet most of the time, especially in the smaller towns, much of the everyday work of the occupation regime (control of work permits, collection of taxes, registration of the population, and other duties) was left in the hands of the local mayor and his administration. In many larger towns as well—for example, Minsk, Borisov, and Stolbtsy—the ghettos were under the direct control of the local city administrations. Mayors like Stanislaŭ Stankevich in Borisov were responsible for closing off the ghettos, requisitioning valuables and money from the inmates, keeping order overall, and helping to prepare the mass shootings of ghetto inmates.[69] In the villages, it was the responsibility of the village elder to ensure that

German demands—from meeting grain quotas to providing lists with the names of young people who would be deported as forced laborers to Germany—could be met. What this meant is that together with the local police forces, the mayors and village elders effectively represented the occupation regime in the localities. They usually had lived in the same town, district, or oblast prior to the war and thus knew both people and places well, a knowledge that was indispensable to the Germans. Of the eighty-nine policemen employed in Borisov district, for example, the absolute majority hailed from the town of Borisov and its surrounding district.[70] The victims, for their part, usually did not know the German killers, but they were much more likely to know one of the local perpetrators.

In Novogrudok, Sulia Wolozhinski Rubin's former boyfriend, a young Pole named Edward Niedzwiecki, was among those who joined the local police in the summer of 1941. A few months prior, he had been arrested by the NKVD, but during the German invasion, he was freed from a prison close to Minsk and returned to Novogrudok. Although Wolozhinski Rubin had ended the relationship before the summer of 1941, he continued to visit her, even after the Wolozhinski family had been forced into the Novogrudok ghetto. It is not clear how long Niedzwiecki served in the police and if he participated in any shootings later on, but at least in the beginning, he benefited materially from his position. As Sulia Wolozhinski Rubin remembered, he "was one of the confiscators of Jewish property. He wasn't poor anymore. Every time he showed up in a different suit." But when he was subsequently caught smuggling food to her sister Ruth in the ghetto, the Germans sent him, as it was rumored, to a work camp in Belgium.[71]

That perpetrators and victims knew each other meant that the violence committed by local policemen was intimate and often personal, in the sense that it was directed against former schoolmates, colleagues, or neighbors. Sofiia Khabai, for example, lived with her family in Minsk, on First Zaslavskii Lane, which later came within the borders of the ghetto. When the ghetto was established, Khabai's non-Jewish neighbors had to relocate to a different part of the town. This included a woman named Adelia, whose sons joined the German-organized police forces. On September 10, 1941, they appeared on First Zaslavskii Lane. The men whom Khabai described as "neighborhood acquaintances [*tovarishchi po sosedstvu*]" assaulted the Jewish residents: "They stole from those who lived with us, violated [*nasilovali*] and brutalized them. When they attacked house No. 6, next to our house [where] old people lived, they broke the nose of the old man, cut off the beard, split the head of the old woman."[72]

That kind of violence, as Sofiia Khabai's testimony makes clear, required actual physical exertion and close encounters with the victims. It also involved not just guns but knives, spades, axes, and stones as well. In some cases, the method of killing suggests that the perpetrators took a sadistic pleasure in their actions. One of the most extreme cases from Belarus (in its post–1945 borders) has been recorded for David-Gorodok, Litman Mor's hometown in Pinsk oblast, located south of the Pripyat river in the historic Polesia region not far from the border with Soviet Ukraine. Before 1939, David-Gorodok (then called Dawidgródek) belonged to Poland; after 1939, it belonged to Soviet Belarus. Unlike Lida or Grodno, bigger towns to the north, the Christian population of David-Gorodok was not predominately Catholic and Polish-speaking but Orthodox and Belarusian-speaking.[73] Here, the German-led killing of the town's male Jewish population and the expulsion of Jewish women and children took on a communal character.

In the early morning hours of August 10, 1941, SS Cavalry Regiment no. 1 arrived in David-Gorodok, and with the help of local policemen, shot the men to death. The women and children were driven out of the town, although it is not clear who was involved in that—only German soldiers and local policemen or local civilians as well. Among the women were Miriam Bragman and her father, disguised in women's clothes: "Along the road we were encountered by a gentile who was inspecting the crowd, and he recognized father. Words were of no avail. He returned with him to town." The women were driven to a manor alongside the river on the way to a nearby town, Stolin. "Meanwhile, the gentiles from the vicinity arrived, and they began to plunder and grab whatever came to hand." At night, Ivan Mareiko, David-Gorodok's German-appointed mayor, came to take a few Jewish women away. It is unclear what happened to them, but it is very likely that they were raped and killed.[74] In the days that followed, local policemen and other town residents hunted down fugitive Jews and tortured them to death. As Meier Hershl Korman recounted: "Baruch Katzman and his two sons were found and killed by Dmitri Pusik. Issur son of Nisson Gurvitch had his eyes gouged out by the Horodtchukas [as the Christian Orthodox town population was called] and his limbs severed one by one." Among the victims were Meier Hershl Korman's children, brutally murdered in full view of the public: "My two children Bracha and Baruch who, thanks to a gentile woman, had fled to the Dubinitz forest, were returned to the town by the gentiles and were cut to pieces in the middle of the marketplace."[75]

Besides serving in the local police forces or holding low-level representative posts in the German administration, there were other ways in which individuals contributed to or participated in German crimes or benefited from the suffering that Nazi rule caused for others. Most commonly, as happened in David-Gorodok, locals took part in the looting and appropriation of Jewish property—in some cases before the owners had been killed; in others, after they had been murdered.[76] After a mass execution, the Germans usually took the best valuables for themselves and left the rest for their local representatives. The city administrations used tables, chairs, and other items from empty Jewish homes to furnish their offices or leased them out to locals, as happened from August 1941 on in Mogilev.[77] When the Jewish community of Mozyr' was murdered in late September 1941, "the Germans allowed the population to plunder the apartments of those who fled into the depths of the country and to plunder the apartments of the Jewish population," the NKVD officer Khmelevtsev reported to Moscow.[78] And after the mass execution of the Jewish community in Kurenits, Vileika oblast, some locals went from one empty house to the next, taking up the floorboards and searching for valuables.[79]

Some people also decided to blackmail Jews in hiding, exploiting their vulnerability. Others denounced Jews to the German authorities, knowing that this would mean their death. During the mass execution of the Jews of Tolochin, Vitebsk oblast, for example, Gutman Aleinikov managed to escape and hide in a drainage pipe under a bridge for two days. A local peasant, however, discovered him and called the Germans, who murdered Aleinikov.[80] In Minsk, Ol'ga Bembel'-Dedok hid her Jewish acquaintance Nina Zhitnitskaia at her home. One of the neighbors reported Zhitnitskaia's presence to the police, and a policeman came and arrested her. She was probably killed soon after.[81] In Grodno, the local staff of the labor exchange (Arbeitsamt), where non-Jews had their labor permits stamped, reported people they suspected of being Jews to the Gestapo. As Chasia Bornstein-Bielicka observed, the Germans were not able to detect who spoke Polish with a Yiddish accent. The local staff, though, "could tell who was faking. The wrong facial expression, a telltale accent, or a question not answered fluently enough would betray you." One of her friends, Sarka Shewachowicz, was caught that way, handed over to the Germans, and killed.[82]

Also vulnerable to denunciations were Soviet officials and party members who had remained in occupied territory. Arsenii Kalinovskii, who spent the first days of the war with his wife's brother in the village of Edino, Minsk oblast, soon decided to return home to Minsk. The reason for that, as he recalled, was that he feared that locals would give him away: "Many in the village knew me as a communist and Soviet official [*kak kommunista i sovetskogo rabotnika*]." One of the villagers had also joined the German-organized police forces.[83] Several cases have been recorded in other parts of eastern Belarus where people reported fellow villagers who were said to have helped the Soviet authorities with the collectivization of agriculture to the Germans.[84] And when Anastasiia Voskabovich's husband—from the village of Blon', south of Minsk—was arrested by the Germans in August 1941, Voskabovich believed that an acquaintance had denounced him. The next day after church, she confronted the person whom she suspected, Pavel Azhgerei, directly. Azhgerei responded that he knew that her husband had cooperated with the NKVD. Pointing to a relative of Anastasiia Voskabovich's, he warned her that the same fate awaited that woman and said that "if he wanted to, he could kill five people right here on the street who were advocates of Soviet power."[85]

What can be said about why individuals joined the local police, served as town mayor, or denounced Jews and communists? In the eyes of the NKVD officers and Soviet officials who were present in occupied territory during the first weeks of the war, individuals who worked as policemen, town mayors, or village elders were mostly ill-disposed toward Soviet power. Curiously, in their reports to Moscow (submitted after they had managed to cross the frontline into the Soviet rear), they did not specifically mention antisemitism as a driving factor. Rather, Soviet officials and NKVD officers wrote of "kulaks," "counterrevolutionary elements," "criminals," and "lowlifes" (*deklassirovannye elementy*) but also of deserters from the Red Army who went to work for the Germans.[86] According to the secretary of the Pinsk regional party committee, a man by the name of Shapovalov, the local policemen in Pinsk oblast were "people who are known kulak and anti-Soviet elements."[87] In the region around Berezino, Minsk oblast, the local German-organized police, according to the NKVD officer Nikolai Zaitsev, consisted "primarily of people who had been repressed by Soviet power, or relatives of repressed people"[88]

The German authorities did indeed try to exploit any existing conflicts or grievances accumulated during Soviet rule. They reopened the churches and declared that they would do away with the collective farms in eastern Belarus—a promise that made a positive impression on the rural population, as the Soviet partisan I. S. Shurman reported from the region around Orsha in Vitebsk oblast a year into the German occupation.[89] In the General Commissariat Weissruthenien, which comprised large parts of western Belarus that had belonged to the interwar Polish state, the attempt to capitalize on negative legacies of Soviet rule had a clear ethnic component. Here, the German authorities at first sought to recruit those locals who self-identified as Poles, believing that these individuals would feel the least loyalty to Moscow.

Within a few weeks, however, German policy toward the Polish-speaking population began to change. The Germans were particularly wary of the Catholic clergy, whom they accused of trying to polonize the region's Belarusian-speaking Roman Catholic population. Ethnic Poles were removed from the police forces and the local administration, as the German authorities (correctly) feared that Polish nationalists would try to use these institutions for their own political aims. They were replaced with ethnic Belarusians, whose national consciousness the Germans deemed low and non-threatening to Nazi rule.[90] Increasingly, members of the local Polish elites—who as a group had already suffered disproportionally in the preceding two years under Soviet rule—also became the target of arrests. A few thousand of them were killed, as happened in Novogrudok in the summer of 1942.[91] Mirroring similar policies pursued by the German imperial army during the First World War, the Nazis even encouraged, within limits, the promotion of a decisively anti-Soviet type of Belarusian nationalism under German tutelage, hoping that it would strengthen the occupation regime. In December 1943, these efforts culminated in the creation of a Belarusian puppet administration, the Belarusian Central Council (Belaruskaia tsentral'naia rada). Headed by Radaslaŭ Astroŭski, the council was a short-lived, powerless institution that consisted primarily of former émigrés and Belarusian nationalists. Many of its members—whose political goal, if always unrealistic, was independent statehood—had a clearly fascist outlook and combined antisemitism with strong anti-Polish, anti-Russian, and anti-Soviet sentiments.[92]

Given the history of Soviet state violence in both western and eastern Belarus prior to the war, the German authorities could reasonably assume that resentment of Soviet rule would lead some individuals to join the occupation regime, just as Soviet officials thought.[93] Holocaust survivors often remembered the men who joined the local police in the summer of 1941 as people who had been known to be antisemites before the war or as disreputable people—local hooligans, drunks, or thieves who enjoyed the power that they now held over other locals.[94] Material incentives probably also played a role: in addition to taking part in the plunder of Jewish property, policemen and mayors received other privileges, such as visits to German brothels and bars. Their families were often exempt from paying taxes or spared deportation as forced laborers to Germany.[95] Yet others were resentful of the Soviet regime and the violence of collectivization and, even if they did not hold a post in the occupation regime, used the opportunities that now presented themselves to settle scores with those they deemed responsible for Soviet crimes, as Pavel Azhgerei did.[96] In the case of Edward Niedzwiecki, Sulia Wolozhinski Rubin offers several clues as to why her former boyfriend might have joined the Novogrudok police. In her memoirs, she describes him as a Polish patriot who was devastated by the loss of Polish independence in 1939. In the spring of 1941, he was arrested by the NKVD but escaped or was freed from Soviet imprisonment when the Germans invaded. In his case, it may have been a combination of different factors—Polish nationalism, resentment of Soviet rule, and material incentives—that explains why Niedzwiecki joined the police. Although he does not appear to have been antisemitic, his new, powerful position soon affected his behavior toward Wolozhinski Rubin. Prior to the war, he had been, in her words, a gentleman, yet after the German arrival, he exploited her new vulnerability by trying to force himself on her, telling her that she would die anyhow.[97]

In many more cases, though, the motives behind people's choices cannot be completely or, for that matter, coherently reconstructed. What to make of, for example, the three NKVD policemen in El'sk raion, Poles'e oblast, who, according to another NKVD officer, entered the German-organized police forces in the summer of 1941?[98] One reason why the issue of motivation is so complicated is that little material exists in which policemen, town mayors, village elders, or others accused of working for the Germans explained their actions themselves. Postwar Soviet interrogation protocols of Soviet citizens accused of collaborating with the Germans during the war usually include a part where the accused are asked to talk about their motivations, but these primary sources come with their own set of problems. Like any legal testimony given by a person suspected of wrongdoing, we can assume that the accused tried to present themselves in as positive a light as possible, thereby not being fully open about their motives. In addition, Soviet state security officers routinely applied a mix of psychological and physical pressure during interrogations, which in turn could (and did) make people provide self-accusatory statements that did not necessarily correspond with what they really thought.[99] It is also important to know that these protocols were not verbatim transcripts of the interrogations (which often lasted several hours and were repeated over the course of several days) but were rather drawn up at the end of each interrogation, not unlike short summaries—making it impossible to know whether the words of the accused as recorded in these protocols were indeed his or her own words or were provided by the interrogators.

The reliability of Soviet interrogation protocols for historical research continues to be a question of much debate.[100] If examined carefully and juxtaposed with other sources, the protocols can provide information on specific events and developments, such as on the activities of local policemen and their involvement in the Holocaust or the destruction of villages.

However, any self-accusatory statements or statements made by the accused regarding their motives during the interrogations cannot be treated as reliable historical sources. This means that we mostly have to rely on what contemporaries thought compelled these people to act that way—that is, we have to rely on the interpretations and explanations offered by others.

The question of motivations also raises another important issue, that of the conditions under which people came to join the Germans and the ways in which these were affected by the changing tide of the war. In the early stages of the war, the members of the local police forces were usually volunteers. Soon after the invasion, notices were put up in Minsk, asking for volunteers to join the police, who then underwent a vetting procedure.[101] Once partisan warfare began to pick up in mid-1942 and the German authorities sought to increase the strength of the local police force, a greater degree of compulsion was used to obtain recruits. Young men were told that if they did not join the police, they or their family members would be deported to Germany as forced laborers. Town mayors, it seems, were usually chosen by the Germans, although it is unclear how many of them volunteered for these positions. The main exception to voluntary recruitment during the initial phase of the war were the much-needed translators, as the police could hardly function without them.[102]

Some of the village elders appear to have taken up their positions of their own accord. In general, however, village elders were simply appointed, either by their fellow villagers on order of the German authorities or by the Germans themselves. This was, for example, the case in Lidiia Kozlova's home village, Osmolovichi, in Mogilev oblast. In mid-August 1941, the Wehrmacht passed through Osmolovichi, yet it was not until September that a group consisting of German officers, a translator, and local policemen arrived in the district. The translator told the assembled inhabitants that the Germans had liberated them from the communists and Jews and it was time to appoint local representatives. "People chose the authorities [*uprava*]," Kozlova recalled. "As mayor—the former secretary of the village council [*sel'sovet*], as the head of the village—the assistant to the agricultural specialist."[103] Kozlova's fellow villagers did not pick local representatives according to their political views but simply because of their expertise—which explains why those who held responsible positions in the rural economy before the war were often chosen for similar posts under the Germans. Therefore, not all of the individuals who came to occupy low-level positions in the occupation regime—village heads, town mayors, and policemen—may have done so of their own choosing. Because of their work responsibilities, they had to become complicit in German crimes (if to varying degrees), but that didn't always mean that they did so on their own initiative. As the partisan I. S. Shurman recalled from Vitebsk oblast, the *starosta* of the village of Iagudove, a man by the name of Svitin, did not actively participate in German crimes. According to Shurman, Svitin knew about the whereabouts of Communist Party members, but he did not give them away to the authorities. At the same time, he "gathered the collective farm members and read the Hitlerite laws to them," suggesting that Svitin complied with (some) German demands.[104] Some also tried to use their positions and the limited agency that they had to help others in need or, once the Soviet partisan movement gained strength, to support the partisans. According to Anna Adamovich, who lived in the small town of Glusha west of Bobruisk, the German authorities simply chose Konstantin Bychkovskii, an unskilled laborer, as mayor because he was a hardworking man. Bychkovskii, however, had ties to the small communist underground and provided its members (of whom Anna Adamovich was one) with documents and permits. In the spring of 1942, he left to join the nascent partisan movement in the surrounding forests.[105]

Considering the many shades of what constituted complicity, it is impossible to say how many locals participated in or contributed to German crimes, especially if we consider not just indigenous participation in the police forces or physical violence committed by civilians but acts such as reporting on a neighbor, blackmailing Jews, and appropriating property. Indeed, when we expand the question of complicity into the much broader but also more nebulous question of entanglement, we can find that simply by way of their profession, many more people came in contact with the occupation regime—which in turn could play out in different ways. Teachers, industrial specialists, and forestry workers were working in institutions that were overseen by Germans and as such had to comply with their demands, even if actual face-to-face contact with their German superiors occurred seldom. Similarly, office clerks in the city administration had usually worked in the same position under the Soviets and had not made an active choice to work for the occupation administration. Still, each office clerk (that is, if he or she did not engage in resistance activities) contributed to the functioning of the occupation regime. The members of housing departments, for example, were usually responsible for the sale of empty Jewish houses.[106] Their choices during the German occupation—and whether they had implicated themselves, legally or morally—would constitute a major source of division in the immediate postwar years, both in more private encounters with other Soviet citizens and in encounters with the Soviet authorities. What is clear, though, is that in every town and district, a small group of people, primarily those who entered the local police forces, assisted the Germans in carrying out the murder of the region's Jewish communities. In that respect, eastern Belarus—the part that had been Soviet for more than two decades before the war—did not differ from western Belarus, which had been Soviet for only two years before the German invasion. More specifically, the participation of the local police in actions against the Jews was not markedly dissimilar in these two sections. In both western and eastern Belarus, some locals, whether willingly or more reluctantly, took an active part in the murder and mistreatment of the local Jewish population, not just in the initial phase of the war but throughout the different stages of the Holocaust.[107]

Where a regional difference can be detected, though, is in the level of local violence against Jews that took place throughout the East European borderlands in the summer of 1941, during the transition from Soviet to Nazi rule. This violence differed from the more institutionalized violence that local policemen later committed on an everyday basis in that it often took the form of a riot or pogrom, understood here as a collective violent action by members of the majority population against a specific minority group, Jews.[108] The perpetrators of these pogroms were usually local civilians, of whom some might join the local police forces or administration later; in other cases, a mix of civilians and local policemen committed the violence. In each pogrom, the level of German presence varied. Some violence was committed before German troops arrived in a particular region or district, while other attacks occurred with their direct participation or presence. Still other pogroms took place after the Germans had shown themselves in a given locality but left shortly thereafter, leaving the town without clear authority for a few days.

In the pre-1941 Belarusian territories, the most extreme cases of local anti-Jewish violence—in terms of brutality, intimacy, and scale—occurred in the region around Białystok (Belostok). This region was annexed from Poland in 1939 and constituted the westernmost part of Soviet Belarus until Moscow handed it back to Poland in 1945. In contrast to the linguistically more mixed countryside farther to the east, the rural population of the Białystok region was in the absolute majority Polish-speaking. This was also the region where German violence against Jews most massively and rapidly accelerated in late June. During the first two weeks of the war, non-Jewish locals (some of them civilians, others already in their position as German-appointed policemen or town mayors) committed individual acts of murder in an estimated thirty smaller towns, sometimes helping Germans kill Jews, sometimes acting on their own. In some cases, the victims were subjected to several weeks of torture before their death.[109] In early July, local violence against Jews reached a peak. On July 5, a small group of Germans arrived in Radziłów, a town northwest of Białystok. The next day, a Gestapo man, with the help of local Poles, assembled the town's Jewish residents on the market square. On July 7, the Germans left and did not return until July 9. On their departure, residents of Radziłów forced their Jewish neighbors into a barn. The barn doors were nailed shut, gasoline was poured around it, and the barn was set on fire. It is possible that the local perpetrators were copying German methods: on June 27, German policemen had killed almost one-third of their Jewish victims that day by burning them alive in the Great Synagogue in Białystok. Anyone trying to escape from the barn in Radziłów was shot by locals or thrown into the flames alive. The hunt for fugitives continued for three days. Estimates of the number who were murdered during these three days in Radziłów range from eight hundred to two thousand.[110] The violence then spread to nearby Jedwabne, where on July 10, a similar massacre occurred. Early that day, a small German unit, probably from the SS, arrived in the small town. Although present, the Germans did not participate directly in the ensuing violence but left the initiative to the mayor, Marian Karolak. Karolak mobilized roughly one hundred local men from Jedwabne and its environs. The men dragged the town's Jewish residents to the main square, where they raped, tortured, and beat some of them to death. They then drove the remaining victims to a large barn and set it on fire. An estimated 1,600 people, Jedwabne's entire Jewish community, were murdered that day.[111]

While the local anti-Jewish violence that occurred in the summer of 1941 around Białystok has been well researched, it is less known that pogroms also occurred in the other western Belarusian regions—although on a much smaller scale, and with far fewer victims. As recalled by Izaak Lichtenberg, in the small town of Lakhva, Pinsk oblast, the civilian population "harassed the Jews for several days before the arrival of the German army on July 7–8. They smashed stores and plundered Jewish property, and they beat up the Jews."[112] Shalom Yoran and his family, who were trying to flee east when the German army started bombing the small town of Smorgon' in northwestern Belarus, were attacked by farmers on their way from Vileika to Il'ia: "There was chaos all around, no one in charge, no one to prevent looting. . . . The fleeing refugees, largely Jews, were vulnerable and easy targets."[113] Other violence was committed after German troops entered a given locality for the first time. According to Ioffe, a lecturer of the Brest regional party committee, in Gorodishche in Pinsk oblast, "in front of the eyes of German troops [*na glazakh u nemetskikh voisk*]," locals organized a "Jewish pogrom" and killed fourteen Jews in their apartments.[114] After the Germans had arrived in the small town Molchad' in Baranovichi oblast on June 29, gangs of local residents—often intoxicated and armed with spades, picks, and axes—roamed the streets. They broke into the synagogue and destroyed the Torah, beat Jews who dared to leave their houses, raped Jewish women, and killed a Jewish family, whose house they plundered. Martin Small, who grew up as Mordechai Leib Shmulewicz in Molchad', also witnessed how local men dragged the town's Orthodox priest, his wife, and two little children out of their home. Taunting them as "Jew lovers," they put the family up against the wall of the Orthodox church, pulled out guns, and killed them.[115]

It is not clear from Small's recollections if Germans were actually present in Molchad' as local gangs attacked and abused their Jewish neighbors. In smaller towns, especially those off the major roads, it was quite common for German frontline troops to pass through, leaving the town without authority for a few days or even weeks until a more permanent German presence arrived. Most local anti-Jewish violence in western Belarus seems to have been committed during that particular time period. In Vidzy, a town in Vileika oblast, for example, locals formed a self-defense force and started arresting, beating, robbing, and murdering Jews before a more permanent German presence was installed in mid-July 1941. Similar incidents in which gangs of locals broke into Jewish homes, robbing and beating their inhabitants and killing some of them, have been recorded for the small shtetls Deliatichi and Korelichi close to Novogrudok, for Stolin to the southeast of Pinsk, and for Kurenits to the north of Vileika.[116]

With respect to local violence against Jews committed in the summer of 1941, then, a significant difference existed within the territories that at the time constituted western Belarus. The violence was most intense in the regions around Białystok, where a systematic and uniform pattern of abuse and murder extended across many small towns.[117] The extent of pogroms in the other regions of western Belarus was more limited, and in each case the number of victims was much smaller. Given the fragmentary source basis, it is often impossible to establish the identity of the perpetrators. In Molchad', Martin Small remembered them as his Polish neighbors; in Lakhva, Izaak Lichtenberg recalled them having been Poles and Belarusians; and in Stolin, Shammai Tokel described those who carried out anti-Jewish violence as a mix of former Soviet prisoners, "hoodlums" from the town and vicinity, and "local peasant gangs."[118] Geographically, three clusters of pogrom violence appeared in areas that differed from each other in terms of the population's linguistic and religious proportions: around Vileika (northwestern Belarus), between and around Baranovichi and Novogrudok (central-western Belarus), and to the east of Pinsk (southwestern Belarus). The latter was part of Polesia, the historical region that extended across the Belarusian-Ukrainian border. In terms of local dynamics of violence, it seems possible that the violence in the town of Stolin in Belarusian Polesia was connected to local pogroms that took place in nearby towns like Berezhnytsia and Sarny just across the border, in the Ukrainian part of Polesia.[119]

In contrast to western Belarus, pogroms against Jews in the summer of 1941 have not been recorded for eastern Belarus. Collective acts of violence against Jews committed by local inhabitants either shortly before or during the first days and weeks of the German conquest of a given town or district have been recorded only for the regions that were annexed in 1939, not for those that had been Soviet for more than two decades prior to 1941. This pattern of local anti-Jewish violence corresponded to the pattern of local violence against Soviet officials: incidents of physical violence against Soviet representatives during the transition from Soviet to German rule have also been recorded only for the western part of Belarus.

To understand why, during the summer of 1941, the extent of local anti-Jewish violence varied within Belarus, it is important to look beyond the borders of the republic. In the other Soviet regions that were under German occupation, pogroms against Jews also occurred mostly in June and July 1941, shortly before or after a region had formally been conquered by the Germans. Primarily, however, this was the case in regions that had been annexed to the Soviet Union only in 1939 and 1940. In the old Soviet regions under Nazi rule (apart from eastern Belarus, this included eastern Ukraine and a small strip of western Russia running from the Baltic to the Black Sea), such incidents appear to have been almost nonexistent. Only a few cases so far are known, for example from the town of Olevs'k, located in the northern part of Zhytomyr oblast just to the east of the pre-1939 Soviet-Polish border. Until early November 1941, when personnel from the German civilian administration arrived, the town was practically in charge of the Ukrainian Polis'ka Sich (Polesian Sich). These paramilitary forces were headed by the nationalist leader Taras Bul'ba-Borovets', who hailed from a nearby village in neighboring Rivne oblast that had belonged to Poland during the interwar years.[120]

How, then, can we make sense of the variation in violence? One explanation that is often offered is the impact that "double occupation" (first Soviet, then German) had on relations between Jews and non-Jews—namely, that in the new Soviet regions, the years of Soviet rule from 1939 (or 1940) to 1941 perpetuated the stereotypical image of Jews as supporters of communism. The summer 1941 pogroms were thus motivated by feelings of revenge against those who supposedly sided with the Soviets.[121] While that may have constituted one of several factors, often overlooked in these debates is the tremendous amount of state violence that inhabitants of the old Soviet territories suffered prior to 1941—indeed, even more than in the new Soviet territories. Moreover, local policemen in the old Soviet territories would later just as actively participate in the ghettoization and murder of the region's Jewish communities, civilians would avail themselves of Jewish property, and people would denounce their Jewish neighbors.[122] Finally, even within the new Soviet territories (apart from western Belarus, these encompassed western Ukraine, Bessarabia, Lithuania, Latvia, and Estonia), levels of local violence against Jews differed significantly from region to region. In terms of intensity, scope, and brutality, local anti-Jewish violence was highest in western Ukraine (eastern Galicia and Volhynia), in the Białystok region, and in the Romanian-administered regions of northern Bukovina and Bessarabia. During the summer of 1941, mass killings of Jews with significant local participation also took place in Lithuania—in particular, Kaunas in late June. In Latvia, however, the level of local violence toward Jews was already lower, perhaps comparable to that in the western Belarusian territories, excluding the Białystok region. In Estonia, whose small Jewish community had mostly managed to flee before the arrival of the Germans and where the German Security Police decided not to incite popular violence against Jews, it was almost nonexistent.[123]

In their study of local anti-Jewish violence in six of the eight former Polish provinces that constituted eastern Poland before 1939, Jeffrey S. Kopstein and Jason Wittenberg have argued that pogroms were most likely to break out in places with large Jewish communities that sought national equality with non-Jews, and where local non-Jews perceived this situation as a threat to their political dominance. The latter then seized on the opportunity that the transition from Soviet to German power offered to rid themselves of their political enemies.[124] For lack of local census data crucial to their research design, Kopstein and Wittenberg could not include Wilno and Nowogródek voivodships, which comprised large parts of the regions that constituted western Belarus in 1941—thus making it difficult to know whether their argument could also apply to the pogroms in these regions. The issue of radical nationalism, though, is an important one. Kai Struve has argued that the number of Jewish victims in the local pogroms was highest (with tens, if not hundreds of victims) when small groups of radical, antisemitic, and anti-Soviet nationalists were involved—with or without German presence and instigation. In the case of western Ukraine, these groups belonged to the Organization of Ukrainian Nationalists (OUN), in the case of Lithuania, to the Lithuanian Activist Front (LAF), and in the case of northern Bukovina and Bessarabia, to Romanian nationalist underground cells that cooperated with Romanian troops and policemen.[125] In the old Soviet territories in eastern Belarus, eastern Ukraine, and parts of Russia that came under German occupation, two decades of coercion and state terror prior to the war had eliminated any political alternatives. The strong presence of the Soviet state security organs also prevented the growth of radical nationalist groups whose members could act as both instigators and perpetrators of more organized local violence—which may be the primary reason why pogroms, with few known exceptions to date, did not take place in the old Soviet territories during the summer of 1941.

Struve's findings also offer a clue for western Belarus. In the predominately Polish-speaking region around Białystok, where levels of local anti-Jewish violence were as high as in western Ukraine, the radical Polish Right, which combined exclusionary nationalism with fervent antisemitism, had a strong support base. By the summer of 1941, the perception that Jews were to blame for Polish suffering was widespread.[126] Stereotypes of Jews as supporters of communism and religiously motivated antisemitism certainly could also be found among the population that lived in the other, linguistically more mixed yet predominately Belarusian-speaking western Belarusian regions. However, the radical Polish Right was much weaker in these regions. The majority of the Belarusian national movement in interwar Poland, in turn, had held strong socialist leanings. While Belarusian proponents of an integral form of nationalism who sought to create an ethnically pure state free of Jews, Poles, and Russians did exist, many of them were émigrés who returned to Belarus in 1941 with the Germans. As a group, they were too weak and small to mobilize segments of the population—and unlike the Organization of Ukrainian Nationalists (which used anti-Jewish and later anti-Polish violence for its own state-building purposes), they lacked paramilitary units by the summer of 1941.[127] The absence of such an extremist nationalist organization that would capitalize on the chaos and confusion surrounding the transition from German to Soviet rule probably explains why no large-scale pogroms comparable to Jedwabne or L'viv have been reported for the western Belarusian regions where Belarusian was the majority language.

At the same time, though, while the presence (or lack) of small, radical antisemitic nationalist groups can help us to understand the variation in scale and intensity of local anti-Jewish violence, it is important to keep in mind that each episode of mass killing had its own situational dynamics, with its own unique set of actors.[128] The interwar history of the town of Grodno, located about fifty miles to the northeast of Białystok, shared many similarities with the latter, including increasing economic tensions between the Christian and the Jewish populations, boycott campaigns against Jewish stores led by the Polish Right, and two anti-Jewish riots. However, pogroms did not occur here during the summer of 1941.[129] Moreover, the extreme brutality with which locals killed their Jewish neighbors in David-Gorodok in early August 1941 cannot be attributed to members of nationalist organizations. According to Jewish survivors, the Belarusian-speaking, Christian Orthodox inhabitants of the town identified as neither Ukrainian nor Belarusian but rather had a strong local identity.[130] One could also speculate whether the length of the interregnum period was usually shorter in the old Soviet territories, most of which were conquered by the German army in the late summer of 1941, at a time when the wave of pogroms that had swept through the new Soviet regions had largely abated—and if so, whether this meant that local potential for anti-Jewish violence was channeled into the local police forces here sooner than in the regions farther to the west.

What seems most plausible, then, is that it was a combination of different factors that accounted for the regional variation in local anti-Jewish violence during the summer of 1941: the extent of German instigation and presence, the social and political effects of prior Soviet rule, the specific local context during the interregnum period, the dynamics of violence that emerged between neighboring towns, and, most importantly, the existence of radical antisemitic nationalists that acted as both perpetrators and instigators of further local violence, drawing in other individuals who otherwise might not have acted of their own accord.[131]

But did the different levels of anti-Jewish violence that could be observed in Belarus during the summer of 1941 also translate into similar differences in interethnic relations during the subsequent years of Nazi occupation, as has been suggested for other East European regions that had, to varying extents, been exposed to Soviet rule prior to the war?[132] In the case of Belarus, Holocaust survivors from both the western and the eastern sections provide evidence of selfless help that was extended by non-Jews: family members and friends, but also complete strangers. This help took various forms: from providing a person with food or shelter for a night to establishing ties with the partisans in the forests or hiding someone for a prolonged period of time in one's house. In providing assistance, these individuals put their own lives and those of their families at great risk: anyone suspected of helping Jews was killed by the Germans. Survivors, however, also recall hesitation, fear, indifference, or hostility displayed by others and the pervasive fear of being detected by neighbors. Consider, for example, Chasia Bornstein-Bielicka and Zinaida Suvorova's accounts of their survival—the former hailing from western, the latter from eastern Belarus.

During the war, Chasia Bornstein-Bielicka from Grodno was active in the town's ghetto underground. The organization was mostly composed of members of Hashomer Hatzair, the Socialist-Zionist youth organization that Bornstein-Bielicka had joined as a teenager before the war. In early 1943, on order of the underground leadership, Bornstein-Bielicka left for Białystok, where she first served as a liaison with the Białystok ghetto underground and then with the mostly Jewish partisans in the surrounding forests. Pretending to be a Polish village girl, she managed to find work as a domestic with an SS officer and later with a German civilian worker for the Wehrmacht before she joined the partisans, who by the end of the war were operating under Soviet command.[133]

In Białystok but also in Grodno, Chasia Bornstein-Bielicka remembered the overall atmosphere as hostile. No one could be trusted, and neighbors could give one away at any given moment if they held any suspicions or doubts. Some locals took great pleasure in Jewish suffering. In 1943, as the destruction of the Białystok ghetto began, Chasia Bornstein-Bielicka witnessed how local crowds gathered at the ghetto's main entrance, laughing and jeering as German soldiers led Jewish orphans—children, toddlers, and babies—to their death.[134] Still, at different moments in time and in different forms, several individuals who knew that she was Jewish provided her with help. One of them was Irena Adamowicz, a Polish Christian woman who was active in the Polish Scout organization. During the German occupation, Adamowicz, who had prewar ties to Hashomer Hatzair, traveled from ghetto to ghetto to help members of the Hashomer Hatzair keep in touch.[135] Another individual who extended help was Chasia Bornstein-Bielicka's former geography teacher from Grodno. They encountered each other in Białystok, when Bornstein-Bielicka, whose papers gave her name as Halina Stasiuk, reported to the town hall to receive ration cards for bread and other necessities. The clerk who took her papers recognized her. Instead of giving her away, he provided her with extra ration cards and offered his help whenever she needed it.[136] Assistance even came from the unlikeliest places. In the summer of 1943, Chasia Bornstein-Bielicka started to work as a domestic for Otto Busse, a German painter who was employed as a civilian worker by the Wehrmacht in Białystok. When he discovered that she was Jewish and learned about her resistance activities and connections to the partisans in the forests, he provided her with food, clothes, and permits that allowed her to use the railroad. Busse also made his typewriter available so that Chasia Bornstein-Bielicka and her friend Chaika Grossman could print anti-German resistance posters and procured a gun and ammunition for her.[137]

Similarly, Zinaida Suvorova from Orsha in Vitebsk oblast was able to draw on the help of several people. After she defied German orders to move into the ghetto, she left with her two little children for the countryside. During the

FIGURE 3. Chasia Bornstein-Bielicka. Reproduced from Neomi Izhar, *Chasia Bornstein-Bielicka: One of the Few. A Resistance Fighter and Educator, 1939–1947* (Jerusalem: Yad Vashem Publications, 2009).

years that followed, Suvorova and her children repeatedly changed location, wandering between towns and villages, afraid of detection if they stayed for too long in one place. As Suvorova recalled, when news of the murder of the Jews spread, "one could hear in the villages that 'the last day of the Jews had come'—many antisemites said this." Many villagers also disliked party members and did not speak well about them.[138] In the beginning, Zinaida Suvorova's sister, Fania, and her children joined her, and for a while, they lived with a stranger, an old man with mental health problems. Later, the two sisters got separated, and Zinaida Suvorova and her children were on their own. As they were wandering from village to village, they spent one night with the family of a friend whom Suvorova knew through her time in the Komsomol. Her friend's mother, as she recalled, was ill-disposed toward Jews and suspected that Suvorova and her children were Jewish, but the friend bluntly told her mother that this was none of her business.

Another woman who helped Zinaida Suvorova was her former neighbor Nadia, with whom she stayed in Vitebsk for a while. When the Germans came to confiscate Nadia's apartment, Nadia and her husband arranged for Suvorova and her children to stay with another friend who lived not far from Vitebsk. So that the neighbors would not notice, she and her children spent the entire winter on the peasant hut's large Russian stove, hidden from view. As Suvorova later recalled, her prewar friendships with non-Jews were crucial for her survival. It also helped that, as she phrased it, "I wasn't taken to be Jewish [*mne ne prinimali za evreiku*]. . . . I had light-colored eyes, light brown hair."[139] Her small children, who knew only Russian, had Russian-sounding names; her little son was not circumcised. Whenever someone asked her children what their names were, Suvorova did not have to be afraid that the children might let Jewish-sounding names slip. Suvorova was fluent in Russian and knew Belarusian, too, which is why she could alternatively pass off as Russian or Belarusian to those who might not have given her shelter had they known that she was Jewish.[140] Similarly, Chasia Bornstein-Bielicka spoke Polish in the Grodno dialect, without a Yiddish accent or idioms. As Chasia Bornstein-Bielicka also had the looks, in her mother's words, of a "genuine Polish girl," she had a better chance than others to survive on what ghetto inmates called the "Aryan side."[141]

Like every survivor's story, Chasia Bornstein-Bielicka and Zinaida Suvorova's accounts are extraordinary tales of human strength and resilience in the face of genocide and mass murder. They speak to the importance of sheer luck and coincidence, an aspect that survivors often stress when reflecting on why they and not others survived. But they are also a testament to the existence of human compassion and kindness, extended under the most extreme, inhumane circumstances. In my reading of these and similar accounts of survivors from both eastern and western Belarus, each case showed a spectrum of human behavior, but each case also fundamentally depended on the individuals involved and the specific circumstances in which these people found themselves.[142]

The existence of a spectrum of human behavior, of course, does not preclude the existence of quantitative differences within it. In her comparison of the two neighboring regions of Bessarabia and Transnistria (which corresponded roughly to the territories of modern-day Moldova and southwestern Ukraine), Diana Dumitru found substantial differences in how the non-Jewish populations treated the regions' Jewish populations during the war. Until the Russian Revolution, Bessarabia and Transnistria were provinces of the Russian empire. During the interwar years, Bessarabia belonged to Romania, and Transnistria was part of the Soviet Union. In the summer of 1940, the Soviet Union annexed Bessarabia, but after the German invasion of the Soviet Union a year later, Romanian troops, with the help of their German ally, brought both Bessarabia and Transnistria under their control. As Dumitru has shown, over the next three years, until the Red Army reconquered the two regions in the summer of 1944, the "civilian population in Bessarabia had a more antagonistic attitude, and the civilian population in Transnistria a more cooperative attitude toward the Jews during the Holocaust."[143] With the exception of the summer of 1941, however, such regional differences cannot be detected clearly for German-occupied Belarus, at least not for the regions that constituted post-1945 Belarus. Where eastern and western Belarus did differ, however, was in the type of support network that people could draw on. As intercommunal relations among certain urban groups in eastern Belarus—younger people, those who no longer practiced a religion, and people who closely identified with the Soviet project—were less defined by traditional social and religious markers of identity than in western Belarus, help was often extended through these networks. Zinaida Suvorova, for example, could draw on the support of individuals that she knew through her Komsomol activities. The case of Minsk illustrates best how high prewar levels of interethnic integration came to shape support networks. On one hand, as Iurii Taits recalled, a "tremendous amount of antisemitism" erupted after the German army entered the city, with children throwing stones at Jews and people insulting others as "kikes."[144] Yet on the other hand, a strong underground movement developed in Minsk during the war. The communist-led ghetto underground organization had close ties to the communist-led, citywide underground organization. Based on prewar party connections but also on friendships, the underground cells cooperated closely, and non-Jewish members helped Jews to flee from the ghetto.[145] It is possible that such regional differences (in terms of support networks) also translated into numerical differences, meaning that overall, more non-Jewish urban residents in eastern Belarus were willing to help Jews than in western Belarus. However, the primary sources do not provide a conclusive picture. If quantitative differences did exist, then these would have been subtler than in the case of Transnistria and Bessarabia, where the contrast was more evident and thus methodologically easier to detect.[146]

The Partisan Movement

Examining the extent of local complicity and entanglement with the German occupiers makes visible that although all inhabitants of the western regions of the Soviet Union found the space within which they could act severely circumscribed by the Germans, that space was almost nonexistent for Jews and larger for non-Jews. Within the significant constraints imposed by the German authorities, non-Jews had a range of options at their disposal and could decide which ones to pursue. Some of the choices that people made were far-reaching, such as volunteering to work in the local police or reporting on Soviet party activists and Jews in hiding. Yet people's choices also included smaller acts, such as taking furniture from a murdered Jewish neighbor's apartment. Complicity was a question of degree—but also one whose extent was not contingent on whether one had voluntarily joined the Germans. Some locals became involved with the occupation regime much more reluctantly, even against their will, when they were appointed by their village communities or coerced by the Germans into serving. Still, forced participation did not prevent them from becoming complicit in German crimes, as was the case with local men who joined the police forces under threat in 1942, yet who nevertheless participated in the killings of Jewish communities. Throughout the occupation, non-Jews continued to have more space for action within which they could act than Jews. Once partisan warfare began to pick up in mid-1942, though, and the German authorities responded with large-scale punitive operations, the space for non-Jewish locals to act also became more limited.

In a speech given on July 3, 1941, Stalin called on the population in German-occupied territory to organize partisan units: "In the occupied regions, conditions must be made unbearable for the enemy and his accomplices. They must be hounded and annihilated at every step and their measures frustrated."[147] Yet how exactly these units were to be organized, who was to provide centralized leadership, and how the population in occupied territory was supposed to hear about Stalin's order was unclear. Meanwhile, some NKVD officers and local party leaders had taken matters into their own hands. When the Germans advanced, they stayed behind—be it because they had decided not to flee, had been unable to do so, or had to abort their flight—and went to the forests, where they tried to form early partisan units.

In early July, when the Wehrmacht was about to arrive in Kirovskii and Bykhovskii districts in Mogilev oblast, local party leaders, together with NKVD officers from other districts, left for the forests.[148] In Poles'e oblast, the head of the regional NKVD ordered all communists to stay and organize underground groups. According to the NKVD officer Nikolai Ermakovich, almost all members of the state security organs of Liubchanskii district in Poles'e oblast became partisans.[149] Individual officers also remained behind as undercover agents. Trying to pass as ordinary civilians, they sought contact with individuals who had worked as informers prior to the invasion and gathered information on the situation in the occupied territories. They also identified and killed individual locals whom they accused of collaborating with the Germans.[150] One of these was Mikhail D'iachkov from Saratov in Russia, who in 1939 was sent to western Belarus to help carry out the express Sovietization of the region. The summer of 1941 found him in Vitebsk oblast. Upon hearing of the German invasion, he decided to form a "destruction battalion" (*istrebitel'nyi batal'on*) whose explicit purpose was to fight internal "wreckers" and "spies."[151] For that, he did not need directives from above: members of the state security organs knew what was expected of them. As D'iachkov explained, referring to the common name "Chekist" for NKVD officers: "My entire life is the life of a Chekist. Beriia raised me exclusively for the fight with the internal counterrevolution."[152]

Apart from state security officers, the first members of the early partisan groups were mostly Red Army soldiers who got trapped behind the front lines. During the first months of the war, the partisans were primarily concerned with their own survival. Scattered throughout the forests, without a steady food supply and in some cases without guns, the men usually had no connection to other units or the Soviet rear.[153] They were also under constant threat of being discovered by German soldiers and local policemen. In Polesia, in the Belarusian-Ukrainian border region, armed groups of locals, perhaps members of the Ukrainian nationalists who had joined the local police forces, were combing the forests, looking for partisans.[154] Once winter approached and living conditions became even more difficult, many units decided to disband. While some men set out to cross the front line into the Soviet rear, others buried or discarded their weapons, and sought shelter in nearby villages, where they helped with farm work.[155] In December 1941, Stepan Shupeniia's unit was located not far from Turov, Poles'e oblast. As he recalled: "We didn't do anything, we took a rest [*otdykhali*] . . . We didn't have contact with anyone."[156] Of the fifteen men in his unit, most decided to try to reach the Soviet rear. But on their way east, some of the men got separated from the group, a few were killed, one man decided to stay with a woman he met in one of the villages, and another returned home to his family in Polesia. Stepan Shupeniia was the only one who eventually managed to cross the front line.[157]

By the winter of 1941, and with the exception of a few units that held out in heavily forested areas, the partisan movement had effectively ceased to exist in the German-occupied Soviet regions. From the spring of 1942 on, however, the number of partisans began to increase. In Belarus, the growth of the movement was initially focused on the old Soviet territories, in particular on Minsk and Vitebsk oblasts, but a few units also emerged in the western regions, most notably around Novogrudok in the dense Naliboki forest, as well as in Polesia. With its vast forests and extensive marshes, the republic offered naturally conducive opportunities for partisan warfare. Outside of Belarus, the growth of the partisan movement was concentrated on the old Soviet territories, again in regions with extensive forests—in particular, northwestern Russia around Leningrad, Smolensk, Kalinin, and Briansk and in the Ukrainian part of Polesia. In most of the rest of Ukraine, the open steppe made it very difficult for partisan units to form. For a variety of different reasons, Soviet partisans would become a noticeable force in the three Baltic republics and in eastern Galicia only during the last stage of the war, shortly before the Red Army reconquered the regions.[158]

One of the factors that contributed to the growth of the partisan movement had to do with frontline developments and an ensuing improvement in communications with the Soviet rear. By late 1941, Moscow was effectively cut off from the occupied territories and received very little to no information on what was happening in the region. In January 1942, however, a gap in the front line around the small town of Surazh in Vitebsk oblast opened up. The "Surazh gates," which existed until September 1942, made it possible for the Soviet rear to establish ties to the nascent partisan units in northeastern Belarus, and to send special agents into occupied territory who were tasked with the organization of new partisan units.[159] During that time, a centralized agency, the Central Staff of the Partisan Movement (Tsentral'nyi shtab partizanskogo dvizheniia) was established in Moscow in May 1942. It was subordinated to the Stavka, the high command of the Soviet armed forces, which was headed by Stalin. The purpose of the Central Staff of the Partisan Movement, which was subdivided into regional branches, was to both direct and control the partisans from the Soviet rear. Throughout 1943, Moscow's organizational control over the movement strengthened. Contact was usually established through special secret agents who were moving back and forth across the front and through radio transmitters. Still, communication with units operating closer to the front lines—in particular, in Vitebsk oblast (due to the Surazh gates)—was more stable than with those in regions farther west and south.[160] As late as January 1943, the Central Staff of the Partisan Movement reported that it had no reliable contact with the partisans in the western oblasts of Belarus. Although the situation improved slowly, the geographical imbalance remained: by January 1944, 70 percent of all Soviet partisans in Belarus were operating in the eastern oblasts, and 30 percent in the western oblasts.[161] As Chasia Bornstein-Bielicka experienced, in the region around Białystok, where the Polish Armia Krajowa was strong and where non-Polish partisan groups consisted mostly of Jews who had fled to the forests, the Soviet partisan movement formally took control over the latter only in the summer of 1944, shortly before the Red Army reconquered the region.[162]

Until the disbandment of the Soviet partisan movement in the summer of 1944, the Central Staff of the Partisan Movement was headed by Panteleimon Ponomarenko, first secretary of the Communist Party of Soviet Belarus. Several of Ponomarenko's close associates from Belarus also worked for the agency. Ponomarenko's deputy from 1943 on was Lavrentii Tsanava, prior to the war head of the NKVD in Belarus, while Petr Kalinin, the second secretary of the Communist Party of Soviet Belarus, headed the Belarusian branch of the partisan movement (Belorusskii shtab partizanskogo dvizheniia). Unlike some leading communists who preferred to limit the Soviet partisan movement to party members, Ponomarenko was an early proponent of expanding the movement's popular basis and repeatedly appealed to Stalin to make this official policy. By the fall of 1942, those efforts had born fruit. From then on, partisan warfare was to become an "all people's war." Consequently, the Central Staff instructed the partisans to mobilize more local men into their ranks.[163]

The main reason for the 1942 growth of the partisan movement, however, was neither ideological conviction nor improved control or direction from the center but rather German conduct in occupied territory. Afraid of partisan resistance, the German authorities pursued from the beginning a harsh line against anyone deemed "wanderers" or "nonresidents" and used this as a pretext to kill Jews and encircled Red Army soldiers.[164] By the spring of 1942, military leaders became too concerned about the high number of former Red Army soldiers who were still living as disguised civilians in Belarusian villages. The Wehrmacht subsequently issued a set of orders instructing all people in occupied territory who were not local residents to register with the authorities. On registration, the men were either interned or deported to Germany as forced laborers. As the partisan Mikhail Peregudovyi recalled from the region around Minsk, once the Germans began the roundups, word began to travel from village to village, and the remaining former Red Army soldiers decided to return to the forest—precisely the development that the Germans had wanted to prevent.[165]

As more and more former Red Army soldiers went to the forests, more and more Jews tried to escape from the ghettos. This was particularly the case in the parts of Belarus under civilian control, where the destruction of ghettos reached its height in 1942. With each new impending mass killing, more people fled to the forests. One of them was Sulia Wolozhinski Rubin, who escaped from the ghetto of Novogrudok to join the Bielski partisans, an exclusively Jewish partisan unit (and eventually the largest in wartime Europe) that was active in the dense Naliboki forest northeast of Novogrudok.[166] But although fleeing to the forests was the only hope for survival, it also carried a risk for those trying to be accepted into otherwise predominately Slavic units: while the movement would ultimately save many of them from certain death, there were also incidents when partisans—probably out of hatred, greed, or distrust—killed Jews who asked to be accepted.[167]

In Nazi thinking, Jews were partisans, and partisans were Jews; both groups needed to be destroyed. In response to increased partisan activity, but also as a preemptive means, the German military began to develop a strategy of indiscriminate violence. One of the early key figures in this process was Wehrmacht General Max von Schenckendorff, the commander of Army Group Center Rear Area, who considered all Jewish men, women, and children active supporters of partisans who needed to be "completely annihilated."[168] He was later succeeded in that role by Erich von dem Bach-Zelewski, Hitler's man for the antipartisan operations in the east. By razing entire villages to the ground—killing their inhabitants, burning down the houses, and seizing the livestock—the Germans sought to cleanse (*säubern*) and pacify (*befrieden*) whole districts that were suspected of harboring bandits (*Banditen*), as they called the partisans.

Wehrmacht and Nazi leaders believed that the annihilation of entire villages would eliminate potential support for the Soviet partisans and deter locals from joining their ranks. While some Belarusian villages had already suffered this fate in 1941, the destruction of villages became more systematic in 1942. The first large-scale antipartisan operation, Operation Bamberg, was carried out in Poles'e oblast from March 26 to April 6, 1942.[169] This isolated region, with its marshes and wetlands and few towns, was impossible for the Germans to control. Among the villages that were razed to the ground was Rudnia in Oktiabr'skii district. As Ganna Goshka, one of the few survivors, recalled, when the Germans and their allies entered Rudnia, they rounded up the villagers in the collective farm's yard and separated the men from the women and children. The women were squeezed into the small firehouse. Meanwhile, the men were led away to a shed. Gunfire opened up. When the women realized that their husbands, fathers, and brothers were being killed, they started to cry and scream. After the murder of the men, the soldiers set the shed on fire. They then took the women, group by group, to an empty house. Ganna Goshka was among the first to be led away. When the soldiers opened fire, she fell to the ground, but she was not hit. Pretending to be dead, she had to witness how the other women were killed, their dead bodies falling next to her. Among the victims was Ganna Goshka's little sister: "The third time round I heard my little sister coming. She is crying very hard because she can see me . . . She fell right here, at my feet."[170]

Across Oktiabr'skii district, village after village was set on fire. According to German sources, 3,500 people were killed in the course of this operation, yet the actual number was likely to have been around 6,000 people, the majority of them local peasants, and a smaller number of fugitive Jews. In some places like Rudnia, they shot people before burning their corpses, but in other villages like Khvoinia, people were herded into houses and barns and then burned alive. In Kovali, little children were thrown alive into the fire.[171] Like the rape of Jewish women during mass killings, the rape of village women and girls was common during antipartisan operations.[172] As German troops were closing in on their homes, people tried to flee for the forests. In Lavstyki, Ganna Paduta was hiding with a few other women in a dense group of bushes on the edge of the village when they heard their neighbors cry and scream in agony: "We didn't see them burn and kill, just heard—they screamed terribly, people screaming. We couldn't hear what one of them was saying, only 'A-a-a!' Only that voice going, that voice. And then that was all—everything went quiet."[173]

By the summer of 1944, approximately 9,200 villages in Belarus had been set on fire, of which 5,295 were annihilated with some or almost all of their inhabitants.[174] The German authorities employed a similar strategy in western Russia, northern Ukraine, Greece, and other occupied regions, yet not on the same scale. In Belarus (in its post-1945 borders), up to 345,000 civilians were killed as a result of German antipartisan operations, some of them Jews but the overwhelming majority non-Jewish rural residents.[175] Usually, it was Wehrmacht troops—sometimes supported by Hungarian, Slovak, Romanian, or other Axis troops—or a mix of SS, German police, and Wehrmacht forces that carried out the destruction of villages. Local policemen also took part in the antipartisan operations, as did other Soviet citizens employed in SS or police battalions. Operation Bamberg, for instance, was carried out by soldiers of the 707th German Infantry Division, the 102nd Slovak Infantry Regiment, and members of the German Police Battalion 315, with the support of local policemen.[176] In the postwar Soviet Union, one of the best-known burned villages was that of Khatyn, northeast of Minsk. On March 22, 1943, 147 inhabitants, half of them children, were herded into a barn and burned alive in retaliation for the killing of a German officer and three subordinates.

FIGURE 4. A village set on fire by Kampfgruppe Schimana, named after its commander Walter Schimana, SS and police leader of General Commissariat Weissruthenien. Army Group Center Rear Area, summer 1943. Courtesy of the Bundesarchiv.

The Khatyn operation was carried out by about 260 men, of whom about 100 were German SS soldiers from the Dirlewanger Brigade, one of the most brutal and notorious SS formations. After the demise of the Soviet Union, it became known that the rest of the perpetrators had been members of Schutzmannschaft Battalion 118, which was mostly composed of Ukrainians (with many of them members of the Melnyk wing of the Organization of Ukrainian Nationalists, OUN-M) but also some Russians and Belarusians.[177] Given that local policemen regularly took part in the cleansing of villages and helped to identify families accused of being partisan-friendly, it was not uncommon that perpetrators and victims knew each other personally. When a group of men in uniform approached the women who were herded into the firehouse in Rudnia, one of them recognized a policeman named Andrei from nearby Smykovichi. She pleaded with him, "Andrei, dear, what will happen to us?" "Nothing," replied the man, but he took his own mother, who was among the women, from the firehouse. Another policeman did the same. As Ganna Goshka remembered, "They got theirs out of the barn and led them away," leaving the other women to die.[178]

Germans, Partisans, Civilians

As long as German violence was mostly aimed at Jews or prisoners of war, the partisans weak, and rumors about the defeat of the Red Army rife among the population, few among the Slavic civilian population had an incentive to expose themselves to the dangers of partisan life.[179] That also applied to party members. In the summer of 1942, for example, the commander of a partisan unit in Vitebsk oblast, a man by the name of Butenko, found out that a fellow comrade by the name of Mal'chevskii was living with relatives in the nearby village of Tadulino in Lepel'skii district (not far from Vasil' Bykaŭ's home village, Bychki). Before 1941, Mal'chevskii had been secretary of the Komsomol in Minsk oblast. But when Butenko requested that Mal'chevskii join his unit, he refused, arguing that his family would suffer German reprisals. At Butenko's insistence, Mal'chevskii eventually consented, but a few days after his arrival in the unit, he and a few other men deserted. One man left a note behind, in which he explained, "I am not leaving the unit because I want to betray it, but only because I am not able to fulfill the partisan chores, as these are very difficult."[180]

Life in the forests was harsh and dangerous, a constant battle with cold, hunger, and lice. Only the young and physically fit could hope to survive the extreme conditions in the forest, especially during the winter, when units built underground shelters (*zemlianki*) to withstand the cold. For certain population groups, above all for the elderly and children, leaving for the forests was never an option. The primary task of the partisans was to fight, to destroy, and sabotage but not to save civilians (with the exception of the Bielski partisans).[181] When the first partisan zones emerged, entire districts under the control of the partisans, it became easier to extend protection to civilians, but the fighting units continued to be composed primarily of men. Many units refused to take in men without guns, let alone families, women, or mothers with children. The latter were usually turned down, as happened to Zinaida Suvorova, who tried to join a partisan unit with her two small children.[182] If women were accepted into the predominantly male units, they found themselves vulnerable to sexual assault and exploitation.[183] This was the case also within the Bielski partisans' fighting unit. After Sulia Wolozhinski Rubin joined in 1942, it soon became clear to her that in order to survive, she needed to become the "wife" of a partisan who could provide her with food, protect her from sexual harassment, and possibly help her get her family out of the ghetto. As she recalled, "there weren't many women; and to get a boyfriend, a protector—a *tavo* in partisan language—wasn't hard. I don't know what or whom I waited for. I fought. Scratched and pushed off."

After Sulia Wolozhinski Rubin chose a man to live with, her status increased immediately.[184]

Once German violence against non-Jewish civilians became much more frequent and widespread, the composition of the partisan units began to change. In 1942, former Red Army soldiers still constituted the majority of Soviet partisans. Within a year, the situation was very different. According to official data compiled by the Belarusian Staff of the Partisan Movement on January 1, 1946, in total, the partisan movement in Belarus comprised 360,491 individuals from the summer of 1941 to its disbandment in the summer of 1944. This included 79,484 partisans who guarded family camps or fulfilled supporting functions, but for whom otherwise no further information exists. For the remaining 281,007 individuals (16 percent of them women), additional information on their ethnicity, gender, social background, prewar profession, and year as well as circumstances under which they joined is available.[185] What the data show is that throughout 1943, when German punitive operations against villages reached their peak, almost 170,000 people joined the partisans. By the end of 1943, most of the partisans active in Belarus were prewar inhabitants of the republic—and most of them peasants, Belarusian-speakers from the villages.[186]

Some people left for the forest because they wanted to evade deportation and forced labor. Others joined the partisans because they had no family and no livelihood to return to after their village had been razed to the ground. One of them was Pavel Pal'tsev from Karpilova village in Gomel' oblast. After German soldiers and local policemen burned down the village, killing most of its inhabitants, he and the other few survivors went to the forests, where they formed a partisan unit.[187] According to the partisan Stepan Plianto, up until the fall of 1942, locals in Mogilev oblast mostly joined their unit because they were fleeing the campaigns for forced labor or their villages had been destroyed.[188] Ivan Danilov from Pinsk oblast joined the partisans because he was arrested by the local police but managed to flee; returning back home was out of the question, as he surely would have been rearrested and killed.[189] Fighting the Germans also offered a way to take revenge for the murder of loved ones or to take an active part in the liberation of one's home region and country from foreign invaders. After the tide of the war turned at the Battle of Stalingrad in the winter of 1942–1943, joining the units was motivated by frontline developments, too. To increase local participation, the partisans also recruited by force, usually young men from the villages who received a "summons" from the nearest unit—and had to fear retaliation if they did not comply. In January 1944, for example, Stepan Shupeniia, by then commander of the partisan forces in Baranovichi oblast, received

FIGURE 5. A woman in front of the remains of a house burned down during German antipartisan operations, Kozlovichi (Kazlovichy) village, Kalinkovichskii district, southeastern Belarus, 1944. Courtesy of the Russian State Archive of Film and Photo Documents.

an order from Moscow to mobilize from districts under partisan control all local men born between 1915 and 1925. The summonses were distributed throughout the villages. According to Shupeniia, 1,500 men were thus mobilized, although a few tried to evade the draft by going into hiding.[190]

The Soviet partisan movement significantly disrupted the workings of the German occupation regime. By the time Nazi occupation entered its last phase, the German authorities had become afraid to venture out into the countryside. In many areas, it had become impossible for them to collect grain and taxes. Throughout 1943, large partisan zones emerged—in particular, around Minsk and Vitebsk but also in the Naliboki forest close to Novogrudok, around Mogilev, and in Polesia. Encompassing entire districts with their villages, the Germans no longer entered these zones, except during large-scale military operations.[191] As successful as the partisans were at unsettling the occupation regime, though, they greatly inflated the number of German military personnel that they killed during their operations.[192] In reality, German soldiers were not easy to attack. Stationed in larger towns or in heavily guarded garrisons, they were well armed and increasingly traveled only in groups. The partisans' main target, therefore, were those who represented the occupation regime in the localities: policemen, mayors, and village heads. As Litman Mor, who escaped from the ghetto in Vilnius to a partisan unit in the Lithuanian-Belarusian border region, recalled: "Our military assignments were focused on eliminating the local police in the small towns of the forest area."[193] Just as it was easier for German soldiers to kill civilians than to inflict losses on the partisans, it was easier for the partisans to direct their actions against local representatives of the Germans than to inflict losses on German soldiers. The partisans also attacked others who were linked to the German authorities—for example, agricultural specialists, translators, and people deemed German-friendly. Since the partisans in Belarus were, by the end of 1943, mostly composed of people from Belarus, locals essentially found themselves fighting against other locals.[194]

What partisan operations against those deemed traitors looked like was described by Mikhail D'iachkov, an NKVD officer and commander of the Second Belarusian Brigade, which was active in Mekhovskii district north of Vitebsk. By the winter of 1941–1942, his small partisan unit consisted of only a few men. D'iachkov had been able to procure two weapons, but the others were unarmed. Under these circumstances, D'iachkov explained, it was impossible to inflict any harm on the Germans, which is why he told his men that instead, "we will destroy and annihilate all scum [*svoloch'*] on our territory." One day, they paid a visit to a village elder, who treated them to moonshine and honey. When they asked him which of his fellow villagers was a scum (*"kto u tebia svoloch' tut?"*), the village elder replied that all of them were good people. But when the partisans questioned some of his villagers, they "told us frankly: that person is a scum, that person is a scum, but not that person." After they had obtained the information, D'iachkov and his men killed three local policemen.[195] According to the Belarusian Staff of the Partisan Movement, between June 1941 and January 1944 (half a year before the movement was disbanded), the partisans in Belarus killed 17,431 local policemen and other "traitors"—that is, they killed almost three times as many Soviet citizens as German soldiers during the war.[196] The actual number of killed policemen and others deemed traitors must have been higher, though, seeing as the numbers for the second half of 1944 are missing. Most of them would have been prewar residents of Belarus. The number of civilians (family members of policemen or village heads but other civilians, too) who died at the hands of partisans has not been established. Just as the Germans had an incentive to report the murder of civilians as the killings of partisans, so did the partisans have an incentive not to report civilian deaths or to disguise them as the killings of German soldiers.[197]

All partisans killed so that *they* would not be killed, but for some partisans, killing local representatives of the Germans was also a means to take revenge, to avenge the death of family members. The partisan units that were operating around David-Gorodok, for example, consisted of both non-Jews and Jews, the latter mostly locals who had fled to the forests. In 1943, they launched an attack on the town, in the course of which several policemen and their families were killed and parts of David-Gorodok set on fire. Their attack can be interpreted not just as an act against local representatives of the German occupation regime but also, at least for the Jewish members of the unit, as an act of personal revenge against individuals who had tortured and murdered their relatives in the fall of 1941.[198] For others, certainly for NKVD officers like D'iachkov, it was a question of us versus them, for or against Moscow, or, as the partisan Shurman put it, "our people" or "enemies."[199] Yet for others, avenging the death of civilians, liberating the region from the Germans, and fighting against those deemed traitors were one and the same thing. Attacking local policemen or village heads was also a way to procure weapons and food.

Still, to think of partisan violence as selective and aimed at specific targets only would be to present a sanitized picture of war. Much of the violence that partisans committed could not be easily rationalized. In a world where—in the eyes of the partisans—every civilian could potentially be a German spy, "treason" was a very flexible term. A person's death sentence was often pronounced within seconds, on the basis of mere suspicion. Varfolomei Lapenko, the political commissar of the Stalin Partisan Brigade, which was active in Vitebsk oblast, recalled how in May 1942, his unit attacked and eliminated (*unichtozhili*) several supposed traitors in Rassonskii district. In the course of their attack, they also destroyed the local dairy and milk delivery point so that the Germans could no longer make use of it. They then called the local population together and told them that if they had any questions, they should turn to the partisans. If they turned to the Germans, they would be shot. As Lapenko remarked casually, "some had to be shot" (*nekotorykh i prishlos' rasstreliat'*).[200] He also personally killed Sazon Khrylev, a former school director, because rumor had it that Khrylev had asked the Germans for a piece of land.[201] One of Shalom Yoran's fellow partisans who was active in the Lithuanian-Belarusian border region close to Lake Naroch' called a peasant a German spy and wanted to shoot him just because that man had been seen entering the local police station to, as it later turned out, request a permit to visit a relative in another village.[202] Nikolai Obryn'ba, who fought in a Soviet partisan unit around Lepel' in Vitebsk oblast, was sent one night by his commander to murder a woman, a refugee from Leningrad, simply because she supposedly had romantic relations with a local policeman in Lepel'.[203] Another time, he received the order to kill the brother of a policeman even though the brother did not work for the Germans. Obryn'ba set out on his mission with a fellow partisan who had to execute a man suspected of being a German informer.[204]

In their retributive actions, the partisans also employed collective punishment, killing not just policemen or mayors but entire families, including children. On September 8, 1942, the wife of the policeman Ivan Abramovich reported to the local military commander's office in Berezino, a town located between Minsk and Mogilev, that because of her marriage to a policeman, partisans had murdered her relatives, nine families in total, who had lived in the nearby village of Shevernichi. Among the victims were her five-year-old daughter, her mother, her sisters, and her sisters' children.[205] In some cases, Soviet partisans burned whole villages to the ground and killed their inhabitants. Drazhno in southern Minsk oblast was one of these. In January 1943, a partisan unit that belonged to the Second Minsk Partisan Brigade had unsuccessfully carried out an attack on the village's large police garrison. Probably in retaliation for the heavy casualties suffered by the partisans, the brigade attacked Drazhno on April 14, 1943. They killed thirty-five villagers, including women and children, and set the houses on fire. Among the murdered was a woman who was active in the Komsomol, the father of the head of the regional Red Army conscription office, and parents of Red Army soldiers who were fighting at the front.[206]

Panteleimon Ponomarenko, the head of the Central Staff of the Partisan Movement and first secretary of the Communist Party of Belarus, knew about such violence from internal partisan reports and understood that these were not isolated incidents. In early 1943, he wrote to the leaders of the partisan movement in Mogilev oblast: "The Central Committee of the Communist Party of Belarus can no longer tolerate the shameful tactic of several partisan commanders to burn down whole villages under the pretense of taking revenge for the presence of a few policemen in the village or with the aim to prevent the Germans from setting up their quarters there. The villages Vydrytsa and Dolgoe with 250 houses and much else were burned down. We also possess numerous documents about the killings of citizens, the rape of women, and the plunder of the civilian population."[207]

Fearing that indiscriminate violence would turn the local population against the partisans, Ponomarenko sought to put an end to it. Throughout 1943, the situation improved: under pressure from the center, many commanders introduced a stricter discipline. As Stepan Shupeniia, the commander of the partisan units in Baranovichi oblast recalled, he didn't tolerate any such behavior: "I shot many people for looting, violence, excessive drunkenness, for unnecessarily shooting on the street, in the villages."[208] Yet despite these draconian measures, there were limits to how much control commanders could exert over individual men. For civilians, the forests continued to be dangerous spaces. Vladimir Rott from Bobruisk recalled that even during the day, people were afraid to go into the forests to collect mushrooms or berries, fearful of whom they would meet there: "Everybody was afraid of the partisans."[209] It was only many years after the war that Vladimir Riso from Vitebsk understood that his mother had been robbed and then raped by partisans after she had left for the countryside to exchange some of their goods for potatoes.[210] Moreover, much of the everyday violence—above all beatings but also sexual assault—that partisans inflicted on civilians occurred when the men, often already drunk, were searching peasant huts for moonshine.[211] Partisan violence against civilians, then, was also generated from the feeling of power that came with holding a gun in one's hand. In turn, locals who witnessed or heard of such acts simply could not justify them as violence against suspected traitors. Trying to capitalize on these conflicts, the Germans created self-defense units from among the local population and established a number of heavily fortified villages (*Wehrdörfer*), whose inhabitants engaged in fights with the partisans.[212] In some parts of Belarus, the situation was further exacerbated by the presence of other armed partisan formations: in Polesia (which during the war constituted part of the Reich Commissariat Ukraine) by Ukrainian nationalist formations, and in western Belarus by the Polish Armia Krajowa. Here, the war behind the front developed into wars within a war, with multidimensional, overlapping conflicts between different political forces.[213]

By the spring of 1943, the Armia Krajowa had grown into a sizable force, not just around Białystok, but also in the region around Baranovichi, Novogrudok, and Vileika—which included the Naliboki forest, where the Bielski partisans and other Soviet units were active.[214] The Armia Krajowa was fighting against the Germans, but it was also fighting for the independence of Poland within the borders of 1939—and thus inevitably clashed with Moscow, which was determined to keep the former eastern Poland. Throughout the spring and summer of 1943, Polish partisans who were active around Novogrudok, Baranovichi, and Vileika reached out to nearby Soviet units, seeking military cooperation against the Germans. When their commanders informed the Central Staff about these efforts, Ponomarenko's instructions—sanctioned by Stalin—were clear: the Polish partisans had to be destroyed.[215] Pretending to be willing to cooperate, Soviet partisan commanders invited Armia Krajowa leaders for talks but then arrested and shot them. Under attack from the Soviet side, individual Polish units—disobeying orders from the central leadership—decided in late 1943 to cooperate with the Germans, who provided weapons and munitions.[216] In their fight against the Armia Krajowa, Soviet partisans killed Polish partisans and local civilians and their families deemed to be supporters, burning down their houses and farms. Among the victims were acquaintances of Zofia Brzozowska, entire families with their children. Czombrów, her grandparents' estate, was burned down by Soviet partisans, as were many of the small manors owned by Poles in the Novogrudok region.[217] The Armia Krajowa employed similar methods, killing local civilians they considered Soviet supporters. Jews who fought with the Bielski partisans or in other Soviet units often recalled the Polish partisans as antisemitic and viewed their attacks as assaults not just on members of the Soviet partisan movement but also—or even primarily—on them because they were Jewish.[218]

What, then, did this mean for civilians? Within the violent triangle between Germans and their local representatives, partisans, and civilians, the last group, obviously, occupied the most vulnerable position. From the very beginning, locals were at the whim of the occupiers. As German punitive operations against villagers began to spread, German violence increasingly also affected the non-Jewish population. The partisans, meanwhile, were officially fighting for the liberation of the Soviet people. Although the extent of partisan violence toward civilians was much more limited than the indiscriminate and large-scale violence committed by the Germans, the relationship between civilians and partisans always remained fragile, unequal, fraught with conflict, and at times antagonistic.[219] This applied not just to individuals who did not identify with the Soviet partisan movement, or else were ambivalent about it, but also to civilians who thought of themselves as supporters of the partisans. The reason for that had to do with the structural imbalance of power, or put more simply, with the fact that one side was armed and the other was not. Consequently, the boundary between the voluntary handing-over of food and livestock and its forceful acquisition was blurred. As Mariia L. described the situation in her village not far from Molodechno, "The Germans came during the day and took from us; the partisans came at night."[220]

Three implications arise from these observations. First, civilians did not only find themselves confronted with demands from the German authorities and local policemen, on one hand, and Soviet partisans, on the other (and depending on the region, from the Armia Krajowa and Ukrainian nationalists as well). Increasingly, the civilian population was also trapped between these sides. If they fulfilled the demands of one group, they had to fear punishment at the hands of the other, and vice versa. In consequence, and adapting a term coined by Lawrence L. Langer, many choices that civilians in occupied territory had to make were "choiceless choices."[221] When confronted with decisions, they faced only options that would have a destructive effect on their personal lives, families, and local communities, as when a village head had to decide whether to hand over villagers as forced laborers to the Germans and fear reprisals from the partisans or refuse to do so and fear German collective punishment.[222] Families who had relatives fighting on both sides, German and partisan, must have been particularly torn. As a political commissar by the name of Romanov observed, in the partisan brigade For Soviet Belarus that was operating in the region around Vitebsk, it was not uncommon "for one brother to be in the unit, the other in the police; or one in the unit, and the father a town mayor, etc." These constellations, as Romanov wrote in his July 1942 report, led to a "difficult intertwining [*perepletenie*] of relations and interests."[223]

Second, if we speak of partisan violence against civilians, it is important to keep in mind that the very same people who suffered from partisan violence could become perpetrators of such violence themselves. Civilians in occupied territory who had their livestock, clothes, or food taken away by partisans, but who subsequently fled to the forests and joined partisan units, inevitably had to depend on food provided by (or taken from) the local population. So as to alleviate the pressure on the local peasant population, some regiments divided the area in which they were operating into different sectors. Every regiment was allocated a sector in which it was allowed to take food. As Litman Mor remembered, "according to partisan rules, we could go in, take food, and get out; it was forbidden . . . to equip ourselves with a stock of food."[224] Civilians, though, had no say in the creation of these rules—and the extent to which individual partisans adhered to them was an entirely different matter.

Third, the structural power imbalance between partisans and civilians in occupied territory means that assessments made by partisans about the extent of local support—and thus about the motives behind civilians' choices—have to be examined critically. As Soviet partisan commanders and state security officers saw it, during the first months of the war, the local population in eastern Belarus was initially wary of supporting the fledgling units. While some were hostile to anyone they associated with Soviet power, most locals were too afraid to act. According to the NKVD officers Golovkin and Gutkin, who in the fall of 1941 found themselves in Gomel' oblast: "the great bulk of the population kept aloof from the partisans, at best being neutral and denying essential support. In a couple of cases, the attitude of the population of some district villages (in the villages Liaskovichi

[and] Makarychi) toward the partisans was outright hostile, looking at them from the German viewpoint."[225]

The overall spirit was defeatist: rumors were flying around that the Red Army had been destroyed, that Moscow had been taken. Some reports also stressed the initial positive impression that the opening of churches and German promises to do away with the collective farms had on the peasants. Within a year, however, the situation had changed: with the exception of some who continued to serve the occupation regime, the local population, according to partisan reports, unequivocally hated the Germans. Although in fear of German reprisals, they supported the partisans.[226] In the opinion of the NKVD officer Gusev, this was the case not just in eastern but also in western Belarus. In April 1943, he wrote to Ponomarenko that "the population of the western oblasts—Poles and Belarusians—are awaiting the arrival of the Red Army and are helping the partisans in every possible way."[227]

However, although German conduct clearly affected local perceptions of the partisans and people's choice to join them, the question of what constituted civilian support for the Soviet partisans was more complex than Gusev and others thought. Juxtaposing two recollections, one by Aleksandra Zakharova and the other by Shalom Yoran, shows this well. Zakharova, who fought during the war as a political commissar in a partisan unit in Gomel' oblast, fondly recalled the selfless help provided by the local population—the same population that the NKVD officers Golovkin and Gutkin had still called unsupportive of the partisans in the fall of 1941. She remembered one person in particular: "There was a woman there alone, without her husband but with her three little children. She never drove us away when we came but lit the stove and cleaned our clothes . . . She gave us all she had left."[228]

Shalom Yoran, who by 1943 was fighting with a Soviet partisan unit in the region around Lake Naroch' north of Minsk, described the situation differently. As he recalled, one of the first and most essential missions of each unit was to acquire food: "Because I had a rifle I was given the job of going to nearby villages at night to replenish our supplies. . . . The villagers close to our woods were supportive of the partisans, though not necessarily by choice. . . . In our designated area we would approach the village leader with a list of supplies we needed. It was up to him to decide how much each villager was to give, and he accompanied us on our rounds."[229]

In areas further removed from the forests, the acquisition of food did not follow this systematic pattern: "Further away, nearer to the German garrisons, the population was more loyal to the Germans, also not necessarily by choice. There, because it was not considered under partisan jurisdiction and not bound by any self-imposed partisan restrictions, any *otriad* [unit] was free to go" and acquire food. Because the partisans had to move more carefully in those areas, they stationed two guard groups at each side of the village before going from house to house, collecting food, clothes, and occasionally livestock: "The peasants protested, argued, pleaded, but were afraid to resist."[230] One of Yoran's fellow partisans, a man named Suvorov, would usually threaten reluctant peasants with his gun, take a grenade out of his pocket and place it casually on the table, or feign a person's execution by shooting through his earlobe. "He threatened to shoot them, to burn them, to take away their possessions, if they didn't hand over their possessions at once."[231]

How local civilians behaved when confronted with partisan demands for food, then, was not just a question of hatred for the Germans, patriotism for their homeland or region, or identification with communism. Rather, it also depended heavily on external factors such as their geographical closeness to either a partisan camp or a German garrison. Stepan Plianto, the deputy commander of a partisan unit that began its activities in the spring of 1942 in Mogilev oblast, suggested a similar dynamic when he remarked that in the districts that were under the firm control of his unit, "without a single German, without a single policeman," it was no longer necessary to go on food procurement missions with a weapon.[232] From such comments we can see that the potential for violence toward civilians, whether at the hands of the Germans and their local representatives or at the hands of the partisans, was higher in the "twilight zones," the regions where power was contested and where locals, caught in-between, had to try to satisfy both sides.[233] But we can also see that, just as with local behavior toward the Germans, we cannot deduce people's motivations for their actions toward the partisans from acts alone. The choice to provide partisans with bread or shelter for a night could be indicative of a whole range of motivations, ranging from fear to sympathy for the Soviets, but taken by itself, it cannot provide clear evidence of any one motive.

During the Second World War, the inhabitants of Belarus found themselves within a world of almost unimaginable, apocalyptic violence. Confronted with an occupation regime that subjected the local population to a regime of utmost brutality, yet also sought the limited engagement of some, people's wartime choices were, first and foremost, shaped by the options offered by the German authorities. But while the occupiers clearly circumscribed locals' space for action, the size of that space was neither the same for everyone nor static over time. Singled out from the beginning for destruction as a group, the space for individual agency was almost nonexistent for Jews. It was, however, larger for non-Jews. Toward the Slavic population, the occupation regime employed a mixture of co-optation and brutality, with violence becoming more systematic and widespread once German antipartisan operations increased in mid-1942 and the campaigns for forced labor intensified. Within the constraints of occupation, non-Jews had a range of options at their disposal. Some of these were far-reaching, such as volunteering to work in the German-overseen local police forces or, quite the opposite, giving shelter to Red Army soldiers, Jews, or partisans and risking their lives in the process. But wartime choices also included smaller, seemingly insignificant acts, such as taking furniture from a murdered Jewish neighbor's apartment or refraining from doing so.

During the chaotic transition from Soviet to German rule, the space for local action was largest, and some people committed violence against Jews and Soviet officials. The level of local anti-Jewish violence was highest in the Białystok region (which the Soviet Union handed back to Poland in 1945). In the other parts of western Belarus, the level of violence was much lower, although small-scale pogroms against Jews also took place, primarily around Vileika, between and around Baranovichi and Novogrudok, and east of Pinsk. For eastern Belarus, local pogroms against Jews during the summer of 1941 have not been recorded. A variety of different exogenous and endogenous factors accounted for the variation of local anti-Jewish violence across the western parts of the Soviet Union during the summer of 1941. What specifically set the case of western Belarus in its post-1945 borders apart from western Ukraine, the Białystok region, and Bessarabia and northern Bukovina was the weakness and relative absence of small groups of radical nationalists who could have acted as potential perpetrators and instigators of local violence against Jews. Once the German authorities installed their administration, though, they could depend in both western and eastern Belarus on a small group of people, primarily local policemen and town mayors, who actively assisted the Germans in carrying out the murder of the region's Jewish communities. In that respect, eastern Belarus did not differ from western Belarus, and Belarus as a whole did not differ from the other Soviet western regions. In their treatment of their Jewish neighbors, the non-Jewish civilian population in western Belarus displayed the same behavioral spectrum as in eastern Belarus, ranging from acts of rescue and shelter to expropriating Jewish property, blackmailing or denouncing neighbors in hiding, or even taking part in the killing process.

Quantitative differences within this spectrum of human behavior (such as that more people in one part of Belarus were willing to help Jews than in other parts, or correspondingly less willing to extend help) could not be clearly detected, at least not for the regions that would constitute post-1945 Belarus. Where a visible difference between western and eastern Belarus did exist, though, was in the support networks that Jews could draw on. In eastern Belarus, intercommunal relations among certain urban groups (younger people, those who no longer adhered to a religion, and people who identified with the Soviet project) were by and large less defined by traditional social and religious markers of identity than in western Belarus, and rates of interethnic integration were higher. Consequently, help was often extended through these networks, thereby reflecting the different prewar legacies of Soviet rule in western and eastern Belarus.

Trying to reconstruct why individuals acted the way they did under the extreme circumstances of Nazi occupation is a complicated task, especially with regard to local perpetrators who committed violence in the name of German power and rarely talked about their own motivations—or if they did, it was only under problematic circumstances such as postwar interrogations conducted by the Soviet state security organs. The act in itself does not tell us much about internal motives and driving factors. What can be said is that when the German army invaded in 1941, people's initial choices were often influenced by their prior experiences with Soviet rule or their relationship to the Bolsheviks. Party members or individuals who held important positions within the Soviet party-state were more likely to flee east, while many who had previously suffered under the Soviets were among those who joined the German-organized police forces. Once partisan warfare began to pick up in mid-1942, however, civilians in Belarus came increasingly under pressure from both sides, German and partisan. At this point in time, the space for individual action was no longer circumscribed by one but by two groups, and in those western and southern regions where Polish or Ukrainian nationalist partisans were active even by multiple groups, all of which were fighting one another in a life-and-death struggle. As a result, people's actions came to be much more determined by situational factors—including the will to survive, coercion, violence, patriotism (which was not identical with belief in communism), or simply by the proximity of one's village to either a German garrison or a Soviet partisan zone. Many choices that civilians were forced to make were "choiceless choices," in which either option might have an equally destructive effect on their families and local communities. As political circumstances, and thus the terms of involvement with both

Germans and partisans, changed over time, individuals reevaluated their previous choices. In short, complicity and entanglement were questions of degree, and both people's decisions and their consequences varied over time. The returning Soviet authorities, though, showed little concern for these moral gray zones of occupation—and did not take them into account when judging a person's wartime behavior after the war.

Chapter 3

Post-1944

The Moment of Return

Chasia Bornstein-Bielicka experienced the end of Nazi rule in the forests of Białystok. After the Battle of Stalingrad, the tide had turned on the Eastern Front. In a series of counteroffensives, the Red Army began to push the Germans from the western regions of the Soviet Union. In the fall of 1943, Soviet forces crossed into Belarusian and Ukrainian territory; roughly six months later, the Red Army had retaken all of Russia, most of Ukraine, and parts of southeastern Belarus around Gomel'. The Soviet High Command then began to direct its forces against Army Group Center, which was still holding on to much of Belarus. On June 23, 1944, almost three years to the day that Germany had invaded the Soviet Union, the Red Army launched Operation Bagration. Within less than two months, Army Group Center fell apart. On July 3, 1944, units of the Belarusian Front liberated Minsk. By mid-August 1944, the Germans had been pushed from all of Belarus—which at the time still included the Białystok region.[1]

A member of the Jewish resistance, first in Grodno and later in Białystok, Chasia Bornstein-Bielicka survived the war under a false identity, posing as a Polish village girl. For many months, she served as a liaison between the Białystok ghetto resistance and the outside world. After the liquidation of the ghetto in the summer of 1943, she traveled back and forth between the town and the surrounding forests, providing the Jewish partisans with intelligence information, food, and weapons. In July 1944, when the Red Army approached the Białystok region, Bornstein-Bielicka joined the partisans, who just a few weeks earlier had come under the command of the Soviet partisan movement. Many years later, she recalled the elation that accompanied the subsequent encounter with the Red Army, a moment of immense delight, carried by a sense of relief and salvation. That evening, her comrades celebrated—going wild with joy, drinking, singing, and firing their weapons into the air. But the moment of happiness also carried an immense sadness. By that time, Bornstein-Bielicka already partly knew what would later be confirmed: that she was the only one of her family to have survived the Holocaust. In the fall of 1944, she set out to return to Grodno, her hometown in western Belarus.[2]

This chapter looks at the moment of return, and the worlds destroyed, worlds in flux, and worlds apart that it revealed. Nazi rule had brought tremendous death and destruction throughout the Soviet western regions. Belarus was among the hardest-hit places. In 1946, an American journalist visited the republic. Shocked by what he saw, he wrote in his diary: "I traveled from one end of this republic to the other, and I can only think of it as the most devastated territory in the world."[3] Most cities lay in ruins, entire rural districts had been burned down, and large parts of the population were uprooted or displaced. Those who survived were not able to settle down quickly. In the first post-occupation years, the region continued to be in motion, as hundreds of thousands of demobilized soldiers and partisans, former forced laborers, reevacuees and refugees were moving into, out of, within, and through the republic.[4] In that experience of migration, the moment of return, first and foremost the much hoped-for reunion with family members, figured prominently. While some people were overjoyed to find their loved ones alive, for others it was a moment of deepest grief and devastation, in particular for Holocaust survivors who discovered that nothing of their prewar worlds remained. Some who were fearful of their wartime pasts sought to evade home and settled elsewhere or fled west as the Red Army advanced. Yet others, such as ethnic Poles from western Belarus, had to ask themselves whether returning home meant resettling to Poland under the conditions of the Polish-Soviet population exchange.

Among those who returned to Belarus were the prewar leaders of the republic, headed by First Secretary Panteleimon Ponomarenko. For the Soviet authorities, the task that lay ahead of them was enormous: to rebuild the Soviet state in an utterly destroyed region and in a time of great flux and population movement. Especially on the lower levels of the party-state, the authorities faced a dire shortage of qualified personnel. Many of those who had occupied these positions prior to the war had been killed or were unavailable in 1944, either because they were still serving in the Red Army, or because they had been assigned to different jobs elsewhere in the Soviet Union. Rebuilding the Soviet state, though, was not just about the reconstruction of institutions and cadres. It was also a question of making sure that any resistance, real or imagined, would be destroyed—and it meant reclaiming authority over a region where the population was overjoyed to see Nazi occupation end, yet where many people in both western and eastern Belarus were apprehensive about the return of Soviet power as such. In turn, party leaders and state security officers were ambivalent about the local population, given its long exposure to German rule. One task therefore lay at the heart of Soviet state rebuilding, in Belarus as in the other western regions of the Soviet Union: investigating what people in Nazi-occupied territory had done during the war.

Homecomings

In August 1944, Petr Lebedev set out to return home, to the village of Ivanovka in Vitebsk oblast. During the war, Lebedev had fought with the Soviet partisans, but in January 1944, he was seriously wounded and flown out to a hospital in the rear. On recovery, he was declared unfit for service in the Red Army and spent the next several months working on a collective farm in the Kuban region. On June 24, 1944, news reached him that Vitebsk oblast had been liberated. Lebedev wrote letter after letter home, hoping to hear from his family, but never received an answer. Finally, in August of that year, he decided to find out for himself.[5]

FIGURE 6. View of central Minsk, July 1944. Courtesy of the Belarusian State Archive of Film, Photo, and Sound Recordings.

After days of traveling by train, by car, and on foot, Lebedev reached the top of a small hill about half a mile away from Ivanovka. He expected to see the village spread out before him, but instead, he saw mostly earth dugouts; only two peasant huts were still intact. When Lebedev approached what had remained of his village, people came running toward him. Shortly before she could reach him, his mother fell to the ground. Lebedev wanted to catch her, but instead he fell down with her: "I kissed my mother, I kissed the earth. My mother hugged me, cried, and kissed my cheeks, forehead, my head." His parents had believed their son to be dead, having been told so by one of his fellow partisans. Embracing his mother and father, sister, and brothers and surrounded by the other villagers, Lebedev walked to the place that was once called Ivanovka: "We were so happy. And our fellow villagers were happy. Everyone thought that their son, brother, husband, or father might just as well return so unexpectedly."[6]

Similarly, when Raisa Khosenevich, who fought with the partisans during the war, returned to Minsk, she didn't know whether her little son Lenya, whom she had not seen for three years, was still alive. When she walked into the yard of the neighbor who was looking after him since her mother-in-law had died of typhus, Lenya, ragged and barefoot, did not recognize her; he thought that his mother was dead. When Khosenevich told the boy that she was indeed his mother, he first mistook her for his father because she was wearing men's clothes: a German army shirt, a padded jacket, old boots. But "then he hugged me and screamed, 'Mama!!!' It was such a scream!" As she recalled, "for a month he didn't let me go anywhere, not even to work . . . It wasn't even enough for him to see me, to see that I was nearby, he had to hold on to me. If we sat down for lunch, he held me with one hand and ate with the other. He only called me 'Mamochka.'"[7]

Many homecomings, however, did not occur quite that soon. As the Red Army reconquered district by district, it carried out an immediate draft among the local male population. After the disbandment of the Soviet partisan movement in the summer of 1944, most of the former partisans also joined the Red Army. Once the war ended, millions of Soviet soldiers were demobilized over the course of the next few years. Several hundreds of thousands of them would eventually return to Belarus.[8] Among them was the future writer Vasil' Bykaŭ, for whom the war had ended in Austria, after which he was transferred to Bulgaria and then Ukraine. When Bykaŭ was discharged in the spring of 1947, he made his way to Belarus to meet his family, whom he hadn't seen in almost seven years. Soon, however, he was called up again for service. This time, the army took him east, all the way to Vladivostok and the Kuril Islands. In 1955, he was finally demobilized from the Red Army and settled in Grodno, where he worked for the local newspaper.[9]

Also returning from the west were civilians, in the majority women, who had been taken as forced laborers to Germany, as well as Red Army soldiers who had fallen into German captivity. The Soviet forces liberated most of them from German camps outside the Soviet Union. Others were liberated on Soviet territory formerly occupied by the Germans. Before repatriation, both groups had to pass through a series of NKVD filtration camps, where officers checked their wartime activities and assessed their political loyalty. Exploited during the war, during their transport back home female repatriates continued to be vulnerable to coercion and violence, this time at the hands of Red Army soldiers and NKVD officers. At the Brest train station, one of the main transit points, cases of rape were frequent.[10] If repatriates passed through Transit Camp no. 316, located close to the train station of Bronnaia Gora in Brest oblast, they had to sleep in earth dugouts, sanitary facilities were missing, and daily meals were cooked with rotten produce.[11]

It is estimated that between 43 and 60 percent of all repatriates were allowed to return home on discharge from the filtration camps. The rest were either drafted into the Red Army, assigned to various labor battalions that were employed across the Soviet Union, or sent to the Gulag.[12] The last fate befell some of Vasil' Bykaŭ's fellow villagers. As he recalled: "Among my young fellow villagers, there were also those who went the whole circle of hell: mobilized in 1941, [followed by German] captivity and concentration camp, liberation from these in 1944, and once more to the front—and then again to the camps. Just this time into the other direction: to Siberia and the Far North."[13]

By late 1946, the vast majority of repatriates had passed through filtration. By then, 215,000 of the 380,000 civilians from Belarus who had been forcibly taken to Germany during the war and an estimated 150,000 former Red Army soldiers from Belarus who had fallen into German captivity had returned to the republic.[14] Mariia Mosina, whose mother was arrested in 1943 on suspicion of ties to the partisans, was one of them. Only a ten-year-old child, Mosina was separated from her family and taken to Germany, where she and other Soviet children were forced to work in a military hospital, cleaning the bathrooms, wards, and operating rooms. The German supervisor treated the children with cruelty and fed them poorly. After liberation, Mosina returned to Minsk, where she was given a place in a children's home. Eventually, her mother, who had survived, was able to locate her there.

The meeting was incredibly moving: "I cannot recall it without tears in my eyes." From then on, mother and daughter were inseparable.[15]

Hundreds of thousands, though, never returned. For the Red Army, individual breakdowns by republic do not exist, which is why any number has to remain an estimate. Overall, it is estimated that at least 700,000 men (and women) from Belarus died as Red Army soldiers at the front.[16] According to the Belarusian Staff of the Partisan Movement, at least 37,378 people, but perhaps many more, died fighting with the partisans in Belarus or went missing.[17] In turn, the Soviet partisans killed at least 17,431 people, but probably many more, who served in the local police or were deemed traitors.[18] It is unknown how many civilians taken as forced laborers to Germany died during the war. Of Vasil' Bykaŭ's male friends from school, not a single one survived. Some died with the partisans, others while serving in the German-organized local police forces, and yet others as Red Army soldiers at the front.[19] As a woman from the village Ratyntsy in Volozhinskii district, west of Minsk, recalled: "Victory!—they said. The men began to come home. But fewer returned than we sent out. Less than half."[20] Her brother Iusik was the first to come back, but he returned disabled; her husband Ivan fell in battle only two months before the end of the war. Many women in the village shared her fate. Among those drafted in the summer of 1944 was Vladimir Grigorovich, the husband of another woman from Ratyntsy. When called up for service, he cried bitterly because he had to leave his small children behind. The unit was about to leave, but he was holding on to his youngest: "He couldn't let go of him, he stood in the column with him . . . The commander yelled at him, and he was flooding the baby with tears."[21] When the soldiers marched out of the village, his wife took her children and ran after them, and Vladimir Grigorovich kept on turning around, trying to catch a glimpse of his family. After a year, she received notice that her husband had been killed not far from Berlin. She would have given everything for his return. "I've never even seen his grave. One of our neighbors came home perfectly healthy, another came home missing a leg. I grieved so much: let mine come back, even without legs, but alive. I'd have carried him in my arms."[22]

The homecoming of a neighbor could be a moment of happiness, but it also served as a remainder of one's own loss, the joy that one would never experience. For people from western Belarus who had relatives deported to the Gulag prior to June 1941, the summer of 1944 brought new hope of receiving news from them, now that the region was back under Soviet rule. For others who returned from the front or evacuation, it shattered all remaining hope of finding loved ones alive. On the communal level, the moment of return also threw into sharp relief that some had lost more than others during the war. While almost every family in Belarus had a son or husband, uncle, or nephew who was killed at the front, inhabitants of the burned villages lost most or all of their families. When the Germans destroyed the village of Zbyshin in Mogilev oblast, the partisan Ivan Savitskii lost twenty-six members of his family, including his father and sister. Alena Bondarchuk's husband returned from the army, but their four children, the youngest only six months old, were killed in the burning of the village of Aleksichi in Gomel' oblast.[23]

As a whole, no other population group in Belarus lost as much as Jews during the war. Of the 1–1.2 million local civilians whom the Germans killed on Belarusian territory (in its post-1945 borders, not including the Białystok region), about half of them, an estimated 500,000–671,000 people, were Jewish, almost the entire Jewish population of the republic.[24] A few survived with the partisans, others like Lev Ovsishcher at the front, and yet others, primarily prewar inhabitants of the easternmost regions like Ovsishcher's parents, in evacuation.[25] Many survivors, though, lost not only their entire families but their communities as well. This was even more so the case for Jews from western Belarus, where significantly fewer people had been able to flee east in the summer of 1941, and where for mostly religious and socio-economic reasons less overlap had existed between Jewish and non-Jewish communities prior to 1941 than in eastern Belarus. When the partisan Raisa Gorodinskaia returned to her hometown of Derechin in western Belarus, she discovered that her entire family—parents, siblings, and other relatives—had perished. "Before the war, Derechin was a friendly, bustling, cultured place. . . . Now we saw a desolated village." The house where Gorodinskaia had grown up was burned down, the family's property looted: "Every corner, every small bush reminded me of my parents, my brothers . . . There my father had worked, there my small brother had played, and there my older brother had worked. And again tears, and memories made my heart heavy. I couldn't accept that they were no longer alive, I couldn't imagine that!"[26]

For Raisa Gorodinskaia, the return to the place that she once called home was an incredibly isolating experience. On seeing the destruction, she realized that nothing tied her personally anymore to Derechin.[27] The same was true for Chasia Bornstein-Bielicka. In the early fall of 1944, she returned with two of her friends, who like her had been in the Jewish resistance, from Białystok to their hometown, Grodno. On her first morning back, Bornstein-Bielicka visited the former main ghetto in the old town, an area of less than half a square kilometer surrounded by a fence. The first stop, as she recalled, were "the ruins of what had been my family's apartment."[28] Inside, she found destroyed rooms: pieces of furniture, shreds of torn clothing, fragments of shattered dishes. A few days later, she and her friends went from house to house in the ghetto, collecting whatever documents and pictures they could find in the looted, empty apartments.[29] It took a while before Bornstein-Bielicka returned to the place where she had grown up. Her family's house on Podolna Street on the outskirts of Grodno was still intact, unlike Raisa Gorodinskaia's, as were all the neighboring houses, the vegetable gardens, and the fruit trees. "Nothing had changed," she recalled decades later, "only we weren't there. The parents, siblings, uncles and aunts, the Chasid family, the seamstress and her daughters, Cebulski the shoemaker, the Littman family—the bakers—the Karons, who had lived further up the street, and the Sokolowskis. Podolna Street was *Judenrein*."[30]

For both women, it was impossible to remain in the towns they used to call home, to live among the constant reminders of the world they had irretrievably lost, especially when they saw that their neighbors' lives had been touched much less by the violence of war. Soon after her visit, Raisa Gorodinskaia left Derechin for good and moved to Baranovichi, a large town in the region. Her partisan connections helped her to find work there, and she shared an apartment with two Jewish friends, also former partisans. However, when her friends decided to relocate to Poland with the aim of emigrating to Palestine, Gorodinskaia did not join them: "I was thankful to the Soviet army that had saved me from certain death." Moreover, she feared antisemitism in Poland. Content to have found some stability in Baranovichi, she was tired of moving around and did not want to be uprooted again.[31] Chasia Bornstein-Bielicka remained for another year in Grodno, studying at a teacher's college, but she had little intention of staying for long. With her entire family killed in the Holocaust, the only thing that kept her there temporarily were her two best friends, Lisa Czapnik and Anja Rod, with whom she had survived the war. Czapnik had always dreamed of living in a communist society, and her sister-in-law Anja did not want to leave without her. Bornstein-Bielicka, in contrast, had been active in the Socialist-Zionist youth organization Hashomer Hatzair. Emigrating to Palestine seemed like the only logical thing to do, something that filled her with a sense of purpose and hope. In the summer of 1945, an acquaintance, a Jewish Red Army officer, smuggled her in a truck across the new Polish-Soviet border. Eventually arriving in Łódź, she began to operate an orphanage for Jewish children whose families had been killed in the Holocaust. In late 1947, after accompanying a group of children from Poland to Germany and through France, Bornstein-Bielicka arrived in Palestine.[32]

The moment of return, then, carried different meanings for different people. While some lost more than others during the war, for most, returning home always carried an element of sadness and sorrow, making visible what was gone and what had remained, what was undergoing change and what had vanished forever. Among the spectrum of individual return experiences were also the reluctant returns, as well as the returns that were avoided—out of fear of one's neighbor or the Soviet authorities or both. Knowing that severe punishment awaited them once the Red Army had reconquered a region, some policemen fled to the forests when the Wehrmacht retreated. A significant number of them left with the German army. The local policemen from Mirskii district, for example, were incorporated into the Thirtieth Waffen SS Grenadier Division and sent to fight in France in the fall of 1944. According to German military reports, during Operation Bagration, 95,900 people considered "armed collaborators," probably Soviet citizens who were members of special SS fighting battalions as well as local policemen, were taken to Germany.[33] After the war, many of them found themselves in Displaced Person (DP) camps in Germany. Some of them were able to immigrate to North America and the United Kingdom, but most Soviet citizens in DP camps under US, British, and French control were transferred under the authority of the Soviets. Those who sought to conceal their wartime activities typically took on false identities, and some people indeed managed to disguise their real selves, even after passing through various filtration and transit camps.[34] Other former policemen went back to Belarus of their own accord, perhaps because they wanted to be reunited with their families, successfully bypassing the official repatriation procedure. Returning to one's prewar place of residence, however, was highly risky: one could hope to deceive an NKVD officer in a filtration camp, but deceiving old neighbors was impossible. The Soviet authorities were aware of such strategies. As an official observed in the summer of 1944 about Bobruisk oblast, "some of the former policemen try to settle in any place just so that they do not have to return home, apparently out of fear of being discovered."[35]

Liavon Shymanets was still a child when his family decided to leave Baranovichi, the western Belarusian town in which they had lived until the summer of 1944. In October 1940, the NKVD had arrested Shymanets's father as an "enemy of the people," but when German planes bombed Baranovichi in June 1941, the prison in which he was incarcerated was hit. In the ensuing chaos, many of the inmates, among them Shymanets's father, managed to escape. During the German occupation, his mother worked for a while as a teacher in an elementary school and his father, an engineer by profession, in the technical school in Baranovichi. According to Shymanets, his family was "connected neither to the Germans nor to the partisans." Regardless of whether that was entirely true, after the return of the Red Army, his father would certainly have been arrested, given that he was able to escape from prison in 1941. It is not quite clear just how the Shymanets family made their way west, whether on their own initiative or as part of a German-organized transport. By the end of the war, however, they had reached Denmark and later continued on to France.[36]

Barys Kit's story of flight and emigration was in many ways similar, although Kit left Belarus not because he had previously been targeted by the NKVD, but because he had every reason to believe that he would be. On the eve of the German attack, Kit, who in the late 1950s would embark on a successful career in the United States in the field of astronautics, was the director of the Belarusian high school in Novogrudok. During the German occupation, he first worked as a teacher and later as the principal of different schools in northwestern Belarus. In 1943, the Germans arrested him and accused him of having ties to the partisans. Kit did not have any connection to partisans, yet suspicion was usually enough: the other men with whom he shared a prison cell in the town of Vileika were shot. In the end, however, the German authorities released Kit from imprisonment. What saved him, as he later found out, were fellow "Belarusian activists" (*belaruski aktyŭ*)—in particular, Kastus' Kasiak, a former student of his who worked in the town administration and who had enough influence with the Germans to get Kit released.[37]

Barys Kit probably knew that his release from prison would have been enough for the returning Soviet state security organs to order his arrest, as were his ties to Belarusian nationalist circles. In June 1944, shortly before the arrival of the Red Army in the city, he attended the Second All-Belarusian Congress in Minsk. The congress brought together roughly one thousand Belarusian nationalists, some of whom held positions in the Belarusian Central Council, the Belarusian puppet administration. The event was saturated with Nazi rhetoric and symbolism, with Radaslaŭ Astroŭski, who headed the council, depicting the German occupation as a period of Belarusian rebirth and proclaiming his belief in a German victory.[38] Although he attended the congress, Kit maintained that he had nothing to do with such people—a claim that seems implausible. From the school that Kit headed during the occupation, a former student recalled, "every kind of politicization was completely absent." It is difficult to say whether that was indeed the case. Still, the mere fact that Kit worked as a school director during the occupation, combined with his attendance at the congress, would have been enough to make him and his family afraid of the Soviet return. Shortly before the Red Army reconquered Belarus, they fled to Germany, where the Kits settled for a few years in Munich before immigrating to the United States in 1948.[39]

Rebuilding the State

As the Red Army advanced into Belarusian territory, not just those who were fearful of their own wartime record fled westward or hid in the forests. Scores of civilians fled to the forests, too, seeking shelter from military operations or trying to escape the last roundups of forced laborers that the German authorities conducted during their retreat. By the time the Red Army entered a town or village, few civilians were present. Slowly, people returned from the woods.[40]

Among the civilian population, the first encounters with the Red Army usually brought tremendous relief. As Nikolai Shabonia, one of the few who survived the burning of the village of Baiki in Brest oblast, recalled: "The moment the Red Army arrived and liberated us—that's impossible to describe! What joy!"[41] In Minsk, people rushed toward the first soldiers they encountered, crying, kissing, and hugging them.[42] Major General Galadzhev,

FIGURE 7. Civilians returning from the forests, 1944. Courtesy of the Belarusian State Archive of Film, Photo, and Sound Recordings.

head of the Political Administration of the First Belarusian Front, described similar meetings with locals in Bobruisk oblast. For Anton Kozlov, a villager from Rogachevskii district, it was as if "someone had lifted a heavy stone" from his heart.[43] A woman from the same district, whose husband was serving in the Red Army, told the soldiers that she had been sure the Soviet forces would eventually liberate her. Sof'ia Ivanova voiced a similar emotion: "We waited for you, our dear liberators," she told the soldiers, "and we believed that you would come. And we ourselves continued to believe in our native Soviet power."[44]

Many, though, were not as enthusiastic as Sof'ia Ivanova about the reestablishment of Soviet rule as such. While there was universal relief at seeing Nazi rule end, beneath the joyful encounters with Red Army soldiers lay much apprehension. In some cases, this was reflected in the language that people used. As Major General Galadzhev noted in his report, in the region around Bobruisk, "when speaking about the Red Army, about our soldiers and officers, not all local residents use the words 'ours' [*nashi*], but more often say 'Russians' [*russkie*] or 'the Reds' [*krasnye*]."[45] Such use of language not only suggested the existence of an emotional distance, it also implied that the Red Army was seen as synonymous with a political power that, if not as foreign as the Germans, was neither native nor local. Yet for others, it was entirely possible to see Red Army soldiers as liberators, as "our soldiers," but at the same time be fearful about the return of communism. Among the rural population in eastern Belarus, this apprehension mostly stemmed from widespread dislike of the collective-farm system. In November 1943, shortly after the Red Army had begun its advance into southeastern Belarus, the NKGB intercepted a letter by a Red Army soldier. In the letter, the soldier talked about his encounters with inhabitants of Belarus. "People are terribly dissatisfied with the collective farms," he wrote. "The first question when we enter a village is—will there be collective farms?"[46]

In western Belarus, locals were likewise apprehensive about the return of Soviet power. For Zofia Brzozowska, who grew up in a Polish-speaking family that owned a small estate not far from Novogrudok, the return of the Red Army marked the beginning of yet another occupation. Brzozowska had lost more relatives and family friends to the Soviets (either in 1939–1941 or at the hands of Soviet partisans) than to the Germans. In her eyes, there was little difference between the two regimes.[47] In contrast, for Sulia Wolozhinski Rubin, who grew up in a Jewish family in Novogrudok, there was a clear difference between the Soviets and the Germans: the Red Army liberated her from a genocidal regime that had not just killed her family but also destroyed Jewish life as such. Yet at the same time, Wolozhinski Rubin detested the increasing feeling of being unfree after liberation, the power of the state security organs, and the constant fear, even as a former partisan, of random arrests.[48]

Among the rural population of western Belarus, the greatest concern was the collective-farm system. With the exception of a few villages, the agricultural sector of western Belarus had, like that of western Ukraine and the Baltic states, remained uncollectivized prior to 1941. Now that the Wehrmacht had been driven from Belarus, many feared that collectivization was only a matter of time. In meetings with Red Army soldiers, villagers asked over and over again: will the collective-farm system be introduced?[49] What further intensified the uncertainty of the situation was the continued existence of anti-Soviet nationalist formations—in particular, the Polish Armia Krajowa. Meanwhile in Polesia in southern Belarus, in the new and old Soviet districts bordering Ukraine, paramilitary Ukrainian nationalist forces gathered local villagers and agitated against Soviet power.[50]

The returning Soviet leadership thus faced tremendous challenges: to rebuild the state amid massive material destruction and immense human losses, at a time of great flux and population movement, and in a region where they faced not only local apprehension but also, to varying degrees, armed resistance. But who were the men in charge of the postwar republic? Of the individuals who by June 1941 had held high-ranking posts in the Belarusian party-state, most had been able to flee east when the Germans advanced. The entire Central Committee of Belarus, the Sovnarkom, and the Supreme Soviet of Belarus left Minsk in the night of June 24–25, 1941, three days before the Wehrmacht captured the capital.[51] Among those who reached the safety of the Soviet rear were First Secretary Panteleimon Ponomarenko and other men in his leadership circle like Central Committee members Nikolai Avkhimovich, Ivan Bylinskii (deputy to the head of the Belarusian Sovnarkom), Grigorii Eidinov, Petr Kalinin, and Nikifor Natalevich (head of the Supreme Soviet of Belarus). Also able to flee east were high-ranking members of the state security organs, including Lavrentii Tsanava, head of the NKVD in Belarus and a member of the Central Committee, and Ivan Vetrov, since 1940 the chief prosecutor of Belarus.[52]

During the war, most members of the Central Committee of Belarus were located in Moscow, where some of them also worked for the Central Staff of the Partisan Movement. Petr Kalinin, for example, headed the movement's Belarusian branch. Others were assigned to positions elsewhere in the Soviet rear or attached to the Red Army. Lavrentii Tsanava initially headed the NKVD's Special Sector (*osobyi otdel*) of the Red Army's Western Front and later its Central Front before becoming deputy to the head of the

FIGURE 8. Panteleimon Ponomarenko. Portrait taken between 1943 and 1945. Courtesy of the Belarusian State Archive of Film, Photo, and Sound Recordings.

Central Staff of the Partisan Movement, who was none other than Ponomarenko. When the NKVD was (again) divided into two bodies (NKVD and NKGB) in April 1943, Tsanava became head of the NKGB (renamed MGB in 1946) in Belarus, a post that he held until 1951, when he left the republic for Moscow. Appointed as head of the NKVD in Belarus was Sergei Bel'chenko, who had headed the NKVD in Belostok (Białystok) oblast from 1939 to 1941. During the war, Bel'chenko, like Tsanava, served for a while as deputy to Ponomarenko, in the latter's capacity as head of the Central Staff of the Partisan Movement. Bel'chenko held the post of head of the NKVD (renamed MVD in 1946) in Belarus until 1953.[53]

After the Red Army drove the Wehrmacht from Belarus, many of the individuals who had constituted the prewar and wartime leadership of the republic returned to Minsk. Some resumed their previous posts, while others were assigned to new ones, usually high-ranking positions. The leadership was exclusively male. Ponomarenko continued to head the Communist Party of Belarus; in February 1944, he was also appointed head of the Belarusian Sovnarkom (renamed Council of Ministers in 1946). Nikolai Avkhimovich remained secretary in charge of cadres and Nikifor Natalevich the head of the Supreme Soviet of Belarus. Grigorii Eidinov became deputy to Ponomarenko in his capacity as head of the Sovnarkom, while Petr Kalinin was appointed the first secretary of the Grodno regional party committee and Ivan Bylinskii the first secretary of the Poles'e regional party committee. Both regions experienced anti-Soviet nationalist resistance; appointing former members of the Belarusian Central Committee to lead their respective regional party organizations showed how serious the situation was. While Ponomarenko and the two other most powerful men in post-1944 Belarus, Tsanava and Bel'chenko, had no family roots in Belarus, others within the leadership did. Avkhimovich, for example, was born in Bobruisk, Natalevich in Orsha, and Kalinin in the Vitebsk region. Other high-ranking communists were likewise natives of Belarus: Ivan Vetrov, chief prosecutor of Belarus from 1940 to 1941 and again from 1943 on, was born in the Mogilev region. In other words, a significant number of men who held important party-state positions in Belarus during and after the war were locals, meaning they had been born or had grown up in Belarus and spoke Belarusian, even if Russian was their primary language of communication. Whether local or not, what all men at the top shared is that they were *vostochniki*, "Easterners," people who hailed from regions that had been Soviet for almost two decades before the war. These men were long-time members of the Communist Party, loyal to the cause, and ruthless, if not outright brutal, in their endeavors. Many of them had, like Ponomarenko and Tsanava, risen to top-level positions during or after the Great Terror of 1936–1938, thus benefiting from the internal party purges.[54]

Much continuity, then, existed on the level of the party-state's leadership—yet the situation was very different at the lower levels, where the authorities faced a dire shortage of experienced personnel. By June 1, 1941, the nomenklatura of Belarus, as people in leadership positions within the party-state apparatus were called, comprised seventeen thousand people. This included all party secretaries, ranging from the Central Committee in Minsk to the regional party committees down to the district and city party committees.

FIGURE 9. Lavrentii Tsanava, 1946. Courtesy of the Belarusian State Archive of Film, Photo, and Sound Recordings.

It also included all leadership positions within the state branch, ranging from the heads of the Supreme Soviet and the Sovnarkom to the heads of the regional, district, and city executive committees. The heads of the regional courts and the military tribunals, the regional and district prosecutors, as well as the heads of the different departments within the NKVD and the NKGB were also considered part of the nomenklatura, as were the heads of the regional planning commissions, Komsomol secretaries, and propaganda lecturers employed by the Central Committee.[55]

During the war, many mid- to low-level nomenklatura members were killed, either at the front, with the partisans, or as civilians in occupied territory. Others, who in the summer of 1941 had managed to flee east, were tied up in the Red Army or rear when the Soviet authorities returned to Belarus. A few had compromised themselves by working for the Germans during the war. Given that official evacuation had been possible only from the easternmost part of the republic, a considerable regional imbalance existed among the evacuated cadres from Belarus: most of them had been employed in positions in Gomel', Mogilev, and Vitebsk oblasts prior to 1941.[56]

In response, the Soviet leaders decided to pursue a manifold strategy. Once the Central Committee of Belarus had established itself in Moscow during the war, the Cadres Department began to gather and compile information on the whereabouts of its party and state workers (*partiinye i sovetskie rabotniki*). While some were sent into occupied territory, with the aim of organizing partisan units, others were selected to undergo special training in the rear to prepare them for future employment in a reconquered Belarus.[57] In June 1943, Ivan Vetrov, chief prosecutor of Belarus, reported that his institution would need at least 660 staff members to be able to function properly. At the time, more than half were missing, which is why 150 new cadres were sent for express training to the Institute of Law in Kazan'.[58] When Soviet forces crossed into Belarusian territory in the fall of 1943, the center dispatched operational groups to the recently reconquered districts. Made up of experienced party-state officials, they were responsible for establishing the basic pillars of Soviet power in the region: creating party and state executive committees and reestablishing the state security apparatus.[59] As the Red Army entered Minsk, along with it came an operational group that acted in the name of Belarus's leadership. The group consisted of seven members, including Ivan Bylinskii, deputy to Ponomarenko; NKGB officer Vasilii Politiko, deputy to Tsanava; and NKVD officer Illarion Ivashchenko, deputy to Bel'chenko. Other institutions such as the procuracy of Belarus also had their own operational groups.[60] One of their main concerns was the composition of the new cadres that had been dispatched from the Soviet rear. The majority of them—in particular, those employed in the district and city institutions—had little to no work experience. Their number was also too low to fill the required number of posts.[61]

The solution, for the time being, lay with the partisans—who, in the eyes of party leaders, had proven their loyalty to the Soviet motherland. After the disbandment of the movement in the summer of 1944, some partisans were recruited for the party-state apparatus. Of the almost twelve thousand partisans who by the summer of 1944 were active in Brest oblast, for example, a bit more than half were drafted into the Red Army, but about one-fifth were assigned to party-state work. This was a pattern that could be observed throughout Belarus.[62] Aleksandr Feigel', who fought with the Soviet partisans in the Lithuanian-Belarusian border region, recalled that after the disbandment of their brigade, the men were assigned to positions in Vidzy, his hometown in northwestern Belarus: "At that time, all former partisans from our brigade worked in Vidzy's party-state institutions. The former commissar of our brigade, Ignat'ev, was appointed as head of the city executive committee. . . . The entire police was made up of former partisans."[63] Similarly, in Vladimir Khartanovich's native Liubchanskii district close to Novogrudok, "Soviet power was rebuilt by partisans."[64] Two days after the former partisan Petr Lebedev returned to Ivanovka in Vitebsk oblast, the secretary of the district party committee visited the village and appointed him secretary of the village's Komsomol. As a brigade leader, he helped to rebuild the collective farm. A while later, the party sent him to attend a six-month training course in Vitebsk oblast, which would mark the beginning of Lebedev's career as a local Soviet party-state representative. He also took part in the collectivization of western Belarus, which began in the late 1940s and was formally concluded in 1953.[65]

Resistance, Real and Imagined

Rebuilding the state was a question of institutions and cadres. It was also, however, a question of making sure that any resistance, real or imagined, would be destroyed. This was the task of the state security organs, since 1943 again divided between the NKVD and the NKGB. The rank-and-file members of the NKVD and NKGB in Belarus came from different parts of the Soviet Union, but like their bosses, they had in common that they were usually *vostochniki*, people who hailed from the pre-1939 Soviet regions. During the war, many of them fought in the Soviet armed forces or with the partisans.[66]

In eastern Belarus, resistance against the return of Soviet rule primarily took on the form of individuals obstructing the reestablishment of the collective farms. For the Soviet leaders, collective farming was not just an immutable component of the economy; it was also a political question. Collectivization had provided the authorities with a lever into the countryside. Consequently, at stake was now the rebuilding of Soviet power at the lowest level, the village. On January 1, 1944, the All-Union Central

Committee and Sovnarkom of the USSR issued a resolution directed at the Central Committee of Belarus (and a similar one for Ukraine). Signed by Stalin and Malenkov, it emphasized that "the most important task" for the returning authorities was the reestablishment of the collective farms.[67] Accordingly, once the operational groups arrived in the villages, they immediately appointed locals as head of collective farms, and requested that the villages hand over most larger animals and farm equipment to the collective. Among the population, this led to much discontent. At the fall 1943 meeting of a collective farm in Krasnopolskii district, to the southeast of Mogilev, some people were said to have declared that life had been better under the Germans and that the "collective farms were taking everything away."[68] Such incidents repeated themselves over the next months. In August 1944, party representatives reported several cases from Minsk oblast in which individuals had spoken out against the collective farms at village meetings or reclaimed horses and other property from the collective farm. At the Krupskaia collective farm, two women resisted physically when party representatives came to request items from them; at the Kombain collective farm, a woman attacked the head of the collective farm with a pitchfork and seriously wounded him.[69]

Through a combination of select arrests and surveillance networks, the Soviet state security organs were able to bring the situation in eastern Belarus under their control relatively quickly. In western Belarus, however, where the Soviet authorities encountered organized armed resistance, the situation was more precarious. After the Germans left, the NKVD and NKGB took over the fight against the Armia Krajowa from the Soviet partisans. In the southern regions bordering Ukraine, they also encountered armed resistance from Ukrainian nationalists (OUN-UPA), and in the northwestern region bordering Lithuania, from Lithuanian partisan units. Throughout the republic, the state security organs were also searching for individuals who had been associated with German-organized Belarusian nationalist organizations.[70]

As the armed wing of the Polish underground that was reporting to the Polish government in exile, the Armia Krajowa was fighting for the independence of Poland in its pre-1939 borders and against the Soviet territorial annexations of 1939. At no point, however, did Stalin consider returning these regions to Poland. On July 23, 1944, Moscow established the Polish Committee of National Liberation (PCNL), an alternative pro-communist Polish government in Lublin, which in turn ceded the disputed territories to the Soviet Union.[71] The exception was the almost exclusively Polish-speaking region around Białystok. In July 1944, the Soviet Union and the

PCNL concluded a border agreement, which led to seventeen of the twenty-three districts of pre-1941 Belostok (Białystok) oblast, including the city of Białystok, and three districts of Brest oblast being handed back to Poland. All the while, most of formerly northeastern Poland remained part of Soviet Belarus.[72] In support of these annexations, Moscow decided to employ a well-tried method: the transfer of select population groups. In early September 1944, several months before the Yalta Conference officially confirmed the 1939–1940 Soviet annexations (and almost a year before the conclusion of the Soviet-Polish border agreement on August 16, 1945, that established the final boundary between the two states), representatives of the future communist Polish state concluded separate yet nearly identical population exchange agreements with Lithuania, Belarus, and Ukraine. In this way, the Soviet government sent a clear message to the Polish resistance and other nationalists who were operating in the Soviet western regions: most of the pre-1939 eastern Polish regions would continue to be a part of the Soviet Union—and there would be no independent Ukrainian, Belarusian, or Lithuanian states.[73]

Under the Polish-Belarusian population exchange agreement, those whom the authorities deemed ethnic Belarusians from the Białystok region and small parts of the Brest region were to be sent east for "repatriation" to Belarus. Those whom the authorities deemed ethnic Poles from western Belarus and who before 1939 had been citizens of Poland were to be sent west for "repatriation" to Poland. Jews from western Belarus were permitted to leave as well, but ethnic Belarusians as well as other inhabitants from western Belarus who were neither Polish nor Jewish were prohibited from leaving, even though they had likewise held Polish citizenship before 1939.[74] By the time the population transfer concluded in December 1946, about twenty-eight thousand people were resettled from the Białystok region to Belarus. In turn, almost 240,000 people were transferred from Belarus to Poland. Two percent of them were Jewish, the rest ethnic Poles.[75] Zofia Brzozowska was one of those who left. Seeing no future in Soviet Belarus—and having lost her father, grandfather, and uncle who disappeared after their arrests by the NKVD in 1940—she applied in early 1945 for resettlement. A few months later, Brzozowska left together with her mother, aunt, brother, and one-year-old son. Her departure from the Novogrudok region remained forever in her memory: "The rye was green and tall, chamomile flowers were blossoming, it was raining. I held my son in my arms, wrapped in a blanket, and cried."[76]

The Soviet leadership was primarily interested in seeing anyone depart for Poland who had belonged to the local Polish elites before 1939. With landowners deported prior to 1941, this meant that those considered undesirable were primarily urban residents, above all former Polish state officials and members of the clergy. Some, like Aleksander Zienkiewicz, a Catholic priest from Novogrudok, were pressured by the state security organs to leave, but many more needed less direct persuasion and left, like Zofia Brzozowska, of their own accord.[77] Others, however, wanted to leave but eventually did not. About 305,000 people, more than half of those who had signed up for resettlement to Poland, had their requests denied by the authorities. These were overwhelmingly rural residents, peasants who self-identified as Poles in their application forms. The authorities, however, declared them to be polonized "Catholic-Belarusians" who had yet to become aware of their "true" ethnicity. In this war-ravaged republic, their manpower was urgently needed.[78] What this shows is that the aim of the Polish-Belarusian population exchange was not to create an ethnically homogenous western Belarus. Rather, the goal was to remove those deemed hostile to the Soviet state who—because of their social authority, educational background, or nationalist sentiments—would potentially have the means to mobilize others against the Soviet state.[79] In contrast, the authorities seemed confident that they could exert enough influence on peasants who claimed to be Poles and turn them into loyal Soviet residents. While pockets of Polish-speaking communities remained in the western Belarusian countryside, the region's urban landscape, already radically transformed as a result of the Holocaust, underwent further changes—ultimately turning a place like Grodno from a Yiddish- and Polish-speaking town into a primarily Belarusian- and increasingly also a Russian-speaking one.[80]

As the population exchange between Poland and Belarus proceeded, the Soviet state security organs were engaged in a fierce struggle against nationalist resistance. By the summer of 1944, the Armia Krajowa counted an estimated thirty-six thousand members in western Belarus—some of them fighters, others civilian supporters. The organization was strongest in the region around Novogrudok, Lida, and Vileika, which had a high concentration of Polish speakers.[81] In their fight, the NKVD and NKGB employed a combination of smaller search-and-destroy missions with larger military operations. The latter, of which some were conducted with the support of Red Army units, usually followed the same pattern. Once a village or district had been identified as harboring members of the Armia Krajowa, the Soviet forces encircled the area at night, making sure no one would be able to escape. In the morning, NKVD and NKGB officers gathered the local residents. While their documents were checked and the houses searched, other troops combed through the forests. The same methods were also

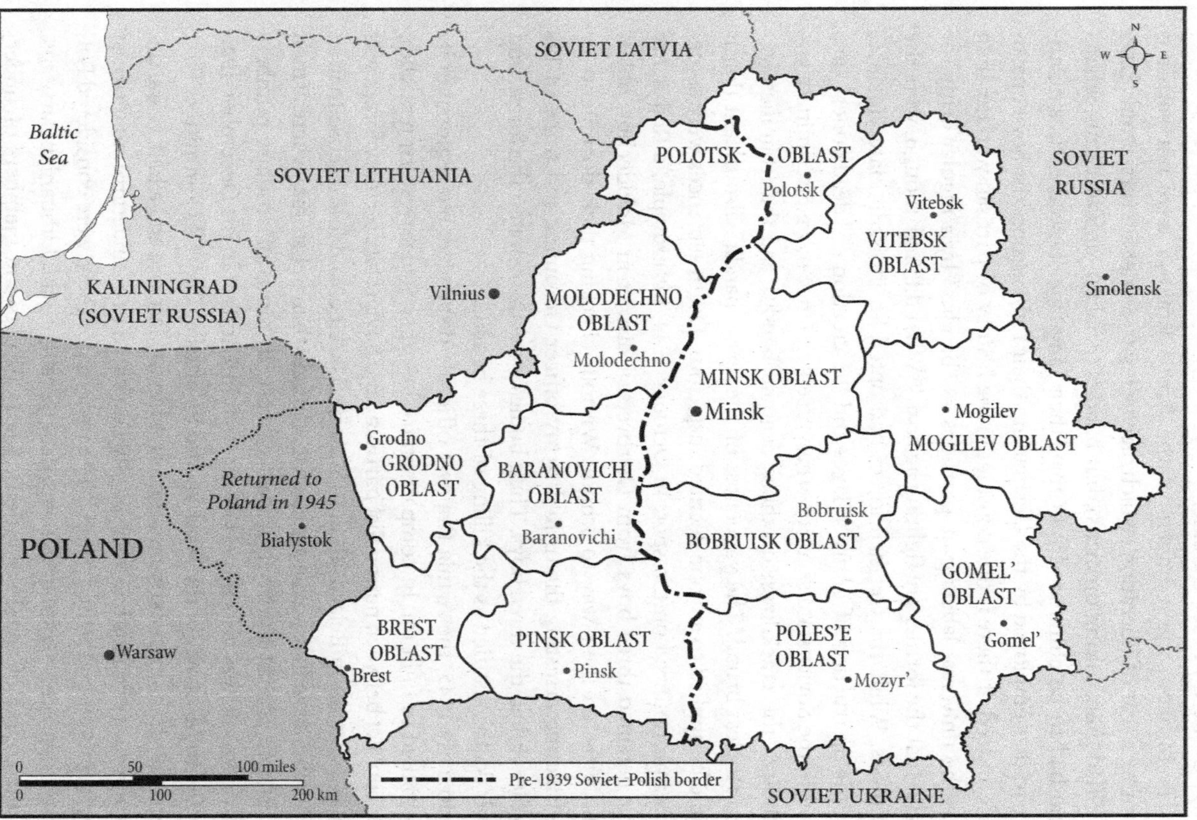

Map 4. The administrative division of post-1945 Soviet Belarus (until the oblast reform in 1954). Map by Mike Bechthold.

employed against the Ukrainian nationalists who were active in the southern Belarusian districts bordering Ukraine, in the Belarusian part of Polesia that OUN-UPA claimed for Ukraine.[82]

For Moscow, the members of the Armia Krajowa were not partisans fighting a war of liberation (which, according to Soviet lawyers, would have justified them taking up arms), but bandits (*bandity*), unlawful combatants who had to be eliminated.[83] In that, their language showed eerie similarities to that employed by the Germans in their fight against the Soviet partisans. Indeed, if there is one constant in the history of partisan warfare, then it is the universal labeling of partisans as "bandits" by a regular army (or state) that the former are fighting against.[84] What differed, though, were the methods. While the German forces had opted for indiscriminate violence, for the destruction of entire villages and the creation of "dead zones" (*tote Zonen*), the Soviet state security organs used violence more discriminately—although the crackdown on those deemed bandits and their families was nevertheless brutal. The vagueness of the term "bandit" also meant that it could be applied to anyone deemed suspicious. Death sentences were sometimes pronounced on the spot. In October 1944, for example, a Red Army unit detained three boys from Ostrovetskii district in Molodechno oblast who were on their way to school. Without checking their documents or considering arresting them, Red Army officer Gorbunov and some of his soldiers killed the three boys. Their bodies were thrown into the forest, and their deaths justified as the killing of three bandits.[85]

In early 1945, the Armia Krajowa officially disbanded, but regional units continued to fight on. In comparison to the other Soviet western republics, the conflict between nationalist partisans and Soviet state security forces was far less intense in Belarus than in western Ukraine, and less intense than in Lithuania as well. It was more intense, though, than in Estonia, where armed resistance against the Soviets was weakest. In terms of absolute numbers of victims, it was also more violent than in Latvia.[86] In his December 1946 report to Moscow on the work of the Belarusian Central Committee, First Secretary Ponomarenko announced that in the last one and a half years, the state security organs had successfully liquidated 814 "underground terrorist organizations and armed gangs." The majority of them were considered Polish groups, others primarily Belarusian, Ukrainian, and Lithuanian partisans. In the course of these operations, 3,035 "bandits and members of underground anti-Soviet organizations" were killed and 17,872 of them arrested. The Soviet forces also arrested 27,950 individuals considered "accomplices" to the nationalists, and another 5,620 people accused of being spies and foreign agents. In turn, anti-Soviet nationalists killed 1,206 people in western

Belarus, not including an unknown number of victims in southeastern Belarus where the Ukrainian nationalists were active. Altogether, up to the end of 1946, at least 4,241 individuals—some of them nationalist fighters, others members of the state security organs, but also many civilians—lost their lives in the conflict. With that, the Soviet state security organs, by and large, managed to contain the threat coming from the different armed nationalist groups active on Belarusian territory, although smaller groups continued to bother the authorities until the early 1950s.[87]

"Servants of the Germans"

The destruction of organized armed resistance, on the whole, combined with the transfer of politically undesirable population groups from western Belarus, marked a major milestone in the process of state rebuilding. At the same time, the problems that the Soviet authorities faced were much more far-reaching. They also persisted way beyond the first post-Nazi occupation years.

In eastern Belarus, local discontent with the collective-farm system continued to be widespread even after individual instances of resistance had been quelled. The quick reintroduction of collective farms exacerbated the dire economic circumstances in which inhabitants of this war-ravaged republic found themselves. In the first years after the war, the peasants received little to nothing in return for their work. As a result, villagers in eastern Belarus experienced the immediate postwar years of scarcity and hunger more severely than villagers in western Belarus, where private farming continued to exist until 1949. In the towns, the stores had little to sell. Trying to get by, some people became seasonal workers at farms in western Belarus or traveled long distances to buy at the western markets, only to resell their products at home for a higher price. In the region around Pinsk, locals encountered "Easterners" who went around the villages, asking for bread.[88] For inhabitants of western Belarus, this only increased doubts about the viability of the Soviet regime. As Ivan Danilov recalled from his village—Osovtsy, not far from Pinsk in southwestern Belarus—for quite a while after the war, many villagers thought that "Soviet power would not hold out for long and that our lands would soon return to Poland." Rumors circulated that another war might break out.[89]

Further intensifying people's perception of political uncertainty was the existence of small groups of men who lived in the forests. In western Belarus, remnants of the different nationalist groups continued to plague the state security organs until the early 1950s. The men directed their attacks mostly at rural party representatives and heads of collective farms or soldiers who were sent to enforce military conscription. Resistance also came from a high-school student underground organization from Molodechno oblast. In 1948, its members, young men and women, distributed anti-Soviet leaflets, calling on peasants to oppose impending collectivization and to take up arms against the Soviets. Arrested and subsequently tried by a Soviet military tribunal in 1950, Rastsislaŭ Lapitski, the leader of the group, was executed, while the other sixteen defendants were sent to the Gulag.[90] Other "forest men"—not just in western but also in eastern Belarus—were an eclectic bunch of demobilized Red Army soldiers, local men and boys who had evaded military draft or compulsory labor recruitment, Soviet citizens who had worked in the German occupation regime, and anyone else who sought to evade the Soviet authorities. Although these men were not necessarily politically motivated, they still disrupted public order, stealing food and clothes from locals.[91] In the cities, it was dangerous to be out in the streets at night. In Minsk, a gang that called itself Black Cat roamed the streets at night. Dressed in military uniforms and pretending to be soldiers, the men mugged people, at times killing just for a coat or a pair of boots.[92]

Deeply worrisome to the state security organs were reports about locals who were said to have unfavorably compared the Soviets to the Germans. At political meetings in Minsk oblast that party representatives conducted in the weeks leading up to the February 1946 USSR Supreme Soviet election, some people—either openly at the meetings or, more commonly, in conversation with neighbors—supposedly said that they would prefer to live under the Germans. A woman from Borisov reportedly told her neighbors that "I lived for three years under the Germans; no meetings whatsoever were conducted, and life was better."[93] Some of these comments contained clear antisemitic overtones, such as when several people, both villagers and townspeople, inquired specifically about the ethnicity of Semen Ginzburg, a candidate for the USSR Supreme Soviet. A few individuals reportedly said that if he were Jewish and not Russian, they would not vote for him, or even expressed regret that "unfortunately, the Germans didn't kill all Jews."[94] Others made it clear that they thought of the elections as a mere farce. Why put up election cabins, a man declared, if everything had already been decided in advance?[95] And a woman in Cherven', a town southeast of Minsk, suggested that the Great Terror was still very much on people's minds when she reportedly said that "soon we will choose representatives to the Supreme Soviet, and then it will turn out that they are all enemies, and others will take their place, but that will not make it easier for us."[96]

For Soviet leaders in Minsk and Moscow, all of these problems were connected—and all of them could be traced back to a common root: the years of Nazi occupation. On June 20, 1944, shortly before the reconquest of Minsk, First Secretary Panteleimon Ponomarenko gave a speech before the Central Committee of the Belarusian Komsomol. He reminded his audience of the task that was lying ahead: "We are currently confronted with having to liquidate the consequences of enemy invasion that exist in all spheres. . . . What are those consequences [*kakie eto posledstviia*]? They consist of the fact that a well-known number of forthright enemies of Soviet power, servants of the Germans, remained behind."[97]

To Ponomarenko, it was clear who the "enemies of Soviet power" (*vragi sovetskoi vlasti*) and "servants of the Germans" (*prisluzhniki nemtsev*) were: they were the "scum" (*svolochi*) that went into hiding when the "kulaks as a class," the "petty bourgeoisie," and landowners were destroyed after the October Revolution. When the Nazis invaded, Ponomarenko declared, these people reared their heads and joined the German side.[98] Speaking before the same audience in March 1945, he again pointed to the "remnants of the shattered kulak class" and "capitalist elements" as "forthright mercenaries of the German invaders." This time, he also included nationalists of various types among the group of familiar enemies.[99]

The belief that the war had helped to reveal enemies in hiding was widespread among the leading Bolsheviks.[100] During the war, the Soviet partisans had killed many of those whom Moscow considered traitors. Still, many more needed to be tracked down, not just because of what they had done during the war, but also because of what they continued to do in the postwar years. As Ponomarenko stressed during a February 1946 party speech which was published a few days later in *Sovetskaia Belorussiia*, the republic's main Russian-language newspaper, those "who worked for the Germans" were to blame for the poor performance of collective farms in eastern Belarus and the delayed collectivization of agriculture in western Belarus.[101] In these speeches as well as in the report on the work of the Central Committee of the Communist Party of Belarus in 1946 that Ponomarenko submitted to the Central Committee in Moscow, he even went further, essentially identifying everything that he believed to have gone wrong as a result of Nazi occupation: "drunkenness and hooliganism" among young people, the "low moral standards" of young men that they displayed in their relationships with women and the family, "decrease in work discipline," "black marketing" (*spekuliatsiia*), and the "squandering and plundering" of state property, renewed religious activity as well as displays of antisemitism but also of "bourgeois-nationalist" and Zionist views.[102]

To overcome these problems, the issue had to be addressed at its core: all "servants of the Germans" had to be detained or destroyed. As the suspected enemies were thought to have gone back into hiding, every adult civilian who had stayed in occupied territory was potentially suspect. Constant vigilance was therefore required—and a tremendous amount of information, too.

Investigations

In their search for "servants of the Germans," the Soviet state security organs drew on a variety of sources, ranging from partisan units, informer networks, and interrogations to captured German documents and witness testimonies provided to the Extraordinary State Commission. During the war, the Soviet partisans had constituted the single most important source of information for Moscow. Once the center had established more or less reliable means of communication with the units in occupied territory, the men provided them with the names of locals who worked for the Germans. The partisans obtained the information through observation and their knowledge of the surroundings, as well as through the interrogation of captured policemen or village heads. Valentin Rusak, for example, had worked from October 1942 on as deputy to the mayor of Baranovichi. In February 1944, Soviet partisans arrested and questioned him about other locals who worked in the city administration. His interrogators made use of a *voprosnik*, a standardized questionnaire that contained almost thirty questions. Some of these were concerned with the relatives of the person under arrest, asking for their names, places of residence, and what they did during the war. As the state security organs were particularly interested in knowing which former Soviet officials had gone to work for the Germans, another question asked specifically about this group: "Who of those formerly employed by the Soviet state [*sovetskie rabotniki*] remained with the Germans, in which position did they work and when?"[103] Rusak did not know any by name, but when asked "Who do you know who worked for the Germans," he provided the names of eighteen locals who he said were agents of the German intelligence service. He also gave a detailed account of the structure of Baranovichi's city administration, its individual departments, and the names of people who headed these.[104]

After the partisans passed the information on to Moscow, the NKVD compiled list after list with the names of those deemed traitors, which included short descriptions of their activities as well as places of residence and a note on the source of this information.[105] The lists were then used by so-called operational-chekist groups that Moscow sent into occupied territory with the order to kill specific people. On November 26, 1942, for example, special agents Fomich and Petrovich assassinated the chief editor of the German newspaper *Novyi put'*, based on information that they had received from the partisans. The man, Aleksandr Brandt, had worked before the war as a Russian teacher in a middle school in Vitebsk. The special agents monitored his movements for about two weeks, then shot Brandt to death in front of his house in Vitebsk.[106]

When the Red Army entered Belarus, the state security organs received even more names and lists from the partisans. After the disbandment of the movement, the partisans' intimate knowledge of the population and the geographical environment continued to be of much use to the NKVD and NKGB. Whether as partisans or as members of destruction battalions (*istrebitel'nye batal'ony*) that were established in recently reconquered territories, the men searched the villages and forests not just for German soldiers, military draft evaders, and nationalist partisans but also for former policemen and others considered German accomplices.[107] The partisan brigade Ponomarenko, operating in the Borisov-Begoml' area northeast of Minsk, reported that from June 28 to July 3, 1944, they were able "to fish out of the forests up to 250 Germans and policemen," whereas the brigade Lopatina operating nearby "fished out more than 200 Germans and policemen."[108] By October 1944, 176 destruction battalions with 16,446 members were operating in Belarusian territory. By the end of 1944, they had arrested 87,408 people, of whom roughly one-third were German soldiers and officers. The rest were Soviet citizens, including 6,308 "German accomplices."[109]

While the destruction battalions were a temporary measure, a more permanent fixture of Soviet life proved equally useful at identifying suspected traitors. In the Soviet Union, every person had to be registered at his or her place of residence, a task that was the responsibility of the regular police (*militsiia*), which from 1938 on was under the NKVD. Similar to the NKVD's surveillance catalogue, the regular police used file cards to systematize the passport and residence information that it collected.[110] When the Soviet authorities returned to the formerly German-occupied regions, the regular police immediately set out to reregister the local population. Day and night, the police in Minsk stopped people in the streets and requested to see their registration papers or passports. They also sought information on where people had worked during the war.[111] As a result, until the end of 1944 and throughout the western parts of the Soviet Union, the NKVD managed to identify more than ninety thousand individuals who were said to have worked in German institutions, served as local policemen under the Germans, or else were considered German accomplices (*posobniki*).[112]

Once Soviet power had formally been restored, the NKVD and NKGB archives returned to Minsk. In combination with the crime surveillance and the passport and registration card catalogues, their archives served as a useful tool to identify and locate individuals suspected of working for the German authorities.[113] Captured German documents and wartime newspapers constituted another source of information. In January 1944, the NKVD's main directorate in Moscow strictly prohibited the destruction of any materials captured or collected from the retreating Germans. Instead, these documents were to be handed over either to the Red Army, if they were of military-operational or strategic interest, or to the different territorial NKVD organizations if they concerned previous military actions not of immediate relevance. The remaining documents, whether coming from "state archives, Soviet institutions, the bodies of the 'self-administration' set up by the German invaders," or other sources were to be "handed immediately" to the local NKVD organs. Its personnel screened the material for the names of Soviet citizens who worked for the German occupation regime.[114] After the NKVD had extracted the information it was looking for, the documents were archived. For decades after the war, whenever a new suspect was discovered or a file reopened, the state security organs continued to make use of the material. As late as 1983, for instance, the KGB instructed the state archive of Mogilev oblast to look through its holdings for information about a man named Mikhail Mikhnevich, who during the war was said to have worked as the director of a middle school located in the village of Veprin in Mogilev oblast.[115]

By the time the Nazi occupation came to an end, the Soviet state security organs could already draw on a substantial source basis. Still, not all potential channels had yet been sufficiently exploited. In the search for "servants of the Germans," local information continued to be key. Some of it was passed on voluntarily, such as when individuals wrote letters to the authorities in which they alerted them to the real, alleged, or surmised wartime wrongdoing of others. Other information was extracted against a person's will, such as when force or the threat thereof during interrogations made a suspect provide names of others.[116] And while some information came from sources like informant networks that were specifically created for that purpose, other information was derived from institutions like the Extraordinary State Commission that, at least officially, appeared to have no connection to the state security organs.

Informant networks were a powerful political tool, not just because they usually led to further investigations and arrests, but also because they created an atmosphere of fear and distrust that played into the hands of those in power. Even if their operational usefulness was not as pronounced as the numbers suggested, the social effect was immediate: because colleagues and co-workers, neighbors, and sometimes even family members had to be suspicious of one another, not knowing which actions or words might trigger arrests, informer networks strongly encouraged conformist behavior. After the war, some inhabitants of the village of Naguevichi, not far from Slonim in western Belarus, strongly suspected that the local shoemaker was an informant but ultimately could not know for sure.[117] While the war destroyed many of the prewar networks, the state security organs managed to quickly recruit new informants and to reconnect with old ones. They probably also drew on the informant networks that the partisans had established during the war.[118] The Germans had used Soviet citizens as informants as well, but their purpose had mostly been to serve as spies within the Soviet partisan units. In contrast, the returning Soviet authorities sought to establish a net of informants in all localities (*naselennye punkty*).[119] As a result, the returning Soviet state was, if indirectly, much more present in the countryside than the German occupation regime ever was during the war. In November 1943, Tsanava informed Ponomarenko that in the recently reconquered eastern districts of Belarus, the NKGB had recruited 602 informants, of whom 266 people were new recruits, while 366 of them had worked as informants before the war. Thanks to the informers, the state security organs had been able to arrest 301 "enemy agents" in October alone, including many individuals who during the occupation had served in the local police or held the post of town mayor or village head.[120] By the end of 1944, almost eight thousand new informants had been recruited in Belarus; by the end of 1947, that number had risen to almost twenty thousand.[121]

While it was the express aim of informants to provide the state security organs with the names of locals considered to have worked for the German authorities during the war, another source, the Extraordinary State Commission (ChGK), at first glance did not seem to have been created for that task—but it came to be utilized for these purposes, too. As early as 1942, Moscow created the ChGK to investigate and establish German crimes committed in the occupied territories and to determine the extent of material destruction. Once the Red Army reconquered a region, local commissions were set up whose members went around the localities, asking people for information about the years of Nazi rule. In Belarus as in the other republics, people provided detailed, harrowing accounts of their experiences. As part of their witness testimonies, some individuals also provided the names of other Soviet citizens known to them who had worked in various capacities for the occupation regime. Overall, according to the ChGK's calculations, several million Soviet citizens contributed to the commission's work, which resulted altogether in more than 250,000 protocols of witness testimonies and declarations of Nazi crimes.[122]

On the surface, the local ChGK commissions appeared to be quasi-independent institutions, with each commission composed of a variety of public representatives, state officials, and nonparty members alike. Internally, however, the power lay with the party and the NKVD. As a rule, the local commissions were headed by a troika of three men: a regional party leader, a procuracy member, and an NKVD officer. In practice, this meant that the ChGK's work in the localities was effectively overseen and controlled by the NKVD.[123] NKVD officers also often collected testimonies from witnesses—and although the latter would not have been aware of the institutional link between the ChGK and the NKVD, they would have recognized the officers by their uniforms. The witness testimonies provided the state security organs with a lot of information on what people had done in occupied territory. On the basis of witness testimonies, for example, the Extraordinary State Commission of Pukhovichskii district, located south of Minsk, was able to compile a list with the twenty-four names of "German-Fascist criminals and their accomplices," including nine Belarusians by nationality.[124] Some of them had been town mayors and as such were accused of having organized the deportation of local citizens to Germany and participated in the destruction of villages deemed partisan-friendly. Another man had worked as a truck driver and was said to have taken part in the shooting of the local Jewish community. The report was signed by the head of the local ChGK commission and secretary of the district's party committee, a man by the name of E. K. Zhur, as well as by three other committee members. One of them, a man by the name of D. M. Ziuzin, headed the district's NKVD organization.[125]

When Panteleimon Ponomarenko, first secretary of the Communist Party of Belarus, returned to the republic in the summer of 1944, he came back to a place that he was determined to at once rebuild and transform. When Chasia Bornstein-Bielicka, a member of the Jewish resistance, returned to her hometown of Grodno in the fall of 1944, she did so in the hope, ultimately shattered, of finding loved ones alive. For someone like the former partisan Petr Lebedev, who was reunited with his family, coming home was a moment of great happiness. For others, though, seeing their neighbors return only served as a reminder of the loss that they had suffered and the happiness they would never experience. Yet others, wary of their own wartime pasts, sought to avoid their wartime places of residence altogether and fled with the German army or took on new identities, afraid to encounter former neighbors or the Soviet state security organs. Inhabitants of western Belarus who, like Zofia Brzozowska, considered themselves Poles or were considered as such by the Soviet state had to ask themselves if returning home meant resettling to Poland. This question—where home was and what belonging implied—was particularly pertinent for Jewish survivors who had lost their entire families and communities.

The moment of return—whether much anticipated, dreaded, or avoided—carried different meanings for different people, party representatives and nonstate actors alike. For private individuals, encounters with the worlds destroyed and the worlds in flux not only made visible just how fragile and transitory feelings of home and belonging were. They also put into focus the worlds apart: that some (in particular, Jews) had lost more than others during the war. Beyond the personal sphere, the moment of return was also one of great political transition and, to varying extents, uncertainty and instability. The postwar Soviet authorities were faced with a host of serious challenges, ranging from armed nationalist resistance in western Belarus to local discontent with the collective farms in eastern Belarus, from widespread apprehension about the return of communism to high crime rates, forest men disrupting public order, and rumors about the viability of Soviet power as such. In the eyes of party leaders like Ponomarenko, all of these problems could be traced back to one common source: the population's exposure to three years of Nazi rule. Investigating what Soviet citizens had done in German-occupied territory was therefore a task of utmost importance, inextricably linked to the reestablishment of Soviet authority in Belarus and the successful rebuilding of its party-state institutions. Correspondingly, the state security organs invested a lot of time and resources in the search for "servants of the Germans." Drawing on a broad range of mostly local sources, they amassed a tremendous amount of information. How to put that information effectively to use, track down suspects, and mete out punishment, though, were another matter.

Chapter 4

Determining Guilt

The Soviet Politics of Retribution

One night in July 1944, a man in a military uniform knocked on the door of an apartment in Minsk, where eighteen-year-old Vladimir Svetlov was living with his parents. Telling Vladimir's mother not to worry, that he only wanted to have a little chat with her son, he took Svetlov away to a half-destroyed building somewhere in the Belarusian capital. Vladimir Svetlov spent the night in a makeshift prison cell. The next morning, Svetlov was greeted by the state security officer Onuchkin: "You didn't think that Soviet rule would return? Well, now you see, we have returned."[1]

Officer Onuchkin first questioned Vladimir Svetlov about his neighbor Gerniak. At some point during the German occupation, Gerniak had been appointed as manager of their residential building and overseen a group of Jews who had to clean the courtyard. After Svetlov told Onuchkin everything he knew about his neighbor, the officer seemed satisfied but then turned his attention to Vladimir. He accused him of having spread anti-Soviet propaganda under the Germans. In fact, Svetlov had kept a leaflet at home, written in Belarusian, that contained nationalist, anti-Soviet slogans. According to Svetlov, a stranger had handed it to him one summer day during the war, when he and some of the other teenagers in his building were hanging out in the courtyard. The stranger had asked him to read the text aloud in front of the assembled group. Svetlov later took the leaflet home, not thinking much about it. It is unclear how the state security organs found out about the incident, but it now served as proof of Svetlov's treacherous activities. "You here are all soaked in fascist stench," Onuchkin told him during the interrogation. "I, however, gave my blood for the motherland, I was twice wounded, I attacked. And now I have to deal with these different kinds of shit."

During his interrogation, Vladimir Svetlov was subjected to different means of psychological torture. As he later recalled, "in the beginning, [they] try to make the person under investigation talk, and then they simply crush him as an individual [*kak lichnost'*], fully demoralizing him. And if he tries to fight against it somehow, they use such swear words [*mat*] that even the most hardened criminal could get envious."[2] After another officer joined the interrogation, the two men played the game of "good cop," "bad cop," alternating between the roles. Officer Onuchkin faked Svetlov's execution but, after counting down to one, chose to strike him on the head with the gun and began hitting his legs. The other officer pretended to come to Vladimir's help. He ordered Onuchkin to stop and, addressing him kindly as "young man" (*iunosha*), asked Vladimir about his family. At that moment, a woman's scream could be heard from one of the other rooms. When the screaming continued, the officer turned to Vladimir and said: "What a great illustration of my words. Did you hear? This is how your mommy too will sing. What a pretty solo it will be."[3] In the end, it was fear for his parents and brother that made Vladimir Svetlov sign a slip of paper saying that he had engaged in treacherous anti-Soviet activity during the war: "I had to save my family. . . . There was no other way out." Within a week of his arrest, Vladimir Svetlov was brought before a military court. After a quick trial, he was sentenced to ten years of forced labor in Vorkuta.[4]

This chapter analyzes the Soviet politics of retribution, from the first reconquest phase in late 1941 to the immediate post-Nazi occupation period and all the way into the 1960s, when a renewed wave of trials took place. The Soviet authorities were determined to punish local participation in Nazi atrocities. At its core, though, the search for those deemed traitors was about defining who had, and who had not, been loyal to Moscow during the war. Serving as proof that Soviet power had fully returned, the prosecution of individuals accused of collaboration with the Germans was inextricably linked to the reaffirmation of Moscow's authority in the formerly German-occupied regions. At the same time, Soviet punitive practices were not static but rather varied over time, alternating between more lenient and stricter, less active and more expansive phases in response to shifting domestic and international circumstances and events. The chapter begins by tracing the evolution of the state's politics of retribution, showing how Soviet punishment of those deemed traitors developed into a process in which different aims and objectives had to be balanced against each other. The focus is on the state and the agents who were most directly involved in the politics of retribution: members of the state security organs, the judiciary and procuracy, and party representatives on different levels of the state apparatus, from Moscow down to the republics.

Given the lack of access to the KGB archives in Belarus and the FSB (previously KGB) archives in Russia, the primary source base remains fragmentary, dependent mostly on top-secret reports by the state security organs, the procuracy, and military courts that were sent to the Communist Party.[5] In contrast, the former KGB archives in Ukraine and Lithuania are relatively open to researchers and allow for cross-comparisons. Yet, even then there are limits to what we can know, considering that it is often not possible to reconstruct the full details of each decision-making process or to identify the specific individuals involved. What the available sources do reveal, though, is that the Soviet Union's punitive practices were not only heavily ideologically inflected. They were also significantly conflicted, torn between ideological imperatives and pragmatic concerns, on one hand, and tensions within ideology, on the other. These tensions were reflected in the treatment of former policemen-turned-partisans, and in the inconsistent treatment of those who had worked as teachers, as agricultural specialists, or in minor administrative positions under the Germans. Public proclamations of the "all people's war" to the contrary, they were also visible in the continued suspicion toward anyone who had lived in occupied territory.

The Evolution of Punitive Practices

On July 3, 1941, Stalin addressed the Soviet people. In his speech, broadcast on the radio, he stressed that the war with Germany was no ordinary war between two armies. Rather, it was a "war of the entire Soviet people" against the Nazis, a struggle against enslavement in which the Soviet Union stood united with all peoples in Europe and America who fought "for their independence, for democratic liberties."[6] In this fight between good and evil, there were no moral gray zones. Consequently, Soviet wartime newspapers and novels portrayed Soviet citizens in occupied territory who were said to support the Germans as the lowest of the low, as "dirty renegades" or "petty kulak carrions."[7] The fight against them, Stalin warned, would be "ruthless." Those deemed traitors deserved only one fate: death.[8]

That punishment would be harsh was repeated over and over again by Soviet party leaders. In a leaflet signed by Ponomarenko and distributed in occupied Belarusian territory in the early months of 1943, the local population was informed about the Red Army's recent military successes. Soon, Ponomarenko wrote, the Germans will "finally be hurled from our Soviet soil." Addressed to village heads (*starosty*), policemen, and "those who are employed in the administration and commandant offices," it warned them: "We tell you openly and frankly: your crime toward the motherland is immense, and if you continue to help the Germans, you will not escape strict punishment."[9]

The prosecution of Soviet citizens accused of what today would be called collaboration (a word that at the time was not yet part of the Russian vocabulary) began in late 1941, after the Red Army, in its first counteroffensive, regained territories in western Russia. It reached its peak in 1943 and 1944, when the Red Army made its biggest advances, and in 1945, the first year after Nazi occupation. The number of arrests remained relatively high until 1952, after which it dropped significantly. According to Soviet sources, from 1943 (the earliest date for which data are available) until the death of Stalin in 1953 (the latest date for which data are available), almost 260,000 of those Soviet citizens who were charged with treason (*izmena rodine*) were specifically accused of "treason and aiding and abetting the German occupiers" (*predatel'stvo i posobnichestvo nemetskim okkupantam*). These numbers, however, do not include those for the year 1944. Assuming that they were as high as those for 1945, one would arrive at 308,000 individuals who, charged with treason, were specifically accused of "treason and aiding and abetting the German occupiers." Indeed, the overall number of prosecuted was probably higher by at least a few tens of thousands, given that the Red Army already began to reconquer parts of Soviet territory in late 1941; therefore, these numbers have to remain estimates.[10]

During the war, the Soviet partisans dealt in their own ways with individuals considered traitors, which usually meant shooting them, sometimes along with their families, thus employing collective punishment. Once Soviet power returned in full force, the state reclaimed its monopoly on violence, and the punishment of suspected wartime traitors was channeled into the military criminal justice system. Those whom state security officers identified as having worked as policemen, mayors, or village heads under the German authorities were charged with treason.[11] In trying its citizens for treason instead of, perhaps, complicity in murder or criminal assault, the Soviet Union did not differ from other contemporary post-occupation states, whether in Europe or Asia.[12]

In Soviet law, treason fell under the category of counterrevolutionary crimes. Counterrevolutionary crimes were a Soviet specialty: whether committed by civilians or members of the military, whether in peacetime or in regions under martial law, they were always prosecuted by military tribunals. Since civilians and not just soldiers were tried in the military courts, civil and military authority was thus fused in Soviet law. Different types of courts existed on different levels of the military and NKVD hierarchy, which operated parallel to the republics' regular courts (*narodnye sudy*) that dealt with civil and ordinary criminal cases. A military court consisted of three judges, or alternatively of one judge and two assessors.[13] In theory, a prosecutor (*prokurator*) and defense attorney had to be present at the trials, but in practice, many trials were conducted in the absence of a prosecutor or defense attorney. The NKVD carried out the pretrial investigations, although the prosecutor—who fulfilled prosecuting, investigative, and protesting functions all at once—could also be involved.[14]

In the words of contemporary leading Soviet lawyers, during the Second World War, treason constituted "the gravest and most heinous offence" of all counterrevolutionary crimes.[15] In the penal code, it was defined as "acts committed by citizens of the Soviet Union to the detriment of the military might of the Soviet Union, to the independence of her state or the integrity of her territory."[16] It made no difference if the accused had held Soviet citizenship prior to 1939 or if they had only become Soviet citizens in 1939–1940, as a result of territorial annexations: the legal system made no distinction between these two groups. Treason was tried under articles 58-1a (for civilians) and 58-1b (for soldiers) if the military court applied the penal code of Soviet Russia. If the penal codes of other Soviet republics were applied, treason was tried under different articles. In Belarus, treason was tried under articles 63-1 (for civilians) and 63-2 (for soldiers). Given that the texts were identical, though, it did not matter which one was used.[17]

Treason carried the death sentence for civilians and soldiers, but if the military court could determine "mitigating circumstances" in the case of civilians, it could lower their sentence to ten years of forced labor. Precisely what counted as mitigating circumstances was left to the discretion of the courts.[18] It was also possible to be sentenced for minor counterrevolutionary activity, which the penal code defined as "relations" with a "foreign state." Depending on the individual case, it was punished with as little as three years of forced labor but could also result in summary execution.[19] At military trials, the defendant had no right to appeal. He or she could only hope that the internal review process (*kassatsionnaia praktika*), whereby the next higher-level military court routinely checked on the rulings made by the lower-level military courts, would find procedural flaws and either change the sentence or hand the case back to the lower-level court or prosecutor. The prosecutor assigned to the lower-level court could also intervene and request that a higher-military court review the case.[20]

Prosecution for treason began in late 1941, after the Red Army regained territories in western Russia. In this early reconquest phase, punishment was particularly strict, as the example of Kalinin oblast shows: half of the defendants charged with treason were sentenced to death. Among them was a woman who had worked as a cleaning lady for the German commander. That trend continued throughout 1942. Soon, however, the center grew alarmed by military tribunal reports that stressed the NKVD's improper classification of crimes and moved to clarify the legal basis of retribution. A divergence arose particularly between the People's Commissariat of Justice and the Office of the Procurator-General of the USSR, on one hand, and the People's Commissariat of Internal Affairs, on the other, with the former criticizing NKVD tribunals for sentencing people without proof of actual crimes or not considering the question of intent. In this regard, these institutions continued an internal conflict that had already existed prior to the war.[21]

The main problem was that the existing law on treason was not very detailed. In that, the Soviet Union did not differ much from other civil law countries—treason is usually an ill-defined, unclear term that is open to multiple interpretations. Not only did the Soviet penal code not specify what was to count as mitigating circumstances, the nature of the crime itself was also only vaguely defined in the text. Consequently, a person who worked as a cook for the Germans could, and was, tried under the same article as a policeman.[22] The case of policemen and village heads seemed relatively easy to judge—in the eyes of the Soviet authorities, those who had held representative posts in the occupation regime were traitors. However, what was one to make of Soviet citizens who worked as office clerks in the district and town administrations—which included departments such as housing, health, finance, and education—and who, in various ways, willingly or unwillingly, became entangled and complicit in German crimes? And what about those whose work brought them in close contact with Germans: for example, translators or newspaper editors, not to speak of the many more who, like teachers or engineers, were employed in German-overseen institutions? In their reports, state security officers and party members often spoke of people who "worked under the Germans" (*rabotali u nemtsev*), but there was no agreement on who was to fall into that category.[23] "Working under the Germans" could be understood in a narrow sense and only refer to policemen, town mayors, and village heads. It could also, however, be understood in a broader sense and include everyone who had continued to work in his or her profession under the occupation regime.

In response, the center issued several directives throughout 1942 and 1943 that were aimed at clarifying the legal basis of retribution. The most important of these was a decree (*ukaz*) of April 19, 1943, which provided the foundation for the Soviet prosecution of German and other Axis soldiers but also applied to Soviet citizens accused of serving the Germans. Formally issued by the Supreme Soviet of the USSR, in theory the highest organ of state power in the Soviet Union, the decree actually originated with the Politburo. It introduced a distinction between "traitors" (*izmenniki,* also *izmenniki rodiny*) and "accomplices" (*posobniki*): traitors were Soviet citizens guilty of murder and mistreatment of Soviet prisoners of war and civilians; they should receive the death sentence. Soviet citizens considered accomplices to these acts were to receive a forced labor camp sentence between fifteen and twenty years.[24]

In practice, however, the April 1943 decree appears to have had only limited effect, as can be deduced from a Supreme Court instruction issued in November 1943. In this document, the Supreme Court criticized that military tribunals classified every action of Soviet citizens deemed to have served the Germans as treason.[25] It therefore saw the need to further specify who traitors were: Soviet citizens who had worked for the Germans in leading positions in the local administration or police; those who had denounced partisans, soldiers, or communists to the Germans; those who had participated in the murder of, as well as violence against, the local population; others who had taken part in the robbery of private and state property; and those who had served as soldiers in the German army. Traitors were to be shot. Accomplices were those who had actively helped the Germans with the reconstruction of industries, transport, and agriculture and with the collection of goods for the Wehrmacht; they were to be sentenced to fifteen or twenty years of forced labor.[26] If civilians, then "traitors" and "accomplices" were to be tried under article 58-1a (or its corresponding republican versions) or under the April 1943 decree. Two groups were to remain unprosecuted: Soviet citizens who had "been employed in administrative positions" under the Germans but who had supported partisans or committed acts of sabotage, and minor employees of the administration, teachers, engineers, or agricultural specialists, as long as they did not commit any crimes.[27]

The November 1943 instruction, it seems, was the most detailed one ever issued by Moscow, reflecting a move toward clarification and systematization. The real turning point in the state's politics of retribution, however, occurred at some point in early 1944. By the late spring, the Red Army had pushed the Germans from western Russia, eastern and central Ukraine, including Kiev, and parts of eastern Belarus around Gomel'. During these first months of 1944, a noticeable change took place: overall, punishment became less strict. As reports by NKVD military tribunals operating in eastern Belarus show, during these first post-occupation weeks and months, the death penalty was less common than one might have expected. Of the 360 civilians who in May and June 1944 were tried under the treason article 58-1a (or 63-1), for example, 9 percent received the death penalty, while the rest were sentenced to a forced labor camp, most of them to ten years and more. Of the 134 people tried under the April 1943 decree, all received forced labor camp sentences.[28] A similar trend—that forced labor camp sentences were much more common than the death penalty—was also observed in Ukraine in the first post-occupation months and years between 1943 and 1945, where around 5 percent of the defendants received the death sentence.[29] In Belarus, the ratio of death penalty to prison sentence dropped even further in the next two years. Of the 3,134 people convicted of "treason and aiding and abetting the enemy" during the second half of 1946, for example, 26 percent were former policemen or members of punitive units (*karatel'nye organy*), and 18 percent were former town mayors, district or village heads, and their helpers (*pomoshchniki*). Among the remaining defendants were people deemed "secret agents," members of the Armia Krajowa, or simply "others." Yet overall, only 4 percent received the death penalty. The rest received forced labor camp sentences, the majority of them ten years in the Gulag.[30]

How can this relative moderation of punishment be explained? Given the difficult archival situation, it is impossible to know for sure, but some explanations are more plausible than others. For one, that punishment became relatively less strict should not be mistaken for an increase in the rule of law. The Soviet justice system in general, and its military tribunals in particular, continued to lack fundamental standards of liberal, rule-of-law-based legal systems such as an independent judiciary, independent defense attorneys, and the assumption of "innocent until proven guilty" that form the precondition for any prosecution to be considered as impartial as possible. During the pretrial interrogations, the state security organs routinely applied different forms of psychological and physical torture. The latter most commonly took the form of beatings, which could be accompanied by other forms of physical abuse or violation, such as pulling out nails or putting out cigarettes on a person's skin. Antonia Galska, for example, who was accused of supporting the Armia Krajowa, was hit repeatedly during her interrogation, as recalled by Armia Krajowa member Irena Krajewska, who shared a prison cell with her in Grodno in late 1944: "Not one square centimeter of white skin could be found on her; that's how terribly she had been beaten."[31] In January 1947, the MVD military tribunal of Mogilev oblast investigated one of its own, officer Aleksei Kikin—not because of the beatings of prisoners as such, but because "the cries and groans of those subjected to beatings reached such levels that they could be heard not just inside but also outside" the prison.[32] The extent to which state security officers applied psychological and physical means of torture depended on each case and on the intensity of the larger conflict. In postwar Ukraine and, possibly, Lithuania, where Soviet forces and anti-Soviet nationalists were engaged in a fierce battle, sexual violence, including rape, was an integral part of Soviet interrogation methods of women who were suspected of working for the anti-Soviet partisans.[33] As the example of Vladimir Svetlov showed, torture (or just the threat thereof) often led to confessions of guilt. In turn, the Soviet criminal justice system considered this sufficient proof. The accused's guilt, in other words, had already been established prior to a trial; the only question that remained was what sentence he or she should receive.[34]

The relative moderation of punishment that began during the first months of 1944 also did not result from a significant improvement in the administration of justice. The conflict between the state security organs and the procuracy continued into the immediate post-occupation years, with the latter repeatedly pointing out the former's improper qualifications of crimes, the lack of thorough pretrial investigations, and the failure to have arrests sanctioned by the prosecutor.[35] Moreover, higher-level military tribunals did not cease to criticize lower-level military tribunals for procedural mistakes made at the trials, including handing out verdicts on the basis of insufficient or contradictory evidence, and complained about the ill-qualified legal staff.[36] It is also important to note that the lessening of punishment toward civilians accused of wartime treason did not go hand in hand with a moderation in punitive practices elsewhere. On the contrary: around the same time, the collective punishment of population groups deemed unreliable or hostile to Soviet power escalated again. In an act of retaliation for alleged collaboration with the Germans, the state security organs deported several non-Slavic communities from the northern Caucasus between November 1943 and October 1944. In May 1944, the entire Crimean Tatar population, almost 200,000 people, was deported, most of them to Central Asia, followed by the deportations of several other Soviet minorities from Crimea.[37] There was also no moderation vis-à-vis anti-Soviet nationalist groups and anyone deemed to be supporting them. In western Ukraine, where the fight was most intense, an estimated 130,295 people, most of them civilians, died from 1944 to 1946 alone in the fight between anti-Soviet nationalists and Soviet forces. About 87 percent of them were killed by Soviet forces, mainly during operations against villages that were considered nationalist-friendly.[38]

Finally, the relative moderation of punishment was temporally limited. In May 1947, with an eye to its international image, the Soviet state abolished the death penalty.[39] As if to compensate, the Supreme Soviet of the USSR and the Ministry of Justice of the USSR soon criticized the military courts operating in the formerly occupied regions for being too lenient with individuals deemed traitors, and in November 1947 issued two corresponding resolutions.[40] In response to the center's criticism, the republics' military courts reviewed their practices and found that too many lower-level courts had taken a "liberal approach" to traitors, as had, for example, the military courts in Molodechno and Polotsk oblast in Belarus.[41] In response, throughout the western parts of the Soviet Union, Soviet military courts quickly began to hand out stricter sentences. Of the 1,211 people who had been convicted of treason in Belarus during the first half of 1947, about 61 percent had received a ten-year sentence, while only about 7 percent had received what after the abolition of the death sentence was now the highest sentence: twenty-five years in the Gulag.[42] A year later, the picture already looked very different. Of the 1,586 people who were convicted of treason in Belarus during the second half of 1948, about 83 percent received a twenty-five-year sentence, while only about 15 percent received a ten-year sentence. These numbers included "members of bandit gangs and spies" and "accomplices of bandit gangs," but not those sentenced under article 63-1 for "aiding and abetting bandit gangs." For the latter, though, the numbers were not vastly different: 70 percent received twenty-five years in the Gulag, the rest ten years of imprisonment.[43] What this means is that the trend toward lower sentences that had existed since 1944 was reversed by 1948. This shift also shows that although the military courts certainly had some leeway in their decisions, Stalin and the Politburo always set the general policy, and the regional courts adhered to it. In January 1950, the death penalty was reinstated for "traitors," "spies," and "saboteurs."

Taking these developments into consideration, the most plausible explanation for the relative moderation of punishment from 1944 to 1947–1948 is that as the Red Army was reconquering more and more territory, Moscow's politics of retribution came to be shaped by tactical considerations about the postwar period that went beyond the need to demonstrate power and reclaim authority. As the example of the "traitor-turned-partisan," discussed later in this chapter, shows, it mattered that the courts increasingly allowed for mitigating circumstances in cases where individuals had gone over to the Soviet side during the war. However, of equal importance was, I would suggest, the regime's self-image. After all, the Soviets saw themselves as liberators even in the territories that had only been annexed in 1939–1940. While it was still important to mete out punishment, the Politburo apparently deemed it sufficient by 1944 to send most of those convicted for treason to the Gulag, not to the gallows. Had the military tribunals proceeded according to the 1943 April decree and the November 1943 instruction, then the number of executions in Belarus would have been higher than the number of executions during the Great Terror of 1936–1938, when an estimated thirty thousand inhabitants of the republic were killed. Executing every village head in the formerly occupied western regions could have had a severely destabilizing effect on local communities, turning people against the Soviet authorities, which would have made it more difficult to portray the regime as a guarantor of justice that meted out rightful punishment. Soviet punitive practices vis-à-vis perceived wartime traitors, then, were not static but rather shaped by a host of different considerations, which had to be weighed against each other. Such a balancing of different aims and objectives also became visible in the question of public versus secret trials.

On Different Ways of Being Public

In general, the prosecution of Soviet citizens accused of wartime treason took place in secret, in quick trials that were neither open to the public nor publicly known. While the war was still being fought, though, the punishment of Soviet citizens in newly reconquered regions was also frequently, and deliberately, conducted in front of local audiences, in the locality where a person had, for example, acted as village elder or policeman during Nazi rule. Many of these public prosecutions were carried out by Red Army military courts as the troops were advancing westward. One such trial is shown in the picture below, taken in the village of Usviat'e in Smolensk oblast (northwestern Russia), which the Soviets had retaken by the fall of 1943. On trial was a man by the name of Bazylev, who during the German occupation had served as the head of Usviat'e village. Bazylev was accused of having given away two Komsomol underground members to the authorities. He is standing in the center-right of the photo, in front of what looks like a jury of three officers, surrounded by at least four armed guards, other soldiers, and what probably were his fellow villagers, most of them women.

The picture suggests just how improvised and quick these Red Army trials were: all that was needed was a table, a couple of chairs, and some paper (the officer in the middle was reading from a piece of paper, possibly the verdict). Such trials probably took place in every district, but certainly in every region throughout the recently reconquered Soviet territories. On October 28, 1943, for example, the military court of the Red Army's 397th

FIGURE 10. Trial of the village head Bazylev, Usviat'e village, Dorogobuzhskii district, Smolensk oblast, Soviet Russia, September 1943. Courtesy of the Belarusian State Archive of Film, Photo, and Sound Recordings.

Rifle Division conducted an open trial in the village of Kliapino in Gomel' oblast. Four local policemen were sentenced to death by hanging.[44] Military Prosecutor A. Valiev recalled a similar trial of a village head in Belarus, which was conducted by the military tribunal of the Red Army's Fiftieth Army. The exact date of the trial is unknown, but it must have been between the fall of 1943, when the Fiftieth Army participated in the reconquest of parts of southeastern Belarus around Gomel', and the summer of 1944, by which time it had been assigned to the Second Belarusian Front that took part in the reconquest of Belarus.[45]

At the trial recalled by Military Prosecutor Valiev, the tribunal likewise consisted of three judges: the head of the military court, the commander of the division, and an NKVD officer. As could be expected from the makeshift format, a defense attorney was not present. The local audience, mostly elderly men and women, testified that the village head had given away Soviet activists and partisans to the German authorities. After the accused fully admitted his guilt, Valiev delivered the closing argument, calling for the death sentence. The verdict was carried out shortly thereafter. In accordance with the April 1943 decree, gallows were erected not far from the village, at the intersection of three roads that saw a lot of troop movement. This was in accordance with the April 1943 decree, in which the Politburo had ordered that executions should take place in public, and that the gallows should be left standing for a few days so that "all understand what punishment means [*kak karaiutsia*] and what kind of retribution awaits everybody who commits violence and reprisals against the civilian population and who betrays his motherland."[46] In front of local civilians and soldiers, as Valiev recalled, the village head was hanged. His body was left hanging for several days, with a sign around his neck that read "traitor."[47]

After the Red Army moved westward, the prosecution of civilians for wartime treason primarily became the responsibility of the state security organs. In the first weeks and months following the reconquest of a region, a select number of trials continued to be conducted in public, but their number was probably significantly lower than during the first wave of quick, improvised Red Army trials. On May 24, 1944, for example, roughly six months after the return of Soviet power to Klimovichi, a small town in the easternmost part of Belarus, the regional NKVD military tribunal conducted a trial of the town's mayor Sharupich, the village heads Tipunov and Voropaev, and the policeman Gomolko. From April to June 1944, at least four other public trials took place in Gomel', Mogilev, and Poles'e oblasts.[48] Once the war formally ended in May 1945, the number of public trials appears to have decreased further, probably because the Politburo in Moscow saw less need to use public executions of those deemed wartime traitors as a means to reassert state authority in reconquered territory. At politically expedient moments, however, the Soviet government decided to open some trials to the public—as the trial that took place on February 18–23, 1946, at Mar'ina-Gorka shows well.[49]

Mar'ina-Gorka is a small town located just south of Minsk and the administrative center of Pukhovichskii district. With its few brick buildings lined along the central square and otherwise mostly wooden one-family houses, it feels much more like a village today, were it not for the abandoned military airfield and dilapidated garrisons on its outskirts. In February 1946, this place was the scene of a public military trial that drew more than ten thousand people from Pukhovichskii and neighboring districts to town. Over the course of six days, and rotating from session to session, they watched the trial of eighteen Soviet citizens who had worked in the local German-organized police forces or as village heads during the war.[50] The timing of their public prosecution, as press coverage makes clear, was not coincidental. In one of its articles, *Stsiag komunizma*, the newspaper of Pukhovichskii district, drew a direct line between the trial at Mar'ina-Gorka and the International Military Tribunal (IMT) at Nuremberg, the trial of major Nazi leaders that the Soviet Union, the United States, France, and the United Kingdom conducted from November 1945 to October 1946. As the German perpetrators were brought to justice at Nuremberg, the newspaper wrote, so were their "faithful assistants" in Mar'ina-Gorka.[51] Locals also would have known of the eight public trials of German military personnel that were held that winter in Soviet cities that had been under Nazi rule or siege during the war, which included a trial in Minsk on January 15–29, 1946.[52] Like the IMT, the trials of German soldiers were covered extensively in the central, republican, regional, and district Soviet newspapers.[53] Even if one was not an avid newspaper reader, it was impossible not to have heard of them: the IMT as well as trials of Axis military personnel were discussed repeatedly at factory or collective farm meetings organized by local party committees. The combination of multilevel trials and press coverage therefore made it possible for inhabitants of Pukhovichskii district to locate "their" trial within the larger national and international context of Soviet retribution and its victory over Germany. Indeed, it was probably not accidental that one of the men on trial in Minsk, Bruno Mittmann, was accused of having committed crimes in Pukhovichskii district—which *Stsiag komunizma* also highlighted in its coverage of the January 1946 trial of German soldiers in Minsk.[54] As a result, Moscow showed itself as a master on both the international and the national stage, merging the IMT, its domestic trials of German soldiers, and its treason trials of Soviet citizens into one narrative of just punishment.

Saying that select postwar trials of Soviet citizens continued to be conducted in public, however, did not mean that they were much publicized beyond the locality in which they took place. While locals in Pukhovichskii district could draw a clear line between the trial of Nazi leaders at Nuremberg, Soviet trials of German soldiers, and the treason trial at Mar'ina-Gorka, this was not possible for newspaper readers in Minsk or Moscow and even for readers in one of Pukhovichskii's neighboring districts. The Mar'ina-Gorka trial found mention only in the district newspaper.[55] It received no coverage in the all-Union press like *Pravda* or *Izvestiia*; in *Sovetskaia Belorussiia*, the main-Russian language newspaper of Belarus; or in *Zviazda*, the republic's main Belarusian-language newspaper. The Mar'ina-Gorka trial was also not mentioned in regional (oblast) or district newspapers, not even in *Kalhasnaia pratsa*, the newspaper of neighboring Osipovichskii district. Even though local audiences were able to attend the trial, knowledge of the trial was supposed to remain limited to Pukhovichskii district.

The only exception to this pattern were two trials that had taken place during the war: the July 1943 trial of eleven Soviet citizens at Krasnodar in southern Russia, and the December 1943 trial of three Germans and one Soviet citizen at Kharkiv in eastern Ukraine.[56] After December 1943, trials of Soviet citizens accused of being traitors and German accomplices were reported neither in the central press like *Pravda*, *Izvestiia*, or *Komsomol'skaia pravda*, nor in the main republican newspapers like *Sovetskaia Belorussiia*, *Sovetskaia Ukraina*, or *Sovetskaia Estoniia*. This differed from the pattern established during the Great Terror of 1936–1938. Following three Moscow trials that saw several prominent party members tried, the authorities subsequently

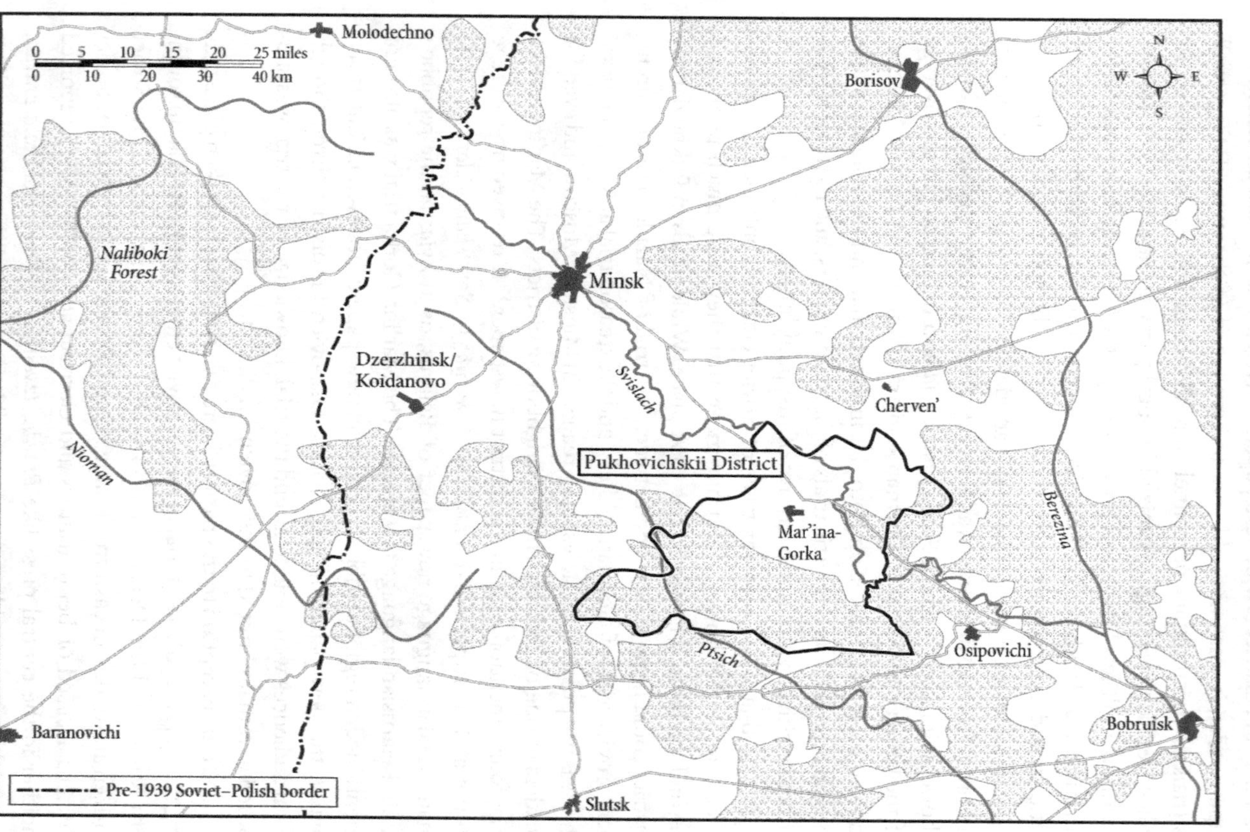

Map 5. Location of Pukhovichskii district, Minsk oblast, 1945. Map by Mike Bechthold.

conducted local public trials of "enemies of the people" and "traitors" in the different Soviet republics. But unlike the postwar trials of those deemed wartime traitors, the local Great Terror trials were also reported in the regional (oblast) press, some even in the main central newspaper, *Pravda*.[57] It was only in 1957, and then more frequently beginning in 1960, that articles about wartime treason trials began to appear in the central, republican, and regional press as well.[58] The March 1962 trial that took place in Baranovichi illustrates this point well. The defendants were four Belarusians who had served in the Thirteenth White Ruthenian Police Battalion under the command of the SS (Schutzstaffel). During the war, they had served as guards in the Koldychevo concentration camp close to Baranovichi. At the time of the 1962 trial, Koldychevo was part of Gorodishchenskii district, which in turn was part of Brest oblast. *Sovetskaia rodina*, the newspaper of Gorodishchenskii district, reported on the trial, as did *Chyrvonaia zviazda*, the newspaper of Baranovichi city, and *Zaria*, the newspaper of Brest oblast. On the republican level, *Sovetskaia Belorussiia* covered the trial extensively, and it even found mention in *Pravda*.[59]

What accounted for this change? Why was the coverage of trials of Soviet citizens accused of crimes in the name of Nazi power no longer limited to district newspapers but instead given multilevel coverage? Although prosecutions of those deemed wartime traitors peaked in 1943–1945, the search continued through the late 1940s and into the early 1950s. In his September 1949 report to Nikolai Gusarov, by then the first secretary of the Communist Party of Belarus, L. Artimenkov, the military prosecutor of the MVD forces in Belarus, wrote that while the "main contingent of the different kinds of traitors of the motherland and active accomplices of the German-Fascist occupiers" had been identified and convicted in the first years after the liberation of Belarus from the Germans, others were still in hiding.[60] Among them was a man named M. A. Slesarevich, who was originally from eastern Belarus. Slesarevich had served as a policeman during the war. He fled with the retreating German army but returned to the republic in 1945. However, he avoided his native district and managed to settle in Grodno with the help of documents that showed his name as Anton Kishkurno. A few years later, the MVD discovered him. Slesarevich was far from the only one. "Currently," as Artimenkov reported in September 1949, "as in the western districts, so in other districts of the republic," the state security organs were uncovering and handing over to the courts those who "at the time had gone into hiding, changed their place of residence, changed their last name and lived semilegally, hoping that in that way they would be able to evade criminal liability."[61]

After Stalin's death in 1953, the number of arrests began to decrease. As part of limited de-Stalinization efforts that saw a range of different prisoners released from the Gulag, the state moderated its punitive policies. In May 1954, the Central Committee in Moscow instructed special commissions, headed by the procuracy, to review the cases of those who had been convicted for counterrevolutionary crimes. This included individuals who had fought as soldiers on the German side or served as local policemen in the occupation regime. Of the individuals who asked to have their cases reviewed, many had their sentences lowered.[62] On September 17, 1955, the Soviet government went one step further and issued a partial amnesty. Any Soviet citizen who had been sentenced to ten years or less for "aiding and abetting the enemy" was released from the forced labor camps, as were individuals who had been sentenced solely on the basis of their service in the German army, local police, or special German formations, regardless of the length of their sentence. However, the amnesty did not apply to those former policemen, SS soldiers, and other Soviet citizens whom the courts accused of the murder or torture of Soviet citizens.[63] A few days later, all remaining German prisoners of war, including those who had been sentenced for the murder and mistreatment of Soviet citizens, were released; by 1956, they had been repatriated to either East or West Germany.[64] Later that year, the Central Committee of Belarus informed Moscow that among the roughly 17,000 Gulag prisoners who by the end of 1956 had returned to Belarus were 6,304 people who had been sentenced for collaborating with the Germans during the war.[65]

Beginning in the late 1950s, the Soviet politics of retribution changed yet again. A second wave of trials began, which lasted well into the late 1980s. While Soviet military trials continued to lack fundamental standards of rule-of-law-based legal systems, the second wave trials differed from the pre-1953 trials of suspected wartime traitors insofar as the documentation collected during the pretrial investigations was much more extensive and systematic. The defendants usually stood accused of having committed violence against Soviet civilians, Jewish and non-Jewish, during the war.[66] This renewed prosecution of Soviet citizens was spurred by a combination of different domestic and international factors. Domestically, the homecomings of those released under the 1956 amnesty ignited local conflicts and led to new accusations from victims, which in turn led to the (re)opening of criminal cases. Heavily discredited by Nikita Khrushchev's Secret Speech, the KGB sought to build a positive public image as an unrelenting hunter of Nazi accomplices.[67] Internationally, the 1961 trial of Adolf Eichmann in Jerusalem brought Nazi atrocities to a global audience. With the rise of

West Germany as a major European power, East-West tensions over the continued employment of former Nazi functionaries in the West German state apparatus increased. Throughout the 1960s, the Soviet government repeatedly accused the West of harboring war criminals and granting them immunity.[68] In its article on the March 1962 trial at Baranovichi, for example, *Sovetskaia Belorussiia* listed Adolf Heusinger and Radaslaŭ Astroŭski among those who had so far escaped justice.[69] Astroŭski—the head of the Belarusian Central Council, the embryonic Nazi-puppet administration—had fled with the Germans and emigrated to the United States in 1956; Adolf Heusinger was a high-ranking Wehrmacht general who bore responsibility for the systematic killings of civilians in Belarus as part of antipartisan operations; after the war, he pursued a high-profile career in the West German army. Like numerous others, Heusinger and Astroŭski were never prosecuted for their wartime activities.[70] In contrast, the Soviet government could demonstrate its firm commitment to the punishment of suspected war criminals. By instituting a new wave of trials of Soviet citizens accused of having committed crimes in the name of German power—and this time making the trials visible beyond the confines of the specific localities in which these had taken place—at least 130 defendants, Soviet citizens, had their names publicly revealed.[71] This deviated significantly from previous practice: from 1944 to the late 1950s, the Soviet authorities had been determined to keep public media references about the involvement of Soviet citizens with the Germans to an absolute minimum, confined to the very local level.

What the mix of public yet not much publicized trials in the first postwar years shows, then, is how carefully the Soviet authorities were circumscribing the public nature of their politics of retribution during that time, weighing different aims and objectives against each other. On one hand, it was important for local audiences to see that the Soviet state was committed to the prosecution of local Soviet citizens deemed to have committed crimes and, through careful newspaper coverage, to enable locals to draw parallels and connections between their local treason trial, the Soviet domestic trials of German soldiers, and the International Military Tribunal at Nuremberg. On the other hand, it seems that the authorities did not want to reveal the full scale and breadth of their politics of retribution. Reporting on the 1940s and early 1950s trials above the level of district newspapers would have revealed the extent to which Soviet citizens, whether willingly or unwillingly, had participated in the occupation regime. At the Soviet Union's eight public trials of Germans soldiers that took place from December 1945 to February 1946, and the nine public trials of German and other Axis soldiers that took place from October to December 1947, any mention of local complicity in the occupiers' crimes was likewise kept out.[72] The discomfort also expressed itself elsewhere. In the early postwar years, the original manuscript of *The Black Book* (Chernaia kniga), an extensive collection of eyewitness accounts of the Holocaust in the German-occupied territories that was compiled by the Soviet Jewish Anti-Fascist Committee, passed through several stages of state censorship. The parts that the Soviet censors crossed out usually referred to the assistance that Soviet citizens had provided to the Germans, or to any manifestations of local antisemitism.[73] Providing specific examples of local complicity would have undermined the regime's narrative of the war as an "all people's war," a war in which the Soviet nation had fought united against the Germans—which is probably also why the authorities were keen to limit knowledge of the local public trials of Soviet citizens deemed wartime traitors to the individual districts in which these trials took place.

Crimes and Choices

Perhaps unsurprisingly, this balancing act was not free from contradictions. First of all, a tension existed between actual versus imagined crimes. The Soviet authorities were committed to punishing local participation in German atrocities: for example, policemen who took part in the killing of the region's Jewish communities or were deployed in punitive raids against villages accused of being partisan-friendly. For the post-1944 trials that were open for local audiences to attend, the state security organs and the political authorities involved in the selection of defendants took great care to choose individuals whose participation in Nazi crimes was, at best, possible to show through witness testimony and documents, or at least highly likely given the positions that they had held in the Nazi occupation regime. Through the presence of witnesses and defense attorneys, the authorities were also careful to project a high degree of legality at these trials. The fact that most of the defendants were locals, meaning they were inhabitants of the respective districts in which they were said to have committed crimes during the war, further contributed to that end, given that other locals usually recognized the defendants on trial and could often link them to actual criminal acts.

In early 1946, for example, the NKVD of Minsk oblast arrested seven men who had worked in the German-overseen police in Dzerzhinsk, a town west of Minsk. Said to have entered the police voluntarily, they were accused of participation in atrocities and violence against civilians, anti-partisan operations, the destruction of villages, and roundups of people to be used as forced laborers—crimes to which they all confessed. In a special report on this group addressed to the Minsk regional party committee, the NKVD officer Krysanov wrote: "We consider it expedient and ask for your directive to hear this case in a public court session [*v otkrytom sudebnom zasedanii*], in the locality where the accused committed the crimes."[74] Similarly, at the February 1946 Mar'ina-Gorka trial, locals both formed the public audience and were on trial: of the eighteen accused men, fourteen were born in Pukhovichskii district (of which Mar'ina-Gorka formed the regional center). Of the 164 witness interrogations that pertained to this case, 140 witnesses were summoned by the military tribunal to testify in court.[75] A number of them had personally suffered from violence: they had repeatedly been beaten by Germans and local policemen, taken to Germany as forced laborers, or had lost family members. One of them was a woman by the name of Nagup', whose daughter had been murdered by Fedor Dubov, one of the former policemen who stood on trial. During her testimony, she asked the military tribunal to publicly hang the accused in Pukhovichskii district.[76]

Yet despite the fact that many of the people who were prosecuted for wartime treason at public trials might have committed some, most, or even all of the specific acts that they were accused of (such as the murder and mistreatment of fellow Soviet citizens), at its core, the Soviet politics of retribution was about defining who had and who had not been loyal to Moscow during the war. In this sense, the search for "traitors" was heavily informed by ideology. Actual criminal acts were prosecuted and punished alongside ideologically inflated acts, as the example of Vladimir Svetlov, with whom this chapter began, demonstrates. Accused of anti-Soviet activity and charged with wartime treason simply because he had kept a Belarusian nationalist leaflet at home, Svetlov received the same sentence as one of the former village heads on trial in Mar'ina-Gorka.

A second tension that ran through the Soviet politics of retribution arose from the issue of moral versus pragmatic choices. Even as Moscow was moderating its punitive practices from 1944 on, it continued to insist that the war was a defining moment in time, one that revealed people's true loyalties. Consequently, the returning Soviet authorities did not show any understanding for the moral gray zones of occupation. Combined with an analysis of the reports on the work of the military tribunals and military procuracy in Belarus, the letters that those deemed "servants of the Germans" wrote to the authorities show this well.

In March 1946, a man by the name of V. Mikhodievskii wrote to the Supreme Soviet of the USSR. Born in Minsk in 1912, Mikhodievskii had worked as a German-language teacher before the war. During Nazi rule, the German labor office ordered him to work as either a teacher or translator. "To work as a teacher meant raising children in the spirit of fascism," he wrote, which is why he chose to be a translator in the industry section of the Minsk city administration.[77] When the Soviets returned, he was sentenced to forced labor in a brick-making plant in Bobruisk, eastern Belarus. As Mikhodievskii wrote: "I work here together with former policemen and their family members, a group of people that I can neither be compared to with regards to my activities under the Germans nor with regards to my moral qualities. . . . The country needs specialists. The schools need teachers. . . . After all, I have the knowledge and the abilities and the strong desire to be of as much use as possible to my country."[78]

In his letter, Mikhodievskii raised an important issue: given the conditions of the German occupation, what constituted guilt? Mikhodievskii maintained that in contrast to the work of local policemen, it had been possible to work in "regular," minor jobs under the Germans (here as a translator within the city administration) without becoming complicit in German crimes. According to him, a clear difference existed between individuals like himself, who in his mind had remained morally untainted, and other locals like policemen and their families, who in his mind had morally implicated themselves. In doing so, Mikhodievskii essentially argued that because of the constraints imposed by the occupation regime, people in occupied territory had no choice *not* to work for the Germans. Yet just what working for the German authorities meant differed from person to person. Some made the choice to support them: these were the policemen, but also people in administrative posts who actively and willingly implemented German policies. Others, according to Mikhodievskii, merely fulfilled their jobs without harboring any political sympathies for the Germans. In his view, it was impossible to say no, but a "yes" carried radically different implications: you could be morally implicated or remain morally untainted.

In his reasoning, Mikhodievskii asked the Soviet authorities to take the circumstances under which he had come to work as a translator into account. A similar argument was put forth in Vasilii Khves'ko's letter to the Supreme Soviet, sent in October 1946 from a forced labor camp in the Far North. Khves'ko was born in the Baranovichi region, which by the time of his birth belonged to the Russian empire. During the German occupation, he worked as the *starosta* of his native village, Dobromysl'. In January 1945, the Soviet state security organs arrested him for treason and sentenced him to forced labor. In his letter, Khves'ko admitted "to being guilty insofar as when fellow villagers chose me for that post, I as a semiliterate unenlightened [*malogramotno-temnyi*] and faint-hearted person was not able to refuse such service as the enemy's accomplice. I stayed and fulfilled my responsibilities as village head."[79] Still, Khves'ko stressed: "I did not cause harm; during my time, killings or arrests of people did not take place in the village, and people and livestock were also not taken to fascist Germany. The village inhabitants can confirm this during the investigation."[80]

It is not known if Khves'ko was pardoned by the Supreme Soviet, and it is impossible to determine if what he wrote was true, just as it is impossible to determine the veracity of Mikhodievskii's letter or find out more about his later whereabouts. What is more important, however, is the way in which both justified how they came to work for the German occupation regime and pointed to external constraints, pressures, and factors—and the only thing that mattered to them was whether the Soviet authorities would consider these in their punishment. While Mikhodievskii argued that he could not have refused an order by the German labor office for fear of negative consequences, Khves'ko pointed to his fellow villagers. Based on the reports that NKVD officers and party representatives who had experienced the first weeks of Nazi rule in occupied territory had sent to Moscow, including to individual Politburo members like Malenkov, the center could indeed have known that many village heads had simply been appointed by their local communities to these posts—and had not volunteered of their own accord. Yet in the reports that military prosecutors and the chief prosecutor of Belarus wrote on the work of the military tribunals from 1944 to 1950, and in particular on the verdicts under review, there was not a single case where such external constraints, pressures, or factors were taken into consideration.[81] The Soviet judiciary did not take into account the circumstances under which people came to be employed by the Germans. Soviet citizens should have refused to enter German service and gone to the forests to fight with the partisans, even if most partisan units only began to exist much later in the war. For the Soviet authorities, people like V. Mikhodievskii and Vasilii Khves'ko had made a moral, not a pragmatic choice.

At the same time, the wartime Soviet state was willing, indeed eager, to coopt into its ranks those whom it considered the worst traitors. These individuals were what one could call "traitors-turned-partisans"—that is, Soviet citizens who had served in the German-organized local police forces (or in other German institutions) but eventually defected and joined the Soviet partisans. Encouraging them to come over to the Soviet side was a deliberate policy, actively promoted by Panteleimon Ponomarenko in his capacity as head of the Central Staff of the Partisan Movement. By the early fall of 1942, this policy had Stalin's approval.[82] Commanders were instructed to infiltrate police units with informers who could organize the defection of policemen to the partisans.[83] According to a July 1943 directive, the aim was to "propagandize broadly" that every return to the Soviet side "has the full possibility to merit the pardon of the Soviet people."[84] To be sure, the state security organs instructed their operational units to interrogate defectors after their arrival in the units and "to carefully check" their "former treacherous activity," at times sentencing them to death.[85] Changing sides, then, was a dangerous task, and few did it in 1942. Throughout 1943, however, the number of defectors grew. From Mogilev oblast, for example, S. A. Mazur, commander of a partisan brigade, reported that several police outposts in Klimovichskii district had joined the partisans.[86] The tide had turned: by then, it was clear that the Soviet Union would win the war. In September 1943, Lavrentii Tsanava remarked on the panic that reigned in a police garrison in Bobruisk: "Large-scale defections to the partisan side were reported." Some even tried to bribe the Soviet agents in charge of organization: "Individual people who wish to come over to our side pay large sums of money to the mediator and middlemen, sometimes even hand them gold."[87]

By the time the Soviet partisan movement was disbanded in the summer of 1944, "traitors-turned-partisans" were not a marginal phenomenon. According to official data compiled by the Belarusian Staff of the Partisan Movement on January 1, 1946, in total, the partisan movement in Belarus comprised 360,491 individuals from the summer of 1941 to its disbandment in the summer of 1944. This included 79,484 partisans who guarded family camps or fulfilled supporting functions but for whom otherwise no further information exists. For the remaining 281,007 individuals (16 percent of them women), additional information on their ethnicity, gender, social background, and year as well as circumstances under which they joined is available.[88] While most came directly "from their place of residence," meaning local civilians not affiliated with the occupation regime, almost forty thousand were former Red Army soldiers who had escaped German captivity or encirclement. Another 29,521 partisans had previously served in the "German army, police, institutions" (*sluzhivshikh v nemetskoi armii, politsii, uchrezhdeniiakh*), which amounted to 10 percent of those partisans for whom such data are available. Most of these "traitors-turned-partisans" were still alive by the late summer of 1944, and more than sixteen thousand of them were eventually drafted into the Red Army.[89]

Of those who survived the war, some might have hoped that the recent heroic part of their pasts would help them to conceal the treacherous part.

Others genuinely seemed to believe that the Soviet regime would forgive them; after all, it appeared to have done so during the war. Ivan Nizov, for instance, was a Red Army officer who early on fell into German captivity. From a prisoner-of-war camp in Prussia, he was taken to Breslau and put into the so-called Radionov Brigade, named after its commander—Vladimir Radionov, a Kuban Cossack and former Red Army officer. In February 1943, Nizov's unit was relocated to western Belarus; six months later, the Radionov Brigade, more than 3,500 men, went over to the Soviet side. For almost a year, Nizov fought with the partisans, reportedly killing many policemen and Germans. When the partisan movement was disbanded, he was arrested for fighting against the motherland and sentenced to ten years of forced labor.[90] In his May 1945 letter to Ponomarenko, Nizov expressed his surprise and outrage at being labeled a traitor: when going over to the partisans, they were told that "with our transfer, we had redeemed our guilt toward the motherland, and that not one finger would be laid on us. But the opposite happened.... Why weren't we arrested on the day when we went over to the partisans?"[91]

The so-called Radionov Brigade, however, was no ordinary Wehrmacht formation. It was the SS brigade Druzhina I, temporarily attached to one of the most notorious SS formations, the Dirlewanger Brigade. In the spring of 1943, the Druzhina men took part in Operation Cottbus in the Begomel'-Lepel' region northeast of Minsk. Operation Cottbus was the largest German antipartisan operation in Belarus, which saw numerous villages burned to the ground and up to thirteen thousand civilians killed.[92] Ivan Nizov, however, stressed that he "never took part in the fight against partisans, neither actively nor passively," and that he also did not participate in any punitive actions against civilians, in particular not in the burning of the village of Azartsy. During his interrogation, he signed a confession, but only so that he could escape "moral and physical abuse by the investigators." The crimes that he was accused of, Nizov wrote, were a figment of his investigators' imagination.[93]

Ivan Nizov probably did not realize this, but he could call himself fortunate. As a member of an SS unit, he usually would have been sentenced to death, but the year that he fought with the partisans counted as a mitigating factor; ten years of forced labor was a light sentence. The same happened to a man called Martynkevich, whom the MVD military tribunal of Bobruisk oblast sentenced in 1948 to twenty-five years in the Gulag. During the war, Martynkevich had served for a year in the German police but then joined the partisans. However, as the MVD military tribunal of Belarus noted during the internal review process, the lower court failed to take into consideration that Martynkevich, after the disbandment of his partisan unit, had joined the Red Army. During his service, he was critically wounded, as a result of which he lost his left leg. He also received several awards. In light of this, Martynkevich's sentence was lowered to ten years.[94]

From a practical point of view, accepting policemen into partisan units made sense. In contrast to civilians, these men were experienced fighters, accustomed to the conditions of partisan warfare (or rather, the fight against it), and in possession of weapons. Although their full redemption was impossible, partial redemption was. As I. Sakharov, head of the MVD military tribunals in Belarus, put it in a secret report in 1949, these men had "partly washed away their guilt toward the motherland with their blood."[95] It is debatable whether this was only a partial legal redemption or also a partial moral one, a question that, because Nizov and Martynkevich's further fates are unknown, has to remain unanswered. Regardless, the postwar treatment of these men remains striking: "traitors-turned-partisans" were the only ones in whose cases Soviet military tribunals systematically took mitigating circumstances into account. Although the Soviet authorities maintained that the war had been a moral test that did not allow for pragmatic choices, they were willing to accommodate their own pragmatic decisions—and did not hold everyone accused of treason accountable by the same standard. These contradictory practices were brought about by the state's balancing of different objectives and interests. As such, they reflected not only tensions between ideology and pragmatism but also tensions *within* ideology. Perhaps no person exemplified this contradiction better than Panteleimon Ponomarenko.

The Ambivalent State

In a speech that Ponomarenko gave in February 1943 in Moscow, in front of the Central Committee of the Communist Party of Belarus, he sent out conflicting signals. On one hand, he evoked existing notions of enemies, in particular that of the kulak, the allegedly rich peasant who, to use Stalin's words, had to be smashed and eliminated as a class.[96] Commenting on the situation in occupied territory, Ponomarenko spoke of policemen, mayors, and village heads as locals chosen by the Germans from among the "remains of the shattered kulak class and bandit-criminal elements," noting that the partisans mercilessly exterminated all "traitors."[97] These images did not fade even as the punishment of the same people believed to be enemies became less strict from early 1944 on—which could also explain why the Soviet authorities had no understanding for the moral gray zones of occupation. In subsequent internal party speeches that Ponomarenko gave over the course of the next three years, parts of which were also published in the newspaper *Sovetskaia Belorussiia*, he repeatedly spoke of "kulaks" who, "as everyone knows," were "the ones who began working for the Germans during the occupation." In that sense, the war helped to reveal that remnants of the "kulak class" had survived in hiding—but that many continued to hide from the authorities even now, in the early postwar years.[98]

On the other hand, though, it was none other than Ponomarenko who had actively pushed for the inclusion of local policemen into Soviet partisan units. By the time of his February 1943 speech, that policy had already been in practice for several months. At the same time, Ponomarenko maintained in his public proclamations that the war was an "all people's war" (*vsenarodnaia voina*). From its very beginning, Ponomarenko played a crucial role in persuading Stalin that Soviet partisan warfare could be successful only if transformed into a mass struggle. In that sense, the recruitment of policemen into partisan units not only followed from pragmatic considerations but also represented the most extreme manifestation of this idea.[99] As the example of Ponomarenko shows, both during and after the war, two beliefs existed at once: that the war exposed mass enemies in hiding, people who had and would always be hostile to Moscow; and that the war revealed people's mass support for Soviet power. The state's politics of retribution, then, reflected more than tensions between ideology and pragmatism, between the regime's high moral standards and the accommodation of its own pragmatic choices. They were also shaped by tensions within Soviet ideology, resulting from two conflicting ideological beliefs. These sets of tensions co-existed and often overlapped, as became visible in the case of "traitors-turned-partisans." The tensions were also evident in the authorities' behavior toward Soviet specialists who had worked in German-overseen institutions—and even in Moscow's treatment of the Soviet population as a whole that had lived under Nazi rule.

According to the Supreme Court's November 1943 instruction, minor employees of the German administration as well as teachers, engineers, and others who had worked in German-overseen institutions were not to be prosecuted if they had not committed any crimes. After the war, the Soviet state usually continued to employ them in their respective fields of expertise, even in positions in which they had worked under the Germans. Teachers are a good example. Of the roughly 4,500 teachers who by June 1946 were working in the schools of Minsk oblast (excluding the city of Minsk), about 3,300 had lived in occupied territory yet had not fought with the partisans. Of those, two-thirds had engaged in farm work, but some

1,100 people had worked in schools or other German institutions.[100] This ratio also applied to other regions. Of the 50,172 teachers employed in Belarus by the summer of 1947, 35,009 had stayed in occupied territory and not joined the partisans. Around that time, the Belarusian Ministry of Education conducted a thorough investigation of all schools and discovered that 2,157 educators had received their training in prewar Poland or during the German occupation. However, the report made no indication that these teachers should be dismissed.[101] Rather, it called for extensive "retraining" (*perepodgotovka*) of educators who had lived in occupied territory. This included extra evening and Sunday lectures on the correct ideological upbringing of children, Soviet patriotism, Marxism-Leninism, and the teaching of history in schools. Instructors were regularly sent out to the republic's schools to monitor the success of the retraining measures.[102]

In continuing to employ people who had worked in German-overseen institutions, the need for qualified labor—in particular, for specialists working in industry, health care, education, and agriculture—played a crucial role. War and occupation had left Belarus utterly devastated, with an estimated 19–22 percent of the population that by the summer of 1941 had lived in the territories that would constitute post-1945 Belarus killed or dead as a result of the war.[103] Among the survivors, the number of locals who had worked under the Germans was significant, as a December 1944 report on the registration of Minsk's population shows. In the five months after the Soviets' return to Minsk, the police registered 100,156 people. Of these, 20,519, about one-fifth of the registered city population, had worked in "German institutions" (*v nemetskikh uchrezhdeniiakh*), although it is unclear from the report what exactly "institutions" meant.[104] If we factor in that not every inhabitant belonged to the working-age population, then the number of those who had worked in German institutions was, in proportion to the overall December 1944 labor force, even higher. For these reasons—the lack of personnel and the fact that many cadres had worked under the Germans—the Soviet state put much emphasis on the education and training of recent high-school graduates. Yet education took time. In the meantime, the Soviet authorities simply could not afford *not* to employ those who had worked in German institutions.

It is, of course, possible that once the first round of postwar higher-education graduates entered the labor force, locals who had been employed in whatever capacity by the German occupation regime were replaced with younger, untainted workers. Unfortunately, the school reports for Minsk oblast after 1946 no longer provide information on how many teachers had not only stayed in occupied territory but had also worked as teachers during that time. However, while the total number of teachers in Minsk oblast (excluding the city) had increased by the beginning of the 1950–1951 school year, the number of those who had stayed in occupied territory had not decreased but was even slightly higher than in June 1946.[105] Obviously, the increase could have been the result of recent graduates who had lived as teenagers in occupied territory but who received their pedagogical training after 1944. Still, having lived under Nazi rule did not categorically preclude one from the educational sector. It is also possible that the teachers' gender mattered. Of the educators in Belarus in 1947, the majority, about 68 percent, were women.[106] It seems that the Soviet authorities took a slightly different view of locals' passivity when it came to women. In their opinion, nothing could plausibly explain why an able-bodied man did not fight with the partisans but remained at home. Women, however, were deemed responsible for the care of children and older relatives. As such, expectations may have been lower that they should live under very difficult circumstances in the forests, without a steady food supply and adequate means of protecting themselves from cold weather, not to speak of sexual harassment. If the authorities indeed held different expectations of men and women, then the teachers' gender may have worked to their advantage after the war, making it possible for women to be employed as teachers even if they had lived under Nazi rule, perhaps even worked as educators during the war.

At the same time, though, the Soviet authorities were highly suspicious of those who had been employed in German-overseen institutions. In their search for "servants of the Germans," the returning Soviet authorities employed a whole range of different methods and sources, ranging from partisan reports, Nazi wartime documents, and letters by Soviet citizens to witness testimony submitted to the Extraordinary State Commission and prewar surveillance and policing tools such as the passport and registration card catalogue and the smaller crime surveillance catalogue. Given the enormity of the task, the NKVD/MVD did not have the capacity to examine every adult's wartime history. Still, throughout the postwar years, its members remained highly alert. In a June 1946 report to the Minsk regional party committee, A. Maksimenko, head of the MVD of Minsk oblast, provided detailed information on some of the current teachers. One woman, Anastasiia Koren'kova from Vitebsk oblast, was accused of having married a German officer during the war.[107] Another woman, Tereza Vykhota, had supposedly told a former student that "in the name of dialectical and historical materialism . . . millions of people died in this war" and that if it were not for the not-yet collectivized agricultural sector in western Belarus, "we would all long ago have died of hunger."[108] Vykhota's husband had been arrested and convicted in 1938. During the German occupation, she taught history in a school in Molodechno oblast and was said to have used "fascist journals" in her classes. Currently, she was a teacher of history and the constitution in a middle school in Minsk. The MVD officer Maksimenko concluded that "teachers who had worked in German-organized schools raised Soviet children in the fascist counterrevolutionary-nationalist spirit, educated them to hate the Communist Party, and made them believe that the German army would bring down the Soviet Union."[109]

It is unknown what happened to the women in Maksimenko's report, although it is very likely that some of them were eventually arrested for their wartime activities. Throughout the postwar years, the Soviet authorities continued to worry that investigations were not thorough enough, and that people who had worked under the Germans might harm Soviet institutions. In a March 1948 report, Military Prosecutor Artimenkov cited the example of Vasilii Rubanov. During the German occupation, Rubanov headed the agricultural department in the administration of Pukhovichskii district. He was accused of having spread anti-Soviet propaganda, punishing locals for not fulfilling his orders, and joining a counterrevolutionary organization, the German-organized Union of the Fight against Bolshevism (Soiuz bor'by protiv bol'shevizma). Although Rubanov left with the retreating German army, he later returned to Belarus and managed to conceal his past. By 1948, he was again working in his field of expertise, employed by the Institute of Agriculture, which was affiliated with the Academy of Sciences. As Artimenkov wrote, the Rubanov case showed that "such specialists, former active accomplices of the German-Fascist occupiers, can not only be of no use whatsoever to those institutions and enterprises in which they work but can also be of harm." This was why, Artimenkov continued, it was necessary to conduct "much more rigorous examinations of the trustworthiness of those specialists" who had stayed in occupied territory and "to determine what they had done during that period."[110] Renewed and recurring examinations also might have been the reason why a lecturer at the Minsk Pedagogical Institute was dismissed from his teaching post in June 1951. As the man wrote in his letter to Nikolai Patolichev, by then the first secretary of the Communist Party of Belarus, "everyone knew that my stay in occupied territory was against my own will." The authorities, however, determined that he had compromised himself under the Germans, and barred him from further pedagogical work.[111]

The state's suspicion, so clearly expressed in Military Prosecutor Artimenkov's report and shared by many Bolsheviks, including Stalin's leadership circle, also extended beyond specialists who had worked in German-overseen institutions.[112] The questionnaires (*ankety*) that one had to fill out before being admitted to university or beginning a new job always asked about the whereabouts of that person during the war, specifically if someone had stayed in occupied territory: "Did you live in territory that was temporarily occupied by the Germans during the [Great] Patriotic War (where, when, and job during that time)?"[113] Those who answered in the affirmative had to fear being denied educational or professional opportunities, even if they had been children during the war. This was the case across the formerly German-occupied regions: in June 1946, for example, N. P. Dolzhenko from Nikolaev oblast in southeastern Ukraine wrote to the Supreme Soviet. A teenager when the Germans occupied his native region, he was drafted into the Red Army in 1944. After the war, his commanders refused him entry into a military training school because he "had lived under occupation."[114] Liubov' I., who during the war grew up in a village close to Mogilev, was also discriminated against. She came to Minsk after the war to work in the automobile factory. In the late 1950s, the factory's party organization discussed whether she could become a candidate for party membership. She was turned down, however, because she had lived in occupied territory: "The things they said to me . . ."[115]

Indeed, people could be denied educational opportunities not so much for what they themselves were suspected of having done as for what their relatives had done. In 1951, for instance, Aleksandr P., a medical student in Minsk, was expelled from university for having hidden crucial autobiographical information—namely, the fact that his father had worked for the Germans as an agricultural specialist. The head of the village council of Chakhets, Aleksandr's native village in Brest oblast, had informed the director of the medical institute about it. Although his father later joined the partisans, as Aleksandr pointed out in a letter to First Secretary Patolichev, he was denied readmission to the university because further investigation uncovered that his father, indeed a former partisan, had refused to enter the collective farm after the war.[116] In this case, the son was held responsible for the actions of his father, a practice already common in the prewar Soviet Union.

The suspicion also extended to those who had survived German camps or ghettos in occupied territory, to Soviet citizens who had been taken to Germany as forced laborers, and to Red Army soldiers who had fallen into captivity. As Litman Mor recalled, a routine question that the Soviet authorities asked Holocaust survivors was, "how did you survive?"[117] Some people experienced outright hostility and discrimination. In a December 1945 letter that the NKVD intercepted, a former forced laborer, a woman by the name of Alekosnok from Minsk oblast, wrote: "Had I known that such a life would await me here, I would never have returned home. Here no mercy is offered to those who were in Germany; people are offended by them; they are not considered human beings."[118]

Depending on whether and under what conditions they had lived under German rule prior to joining the Soviet partisan movement, even former partisans were not above suspicion.[119] This was the experience of Aleksandr Feigel', who fled from the ghetto in Vizdy in northern Belarus and first joined a Soviet partisan unit, then the Red Army. In 1949, while he was still serving in the army, his commander suggested that he enter the Krasnoiarsk automobile technical school. The selection committee, however, rejected him. The reason for that, according to Feigel', was not because he was Jewish: "It turned out that the selection committee did not let those of us pass who during the war had been in occupied territory. . . . During those years, there was much suspicion and distrust of those people who had been in occupied territory. . . . I had been in the ghetto, in camps, and with the partisans. Evidently, the selection committee did not consider it necessary to go into the details, and I as someone who had been in occupied territory during the war was counted among the others."[120]

In light of such widespread and general suspicion, it made sense even for people who had been children during the war to try to conceal their stay in occupied territory—be it out of fear that certain educational or job opportunities might no longer be open to them or because they anticipated unpleasant inquiries. The suspicion was, of course, profoundly at odds with the official narrative of the war as an "all people's war." Yet even if it lost some intensity over the years, it nevertheless lingered on for decades after the war. As with the mistrust of civilians who had stayed in occupied territory, the mistrust of former forced laborers and prisoners of war did not necessarily ebb with time. At the end of the 1970s, while researching in the archives, the historian Aleksei Litvin from Minsk came across a document relating to his former geography teacher. Litvin knew that his teacher had first fought with the Red Army, then with the Soviet partisans, and had more than once been decorated for his service. The archival document, however, indicated that he had also spent ten days in German captivity. When Litvin told his former teacher about his discovery, he did so "without any ulterior motive. But when I saw his reaction, I felt, quite honestly, chilly. His face literally changed. 'Just do not tell anybody,' he asked. He was a party member, but when he entered the party and filled out the biographical questionnaire, he had hidden that piece of his biography because otherwise he probably would not have been accepted." As Litvin noted: "And this was already at the end of the 1970s. One can imagine how people like him felt in the past, in particular in the year of liberation."[121]

The Soviet politics of retribution against those deemed wartime traitors was harsh and often sweeping, but it was not static; it was both clearly ideologically inflected and significantly conflicted. Punitive patterns varied over time, alternating between stricter and more lenient, less active and more expansive phases in response to changing domestic and international circumstances and events. During the first two years of the war, the punishment that Soviet military tribunals meted out to Soviet citizens deemed "servants of the Germans" was often severe and indiscriminate, to the point where Moscow grew alarmed. At the heart of the problem lay a lack of clarity about one crucial question: what exactly constituted treacherous behavior during the war? "Working under the Germans," as party leaders and members of the state security organs called it, was a nebulous, loose category. It could be understood to mean only those who had represented the occupation regime in the localities—policemen, mayors, and village heads—or in a broader sense that encompassed anyone who had worked in German-overseen institutions, including teachers and office clerks. Throughout 1943, several political and judicial central bodies in Moscow issued a series of legal instructions that were aimed at systematization and clarification, and indeed, in early 1944, punishment became less indiscriminate. From that time on, however, Soviet military tribunals also began to hand out lower sentences than they should have, at least according to Moscow's previous instructions. This moderation of punitive practices should not be mistaken for an increase in due process of law: Soviet justice remained illiberal. Rather, it was brought about by shifting political circumstances, which led to a recalibration of state priorities. As the Red Army was reconquering more and more territory from the Germans, retribution evolved into a process in which different objectives and interests had to be weighed against each other: reclaiming authority by way of punishment yet also portraying the Soviet state as liberator and guarantor of justice, while facing a shortage of experienced personnel. A similar mechanism informed the public nature of the Soviet politics of retribution, reflected in the public, yet not much publicized, trials of locals accused of wartime treason that took place throughout the western regions of the Soviet Union in the first postwar decade.

This balancing act, however, was not free of tensions and contradictions. While the Soviet leaders were determined to punish local participation in German crimes, at its core, the search for those deemed traitors was about defining political loyalty. Correspondingly, despite the relative moderation of punishment that began in 1944, the Soviet leadership continued to regard the war as a test that revealed people's true loyalties—and thus showed no understanding for the moral gray zones of occupation. In their rulings, the military tribunals did not take into account external pressures or constraints as mitigating factors and dismissed any recourse to pragmatism as a justifiable reason for people's wartime choices. At the same time, though, the Soviet authorities were willing to accommodate their own pragmatic choices—and they did not hold everyone accused of treason accountable by the same standard. These inconsistent practices reflected tensions between ideology and pragmatism, yet they also arose because of conflicting ideological beliefs: namely, that the war uncovered mass enemies in hiding, while also revealing mass support for Soviet power in the occupied territories. These different sets of tensions—between ideology and pragmatism, and within ideology—co-existed and often overlapped, visible not just in the case of "traitors-turned-partisans," locals who had served as policemen under the Germans and were later accepted into Soviet partisan units, but also in the regime's inconsistent treatment of Soviet specialists who had been employed in German-overseen institutions as office clerks, agricultural specialists, or teachers. Public proclamations to the contrary, the tensions were also at the heart of the continued suspicion toward anyone who had lived in occupied territory. Ultimately, the Soviet authorities—from party leaders to low-level officials, state security officers to members of the judiciary—were unable to establish a consensus on what to think and how to deal with individuals who had lived under Nazi rule. The Soviet state that emerged from the Second World War, then, was able to quickly reassert its authority in the formerly German-occupied territories—yet at the same time ambivalent about its politics of retribution.

Chapter 5

Loss, Grief, and Reckonings

Personal Responses to the Ghosts of War

In the fall of 1944, Litman Mor traveled from Lithuania to southwestern Belarus. Little more than three years earlier, Mor had been a chemistry student at Vilnius University. When the Germans occupied the region in June 1941, he was forced into one of the ghettos that were soon set up in the city. A prewar member of the Zionist youth movement Hanoar Hatzioni, he established ties to fellow members, and together they became part of the ghetto's underground organization. In the fall of 1943, shortly before the liquidation of the ghetto, Mor escaped and joined a partisan unit active in the Lithuanian-Belarusian borderlands. In the summer of 1944, when the Red Army reconquered the region, his partisan unit was disbanded. Soon afterward, the Soviet authorities assigned him to oversee the food industry in nearby Vileiskii district in northwestern Belarus. Mor, however, was anxious to find out what had happened to his parents and siblings, whom he had not seen for more than five years. Granted leave from work, he returned to Vilnius, from where he made his way south. The destination was David-Gorodok, his hometown in Polesia.[1]

Before 1939, David-Gorodok (then called Dawidgródek) had belonged to Poland; after 1939, it belonged to Belarus. Unlike Lida or Grodno, bigger towns to the north, the Christian population of David-Gorodok was not predominately Catholic and Polish-speaking but Orthodox and Belarusian-speaking.[2] Whenever Litman Mor had visited his family before the war, he took passenger trains and, for the last few miles of the journey, a carriage from the closest train station to the town. In the fall of 1944, however, regular transportation did not yet exist. As Mor recalled many years later, "I took the road from Vilna, without having any idea at all of how would I get home. I still say 'home.'"[3] For most of the journey, he rode on cargo trains, hopping on and off different trains. Equipped with papers that showed him as a former partisan, he could travel freely across the region without needing to fear checkups by the police. Mor jumped off a train passing through Lakhva, a town about thirty miles from David-Gorodok, and stayed overnight with a Jewish family. When he told them that he was on his way home, they said, "You don't have to go there, no one has been saved."[4] On their retreat, his hosts added, the Germans had planted mines along the road, and the bridge crossing the Pripyat river was destroyed. With Ukrainian nationalists active in the area, the forests were dangerous places to go through, especially for Jewish survivors. Mor, however, decided to proceed, hoping against hope that someone in his family had survived: "I just couldn't give up . . . I returned because I had to do so, I felt that I must see with my own eyes what happened."[5]

This chapter examines personal responses to the aftermath of Nazi occupation, and more specifically, the ways in which people investigated, addressed, and evaluated the issue of someone else's wartime behavior. How did individuals find out about another person's wartime actions? How did they respond to this information? And how did people try to seek what they perceived as justice and retribution—that is, punishment they believed to be morally right? In contrast to Soviet officials who were preoccupied with the question of political loyalty, for many inhabitants of postwar Belarus, confronting the ghosts of war was a highly individualized process, contingent on a multitude of interacting factors, circumstances, and personal experiences. While the urge for justice and retribution was shared widely, people pursued this goal in different ways: with the help of the state, through nonstate channels, or by a combination of the two. Some confronted neighbors directly, demanding the restitution of property that they had acquired during the war. Others resorted to revenge violence—for example, by beating up a fellow villager accused of having worked for the Germans. Still others chose less physical forms of retribution, such as agreeing to become informers for the state security organs or writing a letter to the state, in the hope that this would help to identify those they deemed traitors and German accomplices. When complicated property conflicts were involved, individuals were likely to pursue justice both through and outside of state channels.

Litman Mor was among those who decided to approach neighbors and acquaintances directly. After days of traveling, he finally arrived in David-Gorodok. He found the two-story brick building of his family's textile store destroyed, but the house where he grew up was still intact. The moment he entered, the emptiness of the rooms overwhelmed him. Nothing of his former life was left, not even a piece of furniture that could serve as a reminder that someone had once lived there: "I went through the empty rooms and didn't know what to do with myself. . . . For the first time ever since I left home, I concretely felt the disaster. During the five years, I had gone through hardships and experienced situations that are even hard to imagine, but this was the first time that I faced the bitter reality, horrible to an extent that cannot be expressed in words. Although I did not have much hope to find anyone of them alive, I felt that my world had shattered."[6]

Litman Mor realized that his family did not survive the war, but before he left town, he was determined to find out what had happened. He first visited "the town's pastor, who used to buy in our store and was on friendly terms with my father." The pastor, however, was reluctant to talk: "He remembered me and did not reject me, but I couldn't learn a thing from him." Mor then sought out a man by the name of Timuch, "who knew me well, since he used to work in our cowshed and was like a member of the family." When Timuch recognized Mor, "he began to make the sign of the cross on his body and yelled: 'Litmanke! I know nothing!'"[7] Litman Mor later found out that during the 1939–1941 Soviet rule of the town, his parents had hidden some items from their store at Timuch's place. That, however, was not on Mor's mind: "Maybe he feared that I came to claim my family's property. But, of course, this did not concern me. I wanted to know what happened. My gentile neighbors' conspiracy of silence provoked me."[8]

Mor continued to walk through his hometown, but the people "that I encountered showed no will to chat with me, and I knew many of them, personally. The meetings were as if friendly, but they did not want to tell anything."[9] After much insisting, Timuch finally told Mor how his father and younger brother Sasha had died: in early August 1941, German soldiers and local policemen, inhabitants of David-Gorodok, had killed them. After that, they drove the women and children, among them Mor's mother and sister Zisl, out of the town. Timuch was not the only acquaintance who began to answer Litman Mor's questions. Slowly, people began to talk—not about what they personally had done during the war, but what Germans and other locals had done: who had served in the local police, how and when David-Gorodok's Jewish population was killed, who had taken pieces of his family's furniture.[10] It is possible that at first locals were particularly reluctant to talk because Litman Mor was a former Soviet partisan: maybe they thought of him as a representative of the Soviet state or even feared reprisal. In his memoirs, Mor did not mention if people in David-Gorodok knew of his partisan past. Considering that Mor had not visited the town for more than five years prior to his return in October 1944, however, they were unlikely to have been aware of his wartime activities. To locals, he was the oldest son of the Jewish family that had owned the town's textile store.

Approaching neighbors and acquaintances, asking them what had happened in a particular place during the war, appears above all to have been done by Jewish survivors. More specifically, it was done by people like Mor who had survived the war elsewhere—be it in the Red Army, with the partisans, or in evacuation—and returned to their former homes in the hope of finding out about the fate of their loved ones. Other kinds of encounters and social interactions likewise prompted conversations about the war years. When in the spring of 1947, Vasil' Bykaŭ returned to his family in Bychki in northeastern Belarus, "fellow villagers came over at night, recent partisans, and recounted how they had survived the war. How much they had been through, how much they had had to suffer! From the Germans, from the partisans, from the *narodniki* [people associated with the administration] . . . Among others also from some people who came from the same villages, in particular from those who up to the war had been Soviet activists and during the war tried hard to serve the Germans."[11]

As Bykaŭ's recollections show, in the immediate postwar years, neighbors and acquaintances who met in social settings could and did talk frankly about the war. That also happened when Ivan Lipai returned home after the war, although he was a different kind of returnee: a native of Novoe Kurgan'e, a village located about halfway between Minsk and Mogilev, and once the head of the local collective farm, he was arrested in 1940 and sentenced to eight years of forced labor in Siberia. After his release in 1948, Ivan Lipai made his way to Novoe Kurgan'e, where his sister Ol'ga still lived. When Lipai asked her about the years of Nazi occupation, she told him that they had hardly ever seen the Germans in their village. Rather, it was the local police who had constantly bothered them—but not only they: "From one side the partisans, from the other, the police. And they were all our folks [*i vse iz nashikh*]. And both groups stole"—mostly food, clothes, and livestock, leaving the villagers with hardly anything.[12]

Such talk about the years of war and occupation, though, was possible only in private, and even then risky. After all, critical remarks in public about the conduct of Soviet partisans would quickly cast doubt on a

FIGURE 11. Vasil' Bykaŭ as a Red Army soldier in Romania, 1944. Courtesy of the Belarusian State Archive of Film, Photo, and Sound Recordings.

person's political loyalties: Why did Ol'ga Lipai mind that the partisans had taken food from her; was she not in support of Soviet power? What Mor, Bykaŭ, and Lipai's recollections indicate, then, is that people mostly spoke about the war at home, among family members, or in conversation with neighbors or fellow villagers. The degree to which they were willing to talk about their own wartime choices also differed: if people talked about taking furniture from Jewish apartments, stealing food from villagers, or serving in the German-organized local police forces, they usually always referred to *other* locals as having done such things, not themselves. As Vasil' Bykaŭ's immediate family had survived the war, though, there was no urgency to find out more about the war years, press for information about the fate of loved ones, or doubt the stories he was told. In contrast, it was precisely his neighbors' unwillingness to talk that made Litman Mor suspicious of their behavior. Compared to Bykaŭ, Mor had much stronger personal motivations to uncover what had happened in his hometown and, especially after he located some of his parents' furniture at a neighbor's house, to determine if the non-Jewish population had benefited from or even participated in the murder of its Jewish neighbors. Even in private, therefore, the ghosts of war—the choices that individuals had made and the choices they had been forced to make during the war—were often not openly acknowledged, or only selectively so. As the example of Litman Mor demonstrates, it needed a lot of personal determination and insistence to overcome people's reluctance to respond to uncomfortable questions, in particular ones that might have brought to light their own entanglement in wrongdoing or crimes.

Distancing, Severing Ties, Leaving Home

When individuals found out or surmised that members of their prewar social communities had become complicit or entangled in the Nazi regime, or that their neighbors had in whatever way taken advantage of other people's plight brought about by occupation and war, they responded in different ways. Some sought comfort in the social relations that had survived, the friendships and solidarities that had not been destroyed by what people had done or not done during the war. Sofiia Brudner, for example, spent the war years with her family in evacuation behind Soviet lines. After the family members' return to Minsk in January 1945, they were able to move back into their prewar apartment, but all of their belongings were gone. Soon, however, the family discovered some of the goods in a neighbor's home. When Brudner's father pointed out that these items belonged to his family, the neighbors refused to return them, saying that they had bought them. Her family decided not to pursue the issue further because, as Brudner explained, "we were not the kind of people to fight with them." While it was very difficult to live with the thought that some of their neighbors could have taken advantage of the plight and suffering of others, the Brudner family did not socialize with anyone they suspected of wrongdoing. Many of Sofiia Brudner's prewar friends, both Jewish and non-Jewish, had been killed during the war, but she remained close to those who had survived, including her best friend, a Belarusian woman who had fought with the partisans. Apart from her family, these friendships provided a great source of strength for her.[13] Indeed, for many, family took on an even greater importance than it might have held previously, with some focusing all their energy on the familial bonds that had survived and others on creating new ones. After the war,

Sulia Wolozhinski Rubin was at first unsure whether to stay with Boris, the man with whom she had entered into a protective relationship after joining the Bielski partisans. Having lost her entire family, however, she ultimately decided to marry Boris, because leaving him would have left her feeling utterly alone in the world.[14]

Often, people cut all ties with those whom they suspected of wartime wrongdoing. Ol'ga Bembel'-Dedok, the artist from Minsk, was convinced that Igor', the nephew of her husband Andrei Bembel', "had besmirched himself, collaborated [*sotrudnichal*] with the Germans."[15] A soldier in the Red Army, Igor' fell into captivity during the war. He survived and after the war wrote to his relatives, explaining that he had tried to kill himself instead of being taken prisoner but had staggered and failed to shoot himself when German soldiers were running toward him. According to Bembel'-Dedok, no one believed his story, but when Igor' came to visit, Andrei Bembel' nevertheless treated him as if he were his own. However, the family soon found out that Igor' had taken on a new last name and now called himself Paletskii instead of Bembel'. Moreover, it turned out that he had worked as a translator in German captivity. His mother was a Russian-German, which is why he knew the language well. Finally, another relative told Ol'ga Bembel'-Dedok that a state security officer had approached her and asked if she had a nephew by the name of Igor'.[16] After all of this became known, Bembel'-Dedok decided to send Igor' a letter: "Igor'! When you came to visit, we received you with open arms; we didn't want to upset you. But now the entire family has discussed the issue of our relationship, and we have decided to cut it off. Do not come to visit us in the future, and do not write letters. You know the reason. You should not be resentful toward us, given that so much seems more than dubious to us."[17]

Not every family member, however, agreed with Ol'ga Bembel'-Dedok. When Ol'ga showed the letter to her sister Anastasiia, she became upset: "Who gave you the right to judge him? You are hurting a person who perhaps his entire life has been suffering from feelings of remorse. Why did you take that role upon yourself?"[18] Ol'ga Bembel'-Dedok explained that "I hate people who served the Germans; I do not want to socialize with those who were associated with the German police or concentration camps."[19] In return, her sister told her that she "cannot at all believe what I say and what they say in the newspaper and in the agitational literature [*agitromany*]."[20] Given how starkly their assessment of Igor's behavior differed, the argument between the two sisters was never resolved. While for Ol'ga Bembel'-Dedok, it was a matter of principle, Anastasiia Dedok was more understanding of the choice that he had made. As Ol'ga Bembel'-Dedok realized on that day, her sister and she "were strangers to one another." For her, this was not simply a question of personality. Rather, in her eyes, the sisters' disagreement over what constituted wartime guilt brought to light their irreconcilable political beliefs: "The issue is not one of difference in character. No, the difference lies in the innermost opposition of ideologies."[21]

Breaking off all social relations, even within families, could also occur several years after the war, presumably once an individual found out or uncovered previously unknown details about a relative's wartime history. In 1951, Nikolai A., the secretary of the Lida district party committee, wrote to the Central Committee in Minsk. He asked to be assigned to a job in another city because his wife had worked as a teacher during the occupation and received a cow from the Germans. "She has discredited herself before the motherland, while I was fighting against the German occupiers at the front," Nikolai A. wrote. "My life with my wife cannot set a good example, and to live well with a person who has worked for the Germans and received a cow from them is simply not possible." In response, the Central Committee in Minsk removed him from his post and assigned him to pedagogical work.[22] Grigorii Zh., in contrast, a former Red Army soldier from Vitebsk oblast, feared that his father's past would stand in his way. In his July 1951 letter to the Central Committee in Minsk, he renounced his father and asked the party to officially acknowledge the act. His father, as Grigorii Zh. wrote, had worked during the war as the head of their native village, Cherepki. For this, he was sentenced to ten years of forced labor in 1944. At that time, Grigorii Zh. had already been drafted into the Red Army, which is why he only heard of his father's imprisonment in 1949. Now that he was to be discharged from the army, he was worried that his father's wartime record would prevent him, the son, to study and work as he liked: "I am a young Soviet person, I must work hard and honestly for the benefit of my motherland; I have to be honest and faithful toward my people, but my father's bad past will hinder me along that path. I thought much about it, and I swore to myself that I am ready to act in such a way that my life is clean and clear and that I won't be connected as a son to such a 'father.'"[23]

Nikolai A. and Grigorii Zh.'s letters are good examples of how individuals drew on Soviet notions of wrong and right wartime behavior when assessing and ultimately judging the wartime behavior of another person. Yet others did not, as Ivan Danilov recalled, citing the case of Stepan Moseichuk who came from the same district in Pinsk oblast as Danilov. During the war, Moseichuk worked in the German police, but instead of fleeing with the Wehrmacht in 1944, he went into hiding—not for a few weeks or months but for fourteen years, during which he lived with his parents in the village of Zelovo. The local inhabitants must have known about it, yet no one reported him to the authorities. Perhaps Moseichuk had been coerced into joining the local police, or perhaps the villagers knew that in 1943, Stepan Moseichuk let Ivan Danilov, who had been arrested by the local police, flee, after which Danilov went to the forests and joined a partisan unit. In 1958, Moseichuk handed himself over to the state security organs, but after a couple of days, he was, for reasons unknown, released from prison and returned to the collective farm. Because he was a dedicated worker, according to Danilov, "the locals treated him with understanding." When he was up for retirement, Moseichuk did not want to claim his pension because he felt that he did not deserve it. The employees of the local rural council, however, saw to it that Stepan Moseichuk received his state pension.[24]

What these different examples and recollections suggest is that for some people like Nikolai A., working as a teacher under Nazi occupation and receiving a cow from the German authorities meant that a person had discredited him- or herself and was no longer worthy of belonging to the Soviet community. For others, such as Moseichuk's fellow villagers and some low-level officials, the fact that he had worked as a local policeman appears not to have been enough by itself to exclude him from their village community. People's responses to someone else's suspected or known wartime behavior, then, depended not just on what the person under scrutiny was thought to have done. As the example of Ol'ga Bembel'-Dedok and her sister Anastasiia shows, assessments of one person's wartime activities could also be widely at odds with one another, leading to much disagreement within families.

In addition to severing connections to specific individuals suspected of wartime wrongdoing, others decided to cut altogether the ties (or rather, the remains of these) that had bound them to a local community. This entailed leaving one's hometown or region—or the Soviet Union itself. When Litman Mor discovered that some inhabitants of David-Gorodok, whether in their capacity as local policemen or civilians, had indeed participated in the murder and expropriation of his family, all social ties that he had once held to non-Jewish acquaintances shattered. During the war, the German-led killing of the town's male Jewish population and the expulsion of Jewish women and children from David-Gorodok in August 1941 had taken on a communal character. Local policemen took part in the shootings and, together with other residents of the town, hunted down Jews in hiding. On discovery, they killed them on the spot with sticks, stones, iron bars, and guns or tortured them to death in the town's marketplace.[25] It is not clear if, during his return to David-Gorodok in the fall of 1944, Mor had yet discovered the full details of how locals had murdered their Jewish neighbors. But what he found out was enough to make him feel completely detached and alienated from the town's residents, regardless of what each had done individually: "I walked about in my town and felt that I was walking about between murderers. I saw in every inhabitant a potential murderer of my family."[26] As he explained, "my hatred toward the locals was not less than my hatred toward the German and Lithuanian murderers who executed the killing in Vilna. My hatred of the Germans was common, not aimed at a specific German. But my hatred of the locals, who murdered my family, was personal."[27] Hoping against hope that some members of his extended family might have survived, Mor returned once more to David-Gorodok in early 1945: "This time, I walked around like in a cemetery. I was completely indifferent. . . . I only knew—I will never return here."[28] Under the conditions of the Polish-Soviet population exchange, he was able to leave for Poland in the fall of 1945. After a journey through several European countries, he arrived a year later in Haifa.[29]

Except for ethnic Poles and Jews from western Belarus, though, leaving the Soviet Union under the conditions of the population exchange was not an option. For Holocaust survivors from eastern Belarus, especially from smaller towns, it was quite common to leave their former homes and try to settle in larger towns or cities.[30] Someone like Lev Ovsishcher, whose postwar army career took him to Moscow oblast, where he was given a spot to study at the Air Force Academy at Monino, did not have to deliberate whether to return to his hometown of Bogushevsk in Vitebsk oblast after the war—and thus did not have to wonder if any former neighbors took part in the looting of his family's property.[31] For others—whether for reasons of resources, job assignments, or sheer circumstance—severing all ties to one's local community by leaving was not an option, but they probably also did not feel the urge to do so. Because non-Jews usually had, on the whole, more of their former lives to go back to, they also might not have felt the same need to sever all ties to their prewar homes as Jews who had lost most or all of their prewar communities—in particular, in the western parts of Belarus from which flight or evacuation had been almost impossible in the summer of 1941. Vasil' Bykaŭ, for example, had little reason to feel estranged from the village collective he returned to, given that he had not lost a loved one to the actions of a fellow villager. In contrast, it was precisely the discovery of local complicity in the murder of his family, coupled with the sense of a strong collective silence, that made Litman Mor feel like an outsider in the place he had once called home. Experiences similar to his help to explain why Jews from western Belarus, who had usually fought with the partisans and were often the only survivors of their families, sometimes did not wait for an official resettlement permit to Poland but decided to find other ways of leaving the Soviet Union—whether that meant being smuggled in a truck across the border like Chasia Bornstein-Bielicka or, like Sulia Wolozhinski Rubin, managing to obtain forged repatriation papers through a Polish acquaintance who worked as the head of the repatriation committee in a town not far from Novogrudok.[32]

Seeking Justice and Retribution

Among the many responses to the known or surmised wartime wrongdoing by members of a prewar social community, one was widely shared by inhabitants of Belarus, as in all countries that had been occupied during the war: the urge to seek justice and retribution—that is, punishment that they believed to be morally right.[33]

In its most immediate and extreme form, retribution meant violence that was not sanctioned by the state. In October 1945, a Soviet official informed the Central Committee in Minsk that in several eastern Belarusian districts, returning former policemen had recently been beaten up by other locals. Cases of murder were also recorded.[34] One of the victims was a man by the name of Brukhovskii who had returned to Rogachevskii district in Gomel' oblast, reportedly bringing with him "seventeen suitcases full of possessions and also a cow and other household items." On his arrival in the Dvoretskii rural council, he was greeted by members of the collective farm. During the war, Brukhovskii was said to have reported local partisan families to the Germans. For that, his fellow villagers "took away his possessions, beat him half to death, and then brought a rope and tried to string him up." The head of the village council intervened, however, and handed Brukhovskii over to the NKVD.[35] In the same district, residents of the village of Rudnia-Kamenka had discovered a policeman in hiding. They locked him up in the bathhouse and "after breakfast, lunch, and dinner, they beat him up, everybody as much as he could." This continued for three days until the NKVD arrested the man.[36]

When revenge violence (or wild retribution) confined itself mostly to beatings, the NKVD usually tolerated it for a while. However, there were limits to what was permissible. In October 1944 in the village of Studzenka to the north of Borisov, three former partisans killed V. Adameiko, a fellow villager, on the grounds that he had "betrayed the motherland during the German occupation." While such killings were standard during the war, they now challenged the state's monopoly on force. The three men were consequently arrested, although it is very likely that their partisan years were later taken into account, lowering their sentence significantly.[37] In the fall of 1944, for example, Mikhail Kurbachev, head of the collective farm Gigant in Vitebsk oblast, was prosecuted for killing his fellow villager E. Shabuneva and her two daughters. However, the procuracy of Belarus informed Panteleimon Ponomarenko, first secretary of the Communist Party of Belarus, that the court had taken mitigating circumstances into account, given that from 1942 on, Kurbachev had fought with the partisans. The Germans had arrested his wife and two daughters in retaliation, and the women had been missing ever since. E. Shabuneva, by contrast, was the wife of a former policeman who was killed in 1942 by the partisans. According to the procuracy, many of her relatives had worked for the police and left with the Germans. In light of this, Kurbachev was released from custody on the condition that he not leave his rural council.[38]

Although most revenge violence took place in the immediate post-occupation weeks, it was also committed many years after the war. In August 1956, the state security organs reported a murder that had recently taken place in the village of Ozarichi in Brest oblast (until 1954 Pinsk oblast). The victim was a man who, sentenced to forced labor in 1944, had just been released from the prison camps. A few days after his return to Ozarichi, he was killed by his neighbor, who accused him of complicity in the 1942 murder of his father and grandfather at the hands of the Germans.[39]

Revenge violence was, of course, not unique to Soviet Belarus but occurred in all societies that had been under foreign rule during the Second World War.[40] What differed, however, was its extent. In places where large-scale expulsions of ethnic minorities occurred, above all in East-Central Europe, revenge violence became a part of these processes.[41] In the case of Belarus, it appears to have been a rather limited phenomenon. In part, this may have been because many local policemen or others who feared retribution at either the hands of the Soviet authorities or their neighbors had left with the Wehrmacht or avoided returning to their hometowns and villages. Pavel Pal'tsev, who survived the burning of Karpilovka village in Gomel' oblast, recalled that one of the local policemen who helped German forces carry out the killings of Karpilovka's villagers was a man by the name of Los' from nearby Smykovichi. Pal'tsev knew him personally, as they had worked together before the war. After the war, Los' intended to return to his home village. "The inhabitants of Smykovichi were going to kill him, but he guessed it and got out," eventually settling in the Komi Autonomous Republic.[42] It is also possible that the strong presence of the Soviet state security organs prevented or deterred locals from committing spontaneous acts of retribution. In Belarus, the state security organs were able to eliminate anti-Soviet nationalist groups sooner than in Ukraine and Lithuania. By late 1946, they had by and large contained the threat coming from Polish and Ukrainian partisans. Although small armed groups continued to bother the authorities into the early 1950s, this nevertheless meant that the state had succeeded fairly quickly at curtailing possibilities for violence by nonstate actors.[43]

Yet it is also likely that revenge violence was more frequent in post-Nazi occupation Belarus than primary sources suggest. After all, reports of such violence have to be read through the lens of the Soviet authorities. Not only was it up to those in power to decide whether beatings would be tolerated or mitigating factors considered in cases of murder, but it was also up to the state security organs and party-state representatives to interpret such acts either as cases of justified (thus retributive) violence or as cases of "banditry." Indeed, *banditizm*, as the Soviet authorities called it, was a widespread phenomenon in the formerly German-occupied Soviet regions. Most often, the term was applied to the Polish, Ukrainian, and other anti-Soviet partisans fighting in the western borderlands. Other "bandit" groups were composed of an eclectic bunch of demobilized Red Army soldiers, local men who evaded the military draft, and Soviet citizens who had worked in the German police or administration. Although these men were not necessarily politically motivated, they disrupted public order, stealing food and clothes from locals, at times killing people.[44]

As "banditism" was such a broad category, it is plausible that the NKVD identified some revenge violence as banditry rather than retribution, given that the relevant acts had been committed by the "wrong" kind of people. In particular, during the first two years after the war and in the countryside, former Soviet partisans occupied many low-level party-state positions in Belarus. By April 1, 1945, for example, 40 percent of Soviet officials in leadership positions in the regional, district, and city executive committees in Belarus were former partisans.[45] In that light, assaults by "bandits" on local party-state representatives (especially common in western Belarus) may in fact have been motivated by a desire to seek revenge for the wartime behavior of these former partisans-turned-Soviet officials. The August 1944 attack by former policemen on the small town of Selets in Berezovskii district in

Brest oblast, for example, which resulted in a fight between these on one side and former partisans as well as armed townspeople on the other, may have been an act of revenge for violence committed by partisans on local civilians (here the families of policemen) during the war. The same could have been true for the group's assault on the former partisan S. Dymsha, which took place in the nearby village of Strigin and left Dymsha wounded, yet alive.[46] "Bandit" attacks, some of them deadly, on low-level party-state representatives in Baranovichi oblast throughout the fall of 1944 may have been similarly motivated.[47] Reports by the NKVD interpreted these attacks as acts aimed at preventing the full reestablishment of Soviet power, yet they may have included aspects of revenge violence, acts that would have been justified in the eyes of those who committed them but not in the eyes of those in power.

Testifying, Informing, Writing Letters

Beyond revenge violence, individuals pursued many other, less physical—or, one could say, more mediated—means of retribution in postwar Belarus. These, in turn, often brought them into contact with the Soviet state. In their efforts to determine what Soviet citizens had done under Nazi rule, the returning Soviet authorities relied heavily on local information, on an assortment of names, clues, and stories provided by inhabitants of the formerly occupied regions. I am deliberately not using the term "knowledge" here, as this could imply that what was conveyed was always accurate or true. Some of this information was provided unwillingly, such as when torture during pretrial interrogations made people provide or fabricate incriminating material about friends or neighbors, as in the case of Vladimir Svetlov, or when people were blackmailed into becoming informers. Others did so on their own initiative—for example, when they approached their local Extraordinary State Commission and gave testimony about the years of Nazi occupation, including the names of those they accused of having worked for the Germans. Yet others, when approached by the NKVD/MVD, asked to be allowed to testify in court.[48] As the NKVD of Minsk oblast prepared the February 1946 public trial of former local policemen and village heads at Mar'ina-Gorka, for example, it selected 140 witnesses to appear in court. According to internal reports, an additional fifty-two people had asked to be heard, but their wishes could not be accommodated.[49] When the witness Nagup', whose daughter had been murdered by the policeman Fedor Dubov, asked the military tribunal to publicly hang the accused in Pukhovichskii district, the audience applauded. Likewise, when the prosecutor asked for the highest punishment to be applied, the more than two thousand local inhabitants present at this point met his request with "approval and applause."[50] As Dubov was among the five defendants who received the death sentence, it is very likely that the witness Nagup', the mother who had lost her daughter, felt that Dubov received the punishment he deserved, perhaps even viewed the Soviet judges and prosecutor as guarantors of justice. The Soviet state, in turn, was not only able to provide local victims with a space to voice demands for punishment but also demonstrated that their voices were being heard.[51]

Finally, some people decided to search for suspects themselves. After his return to David-Gorodok, the Red Army soldier Aharon Moravtchik—who had lost his wife, four children, and extended family in the Holocaust—vowed to himself that he would track down a group of locals who had actively helped to murder the town's Jewish population. These men and women, including Mayor Ivan Mareiko and several local policemen, had fled west with the German army in 1944; Moravtchik suspected they were in Poland. As a pre-1939 citizen of Poland, Moravtchik signed up for the population transfer to Poland. A random encounter with someone from David-Gorodok at a market in Wrocław led to that person's arrest, which in turn revealed that Mareiko was living in Warsaw. Hoping to be able to find him, Moravtchik traveled several times to the Polish capital. In the end, a secret agent who also happened to be Jewish was able to locate David-Gorodok's former town mayor in a small town near Warsaw, where the latter was working as a medical doctor. Mareiko was subsequently arrested, as was the lawyer Evgenii Iavplov and his wife, Marusiia, who were hiding in a small village near Zielona Góra in Silesia. During the war, Evgenii Iavplov was part of the group of locals who represented the German occupation regime in David-Gorodok. Marusiia, as Aharon Moravtchik wrote, had killed Jewish children by throwing them alive into the town's river. Due to Moravtchik's efforts, the Polish secret police was able to identify and arrest at least a dozen individuals from David-Gorodok and its environs. They were extradited to the Soviet Union, where they were put on trial.[52]

Apart from helping to uncover suspects or testifying to the authorities, some individuals also sought to find justice for themselves through means that, because of their negative moral connotations, are usually not thought of as such. One way of doing this was to agree to become informers for the state security organs, in the hope that this would lead to the punishment of locals they believed to be guilty of crimes committed in the name of German power. Sofiia Khabai was approached by an NKVD officer shortly after her return to Minsk in the summer of 1944. Born in 1914 into a Jewish family in

Minsk, she lost almost her entire family during the war, including her two children and husband. Khabai's infant son Lenichka, her sister Khasia and her son, her father, her father's two brothers with their families, her cousin Pesia and her two children, her husband's brother and his family: all were killed in the Minsk ghetto. Shortly before the Wehrmacht arrived in Minsk, her mother and her other two sisters were able to catch a train heading to Ufa; their further fates are unknown. During the chaos of the invasion, Sofiia Khabai's older son Iasha was evacuated with his day-care center from Minsk, but his further fate is also unknown. Her husband, Abram Weingauz, was drafted into the Red Army on the first day of war and died at the front. Of her large family, only her brother Naum Khabai, a Red Army soldier, returned after the war.[53]

Sofiia Khabai herself survived by fighting with the Soviet partisans. In 1943, with the help of a non-Jewish acquaintance who had ties to the partisans, she escaped from the Minsk ghetto and joined a unit in the nearby forest. In the summer of 1944, shortly after the Red Army had reconquered the capital, she returned to her hometown. When Khabai entered Minsk, she ran into non-Jewish neighbors on Dimitrov Street: "They looked at me in surprise and said: 'They beat them and beat them but did not finish the kikes off' [*Bili, bili, ne dobili zhidov*]."[54] Her family's home on First Zaslavskii Lane, which had been within the borders of the ghetto during the war, was still intact, yet the people who now lived in it did not want to let her in. "This is not your house, go away from here," they told her.[55] Overwhelmed, exhausted, hungry, and tired, Sofiia Khabai sat down on the side of the street and cried, until her neighbor Natasha invited her into her house and offered to let her stay there until they managed to evict the people currently living in the Khabai house. Only two weeks later, Sofiia Khabai was able to move back into her old home, although the previous inhabitants, on vacating the place, completely emptied it of furniture and other household items.[56]

Probably not long after Sofiia Khabai had moved back into her house, she was standing at its gate when she saw men in army uniforms conducting a search of her neighbor's place, a woman by the name of Vasilevskaia. Vasilevskaia, it seems, was under suspicion of having stolen or in some other way acquired items during the war that had once belonged to Jews. The NKVD officers called Sofiia Khabai into Vasilevskaia's house and asked her to serve as a witness when "they wrote up a report on how many Jewish goods (tableware, blankets, clothing) there were. Afterward, the major asked me how I had come to this place and I briefly told him. He gave me a summons and instructed me to appear tomorrow on Uritskii Street," where the NKVD was located. At her meeting the next day with the same major, Sofiia Khabai was questioned thoroughly and then recruited under the code name Roza. She did not refuse, as she saw it as a chance to seek the punishment of locals who helped the Germans to murder her family: "I was supposed to communicate with a lieutenant and, in connection with the fact that I had been in the ghetto, was to take revenge on the enemies that were residing in Minsk. Of course, I did not refuse, for my blood was boiling and I wanted to take revenge [*mstit'*] on many people."[57]

The first person that Sofiia Khabai informed on was her neighbor Adelia, whose sons had attacked Khabai's Jewish neighbors in the fall of 1941, looting their property and killing some of them.[58] Soon thereafter, the NKVD conducted a search of Adelia's house: "They found many leather jackets, coats, suits, and many other different things—a whole carload full. After that, Adelia would not leave me alone, would not let me pass, called me every kind of name." Yet when the NKVD summoned Adelia "and warned her that if she were to harm me she would be taken in, she kept quiet and hid from me."[59] Another neighbor that Sofiia Khabai reported on was a man by the name of Adam who lived in the house right next to her. During the war, his daughter had married a local ethnic German who worked in the Minsk Gestapo. "The Jews came to his wife to exchange clothes for flour, and he shot them. At night they attacked houses, surrounded them, murdered all, and took all the furniture home with them." When the Red Army advanced, the local ethnic German fled west with the Wehrmacht, while his wife and her father Adam stayed in Minsk. "I could not keep quiet about this; the wife was arrested, and the father died as a result of the experience [*umer ot perezhivanii*]."[60] The NKVD even issued Sofiia Khabai a special permit so that she could go to the movies, with the aim of recognizing people in the audience who she suspected or knew had stolen or acquired Jewish property items during the war: "I recognized a lot of bandits-bloodsuckers, my soul could not be silenced. For my excellent, sincere work, the NKVD presented me with a gift on the occasion of a holiday, a small box of imported smoked lard, canned goods, sugar, and other items. I had the telephone number of the lieutenant and whenever it was necessary for me to report something, I called him."[61]

Sofiia Khabai continued to work for the NKVD until the birth of her daughter, when she decided to quit and was released from her duties. Her recollections make clear that people did not always need to be blackmailed or coerced into becoming informers. For someone like Sofiia Khabai, it offered an opportunity to seek both personal revenge and the state's punishment of locals who had actively taken part in murder, personally brutalizing and killing Jewish neighbors or acquaintances. Informing on people was also a way to hold responsible those people who had looted Jewish houses, amassed furniture or clothes for their own use, or made money by selling the goods on the local market.

It is not implausible to think that the NKVD intentionally recruited informers among Jews, knowing that of all population groups, they had suffered the most during the war—and thus assuming that survivors would have a strong self-interest in seeking justice for the crimes that not just Germans but also some locals had committed. In the case of Sofiia Khabai, these thoughts might have been on the NKVD officer's mind when, after hearing about her family's fate, he summoned her to the NKVD with the intent of recruiting her. Moreover, she had been a Soviet partisan, which in the eyes of the authorities must have made her reliable. It is known from the post-1944 western Ukrainian case that the NKVD indeed took advantage of conflicts between locals, in this case Poles and Ukrainians. Under mortal threat from Ukrainian nationalists (OUN-UPA), Polish-speaking peasants, usually the minority group in the countryside, became NKVD informers in the hope that the Soviet state security organs would eliminate the Ukrainian nationalist threat, as they eventually did. The NKVD deliberately sought to capitalize on violent local conflicts, strategically playing hostile groups against one another and thereby increasing the possibility that one group would eventually find common ground with the Soviets—which is why it is not impossible to think that the Soviet state security organs employed a similar strategy with respect to Jewish survivors.[62] At the same time, the NKVD did not need to target specific groups or individuals in its efforts to obtain information on people's wartime histories. That information also reached the authorities through letters that individuals sent to them.

Writing letters to high-ranking party-state representatives was a widespread practice in the Soviet Union. Seen by officials as a convenient tool to receive information about the inner workings of society and the activities of low-level officials, as "signals from below," the state actively encouraged its citizens to send complaint letters (*zhaloby*, often also translated as petitions). Throughout the 1930s, it further set incentives to do so when it increasingly softened the sanctions for submitting false information or slander.[63] Once the Nazi occupation came to an end, numerous individuals turned to the authorities to inform them about the wartime activities of former neighbors, fellow villagers, co-workers, or acquaintances. On December 26, 1944, the Red Army soldier Kovalev from Mogilev sent a letter to Georgii Malenkov in Moscow. The soldier wrote the letter on behalf of his father, who had been arrested by the NKVD on charges of treason. Kovalev maintained that his father had fought with the partisans and that the arrest was unjustified. Why, he asked, did the NKVD go after "soldier-partisan families" when the families of policemen and village heads were still running around town? He then provided names, accusing one "former kulak" Beseda, now the head of the collective farm Put' sotsializma, of concealing that he had worked for the German authorities during the war, and he claimed that the policemen Emel'ianov, Timofeev, and Sibakov were still "sitting at home."[64]

Similarly, when Boris Lozhechnik wrote to the Presidium of the Supreme Soviet of the USSR in April 1946, he did so because he felt that the Soviet authorities had wronged him. Recently demobilized from the Red Army, he had returned to the town of Krupki in Minsk oblast, where he intended to build a house for himself. Not much later, however, the Soviet authorities found out that during the German occupation, Lozhechnik had worked as the "head of a street" (*starosta ulitsy*) in Krupki for several months and that he had been employed as a tailor for the local police, probably sewing and repairing police uniforms.[65] After this information was uncovered, the Krupki district executive committee prohibited him from building his house and revoked his right to reside in the town. Lozhechnik, however, felt that the decision was unjustified. As he emphasized in his letter, during the war, the town administration had simply assigned him to work as head of a street. Moreover, "I did not fulfill the orders of the German invaders to supply horses and goods for the German army, and I also hid a Jewish family. Besides, in the part of the street where I was the overseer lived partisan families (the Zaitseves, the Ermoloviches) whom I knew very well, which is why I did not report on them; quite on the contrary, I gave the partisans some information on the location of a major German unit."[66]

At the same time, Lozhechnik claimed that "people are presently working in regional institutions who really did actively help the German invaders." He then identified six people, although he stressed that this was "by far not a complete list of the names." Among those whom he identified was a man named Vainovich and a man named Arkadii Bokuts'. Both of them were accountants currently working in Soviet institutions, yet according to Lozhechnik, they had worked in the same positions for the German authorities. Although the Germans had killed the Jewish wife of Arkadii Bokuts', "for his good work, he received a cow and now Bokuts' works as the head accountant of the district industrial plant." Another person whom Lozhechnik accused of receiving German rewards for his work was a man called Bumilovich. As the head of the local school district and school director under Nazi occupation, he had allegedly received "a German medal" and now worked as a teacher in a Soviet school. A woman by the name of

Beliakova had, according to Lozhechnik, worked as a translator for the German authorities and was presently employed in the construction department of Krupki's district executive committee. Yet how is it, Boris Lozhechnik asked, that these people "are absolutely not being accused for having, in one way or another, helped the German occupiers"; how come "the Krupskii district authorities discovered that I, Lozhechnik, was the only one who worked for the Germans?"[67]

In the scholarly literature, letters such as those by Kovalev and Lozhechnik have often been understood as denunciations, described as a "written communication to the authorities, voluntarily offered, that provides damaging information about another person."[68] A denunciation implies that individual A, driven by base motives, betrays individual B by passing on yet unknown information to the authorities that will ultimately harm person B. However, what one person perceives as a denunciation could be understood by another person as a way to seek justice for wrong that was done. Kovalev, for example, objected in his letter not just to what he perceived as the state's unjustified treatment of his father. Like Lozhechnik, he also turned to the authorities because he wanted punishment for acquaintances whom he believed guilty of wartime wrongdoing. In turn, the individuals that Kovalev and Lozhechnik reported on would certainly have thought of their letters as denunciations. Whether one defines a letter as a denunciation or as a rightful means to seek justice as one sees it, then, is in itself contingent on one's perspective.

Property Restitution

In addition to pursuing revenge privately, then, individuals also sought retribution through state channels, whether by informing and reporting, writing letters, or testifying in front of a commission, even in court. In doing so, some found that their individual notions of what constituted morally right punishment overlapped or were congruent with those of the Soviet regime. Yet while it was relatively easy to draw the attention of state officials, interaction with the authorities could be tricky: there were boundaries to what could be said and done, and investigations could backfire on those who initially set them in motion. Nowhere did this become more visible than in the ubiquitous property conflicts.

The death and displacement of hundreds of thousands of people—in particular, the region's Jews—and the destruction of houses as a result of military operations or German punitive actions meant that a lot of property—be it apartments, furniture, or clothes—passed through many different hands during the war. The appropriation of items, whether state or individually owned, began as soon as the local party leaders had fled their towns or districts. In Pinsk, Bobruisk, and many other towns in western and eastern Belarus, locals took advantage of the resulting power vacuum, ransacking shops and emptying private apartments.[69] Once the Wehrmacht arrived, German soldiers themselves looted private homes, stores, and warehouses, at times allowing locals to take what was left. After the mass executions of Jewish communities, the Germans usually took the best valuables for themselves and left the rest for their local representatives. Tables, chairs, and other furniture from Jewish houses were also frequently used to furnish the office of the city administrations. In some cases—as happened in Ushachi, south of Polotsk—local residents opened up mass graves to search for gold and other valuables.[70] In the countryside, much of the property that changed hands during the war was livestock: cows, horses, and pigs. German soldiers and local policemen regularly stole food and livestock from rural inhabitants. Those considered to be partisan families or partisan villages suffered the most. The Soviet partisans also took food and livestock by force: not every rural inhabitant was willing to give his or her only cow, on which people's families depended for survival, to the partisans. Since the partisans were armed, the boundary between the voluntary handing-over of food and livestock and its forceful acquisition was in any case blurred.[71]

Yet not every property acquisition during the war was accomplished through coercion. In a wartime economy in which locals depended heavily on trade with other locals but also with German soldiers, many items that were originally looted ended up being resold or swapped for others. The items that Jews in the ghettos traded with local non-Jews in exchange for food could also be bought there, making it impossible to trace the circumstances under which they were first acquired. Some locals simply moved into empty Jewish houses after their owners had been murdered, as Ol'ga Bembel-Dedok recalled from a conversation with an acquaintance in Minsk, who told her that their "house burned down and now we moved into an empty Jewish one."[72] The city administrations also put up Jewish houses for sale, as the administration of Mogilev did in the spring of 1942, thereby generating several tens of thousands of rubles for the occupation regime.[73]

Precisely because so many items had passed in various ways through many hands during the war, what belonged to whom was an inherently difficult and at the same time highly contentious question in the immediate postwar years. It was so not just because in a country ravaged by war, there existed a dire shortage of housing and livestock. Rather, it was a deeply personal and at the same time highly political question, given that it went to the heart of someone's wartime behavior. Why did you move into a new apartment during the war—because the Germans had burned down your house as punishment for ties to the partisans, or because the partisans had burned down your house as punishment for ties to the Germans? Or because a bomb had destroyed your house, and you simply needed a new place to stay? Property conflicts, moreover, were not limited to housing questions. How did you come to acquire new furniture and clothes? How did you come to own a cow during the war—did you take it from the collective farm after the Soviet state took it from you during the collectivization of agriculture in the 1930s? Or did you receive it from the Germans for services rendered to them? And if you bought it from someone, how did that person acquire it?

These questions inevitably arose when trying to solve postwar property conflicts, which is why we can read them as one of the ways in which individuals in Belarus grappled with the ghosts of war, people's wartime choices. Sorting them out was an inherently difficult task. Especially for Jewish survivors, it was very painful to find neighbors living in their houses or among their furniture—precisely because, as the recollections of Litman Mor show, it opened up the question to what extent these neighbors had benefited from the exclusion, expropriation, and killing of Jews—indeed, might even have personally taken part in their murder. In some cases, individuals tried to solve property issues privately, by asking those who were now in possession of their items to return them.[74] Some Soviet partisans took advantage of the power and high social status bestowed on them by the Soviet state (and derived from the rifles still worn around their shoulders) to more or less seize their property by force.[75] Others who knew that they wanted to leave the Soviet Union had no interest in reclaiming furniture.[76] Often, however, returning evacuees, Red Army soldiers, Holocaust survivors, or partisans turned to the state, asking the authorities to settle the question of ownership in their favor.[77] They could do so because even though the regime had abolished private property in land after the October Revolution and much housing and many businesses had been nationalized, ownership of small, single-family homes was not abrogated. Individual ownership of household items, furniture, clothes, or small farm animals also continued to exist. It was called "personal property" (*lichnaia sobstvennost'*) in contrast to "socialist property" owned by the state.[78] After the war, individuals could therefore appeal to the Soviet state to have their personal property returned to them, and they could appeal to have their prewar occupancy rights reinstated, even if the state formally owned the apartment.[79]

The regular courts (*narodnye sudy*) also presided over many property disputes. This is what happened to Zinaida Suvorova. When she tried to reclaim her mother's house in Orsha from a woman whose husband had left with the Wehrmacht, the woman responded by saying that the house was hers and that she wouldn't vacate it. She also threatened to kill Suvorova. When the case ended up in court, Zinaida Suvorova was declared the rightful owner. What may have helped was that the judge was a former partisan, a man by the name of Shugailo, whom Suvorova knew personally, and who had privately assured her not to worry, the house would be returned to her.[80] In other cases, some claimants wrote to party leaders, hoping their intervention would help them in court, even lead to a reversal of decisions. Matvei Zinkevich from Vileika in northwestern Belarus, for instance, appealed to Ponomarenko for support. During the war, Zinkevich had fought with the Red Army, while his family was in evacuation in Central Asia. In the summer of 1941, they had left their possessions with a neighbor who, as Zinkevich stressed, "did not defend the motherland but on the contrary worked for the Germans." On his return, he confronted his neighbor, but the latter refused to return the possessions. When the case went before the court, the judge did not decide in Zinkevich's favor. As the case would be heard again soon, Zinkevich implored Ponomarenko to support him, a "defender of the motherland," against someone who had "helped the fascists and undermined the Soviet Union, who did not come to the aid of his motherland."[81]

Referring to someone else's compromised wartime history in contrast to one's own impeccable record was, of course, a way to underscore the legitimacy of one's claim. Still, as Zinkevich's letter suggests, trying to have property returned was also a means to seek justice, to ensure that those who were accused of having taken advantage of the absence, displacement, or murder of other locals would not continue to benefit from it. Even if the larger question ("what did the people who now call our belongings theirs do during the war?") was not always voiced as explicitly as in Zinkevich's complaint to the authorities, it was implicitly ever present. At some point or other, in private or in court, war-related property conflicts inevitably had to bring up the question of someone's wartime behavior.

What added a layer of complexity to these conflicts was that their (attempted) settlement took place in the first tumultuous post-occupation months. After the German army had been driven from Belarus, local village and district authorities engaged in their own processes of retribution by taking livestock from families suspected of German-friendly attitudes and giving it to families who had supported the partisans.[82] These retribution processes, it seems, originated on the initiative of local officials—in particular, former Soviet partisans—and were only ex post facto authorized by regional or central authorities. In Oshmianskii district in Molodechno oblast, for example, the eleven members of the district executive committee decided to claim several cows for their families. One of the locals who had his or her cows taken away then lodged a complaint against the Oshmiany district executive committee. The Molodechno regional party committee consequently looked into the issue, but it established in September 1945 that the complaint was unjustified. Given that the eleven members of the Oshmiany district executive committee were all former Soviet partisans whose "families had especially suffered under German occupation," the men were allowed to keep the cows.[83]

As the case of Oshmianskii district shows, at times, personal and institutional means of seeking retribution did not only intersect and overlap but were also identical. Such fusion of the private and the official was best embodied in the figure of the former partisan-turned-Soviet official who used the formal power that his position bestowed on him to pursue justice for personal grievances or wrongdoing that he felt his family had suffered during the war. On a spectrum that ranged from illegal to legal property confiscation, these redistribution processes therefore occupied a middle ground. Just as common, though, were the practices located on both poles of the spectrum. While individuals whom Soviet courts convicted of wartime treason had their property officially confiscated, policemen and state security officers simply claimed valuable items or apartments for themselves. Often in an intoxicated state, they entered houses and took clothes, shoes, tobacco, or alcohol by force—from anyone who owned an item they desired, not just from those whom they deemed to have sympathized with the Germans.[84] As Ivan Vetrov, chief prosecutor of Belarus, wrote in a report to Ponomarenko in December 1944, such violations of socialist law "have taken on a widespread character, especially in the western oblasts" of the republic.[85] Officially, all property items that the state considered ownerless had to be collected by the local authorities. If not reclaimed in time, they became state property that could be sold. Informally, though, party-state representatives and state security officers kept items considered ownerless for themselves or sold them on the black market. One of the most spectacular cases was that of a man by the name of Karpenko, head of the Bobruisk city NKVD, whom the prosecutor's office accused of employing his staff solely to collect ownerless property without doing the required paperwork. In his office, Karpenko had stored several valuable couches, gramophones, records, cigar boxes, and much more. When the prosecutor's office decided to check on the warehouse in which ownerless property was supposed to be kept, Karpenko, as Vetrov wrote, "for two days was unable to find the worker in charge of the storage."[86]

For Red Army soldiers, returning evacuees, or Holocaust survivors, this meant that they not only found themselves writing letters to Minsk to reclaim their belongings from former neighbors. They also appealed to the leadership to have property returned that lower-level Soviet officials had claimed in the name of the state. Their efforts, however, often proved unsuccessful.[87] In the case of Jewish petitioners, the reason for that, it seems, had less to do with structural or individual antisemitism on part of individual officials in the housing department (although the latter cases also seem to have existed).[88] Rather, the question of property restitution was primarily an issue of social status and privilege: if a state security officer lived in one's prewar apartment or if the apartment was taken over by a party-state institution, it was practically impossible to have it returned, regardless of whether in the eyes of the authorities, the petitioner had proven his or her worth during the war. The same held true if a Red Army soldier or his (or her) family now lived in one's apartment. At the same time, Red Army soldiers, Soviet partisans, and their families—both Jewish and non-Jewish—who sought to have their prewar housing returned had much higher chances than someone who did not fight during the war.[89]

On a practical level, then, the return of Soviet power made the immediate question of ownership even more complicated than it already was. But the core of the problem lay elsewhere. When locals engaged the state, trying to use its apparatus to their advantage, they had no choice but to work with Soviet normative categories, with the authorities' notions of right and wrong wartime behavior. In consequence, it was, of course, impossible to seek justice for wartime wrongdoing believed to have been committed in the name of the Soviet state. A peasant could not complain to Minsk, for instance, that Soviet partisans had stolen his cow during the war. In doing so, he cast suspicion on himself: How come he had not given the cow voluntarily to the partisans? Did he not support Soviet power? Appealing to the authorities to reclaim property that people believed was unlawfully taken by local Soviet officials in the first post-occupation months was also dangerous. After all, investigations would ensue, which could backfire on those who had sought justice from the state. When F. Borisevich from Slutsk, a town to the south of Minsk, wrote a letter to Ponomarenko, complaining that NKVD officers had taken several of her possessions, among them money and clothes, the Slutsk authorities began to look into the issue. They found out that Borisevich's husband had been arrested in 1937 and sentenced to forced labor. During the war, Borisevich had shared a house with two local policemen, one of them her grandson, who stole from "partisan and Jewish families." In the spring of 1945, the Slutsk authorities concluded that she had acquired most of her possessions unlawfully during the war, and they decided to pass the case on to a court.[90]

Individuals who felt that Soviet power had done them an injustice therefore resorted to particular strategies to voice their problems: they wrote letters to party leaders in which they accused others of being German accomplices. Doing so was also a means to try to settle conflicts within local communities, often surrounding property issues, or between individuals and low-level officials.[91] According to Vitalii A. from Slonim, in the immediate postwar years, it was easy to get rid of someone against whom one held a grudge.[92] One way of doing so was to say that he or she helped the Germans—at least that is what, according to internal party reports, the former Red Army soldier Aleksei Vasil'ev had intended to do when he wrote to Ponomarenko in April 1946. In his letter, Vasil'ev criticized the head of his collective farm in Orshanskii district, Nikolai Visloukhov, for not letting him work on the collective farm. When he complained to the village council and the district executive committee, no one responded—but according to Vasil'ev, that was not surprising, given that the local system functioned on connections alone (*po blatu*) and Visloukhov's relatives worked in these institutions. In fact, one of them, Fedor Borozdnov, was a German "henchmen" who had somehow managed to obtain partisan documents for a half a liter of vodka. According to Vasil'ev, these were "people of un-Bolshevik, of fascist upbringing, the Soviet nation needs to punish them severely, and such people still work in the Soviet apparatus."[93]

In its report to Minsk, though, the Orsha district party committee dismissed the accusations as unfounded. Nikolai Visloukhov was a decorated veteran, and his father had already joined the partisans in the summer of 1942. Instead, the local authorities pointed out that Vasil'ev claimed the post of head of the collective farm for himself, but seeing as he was constantly drunk, had twice lost his party card, and thus had been excluded from the party, he ought not be given that job.[94] In a similar vein four years later, a group of villagers informed the MVD that a woman called Nadezhda Kulak had denounced partisans to the Germans. After investigations were conducted, however, the MVD concluded that the allegations were unfounded and that the real conflict lay elsewhere: Aleksandr Smolik, one of the villagers who reported Nadezhda Kulak, claimed that her horse belonged to him.[95]

As the examples of Aleksei Vasil'ev and Nadezhda Kulak's fellow villagers show, trying to use wartime enemy images (the German accomplice, the traitor) as rhetorical tools to try to settle personal conflicts or to seek punishment for what they perceived as unfair treatment at the hands of local officials remained a risky thing to do. People who in that way tried to play the system to their advantage did not always succeed. The Soviet authorities, in contrast, always benefited from the information they acquired. Letters like the one by F. Borisevich prompted the NKVD/MVD to start investigations, which in turn revealed information about her wartime doings that had so far been hidden from the state. Without her complaint, Borisevich might have been able to keep her compromised past concealed. Beyond providing clues and signals from the localities, there was also another, seemingly less evident yet all the more crucially important dimension to these letters: on a more abstract level, complaint letters to the regime acknowledged that the state alone had the means to settle the conflicts and issues brought forward by the authors. The importance that this affirmation of Soviet state authority had should not be underestimated—in particular, when considering how rapidly institutions in the western regions had collapsed in the summer of 1941. In that sense, and regardless of the author's intentions, each letter to the state contributed to the rebuilding of Soviet power in the aftermath of Nazi occupation. Unintentionally, then, confronting the past had a regime-stabilizing effect: instead of leading to the creation of more liberal, open spheres, it strengthened the mechanisms of power in this dictatorship.

Wartime Behavior, Postwar Belonging

Individuals in postwar Belarus sought justice and retribution in different ways, which included confronting neighbors with questions, committing revenge violence, or demanding the restitution of property. While some turned to the state for help, others chose nonstate channels, and still others opted for a combination of the two. In contrast to the Soviet authorities—who pursued the issue of someone's wartime behavior openly, with determination—in social encounters or private settings, people often posed the question of another person's actions less explicitly, behind his or her back. If they were the ones who had stayed in occupied territory, then they talked about their neighbor's actions, about who had served in the German police or had taken Jewish property. Former partisans would talk about their experiences in the forests fighting the Germans and local policemen, but unsurprisingly, people did not like to raise the question if they themselves had somehow become implicated in wrongdoing, not to speak of active misdeeds. Most confronted the ghosts of war only selectively and usually sought to avoid questions of personal guilt and responsibility altogether. Approaching people directly, asking them what had happened in a particular place during the war, appears above all to have been done by Holocaust survivors like Litman Mor, who had strong personal motivations to do so: he wanted to find out about the fate of loved ones, and he suspected that former neighbors or acquaintances had been complicit in German crimes. Above all, such efforts revealed just how fractured, divided, or destroyed the webs of individual relations were that had once constituted a social community. This also could have been the reason why people who had no immediate reason to doubt the stories that they heard from neighbors or family might have preferred not to press anyone on the issue.

Investigating, addressing, and evaluating someone else's wartime behavior was a highly personal process, contingent on a multitude of interacting factors, circumstances, and personal experiences. One's attitude toward the Soviet state as well as the ways in which the war had transformed it mattered greatly, yet so did a person's social relations from before the war, his or her wartime experiences, and the extent of individual suffering and loss. Consequently, the variety in personal responses to the aftermath of Nazi occupation cannot simply be attributed to differences between inhabitants of the part of Belarus that had been Soviet for more than two decades before the war and inhabitants of the part that had been annexed only in 1939. East/west differences certainly existed with regard to state policies and practices, given that the Sovietization of the regions that were annexed in 1939–1940 could be thoroughly carried out only after 1944. One would probably have assumed that these were also reflected in the personal ways in which inhabitants of Belarus responded to the aftermath of Nazi occupation: for example, that people from eastern Belarus were more likely to turn to the state than inhabitants of western Belarus or more likely to agree with the authorities' categories of right and wrong wartime behavior—and thus also more likely to find moral justice through the Soviet state. Given the lack of quantitative empirical data, this is, of course, impossible to rule out entirely. The local context was undoubtedly of great importance in each individual case. Still, I could not detect any clear east/west differences in the available source material. What is noteworthy here is not the existence but rather the absence of a pattern that one would have expected to see.

A general pattern that can be detected in people's personal responses to the aftermath of Nazi occupation, however, is that for many inhabitants of Belarus, wartime behavior and postwar belonging were intertwined issues. While state officials insisted that the war had been a moral test, individuals who lived under Nazi rule often argued that for the sake of survival, it had been necessary to make pragmatic choices—yet this did not mean that they had morally compromised themselves. As a result, civilians with direct experience of what it meant to negotiate life under the German authorities often had a much more complex and nuanced understanding of other people's choices than Soviet party-state representatives or others who spent the war in the rear. At the same time, there nevertheless existed much divergence on these issues, too, as the example of Ol'ga Bembel'-Dedok and her sister Anastasiia showed. Both sisters lived in Nazi-occupied territory, but when it came to judging the choice that their relative Igor' had apparently made (to escape the conditions of the German prisoner-of-war camps by working as a translator), they held diametrically opposed views: while Anastasiia was much more understanding of his choice, Ol'ga Bembel'-Dedok deeply resented Igor' for his actions and no longer deemed him worthy of being a member of their family.

In addition, people's understandings of postwar belonging were also informed by gendered perceptions of right and wrong wartime behavior. While able-bodied adult men who had lived under Nazi rule were generally expected to have joined the partisans, women who stayed in occupied territory were, as elsewhere in Europe, accused of "horizontal collaboration"—not just by the returning Soviet authorities, reevacuees, or others who experienced the war elsewhere but also by those who had experienced Nazi rule themselves. Regina Bakunovich, for example, was a child when the Germans occupied Minsk. On her street, German soldiers regularly went from house to house, asking the women if they could wash their clothes. Whether "washing clothes" was also a euphemism for prostitution is not clear from her recollections, yet regardless of the different kinds of contact between local women and German soldiers, "after the war, all the women who had provided services to the occupiers were indiscriminately called 'German mattresses' [*nemetskie podstilki*]. With ease and without empathy."[96] Her father was among those who applied that word to female neighbors or acquaintances: "In our house lived the Marchenko sisters, and even in my presence, my father did not scruple to call them 'mattresses.'"[97]

Although people's prejudices toward those who had lived in occupied territory did not always have to be articulated fully, biases nevertheless lingered in the background, with the potential to appear at any given moment, often during small, everyday social conflicts. As Asia L. remembered from her youth in postwar Belarus, "even in private conversations, when people were arguing or fighting, among themselves, they would say: 'well, you were under occupation [*ty byl pod okkupatsiei*].'" If a person wanted to cast doubt on someone else's character, all one had to do was add: "He is that kind of a person [*on takoi*], he was under occupation—and then and there, he was considered suspicious." Such comments, Asia L. recalled, could be heard often.[98]

Without a doubt, having lived in occupied territory carried a clear stigma in the postwar Soviet Union. Depending on the individual circumstances, this not only affected neighborly relations and career prospects but also shaped social dynamics of inclusion and exclusion. Social interactions and encounters, both in public and in private, therefore also showed that for many people, actual, alleged, or surmised wartime behavior and postwar belonging were intertwined issues—whether that meant belonging to a family, a local community, or the Soviet nation.

Chapter 6

Belarus, the Partisan Republic

Narrating the Years of War and Occupation

In 1964, Petr Kalinin, a member of the Central Committee in Minsk from 1940 to 1952, published a book on partisan warfare in Belarus during the Second World War.[1] As Kalinin wrote, "all attempts by the Hitlerite commanders to get the local population, prisoners of war, and the so-called 'volunteers' from Lithuania and Ukraine to join in the fight against the Belarusian partisans failed spectacularly."[2] Every Soviet citizen had stood firmly behind the partisans: "The partisan movement on the territory of Belarus resulted in an all people's war."[3] Indeed, it served as proof of the moral superiority of the Soviet people: It "elevated our people to such heights of moral spirit that only the Soviet people, the working people [*narod-truzhenik*], the heroic people [*narod-geroi*] could achieve."[4]

Kalinin had no personal knowledge of what it meant to be a partisan living in the forests, just as he had no personal knowledge of life as such in German-occupied territory. During the war, he had directed the Belarusian branch of the Soviet partisan movement, but he had done so from the safety of the Soviet rear. His book was unremarkable insofar as its main theme—that the partisan movement in Belarus had the full support of the local population—was hardly new. The republic's postwar leadership, headed by First Secretary Panteleimon Ponomarenko, had actively promoted this message from early in the war. Kalinin's book was also just one of many among the partisan and war memoir literature that began to proliferate in the early

1960s. What turned out to be significant about Kalinin's book, however, was its title, given that it cemented Belarus's place within the larger Soviet narrative of the war: *Partizanskaia respublika*, the "Partisan Republic."

This chapter examines the early beginnings of the Partisan Republic narrative—which entailed narrating the partisan movement, which in turn involved crafting an official image of the behavior and attitude of Belarus's population under German rule. By narration, I mean the process of giving shape to a story so that its plot appears structured and coherent. Within the Soviet representation of the war as an "all people's war" (*vsenarodnaia voina*), Belarus's specific contribution came to be the "all people's partisan war" (*vsenarodnaia partizanskaia voina*) that was made possible through the undivided support of the Belarusian people (*belaruski narod* in Belarusian, *belorusskii narod* in Russian). Both Moscow and Minsk maintained that with the exception of a few traitors who thereby had proven that they were never part of the Soviet nation, even in western Belarus, people stood firmly behind Soviet power. In that sense, narrating the years of war and occupation was also about the creation of a new linear story of Soviet Belarusian statehood—one that firmly united eastern and western Belarus under the banner of the "Partisan Republic."

Constructing and upholding an image of Belarus as the place where the "all people's partisan war" had been fought, however, produced its own set of internal contradictions, distortions, and omissions. As acts of public remembrance contributed to public silencing and forgetting, party leaders increasingly omitted Jewish and Polish inhabitants of Belarus from the official war memory—as resisters but also as victims, thereby revealing the mechanisms of inclusion and exclusion that underlay the postwar memory-making process. By presenting the Soviet partisan movement in Belarus as a mostly male, ethnic Belarusian or at best an East Slavic undertaking, the authorities also marginalized the contribution of female partisans. At the same time, even many ethnic Belarusians found that their actual experiences were not reflected in the state's narrative, which left no space to acknowledge that the relationship between Soviet partisans and civilians in occupied territory had been fragile, unequal, fraught with conflict, and at times antagonistic. This chapter identifies the many discrepancies that existed between official commemoration and private memories of the war, between postwar representation and actual wartime experience—and between the ways in which a small circle of high-ranking party members who had helped to direct the partisan movement from the Soviet rear styled themselves as partisans, while removing many rank-and-file partisans who had actually fought in the forests from local positions of power. Yet the chapter also demonstrates that Soviet official memory was not static—and that it was frequently contested. As the lobbying efforts by surviving members of the 1941–1942 Minsk underground show, it was possible to challenge parts of the official narrative while striving to be included in it. After two decades, the resistance organization went from being deemed the work of provocateurs and traitors to the heroic achievement of Soviet patriots. That such a radical reinterpretation became possible had largely to do with power shifts in the Politburo in Moscow, combined with personal rivalries and changes in the larger Soviet war narrative that became more personal and inclusive beginning in the late 1950s. However, this could not have occurred in the first place had it not been for the complaint letters and petitions that former underground members sent to the republican and central authorities. Investing in the war narrative, then, did not necessarily preclude diverging opinions, and within certain limits, people were able to test the boundaries of the narrative to see whether they could be stretched or altered.

The Partisan Republic

On May 9, 1945, the city of Minsk celebrated the Soviet victory over Nazi Germany. On that day, as *Sovetskaia Belorussiia* reported, flags were hanging from factories, state institutions, and private houses, while the portraits of Politburo members adorned the streets. At noon, seventy thousand people gathered on Lenin Square to hear party leaders give speeches. Vasilii Kozlov, first secretary of the Minsk regional party committee, opened the meeting by paying tribute to Stalin: "You are the pride of the people, you are the wisdom of the people, you are their conscience! . . . Glory to you, the great, wise father who led our country to victory!"[5] The party leaders of Belarus then highlighted the achievements of the Red Army and the Communist Party, but they also stressed the contributions to the war effort made by countless individuals in Belarus, partisans and civilians. While the depiction of the civilian population was cast in gender-neutral terms, the partisans were portrayed as an all-male force, thus erasing female partisans from the historical record. Panteleimon Ponomarenko concluded the meeting by emphasizing that "hundreds of thousands of glorious sons of the Belarusian people joined partisan units. . . . Millions of people from Belarus [*milliony belorusskogo naseleniia*] helped the Red Army and the partisans, with an inextinguishable faith in the quick defeat of the German aggressors and the resurrection of Soviet power."[6]

Whether in *Sovetskaia Belorussiia* or in regional and district newspapers, in Russian-language or Belarusian-language publications, such remarks on the

СОВЕТСКАЯ БЕЛОРУССИЯ

От всего сердца

Привет навсегда свободной Белоруссии!

Солнечный день Белоруссии

Примите наше рукопожатие

Смерть немецким оккупантам!

За нашу советскую Родину!

Будь благословенна, Беларусь!

Председателю Совета Народных Комиссаров БССР тов. Пономаренко

Председателю Президиума Верховного Совета БССР тов. Наталевичу

Секретарю Центрального Комитета КП(б) Белоруссии тов. Киселёву

Незабываемые дни

Цвети, Советская Белоруссия!

FIGURE 12. Celebrating the first anniversary of the liberation of Soviet Belarus on July 3, 1945. Soviet partisans greet Red Army soldiers underneath a flag that reads "Death to the German occupiers! For our Soviet motherland!" *Sovetskaia Belorussiia*, July 3, 1945. Courtesy of the National Library of Belarus.

mass participation and contribution of "ordinary" people to victory remained a standard feature in the Belarusian press, from the end of the war until the demise of the Soviet Union and beyond. Until limited de-Stalinization set in in the mid-1950s, Stalin's contribution to the victory always towered over everyone else's. Yet even in the late 1940s and early 1950s, ordinary people were not entirely erased from the war narrative.[7] In newspaper articles, their achievements were commonly mentioned in the bottom half of the text, after Stalin, the Communist Party, and subsequently the Red Army each had received praise. The image of the war as an "all people's war" continued to be used widely, as was the image of the war as an "all people's partisan war." Moreover, discussion of the partisans' feat was not limited to articles linked to specific war events like Victory Day on May 9 or the Liberation of Belarus on July 3. In addition to separate articles on the history of the partisan movement itself, it was, as a rule, included in articles on other major Soviet memorial days such as the Day of the Reunification of Belarus on September 17 (as the annexation of northeastern Poland in September 1939 was officially called) or the anniversary of the October Revolution on November 7.[8]

On September 16, 1945, for example, T. S. Gorbunov, the secretary of the Central Committee of Belarus who was in charge of propaganda, published a long article in *Sovetskaia Belorussiia*. The next day, September 17, he wrote, was a special day, the day on which the "Belarusian people, together with all people of the Soviet Union, celebrate the sixth anniversary of their reunification in a united Belarusian Soviet state." Liberated in 1939 from Poland's "Great Power colonial politics," from the yoke of the landowners and Polish nationalists, western Belarus came under German rule in 1941. "But the workers in the western regions, having experienced the joy of a free life under Soviet power, actively fought from the first day, and together with the entire Belarusian people, against the German-Fascist invaders."[9] Similarly, *Grodnenskaia pravda*, the main newspaper of Grodno oblast, celebrated the day with a tribute to Stalin as "the founder of the Belarusian state, the liberator of Belarus." Following his call, during the war, "the Belarusian people rose with arms in their hands to defend their motherland." In the villages of Karpovtsy, Novoselki, and others in Volkovysskii district, "the best people went to the forests" and the remaining population, children and grown-ups, did everything they could to support the "people's avengers."[10] The partisan movement thus not only reflected the unity of the Belarusian people but also demonstrated the profound commitment of the population of western Belarus to the Soviet Union.

The image of Belarus as the heart of the Soviet partisan movement, as the place where the population had risen in a joint effort against the Germans was also disseminated beyond the borders of the republic. An article published on January 2, 1949, in *Pravda*, which celebrated the thirtieth anniversary of the founding of Soviet Belarus in 1919, highlighted that "the all people's partisan war, which developed on Belarusian soil temporarily occupied by the enemy, represented a significant contribution to the common cause of defeating the horde of German-Fascist robbers."[11] The same applied to the memoir literature. One of the first books on the partisan movement, published in 1949 by none other than Lavrentii Tsanava, by then head of the MGB in Belarus, stressed that "the partisans of Belarus, led by the Bolshevik party, gained the universal love of the people." In mid-1942, the transformation of the movement into an all people's war had required the creation of a central agency, the Central Staff of the Partisan Movement, that had coordinated the partisans from the rear.[12] This leadership, Tsanava claimed, "made it possible to involve broad sections of the population" in occupied territory in the fight against the Germans.[13]

Within the official Soviet image of the war as an all people's war, then, Belarus's specific contribution came to be the all people's partisan war that had been made possible through the undivided support of the Belarusian

Да здравствует воссоединенный белорусский народ!

Пролетарии всех стран, соединяйтесь!
Коммунистическая партия (большевиков) Белоруссии.

СОВЕТСКАЯ БЕЛОРУССИЯ

ОРГАН ЦК КП(б) БЕЛОРУССИИ, СОВНАРКОМА И ПРЕЗИДИУМА ВЕРХОВНОГО СОВЕТА БССР

№ 177 (1082) Воскресенье 16 сентября 1945 г.

Цена 20 коп.

17 сентября 1945 года исполняется шестая годовщина воссоединения белорусского народа.

Слава создателю Белорусского Советского Государства, великому вождю и учителю Генералиссимусу Сталину!

Великий праздник

FIGURE 13. A Red Army soldier, a young woman, and a peasant in traditional Belarusian dress hold up a flag with an image of Stalin to celebrate the sixth anniversary of the Day of the Reunification of the Belarusian People. *Sovetskaia Belorussiia*, September 16, 1945. Courtesy of the National Library of Belarus.

people—not just in the old part of the republic but, as Minsk and Moscow maintained, also in the regions that had only been annexed from Poland in 1939. This narrative, actively promoted by Ponomarenko during the war, remained present in Soviet rhetoric throughout the postwar decades. From the 1960s on, it was modified and became more personal and individualized, but the central message remained the same. The shift toward the personal was the result of changes within the larger Soviet war narrative following the death of Stalin in 1953. With Nikita Khrushchev's speech at the Twentieth Party Congress in 1956, the party leaders initiated a tortuous and often contradictory process of rethinking the Stalinist past. This process involved a reappraisal of Stalin's role in the war, and it shifted the war narrative's main focus to the Soviet people, thus encouraging a more inclusive interpretation of the victory.[14] For Belarus, this meant that instead of general references to the Belarusian people as a whole, newspapers now began to single out select "ordinary" individuals for their specific deeds during the war. In 1960, *Sovetskaia Belorussiia* began to publish a new series titled "The People Remember" ("Narod pomnit"). Most of the articles were concerned with the Second World War and with the selfless and heroic, yet always pro-motherland and pro-Soviet, acts of individual locals or groups. In August 1960, for instance, "The People Remember" told of a girl from Belarus who had helped partisans and individuals who had escaped from German camps, for which the Germans killed her in 1943.[15] In December 1960, the series focused on the story of a peasant couple who had saved the daughter of a communist during the war, and the mother of a partisan who was shot by the Germans was remembered for her sacrifice, while a "Narod pomnit" article in May 1961 described how a woman had saved a young partisan.[16] Such accounts gave a face, or rather individual faces, to the victory. In doing so, they made it possible for people to identify with the ordinary heroes singled out in "The People Remember," with people who could have been their neighbors or fellow villagers. As part of the shift toward a more personal narration of the war, party leaders in Moscow also encouraged the publication of memoirs from Red Army soldiers and partisans. More and more personal accounts began to appear from the early 1960s on, of which Petr Kalinin's memoir *Partizanskaia respublika* was just one. It was, however, an important one, given that it assigned Belarus a special and unique name: the Partisan Republic.[17]

Remembering, Silencing, and Distorting

Constructing an image of Belarus's population as having stood firmly behind the Soviet partisans, however, did come with its own set of internal contradictions, omissions, and distortions of the historical record. One problem was that it was unclear just who "the people" in the "all people's partisan war" were. At the heart of the issue was the term *narod*, and the fact that it, just like *the people* in English or *das Volk* in German, carried more than one meaning. In the Soviet Union, it was clear who the "Soviet people" (*sovetskii narod*) were: those who held Soviet citizenship. Yet just like *russkii narod* or any other combination of *narod* and an adjective that referred to one of the Soviet nationalities (what today would be called ethnicities), *belorusskii* (or *belaruski*) *narod* allowed for more than one interpretation. Depending on the context, it could potentially mean everyone who was a resident of Belarus, regardless of the nationality that Soviet citizens had inscribed in their passports. Yet it also stood for those whom the Soviet state considered to be Belarusians by nationality (ethnic Belarusians). It was therefore only logical that the all people's war narrative reflected this linguistic ambiguity. If left without further specifications, it conveyed inclusiveness, but the multiple meanings inherent to *narod* meant that the audience could interpret it in different ways. Political leaders like Ponomarenko, however, repeatedly used *belorusskii narod* in a way that conveyed a clear ethnic connotation. In his July 22, 1941, article in *Pravda* on the inception of the partisan movement, for example, Ponomarenko stressed the "bravery of the Belarusian people" (*muzhestvo belorusskogo naroda*). As he wrote, "the Belarusian people [*belorusski narod*] have witnessed more than one invader in the course of the century, but never have these [invaders] been able to overpower these people [*narod*], a people who always held the closest ties and kinship [*rodstvo*] to the brotherly Russian and Ukrainian people. . . . And now the entire Belarusian people rose to fight for the defense of their native soil, motherland, their property, their wives, mothers, and children."[18] That Ponomarenko understood "Belarusian people" in an ethnic sense becomes clear through his reference to kinship, to the shared ancestry of the three Eastern Slavs. This view was even more pronounced in a speech that he gave in March 1945 before the Central Committee of the Belarusian Komsomol, when he declared that "the Belarusian people [*belorusskii narod*] have a heroic past. They stem from the Kievan Rus', from which three people emerged: Russian, Ukrainian, and Belarusian."[19]

What were the implications of this? Precisely because a party leader like Ponomarenko, both in public and in internal party speeches, used *belorusskii narod* in such a way that it carried a clear ethno-national meaning, his audience could interpret the "all people's partisan war" as the sole achievement of ethnic Belarusians. According to data compiled by the Belarusian Staff of the Partisan Movement in January 1946, of the 281,007 partisans who between 1941 and 1944 were active on Belarusian territory (not counting the additional 79,484 partisans for whom no further information exists), 71 percent were ethnic Belarusians ("Belarusians by nationality").[20] Still, the 30 percent non-ethnic Belarusian partisans—Russians, Ukrainians, Jews, Poles, and others—vanished from the picture, just as the diversity of Belarus's population vanished from the war narrative.[21] Moreover, in newspaper articles, the war behind the front was usually not only coined the "partisan war of the Belarusian people" (*partizanskaia voina belorusskogo naroda*) or the "struggle of the Belarusian people" (*bor'ba belorusskogo naroda*). The partisans active on Belarusian territory were also often simply called "Belarusian partisans" (*belorusskie partizany*).[22] On October 24, 1944, for example, *Sovetskaia Belorussiia* announced the opening of an exhibition titled *The Weapons of the Belarusian Partisans* (Vooruzhenie belorusskikh partizan) in the Museum of the History of the Great Patriotic War, which had recently been opened in Minsk. Given the ethnic-national connotation of the adjective "Belarusian," the exhibition's title suggested that the partisans had been exclusively ethnic Belarusians.[23]

Ultimately, the ambiguities inherent in the notion of *narod* left it up to the newspaper readers to interpret it in an inclusive, nonethnic sense or in a more exclusive, ethnic sense. Ponomarenko (who was neither ethnically Belarusian nor born in Belarus), though, clearly understood *belorusskii narod* in a more exclusive, ethnic sense. In doing so, he implied that the partisan war against the German forces had been the sole achievement of ethnic Belarusians. What is more, he also spoke about the murder of Belarus's Jewish communities in a way that made it possible to interpret his words to mean that instead of Jews, ethnic Belarusians had been killed.

On May 17, 1942, Ponomarenko published an article in *Krasnaia zvezda*, the main newspaper of the People's Commissariat of the Armed Forces. "Never before in its entire national history," wrote Ponomarenko, "have the Belarusian people [*belorusskii narod*] been exposed to such massive danger as is currently the case. Being under the German-Fascist yoke means for the Belarusian people not just the loss of any freedom and national self-determination, not just a poverty-stricken, half-starved, servile existence, but its outright physical extermination. At stake here is, in the full sense of the word, the life or death of the nation [*Rech' idet v polnom smysle etogo slova o zhizni ili smerti natsii*]."[24] Ponomarenko then gave examples of the extermination of the Belarusian people from towns in eastern Belarus:

> In the town of Petrikovo, the Germans shot the majority of women, while the children were thrown alive into the river. In El'sk, the

> Germans put more than five hundred women and children on a boat and for six days drove the hungry ones along the river Pripyat, then drowned them. In Surazh, the Germans forced seven hundred people into a mine-studded ravine. Those who escaped after the explosion of the mines were shot by the Germans with machine guns. In Shklov, the Germans shot six thousand men and women. The children were thrown alive into the pit together with their murdered parents and covered with soil. For three days, the earth moved on the grave—the children who were buried alive died in horrible agony. Such mass executions were carried out by the occupiers in Minsk, Vitebsk, Orsha, Liozno, Cherven', Glusk, Slutsk, Bykhov, Beshenkovichi, Bobruisk, Polotsk, Lel'chitsy, and other towns and rural communities in Belarus.[25]

Concluding his list of examples, Ponomarenko wrote that in total, "the Germans tortured, shot, strung up, and burned alive more than 700,000 inhabitants of Belarus [*zhiteli Belorussii*]."[26] Alongside "Belarusian people," Ponomarenko thus also used the more neutral term "inhabitants of Belarus." Still, he failed to mention that all of the examples of the physical extermination of the Belarusian people that he provided were examples not of mass executions of ethnic Belarusians but of mass executions of Jews.[27] Although non-Jewish civilians were also among the early victims of German violence, it was only in the spring of 1942 that the number of non-Jewish victims grew, once German forces began to systematically burn down entire rural districts during their antipartisan operations. Moreover, the examples that Ponomarenko provided were not of villages but of towns, the sites of the mass murder of Jews. Ponomarenko knew this well from early wartime reports by Soviet officials and state security officers who personally experienced the situation in occupied territory. Their accounts provided detailed information on the behavior of the German occupation regime toward the local population, including references to the torture and killings of Jews.[28] In his December 1941 report on what he had witnessed in El'skii district in Poles'e oblast, the NKVD officer Vasilii Zasukhin captured the situation in eastern Belarus in the fall of 1941 in one sentence: "The Jewish population is being annihilated in its entirety."[29] Indeed, already on August 19, 1941, Ponomarenko himself had sent a report to Stalin on the situation in occupied Belarus: "The Jewish population," he wrote, "is subjected to merciless extermination."[30]

To put the different pieces together, when writing in May 1942 about Belarus that "the life or death of the nation" was at stake, Ponomarenko knew that the specific examples provided to underline his point were examples of mass executions of Jews, yet he did not mention this. This was not unusual. Soviet wartime media often concealed that the Germans were deliberately killing Jews and thereby universalized Nazi victims, although a few articles mentioning the execution of Jews were also published during the war. The Holocaust was not entirely omitted from Soviet media, but it was carefully circumscribed and clearly marginalized.[31] In that sense, Ponomarenko's *Krasnaia zvezda* article could be interpreted as yet another example of many that concealed the special plight of Jews under Nazi occupation. Still, the article receives a different twist if we consider that Ponomarenko had previously both publicly and internally spoken about *belorusskii narod* as an ethno-national concept. Seen in this light, Ponomarenko's comments suggested that in El'sk, Shklov, and Surazh, the German forces had not so much killed unidentified Soviet citizens but rather ethnic Belarusians. Moreover, knowing that Ponomarenko had previously implied that the partisan war was the achievement of ethnic Belarusians, it would be implausible to argue that all of this was done unintentionally. Instead, Ponomarenko appears to have deliberately played with the ambiguous meaning of *belorusskii narod*, thus excluding Jews as both victims and heroes from the official narrative, even early in the war.

What accounted for this behavior? Karel C. Berkhoff has suggested that antisemitism both within the Central Committee in Moscow and as a mindset among Soviet citizens partly explained the highly selective wartime reporting about the Holocaust in the Soviet media.[32] To motivate the mostly Slavic soldiers, it may have seemed more useful to Stalin and other leading communists to make it appear as if Slavic people were the primary victims of German occupation, or at least not to highlight the fact that proportionally, Jews suffered most of all population groups. Ponomarenko's personal bias toward Jews and Poles, possibly even antipathy toward them, probably also played a role. When Hersh Smolar, who during the war had been one of the leaders of the communist-led underground organization inside the Minsk ghetto, returned to the city in 1944 and sought an encounter with Ponomarenko, he found the first secretary unsympathetic to the plight of former Jewish partisans and outright suspicious of Jewish nationalism. Smolar had initiated the meeting together with fellow Jewish partisans to alert Ponomarenko to the dire material circumstances in which these individuals lived (which were exacerbated by the fact that most of them did not have surviving family members who could support them). When Smolar was finally granted a meeting with Ponomarenko, the first secretary accused him of kindling Jewish nationalism and warned him that strict measures would be taken against it. To Smolar's remark that Hitler had pronounced a death sentence on all Jews, Ponomarenko responded that it would be better to contribute to the building of socialism.[33] As handwritten notes among his personal archival files attest, Ponomarenko believed that the low percentage of Jews and ethnic Poles within the partisan movement in Belarus resulted from their lack of Soviet patriotism—which led him to conclude that, as he wrote in response to an August 1946 draft copy on the ethnic composition of the partisan movement in Belarus, "Poles and Jews did not take an active part in the partisan movement."[34]

The process of omitting Jews as both victims and fighters from the official war narrative continued in the immediate postwar years, although exclusion was not yet total. On May 8, 1945, under the headline "We Won't Forget, We Won't Forgive," *Sovetskaia Belorussiia* informed its readers in several articles about a new exhibition that had opened in the Museum of the History of the Great Patriotic War in Minsk.[35] The exhibition focused on the atrocities that the Germans had committed in occupied Belarus. One of the articles—written by S. Levina, who was part of the museum's young (and mostly female) academic staff—described the life and death of Jews in the Minsk ghetto, explaining how the Germans had forced the city's Jewish population into a ghetto and then proceeded to murder them in waves.[36] The history of the Minsk ghetto was also featured in the museum itself.[37] As elsewhere throughout the formerly German-occupied territories, Jewish survivors in Belarus were able to erect several small memorials, including one in Minsk in 1946, to the memory of the Jewish victims who were killed by the Nazi regime. That the local authorities in Belarus permitted these memorials, yet at the same time rejected similar Jewish monuments in other towns, shows that a centralized policy on Jewish postwar memorial activities did not exist during this time.[38] In 1948, Hersh Smolar's memoir on the communist-led underground in the Minsk ghetto, which had appeared two years earlier in Yiddish, was translated into Russian and published by the state-owned publishing house Der Emes.[39]

With the onset of state-sponsored antisemitism in the late 1940s, however, partial exclusion and limited official remembering of the murder of Belarus's Jewish communities changed to overt exclusion and silencing. At the end of April 1948, the Central Committee in Minsk sent a special party commission to the city's Museum of the History of the Great Patriotic War. After its review of the museum, the committee concluded that the exhibition placed too little emphasis on the role of Stalin and the Red Army and too much emphasis on people's experience of Nazi occupation. The curators were subsequently forced to remove those parts of the exhibition that dealt with the Minsk ghetto, and members of the museum's academic staff who had lived under German rule or had suffered prewar Soviet political repression were released from their posts.[40] Initially, it seemed as if Jewish partisans would constitute an exception to the omission of Jews from the larger Soviet war narrative. In 1949, when Nachum Alpert was looking for a publisher for his book on the destruction of the Jewish community of Slonim, the editor of the Soviet Yiddish journal *Heymland* explained to Alpert that "they were no longer permitted to put out anything on the 'ghetto' theme, since they had already published books about the ghettos" in Vilnius, Kaunas, Minsk, and Warsaw. However, they could publish the second part of his book titled "In the Forest" because "so far they still had permission to publish material about the Jewish partisans."[41] The editor turned out to be mistaken. Alpert's account was never allowed into print, just as the book *Partisan Friendship* (Partizanskaia druzhba), which was compiled by the Soviet Jewish Anti-Fascist Committee and described Jewish contributions to the partisan movement, was halted after the destruction of the committee in November 1948.[42]

The omission of Jews from the partisan narrative continued in the next decades, even after the war narrative began to place greater emphasis on the achievements and sufferings of "ordinary" Soviet people following Khrushchev's 1956 Secret Speech. In his 1968 version of his book *Partizanskaia respublika,* Petr Kalinin remarked on the ethnic composition of the movement that—apart from Belarusians—the units were composed of "more than fifty thousand Russians, thousands of Ukrainians, Latvians, Lithuanians, Estonians, Georgians, Armenians, Azeris, and representatives of other nationalities of our great motherland."[43] Kalinin even singled out twenty-five German, eight Austrian, six Yugoslav, and two Hungarian citizens who had received awards for fighting with the partisans. Yet he did not make any mention of Jews, even though being Jewish counted as a nationality in the Soviet Union, and even though the number of Jews in partisan units in Belarus was higher than the numbers of any of the Baltic or Caucasian nationalities.[44] Poles—after Belarusians, Russians, Ukrainians, and Jews the fifth largest ethnic group within the partisan movement in Belarus—were not entirely forgotten in Kalinin's account. However, he did not include them among the list of Soviet nationalities that had fought as partisans in Belarus but rather made it seem as if they had done so solely as non-Soviet citizens.[45] Similarly, in his 1986 book on the partisan movement in Belarus, Ponomarenko wrote that the largest group within the partisan movement had been Belarusians, followed by Russians and Ukrainians. However, he failed to mention that there had been others as well.[46] The partisan movement had become a male and an East Slavic (yet primarily Belarusian) achievement.

Living with the Unspeakable

Apart from increasingly omitting Jews and Poles from Belarus's war narrative as both fighters and victims, the postwar reality was such that many people's actual wartime encounters with the partisans did not fit into the one-dimensional, exclusively positive story that the Soviet authorities presented. If there was one experience that was shared widely by the majority of rural civilians in occupied territory, it was that of partisans coming and taking food, clothes, and livestock. This was, in many ways, inevitable: living in earth dugouts in the forests and changing locations whenever local police or Germans came too close, these men and women did not have the means to keep their own livestock or grow their own produce. All the while, the Wehrmacht was supposed to feed itself off the land, and although the occupation regime imposed strict grain delivery quotas on the villages, German soldiers often simply robbed locals of food and livestock. During the day, the Germans and local policemen raided the villages; at night, the partisans did so. As excerpts of letters by local civilians show, the villagers, who were struggling to feed their families, suffered from the demands from both sides.

In August 1944, the NKGB intercepted a letter by a man by the name of Slovinskii, who lived in the village of Rotan' in Krupskii district, located halfway between Minsk and Vitebsk. He wrote: "The partisans plundered all the people [*ves' narod*]. From us they took the cow, swine, lambs, and all clothes; they even took them from our bodies."[47] Slovinskii was not the only one who wrote about the partisans in this way; indeed, several letters that the NKGB intercepted that month alone in Minsk oblast told of such incidents. V. Belous, a resident of Kopyl'skii district southwest of Minsk, wrote: "For three years, we took it from the Germans [*ot nemtsev dostavalos'*] and from ours [*ot svoikh*]; there were cases when the partisans put [someone] against the wall and shot [that person]. Not to say anything about [them] taking men's clothes, women's clothes, everything that fell into [their] hands." Commenting on the situation in the recently liberated region, he continued: "Right now, things are also bad: the partisans stole four sheep, the Germans took away one, and only one cow remained, all bread was taken for the collective farm, and I don't know what will happen further, maybe they take away the last cow, well alright may they take it if there is a law for that."[48]

Similarly, M. Birilo, who lived in the village of Dobrynovo in Dzerzhinskii district to the west of Minsk, wrote about how he and his mother managed to keep the partisans from taking their horse. "Every night, the partisans bothered mother: 'Give us a cow, everything,' so mother took off through the window, and I rode the horse every night and returned in the morning, as if I were going to work on the field."[49] According to Birilo, after the German occupation was over, the partisans continued to harass locals, now in their capacity as party-state officials: "Now these bloodsuckers, bandits, criminals are sent to the front and put in the district party committee with the authorities [*u vlasti*]." Van'ka Komarovskii, a former partisan, was working in the district party committee, while "Lidka Mikhalkova [was] the head of the rural council, Stopka Shabalinskii—the head of the collective farm. These days, they are pulling everybody into the collective farm [*vsekh stiagivaiut v kolkhoz*]."[50]

The NKGB passed the excerpts from Slovinskii, Belous, and Birilo's intercepted letters on to Comrade Kozlov, first secretary of the Minsk regional party committee. One can reasonably assume that reading about people's negative descriptions of Soviet partisans only increased the suspicion that party leaders harbored toward civilians who had stayed in occupied territory. But the discrepancies that existed between the official narrative of the war—according to which peasants had willingly provided the partisans with their last pieces of food—and villagers' personal memories of partisans raiding their villages for food or moonshine could not be acknowledged by the Soviet authorities after the war, certainly not publicly but also no longer internally. For decades after the war, partisan misconduct and violence toward civilians remained a political taboo. While stories were, as the letters show, shared within families or among neighbors and friends in private settings, it was impossible to voice them in more public settings for fear of attracting the attention of the authorities. For those who had suffered from partisan violence, it must have been very difficult to see former partisans celebrated as heroes and avengers of the people, thereby prolonging or deepening the feeling of powerlessness that they had experienced during the war when faced with demands from the partisans.

With the onset of perestroika in the mid-1980s, the boundaries of what was permissible to say expanded. After the dissolution of the Soviet Union, historians, politicians, and public intellectuals in newly independent Belarus began to engage in a public reassessment of the republic's history, including a modest reappraisal of the partisan movement. For the first time, a ninth-grade textbook included a few references to robberies and violence committed by partisans against the local population. With the election of Aleksandr

Lukashenko as president in 1994 (since then, he has been the authoritarian ruler of Belarus), however, these references were omitted from the textbook.[51] With some modifications—slightly more nationalistic and with an altogether more negative assessment of Lithuanians and Ukrainians—the Soviet version of the "all people's partisan war" continues to be taught in schools and universities throughout Belarus today. While dissenting voices exist, mostly articulated through alternative print and online media outlets, the official media, politicians, and historiographical mainstream depict the partisan-civilian relationship in an exclusively positive way.[52] According to a popular history textbook, issued under the auspices of the National Academy of Sciences, that advanced university students would consult, "the partisan war . . . represented a deep manifestation of the people's patriotism. . . . Despite the brutality of the occupation regime, the Belarusian people did not fall on their knees, did not submit to the enemy. Belarus soon transformed into one united fighting camp."[53]

How individuals in postwar Soviet Belarus who experienced threats or violence at the hands of Soviet partisans dealt with these discrepancies between official and personal memory and perhaps even tried to make sense of them is a difficult question. In a state where nonparticipation in the official narrative would have carried high costs, people on the whole conformed to what was expected of them: they participated in the official victory celebrations, gave the right kind of answers on high school or university history exams, or attended lectures in factories without outwardly objecting to the content of the war narrative. While some whose own wartime experiences conflicted with the official version probably continued to live with unresolved resentment, others may have tried to suppress it. Some may have agreed to say and do certain things in line with the official version of the war because they saw it as a means to social advancement, while for others it ensured inclusion in Soviet society and its projected unity, something that individuals may have found comforting after the divisions of the war. Yet others may have selectively appropriated some aspects of the war narrative while secretly objecting to other parts. After all, the "all people's war" assigned a meaning and purpose to the death and destruction brought about by war and occupation. For families who had encountered partisan violence in occupied territory, yet also lost a son or father fighting at the front, for example, receiving official state recognition of their loss may have helped them in their grief. Seen in that light, taking part in the Victory Day celebrations on May 9 each year could, from the outside, be interpreted as an act of concurring with the regime's version of the war. On the inside, however, an individual could primarily think of May 9 as a day to honor the dead and mourn the loss of loved ones, regardless of how he or she related to Soviet power. Perhaps this is also what Svetlana Alexievich had in mind when, traveling through the Belarusian and Russian countryside in the late 1970s and early 1980s, she observed that "in our villages on Victory Day there is weeping, not rejoicing. Many weep. They grieve."[54]

Lastly, one way in which individuals may have been able to accommodate their own wartime experiences with the official narrative has been suggested by fieldwork that the historian Ales' Smalianchuk conducted in the region around Slonim in western Belarus and in the region around Mogilev in eastern Belarus. In his interviews with rural residents, he detected two dichotomies in his respondents' memory of the partisans operating in their area. For one, both in the east and the west, locals drew a sharp distinction between partisans that they considered "one's own" or "ours" (*svoi, nashi*) and those that they thought of as "strangers" (*chuzhie*). *Svoi* and *nashi* were local men or boys who had either voluntarily joined the partisans or had been forcefully mobilized—that is, who had received a summons from the nearest partisan unit and had to fear violence if they did not comply. While *svoi* and *nashi* were familiar to locals, known to them as sons, husbands, cousins, or fellow villagers, *chuzhie* were strangers, whether they hailed from another region or from other Soviet republics.[55] In addition to the "ours-strangers" distinction, Smalianchuk detected a second dichotomy. Both in eastern and western Belarus, his respondents repeatedly differentiated between "bandits" or "hooligans," on one hand, and real "partisans," on the other. *Bandity* were the ones who had taken food from locals without asking, whereas the *partizany* had asked for food. Yet not every "stranger" was a "bandit," while "ours" [*svoi, nashi*], in turn, were also often considered "bandits" and "hooligans."[56] In interviews that Volia Shamalava conducted from 2002 to 2007 in different villages in Brest, Grodno, Gomel', Minsk, Mogilev, and Vitebsk oblasts, the respondents also drew a distinction between "partisans" and "bandits."[57]

It is impossible to know, of course, whether this is how the interviewees thought of partisans during the war, or whether they only drew the distinction later. However, the interview with Yurii Taits that a member of the Commission of the Great Patriotic War, an oral history project run by Isaak Mints of the USSR Academy of Sciences, conducted in August 1944, suggests that such images already circulated during the war. Taits was a Jewish doctor from Minsk and a member of the Minsk ghetto underground organization. In November 1942, he escaped from the ghetto and joined partisans in the nearby forests. As he recalled, in the first year of the war, the city's Jewish population was initially reluctant to flee to the forests. Some who tried were caught and killed by partisans, which is why "the impression arose that

Jews should not go to the partisans, because the same was awaiting them there as in the ghetto." According to Taits, the problem was that among the first partisan units "there were truly patriotic partisans [*nastoiashchie patrioty-partizany*] and there were bandits." The latter group, which he subsequently also called "partisan-bandits" (*partizany-bandity*), were the ones who bore responsibility for the killings.[58]

It is conceivable, then, that differentiating between "partisans" and "bandits" was an attempt to reconcile the seemingly irreconcilable, a coping mechanism for people to make sense of the violence of the war. Threats or violence against civilians, in that mode of thought, were committed only by bandits—that is, by people who formally may have belonged to the partisan movement yet in the eyes of civilians were not deserving of the name because of their behavior. "Real" partisans were people who did not commit violence against civilians—and thus were worthy of recognition and praise. Given that the official war narrative commemorated only the feats of the "real" partisans, it would have been possible to at once publicly honor these men while rationalizing abuse experienced at the hands of other partisans as acts of people who were not real partisans but bandits, and thus not part of the "all people's partisan war" narrative. Bandits existed, from this viewpoint, but they stood outside the postwar community of heroes.

Cadres and Partisans

For the leadership of postwar Belarus, narrating the years of war and occupation entailed narrating the partisan movement, which in turn entailed crafting an official image of the behavior and attitude of Belarus's population under German rule: a population that, with the exception of a few traitors, stood united behind the Soviet partisans—in the old, eastern part of the republic but also in its new, western half. Sanitized of the moral gray zones of occupation and of the fraught relationship between partisans and civilians, and increasingly ethnicized in terms of both heroes and victims of the war (with Jews and Poles excluded from the narrative), the "all people's partisan war" assigned Belarus a special place within the larger Soviet narrative of the Second World War.

Given the centrality of the partisan image to Belarus's postwar statehood, one might think that former partisans also constituted the institutional backbone of its postwar party-state apparatus; in other words, that many officials had fought as partisans during the war.[59] That, however, was only partly the case. On the levels of the republic and regional leadership, many key figures were indeed linked to the partisan movement. In addition to First

Secretary Panteleimon Ponomarenko, who had headed the Central Staff of the Partisan Movement, this category included Lavrentii Tsanava, the head of the NKGB and subsequently MGB in Belarus until 1951, who had served as Ponomarenko's deputy during the war. Sergei Bel'chenko, who headed the NKVD and subsequently MVD in Belarus until 1953, had likewise served as deputy to Ponomarenko during the war.[60] In the immediate postwar years, then, the three most important men in Belarus had held important leadership positions within the Soviet partisan movement. Other former partisans included Petr Kalinin, head of the Belarusian branch of the partisan movement during the war, who from 1944 to 1948 served as first secretary of the Grodno regional party committee. In 1948, Kalinin moved to Minsk where he became deputy to the head of the Belarusian Council of Ministers, a post that at the time was held by Ponomarenko.[61]

In 1947, Moscow dismissed Ponomarenko from his position as first secretary (although not yet as head of the Council of Ministers) and replaced him with Nikolai Gusarov. Gusarov had spent most of his party career to that point in Perm' oblast, in the foothills of the Ural Mountains, and had neither been connected to the partisan movement nor more generally to Belarus. Decades later, Ponomarenko still held a grudge against Gusarov because the latter supposedly wanted to remove many former partisans from the party-state apparatus, deeming them unqualified for the job and claiming that they had gotten there only through personal connections. However, according to Ponomarenko, Gusarov failed to implement these changes.[62] In 1950, Moscow removed Gusarov as first secretary and replaced him with Nikolai Patolichev, who, like Gusarov, was a newcomer to Belarus and had no ties to the partisan movement. It was only in 1956, when Patolichev was replaced with Kirill Mazurov, that a former member of the Soviet partisan movement again ascended to the top post. As head of the Belarusian Komsomol since 1942, during the war, Mazurov was responsible for the organization of Komsomol underground activities in occupied territory and as such a representative of the partisan movement. He became a member of the Central Committee of Belarus in 1947, and from 1950 to 1953, he served as first secretary of the Minsk regional party committee, the most important regional leadership position in Belarus.[63] Mazurov, in turn, was succeeded by Petr Masherov, who had commanded a Soviet partisan unit in Belarus. In the immediate postwar years, Masherov held various party-state positions, steadily rising through the ranks. From 1955 on, he was first secretary of the Brest regional party committee, and in 1959 joined the Central Committee of the Communist Party of Belarus. Three years later, he was appointed second secretary of the Central Committee, and in 1965 he took over the leadership, a post that he held until his death in a car accident in 1980.[64] As Mazurov and Masherov ascended to power, their protégées, party members who were connected to them in patron-client relationships through their shared wartime experiences, also climbed up the ladder, taking up important positions within the Soviet party-state.[65]

Power in postwar Belarus, it seems, was firmly in the hands of former partisans. Yet although that held true, to a large extent, for the republican and regional leadership, it was not the case for the lower levels of the party-state apparatus. When the partisan movement disbanded in the summer of 1944, many former partisans did at first take over party-state responsibilities. Faced with a dire lack of cadres, their appointment seemed perfectly in line with the official narrative: who, if not those who during the war had fought in the name of Soviet power against the Nazis, should represent the Soviet state in the recently reconquered territories? This was a pattern that could be observed throughout Belarus. By late August 1944, thirty-two of the thirty-seven employees of the party committee and the executive committee of Oktiabr'skii district in Poles'e oblast were former partisans. The district's party secretaries in charge of the recruitment of new personnel were two former partisan commissars, a man by the name of Grib and another by the name of Kamotskii. The head of the district executive committee was a man called Putiago, during the war commander of a partisan brigade. In neighbouring Petrikovskii district, the picture was quite similar: of the twenty-five employees of the district's party-state executive committee, 84 percent were former partisans.[66] Similarly, further west in Slonimskii district, of the thirty-one men who in December 1944 attended courses offered by the district party committee and of whom the majority occupied party-state positions (including as head of the district party committee's organizational department and as head of the district Komsomol), only five did not fight with the partisans.[67]

In the weeks and months immediately after the Red Army returned to Belarus, former partisans thus represented a crucial support base, forming the backbone of the Soviet state at a time when the leadership in Minsk and Moscow had to deal with severe personnel shortages. In subsequent years, though, the cadre composition changed significantly. Many former partisans were released from their posts and replaced either with recently demobilized Red Army soldiers or with people who had spent the war years in the Soviet rear. By April 1945, for example, 55 percent of the cadres in the Bobruisk state apparatus had fought with the partisans during the war.[68] By July 1946, the number was down to 36 percent, and it continued to drop slightly in the next two years.[69] In other regions, the trend was similar. By January 1949, of the 5,159 individuals who held leadership positions within the republic's state apparatus (from heads of the regional executive committees down to heads of city councils), only 19 percent had fought with the partisans.[70] Contrary to what Ponomarenko later claimed in his memoirs—that it was his successor Nikolai Gusarov who wanted to remove former partisans from the party-state apparatus—it was, in fact, under Ponomarenko that the removal of former partisans from mid- to lower-level positions began.

What accounted for this change in the cadre composition? One reason must have been that many former rank-and-file partisans lacked any experience working in Soviet party-state institutions. Of the 281,007 partisans in Belarus for whom the Belarusian Staff of the Partisan Movement held occupational data, 39 percent had been peasants prior to joining the movement. Party-state workers constituted less than 3 percent.[71] Another reason was leniency with one's subordinates as a result of protectionism. Semen Evdachkov, for example, had been a party member since 1927. During the war, he commanded a partisan unit in Kormianskii district, not far from Gomel'. When the Red Army reconquered the region, Evdachkov returned to his prewar post as head of the executive committee in Kormianskii district. In this capacity, he pulled former partisans from his unit into the district's party-state administration. As I. Tur, head of the Gomel' regional party committee, remarked in a July 1946 report to Minsk, "many district employees, heads of the village councils, and collective farms are former partisans of the Voroshilov unit." Yet precisely because of their shared wartime experience, Evdachkov had failed to hold them to a high standard: "Comrade Evdachkov identified with them in the sense that he was blending in with this group, he was not very demanding with them, there was no acuity when dealing with issues." This, in turn, had negatively affected the workings of the local administrative apparatus—which is why the party leaders of Gomel' oblast "deemed it necessary" to remove him from his post in Kormianskii district.[72]

Another common complaint that was lodged against former partisans was that their wartime records had not been checked thoroughly enough. In February 1945, the Cadres Department of the Communist Party of Belarus sent a report to the Buro of the Central Committee in Minsk. It criticized the Minsk regional party committee for having recommended a man by the name of Danil'chik as second secretary of the party committee of the town of Cherven'. Danil'chik had worked in the party-state apparatus before the war, yet during the war, as the Cadres Department wrote, "he stayed in occupied territory and lived in the village of Veski . . . where he would get drunk with the German henchman-translator Pliatsevich, who has left with the Germans, and the mayor Nikinchik." At some point, Danil'chik was arrested by the German authorities, but "after twelve days was released and lived legally in the village Veski and continued to drink with the aforementioned people. In December 1942, he was taken by force [*pod oruzhiem*] into a partisan unit."[73]

Two aspects of Danil'chik's wartime history made him particularly suspect. In the eyes of the Soviet authorities, having been arrested by the Germans but released shortly thereafter strongly suggested that Danil'chik must have struck a deal with the occupiers; how was it otherwise possible that he, a Communist Party member, was able to live unencumbered in occupied territory? Moreover, even though Danil'chik eventually fought on the Soviet side, he had to be coerced into doing so—which clearly raised the question why had he not joined the partisans voluntarily. But the case of Danil'chik also pointed to a larger structural issue. Seventy-one percent of partisans who were active in Belarus during the war became a part of the movement only in 1943. Since most of the partisans had been prewar residents of the republic, and since most of them were ethnic Belarusians from the villages, this meant that by the time they joined the movement, they had already lived for quite a while as civilians under Nazi rule.[74] But what had they done during that time—and why had they not joined the movement earlier? While the Soviet authorities regarded former partisans overall as more trustworthy than the rest of the population that had lived in occupied territory, they were not per se above suspicion.[75]

Taken together, these different factors—lack of qualifications and work experience, incidents of protectionism, and suspicion toward partisans who prior to joining the movement had lived for a significant time as civilians under Nazi rule—explain why in the immediate postwar years, the Soviet authorities removed many former partisans from party-state positions. Although the regime outwardly celebrated rank-and-file partisans as defenders of the Soviet motherland, internally it remained ambivalent toward them. Overall, the need for personnel did not take priority over the issue of the reliability of those who had stayed in occupied territory, even in the case of partisans. As a result, postwar Belarus was often led by individual former partisans, but just a few years into the postwar period, the mid- to lower levels of its party-state apparatus were no longer primarily staffed with them.

Moreover, even at the level of the leadership, the partisan legacy was more complicated than it seemed at first glance. Very few of the men who in the first ten to fifteen years after the war belonged to the leadership of the republic had actually fought in the forests themselves. Kirill Mazurov, who became first secretary in 1956, constituted an exception, as did his successor Petr Masherov. Those who were in power in the late Stalin years—men like Ponomarenko, Tsanava, Bel'chenko, Kalinin and others—had indeed directed (or helped to direct) the Soviet partisan movement. However, they did so not from the forests and marshes of Belarus but from Moscow, from the safety of the Soviet rear.[76] In an ironic twist, these men used the official war narrative to boost their credentials as former partisans who were leading the republic where the "all people's partisan war" had taken place, yet they had no personal experience of what it meant to be a partisan living and fighting in occupied territory.

Contesting Official Memory

In postwar Belarus, just as in the other western republics of the Soviet Union, significant discrepancies existed between public and private memories of the war, between the complex reality of life under Nazi rule and the one-dimensional version of the war that the authorities upheld. Still, Soviet official war memory was not static—and within limits, it could be contested. The lobbying efforts of members of the 1941–1942 Minsk underground demonstrate this well.

In late 1959, the Presidium of the Central Committee in Moscow received a long letter from Minsk. Signed by forty-seven people who described themselves as "members of the wartime Minsk underground," the women and men appealed to Nikita Khrushchev, first secretary of the Communist Party of the Soviet Union, to send a special commission to Belarus. The aim, they requested, should be to "investigate the activities of P. K. Ponomarenko" both during and after the war.[77] In their letter, the authors provided information on their own underground activities and laid out their accusations against Ponomarenko. When the German army conquered Minsk on the eighth day of the war, they wrote, "no evacuation whatsoever of the population and of the city's resources was organized because Ponomarenko was the first to flee in panic from the city, on the third day of the war." A majority of the city's population stayed behind, "among them many communists and Komsomol members, who in response to the call of our party and from the first day of the occupation began to organize a city underground."[78] In early November 1941, they established the "Minsk underground city party committee of the Communist Party of Belarus" (Minskii podpol'nyi gorkom KPB) with its own Komsomol underground organization. Throughout 1941 and early 1942, the underground committee helped to establish ten partisan units and supplied these with weapons and medical supplies. The members of the underground also printed and distributed their own newspaper, *Zvezda*.

When the Red Army reconquered the city in July 1944, the surviving members were overjoyed—but their joy did not last long. As they described in their letter to Khrushchev, "by order of Ponomarenko and his friend, former Minister of State Security Tsanava," many of the underground members were arrested by the state security organs. "An unprecedented hunt began for the city patriots and partisans from the units that the Minsk underground had organized. Already in 1942, Ponomarenko . . . called the Minsk underground provocateurs, the work of the Gestapo."[79] Over the years, Ponomarenko's opinion of the Minsk underground remained unchanged. For more than fifteen years, the underground members wrote, "Ponomarenko and his closest friend Tsanava have covered the patriotic activities of the underground members of Minsk with spittle"—which is why they beseeched Khrushchev to intervene on their behalf and "to bring an end to the shameful hassle over the heroic action of the Minsk underground members."[80]

The letter was not the first one that former members of the 1941–1942 Minsk underground had sent to Soviet leaders in the hope that their plea for recognition would be heard. In 1949, some of them wrote to Stalin, and in 1956, to Khrushchev. In both cases, the center instructed the Central Committee in Minsk to look into the issue, but the investigations went nowhere. In 1958, the members of the underground sent yet another letter to Moscow, addressing the Presidium of the Central Committee, which subsequently instructed Minsk to create another special commission to investigate the claims. This time, the commission confirmed the existence of an early communist-led underground in the Belarusian capital. Soon thereafter, however, the decision was nullified by, it seems, the Central Committee in Minsk—against which the underground members protested by sending the above-cited letter to Khrushchev. In response, the Central Committee in Moscow took action and established that, indeed, there had been an early communist-led resistance in Minsk.[81] This resistance had begun in the form of small, loosely connected conspiratorial groups. By the fall of 1941, its members had organized themselves into a Minsk-wide underground organization, of which one unit was active in the ghetto, under the leadership of Hersh Smolar. The German forces destroyed this first city-wide underground in late March and early April 1942, yet a second Minsk underground organization soon took form. In the fall of 1942, the German authorities uncovered that group, too, and arrested and killed many of its members. With that, the 1941–1942 Minsk underground ceased to exist. Those few who were able to escape fled to the nearby forests, where they formed or joined partisan units.[82]

In October 1943, the Central Committee of the Communist Party of Belarus ordered the creation of a third Minsk underground committee, yet this organization did not operate in the city itself but instead was located in the nearby forests. In the eyes of Ponomarenko, Tsanava, and other party leaders in Belarus, this third committee was the only legitimate Minsk underground organization that had existed during the war. They considered the first and second committees (the 1941–1942 Minsk underground) the work of "spies" and "traitors." They also did, as the authors of the 1959 letter to Khrushchev correctly claimed, arrest many of its few surviving former members, some already during the war, others in the immediate postwar period.[83]

Why did men like Ponomarenko and Tsanava deny the 1941–1942 Minsk underground its legitimacy, claiming it had been a German operation? The spymania that was so prevalent on both the Soviet and the German sides, the fear that the other was undermining one's own groups, could have played a role. Through secret agents who reported to the NKVD, Ponomarenko heard about the destruction of the second Minsk underground in the fall of 1942.[84] In April 1943, one of the agents reported that he had met surviving underground members among the partisans. According to the agent, the surviving members suspected that some of their own, including one of the organization's central figures, the communist Ivan Kovalev, had given the organization away to the Gestapo.[85] However, it seems likely that the main reason why Ponomarenko denied the existence of an early resistance organization was that it cast a highly unfavorable light on the leaders of Belarus. After all, as the letter to Khrushchev pointed out, the leadership had indeed fled the capital three days before the German arrival. In his postwar speeches, Ponomarenko repeatedly stressed the success of the party's evacuation measures, but he did not mention that these had mostly taken place from the easternmost part of Belarus, which the Wehrmacht conquered only several weeks into the war. That the population and, above all, children of Red Army soldiers were among the first to be evacuated from Minsk, as Ponomarenko later suggested, was one of many falsifications with which Soviet leaders tried to cover up a behavior that they would have deemed cowardly at best and treacherous at worst if others had acted in the same way.[86] As many in the post-1944 leadership circle around Ponomarenko had also belonged to the leadership before June 1941, public recognition of other people's early resistance to the German occupiers would have amounted to an acknowledgment of their own weakness in the summer of 1941. In addition, given that many of the activists in the 1941–1942 Minsk underground were low-level Soviet party-state representatives or not even party members at all, highlighting their achievements would have made the population of

Belarus wonder why high-ranking party officials could not likewise have stayed and fought in occupied territory instead of fleeing to the Soviet rear.

Last but not least, there was the risk that the underground members, once in the eye of the public, could challenge Moscow's claim that the Communist Party had from early on directed all resistance activity in occupied territory. That, however, was not the case. The 1941–1942 Minsk underground was the result of individual initiative on the ground. From its very beginning to its destruction in the fall of 1942, the underground members operated without guidance or support from Moscow. Arsenii Kalinovskii, who prior to the war had worked in the Minsk city administration, recalled how in the summer of 1941, he and three fellow comrades decided to begin conspiratorial activities of their own accord. They did so because there were no superiors left from whom they could have taken orders: "No one was able to give us any other directives."[87] Similarly, Hersh Smolar's account about the activities of the underground in the Minsk ghetto made it clear that its members, lacking central directives or guidance from above, acted on their own initiative.[88] It was only in September 1942, shortly before the destruction of the second Minsk underground, that one of its members, Khasia Pruslina, was able to establish contact with the Soviet rear, via a partisan unit that was operating in the vicinity of Minsk and that had contact with Moscow through radio telegram.[89] This meant that the leaders of Belarus could not credit themselves with the early resistance activity that had taken place in the republic's capital—an embarrassment to them and one that had to be concealed.

Apart from Ponomarenko and Tsanava, another man who was instrumental in upholding the view that the 1941–1942 Minsk underground was a German operation was Vasilii Kozlov, since 1949 a member of the Buro of the Central Committee of the Communist Party of Belarus. In the fall of 1943, Vasilii Kozlov became the head of the third Minsk underground organization, which was created under the control of the Central Committee of Belarus and operated from the nearby forests, not in the city itself. As a decorated Hero of the Soviet Union, Kozlov occupied a prominent position within the partisan war narrative. In their 1959 letter to Khrushchev, the former members of the 1941–1942 Minsk underground criticized the "Kozlov cult" (*kul't Kozlova*) in Belarus, especially since, as they wrote, "all Belarusian partisans know that for all of 1941 and for the greatest part of 1942, V. I. Kozlov's group was lying low in the impassable Polesian marshes and did not play any special role in the creation of the partisan movement in Minsk oblast."[90] Kozlov, then, had much to lose: not just his status as head of the supposedly only Minsk underground organization, but also his alleged early partisan feats. This is a likely explanation for why, throughout the 1940s and 1950s, he and others repeatedly blocked or ignored requests by former members of the 1941–1942 Minsk underground to reconsider their cases.[91]

After the Central Committee in Moscow decided to recognize the 1941–1942 Minsk underground as an early communist resistance organization, 113 of the roughly 126 underground members who had been arrested after the war were rehabilitated, some of them posthumously.[92] A long article on their resistance activities—published on June 3, 1960, in *Pravda* and two days later reprinted in *Sovetskaia Belorussiia*—marked the beginning of public acknowledgment of the underground organization. The author of the article, Ivan Novikov, was the Belarus correspondent for *Pravda*. He portrayed the members of the underground as true Soviet patriots, members of the party and the Komsomol, and singled out some of them by name—but he did not mention that the underground had existed within the ghetto, too, or that many women had been among its members.[93] Around that time, it seems, Novikov established contact with the former underground members. Based on their recollections, he published two books on the underground and one on *Minsk, the Hero City* (a title the city was awarded in 1974).[94]

Yet even after the official decision in 1960 to recognize the 1941–1942 Minsk underground, some of its former members still had the stigma "traitor" attached to them. Subsequently, the Communist Party of Belarus convened three more special party commissions in 1978, 1983, and 1990 to settle the remaining contentious issues. For one, there was the question of what Ivan Kovalev, the communist accused of having betrayed the underground, had done during the war. Until the late 1980s, the official position was that Kovalev had given away the organization by going over to the German side, giving anti-Soviet speeches and eventually traveling to Berlin. In 1990, however, the fourth special party commission concluded that when the German authorities arrested Kovalev in the fall of 1942, he did not give the underground away before being killed by the Germans; from then on, he was no longer deemed a traitor but regarded as a hero.[95]

The second issue that the special party commissions had to determine was that of rightful membership: who could and could not call themselves former members of the underground. Once the record was set straight, more and more people wanted to be officially recognized for their activities. While the 1978 commission established that the early Minsk underground had consisted of three groups, the 1984 commission already revised these findings significantly. It found that ninety-five underground groups and twenty-three underground organizations with 1,630 people had been active in the Belarusian capital. Another four thousand people were deemed "candidates to be called members of the Minsk underground," which probably meant that their wartime histories still needed to be investigated thoroughly to see whether they fulfilled the party's criteria to be called former underground members.[96]

Within forty years, then, the 1941–1942 Minsk underground went from being seen as the work of provocateurs and traitors to the heroic achievement of many individual Soviet patriots. What this shows is that it was possible for individuals to dispute particular aspects of the official war narrative while striving to be included in its larger version. Moreover, people were able to test the boundaries of the narrative to see how far these could be stretched or altered, and, like the members of the 1941–1942 Minsk underground, to invert the official interpretation of their wartime activities from treacherous to heroic. At the same time, the success of their efforts also depended on developments that were outside their control—yet that turned out to be to their advantage. That the larger Soviet war narrative became more popularized and inclusive after Khrushchev's Secret Speech in 1956 certainly played a role. A similar, and probably even greater, impetus was the power shift that took place around that time within the Politburo in Moscow—as well as the personal rivalry between Khrushchev and Ponomarenko, which by the late 1950s had worked against the latter.

From 1938 to the late 1940s, Ponomarenko was the most powerful man in Belarus. In 1950, he left the republic for Moscow to take on the post of minister for the procurement of agricultural goods. After 1956, his political star began to sink. Before retiring to his dacha near Moscow, he served as ambassador to several different countries—certainly not a low-level job, yet one that was far removed from the everyday operational work he had done in earlier years. Lavrentii Tsanava fared much worse. In October 1951, he was promoted to deputy head of the MGB of the USSR, but during the power struggle following Stalin's death in March 1953, his career came to an abrupt halt. He was arrested in April of that year for the 1948 murder of the Jewish actor Solomon Mikhoels in Minsk and subsequently died in prison in 1955.[97] By 1960, therefore, two of the main obstacles that had stood in the way of the rehabilitation of the 1941–1942 Minsk underground were no longer as insurmountable as they had once been.

Still, just because Ponomarenko left for Moscow in 1950 did not mean that he no longer wielded any influence over politics and intrigues in Belarus. The authors of the 1959 letter to Khrushchev noted that "it is in principle not possible for the issue of the Minsk underground to be decided in Belarus," given that the "people who in Belarus are called Ponomarenko guys [*nazyvaiut ponomarenkavtsami*]" continue to exercise a "commanding influence."[98] Provided that a person moved up in the party-state hierarchy, patronage networks ensured that the person remained influential in his former position, city, or republic even if no longer physically present—just as happened after Ponomarenko's departure for Moscow in 1950. It must have been precisely the personal allegations against Ponomarenko, however, that helped the 1941–1942 Minsk underground be finally recognized in 1960. When its former members turned to Khrushchev, they did so because he, as first secretary of the Communist Party of the Soviet Union, was the most powerful person in the country. What they may not have known was that Ponomarenko and Khrushchev were old rivals. In Ponomarenko's words, Khrushchev was an "old Trotskyist" with whom he had a strained relationship that only deteriorated when Ponomarenko became the head of the Central Staff of the Partisan Movement in 1942, an appointment that Khrushchev supposedly disapproved of. According to Ponomarenko, the friction between the two men had its origin in territorial disputes: in 1940, Khrushchev, then first secretary of the Communist Party of Ukraine, tried to get Stalin to transfer to Ukraine parts of the newly acquired southwestern Belarus, including the city of Brest. Khrushchev did not succeed, but after that, he and Ponomarenko were locked in an antagonistic relationship.[99]

Until the early 1950s, the two men were more or less equal in terms of where they stood in the party hierarchy—although if we count the number of meetings that a leading communist had with Stalin as a reflection of that person's power, Khrushchev was more powerful during the war than Ponomarenko.[100] After Khrushchev became first secretary of the Communist Party of the Soviet Union in 1953 and, more importantly, after he subsequently won the leadership struggle with Georgii Malenkov, Ponomarenko's patron, the differences in power between Ponomarenko and Khrushchev became significant.[101] But although Khrushchev had clearly overtaken his old rival, he probably did not like to hear that Ponomarenko still exerted considerable influence in Belarus. According to the former underground members, Ponomarenko considered "the mass partisan movement in occupied Belarusian territory his personal achievement and that of people who are close to him."[102] It is not implausible that such claims spurred Khrushchev to order investigations into the case. By overturning the judgment on the history of the 1941–1942 Minsk underground, the Politburo in Moscow could put both the leadership in Belarus as well as its patron Ponomarenko, at that time Soviet ambassador to the Netherlands, in their place.

From early in the war, Panteleimon Ponomarenko was a proponent of the idea that the partisan struggle in occupied territory should be transformed into a war that mobilized the entire population against the Germans.

An outsider to Belarus when he arrived to take up the post of first secretary in 1938, during the war years, Ponomarenko seized the chance to portray himself as the father of ethnic Belarusians. Although not alone in this endeavor, he was instrumental in shaping a specific Soviet Belarusian war narrative in which the Belarusian people, finally liberated from the Polish yoke and unified in one state, had stood united behind the Soviet partisans, thereby demonstrating their commitment to the Soviet Union. Yet because "the people" could be interpreted either in an inclusive, multiethnic sense or in an exclusive, monoethnic sense, it was never entirely clear just who belonged to "the people" and who did not. By deliberately playing with the ambiguity inherent in "Belarusian people," Ponomarenko made partisan warfare in occupied territory appear to be the sole achievement of ethnic Belarusians. He also wrote about the murder of Belarus's Jewish communities at the hands of the German occupiers in a way that implied ethnic Belarusians, not Jews, had been killed. While "hierarchical heroism and universal suffering" continued to be the cornerstones of the larger Soviet war narrative, as Amir Weiner has shown, what Ponomarenko did was more than universalizing the victims by omitting their ethnicity and instead speaking of them as "peaceful Soviet citizens."[103] It was a distortion of the historical record that assigned Jewish victims a Slavic ethnicity. From the late 1940s on, such distortions turned into the outright omission of Jewish residents of Belarus, who, like the republic's ethnic Poles, were excluded as both victims and resisters from the "all people's partisan war."[104]

The Soviet narrative of the years of war and occupation, however, went beyond the omission of certain population groups. It also strove to overcome one major obstacle: that until the end of the war, the actual relationship between partisans and civilians in occupied territory had been fragile, unequal, fraught with conflict, and, at times, antagonistic. If there was one experience that was shared widely by the majority of rural civilians in occupied territory, then it was that of partisans taking their food, clothes, and livestock against their will. Individuals tried to make sense of the discrepancy between official and private memory by distinguishing between "real" partisans (who could be honored) and "bandits," thereby attempting to rationalize the abuse they had encountered at the latter's hands—yet even this reframing of their wartime experiences could be articulated publicly only at the cost of exclusion from the larger political community. The exclusively positive depiction of the partisan-civilian relationship has proven incredibly resistant to political and societal change and continues to form the core of the war narrative in today's independent Belarus. This is even more remarkable given that internally, the postwar Soviet authorities remained ambivalent toward the bulk of partisans who had fought in occupied territory. From the summer of 1944 on, after the Red Army's return to Belarus, many rank-and-file partisans initially constituted the institutional backbone of the regime, but within a year, a substantial number of them were removed from their positions. The postwar leaders of the republic, in turn, had often helped to direct the Soviet partisan movement during the war, but they had done so from the safety of the Soviet rear. Belarus, the Partisan Republic, was led by men who styled themselves as partisans yet usually had no personal experience of what it meant to live in the forests—while dismissing those from local positions of power who had actually fought against the German forces in occupied territory.

Much of the Soviet regime's narrative of the years of war and occupation, then, ran counter to private memories of the war, and significant discrepancies existed between the complex reality of life under Nazi rule and the one-dimensional version of these years as presented by the authorities. Nevertheless, Soviet war memory as such was not static, and within limits, it could be contested and reshaped. As the lobbying efforts by surviving members of the 1941–1942 Minsk underground demonstrate, it was at once possible to challenge parts of the official narrative while striving to be included in it. After more than twenty years, the underground was recognized as an official communist resistance organization; after forty years, it had firmly turned from the work of alleged traitors to the feat of heroes. This radical historical reinterpretation became possible due to a combination of several factors: individual persistence from below, a general shift in the Soviet war narrative that became more popularized and inclusive from the late 1950s on, and, most importantly, power shifts in the Politburo in Moscow combined with a personal rivalry between Nikita Khrushchev and Panteleimon Ponomarenko, which worked to the detriment of the latter. Once the father of the Partisan Republic, Ponomarenko spent the last years of his life, and the last years of the Soviet Union, at his dacha in Moscow. Resentful and bitter, he kept a portrait of Stalin in his study and employed the help of professional historians to write his memoirs, trying to change a war narrative that he had lost control over.[105]

Afterword

As the Second World War came to an end, hundreds of thousands of individuals were prosecuted for their wartime activities in almost all former belligerent countries across Europe and Asia. This global moment of post–Second World War justice involved numerous countries on several continents, saw the emergence of international criminal law, and witnessed public and official discourses on collaboration transcend national boundaries.[1] The moment was arguably also a global one because war and occupation had brought about similar challenges and structural conditions in both Europe and Asia. Very different states and societies, ranging from democratic to authoritarian to totalitarian, now found themselves confronted with similar issues—how to punish enemy soldiers they deemed responsible for wartime atrocities, and how to punish alleged traitors and collaborators among their own citizens. In response, all of them chose to rely on the same means: the criminal justice system.

As one of the countries that was hit hardest by the apocalyptic violence of war and occupation, the Soviet Union was a part of this global reckoning in multiple ways. Together with its three Western Allies—the United States, the United Kingdom, and France—the Soviet Union organized and participated in the 1945–1946 trial of major Nazi leaders at the International Military Tribunal at Nuremberg.[2] While Moscow's involvement at the 1946–1948 International Military Tribunal for the Far East at Tokyo was minimal, largely due to the powerful position of the United States in East Asia, it took a much more active role in the prosecution of lower-ranking Axis military personnel suspected of wartime atrocities. Once the tide of the war turned at the Battle of Stalingrad in the winter of 1942–1943 and the Red Army began to reconquer more and more territory, Soviet military tribunals prosecuted Axis soldiers (primarily German nationals but also Austrian, Hungarian, Romanian, Japanese, and others who had served in the Wehrmacht or in the armies of German allies) for their wartime conduct.[3] These trials, nineteen public ones and a large number of secret trials, resembled the Soviet treason (or collaboration) trials in many respects. Like the collaboration trials, the extent, intensity, and publicity of the Soviet prosecutions of Axis soldiers were informed by a host of domestic and international considerations. Discursively, they were linked to Moscow's participation at the IMT, and more generally to the Soviet Union's role as one of the main victors and victims of the war. Just like at the public collaboration trials, the members of the Soviet military tribunals took great care to project a high degree of due process at the public trials of Axis soldiers, which always included the presence of witnesses and defense attorneys. Yet also like at the collaboration trials, the guilt of the accused had already been established prior to the trials; the question was only what sentence they should receive.[4] Both types of trials lacked fundamental standards of rule-of-law-based legal systems such as an independent judiciary, independent defense lawyers, and the assumption of "innocent until proven guilty" that form the precondition for any trial to be considered as impartial as possible. In consequence, neither Soviet trials of Axis soldiers nor trials of Soviet citizens deemed wartime traitors fulfilled the criteria necessary to establish beyond doubt an individual's criminal responsibility.

At the same time, the Soviet politics of retribution were more complex than the notion of "show trials," commonly associated with Soviet legal spectacles, suggests. Examining the place of the Soviet Union within the global moment of post–Second World War justice calls into question a dichotomy that continues to underlie scholarly thinking within international legal history, and that is the dichotomy between "good" political trials that, despite shortcomings, promote liberal values and "bad" political trials that merely serve propaganda and terror purposes.[5] In his book on the politics of war crimes tribunals, Gary Jonathan Bass has taken this farthest by arguing that only liberal states conduct genuine war crimes trials, whereas illiberal states only conduct show trials.[6] The historical example for show trials that is usually cited is the series of public trials of alleged state enemies that the Soviet government conducted in the 1930s—in particular, the three 1936–1938 Moscow trials of prominent Bolsheviks. These trials were entirely staged: scripted, with fabricated acts and likewise fabricated evidence, predetermined outcomes, and lack of independent judges and defense attorneys.[7]

However, the dichotomy between "good" and "bad" political trials, "good" war crimes trials and "bad" show trials, does not adequately reflect the variety among the trials that took place in the aftermath of the Second World War. Given the trials' complexity, it would instead be more appropriate to conceive of them as located along a spectrum marked by two poles. On the left was the ideal-type liberal trial, impartial and solely based on the rule of law, thus representing the ultimate, if in reality probably unattainable, model of what a liberal trial should look like. On the right was the classic show trial: politics unconstrained by judicial process, a scripted trial with fabricated allegations and predetermined outcomes (historically represented by the 1936–1938 Moscow trials). Depending on the degree to which a trial complied with standards of the rule of law, each trial that took place in response to the violence of the Second World War could then be placed along that spectrum. Doing so would show just how legally flawed the global moment of post–Second World War justice was. Of the trials of suspected traitors and collaborators that democratic states held in postwar Europe, many were located toward the illiberal end of the spectrum.[8] Similarly, the Western Allies' war crimes trials in Europe and Asia often did not live up to the liberal legal standards that these countries sought to achieve at home. A mix of procedural shortcomings, including looser rules of evidence or denial to suspects and defendants of the same rights that Western Allied country nationals were granted in domestic courts, usually accounted for that.[9] The American judges at the 1946 Mauthausen trial that saw SS concentration camp personnel prosecuted spent on average four hours to consider a defendant's case before handing down dozens of death sentences. Prior to the trial, some investigators applied dubious interrogation techniques bordering on torture.[10] In Asia, the trials of Japanese military personnel were often used by European colonial empires (France, the United Kingdom, and the Netherlands) as a means to reassert their authority in colonies that had been under Japanese occupation during the war.[11]

Clearly located at the end of the illiberal spectrum were Moscow's trials of both Axis soldiers and Soviet citizens deemed wartime traitors. In one crucial respect, though, the Soviet prosecution of Axis military personnel (if less so the treason trials of Soviet citizens, which would have to be assessed on a case-by-case basis) was distinct from Soviet prewar justice. The difference lay in fabricated (or imagined) versus actual and visible acts, and in the extent to which almost everyone in occupied territory had suffered under the Germans. At the public trials of political enemies that took place in the interwar years, the defendants were accused of acts such as industrial sabotage or plotting against the Soviet government that had as a whole not taken place. In contrast, the kind of acts that the defendants at Soviet trials of Axis soldiers were accused of had, of course, been committed. This included killing captive Red Army soldiers, Jews, or other civilians; rounding up people for forced labor in Germany; or participating in punitive raids that saw entire villages razed to the ground. In consequence, the Soviet prosecution had no difficulty in presenting evidence of atrocities committed by German or other Axis military personnel.[12] What was much more difficult was to provide material that testified to the defendants' *personal* participation in these acts—a problem that state security officers were keenly aware of, as internal reports leading up to the trial of thirteen Hungarians and three German nationals that took place on November 17–25, 1947, in the Ukrainian town of Chernihiv show.[13] However, their difficulties in conjuring evidence attesting to an individual's criminal responsibility do not seem to have affected public perceptions of Soviet justice. According to NKGB reports, the absolute majority of the six hundred local inhabitants who attended the January 1946 trial of German soldiers at Mykolaiv, Ukraine, approved of the trial. Their comments, collected by state security officers disguised as civilians and other informers, had a "patriotic character, expressing a desire for just retribution."[14] Indeed, for some, Soviet justice was too lenient: at the Mykolaiv trial, workers of Factory no. 445 were reported to have said that Soviet courts were "unnecessarily humane toward the Germans," while another worker, during a break, asked his neighbor: "Why mess around with them for long? Kill them, like dogs, indeed all of them. Are these even people?"[15] Similar comments were recorded at the November 1947 Chernihiv trial. As the MGB officer Fedorov wrote in his report on the trial: "Many workers of Chernihiv expressed their regret that the death sentence has been abolished and that the fascist occupiers will not be hanged."[16]

Mood reports by state security officers and their informers are undoubtedly a difficult source and thus have to be treated with a lot of caution. There was no guarantee that informer reports were accurate, and that people had indeed said what they were alleged to have said. Since the existence of informer networks was known to everyone, it is also possible that a person told someone whom he surmised of being an informer what he assumed the other wanted to hear. People's expectations could have affected their behavior, and depending on whom they spoke to, they adjusted their comments accordingly. Yet even in cases when observers otherwise sensed that the proceedings were predetermined, they usually deemed the Soviet trials justified and right. Edwin L. James, the *New York Times* correspondent present at the public trial of three Germans and one Soviet citizen that took place in December 1943 at Kharkiv in Ukraine, thought that the trial was a "red propaganda coup," but it was "justified propaganda, which is perhaps without equal in this war."[17] This was also how the American journalist Edmund Stevens experienced the Kharkiv trial: "During the recesses, I discovered that many of the people in the audience had personal knowledge or experience of the events and atrocities described. . . . Several times during more gruesome bits of evidence there were stifled sobs from some woman."[18] According to Stevens, the local audience knew what verdict the defendants could expect: "The court and the people watching knew what was coming. Most of them had seen the four gallows-trees being erected in the center of the market place."[19] The continuities with prewar Soviet justice may not have been lost on the audience; they were certainly not on Stevens, who had also attended the third Moscow show trial in March 1938.[20] Still, because of the existence of atrocities on such a tremendous scale—combined with the extent to which almost everyone in occupied territory had personally suffered under German occupation—this did not seem to have mattered much, if at all. As the example of the Soviet Union therefore indicates, within the global moment of post–Second World War justice, the acts that had been committed could, and did, legitimize a significant lack of the rule of law.

This book's main narrative began with the lives of eight individuals: Ol'ga Bembel'-Dedok and Vladimir Khartanovich, Chasia Bornstein-Bielicka, Litman Mor and Zofia Brzozowska, Vasil' Bykaŭ, Lev Ovsishcher and Zinaida Suvorova. Strangers to one another, their personal lives did not intersect, or at least not in ways of which they were aware. They spoke and wrote in different languages—Belarusian, Polish, Yiddish, and Russian—and they had been raised in different religions: Russian Orthodoxy, Roman Catholicism, and Judaism. What they had in common, though, was that they called the same multilingual, multireligious East European borderland their home.

On the eve of the German invasion of the Soviet Union, six of these eight individuals were in Belarus, one in Lithuania, and another in central Russia. Ol'ga Bembel'-Dedok lived with her two small children in Minsk; Chasia Bornstein-Bielicka went to school in Grodno, where she secretly continued to meet with her fellow members of the Socialist-Zionist youth organization Hashomer Hatzair; and Vasil' Bykaŭ studied for a year at the Vitebsk Art College. Vladimir Khartanovich, who hoped to become a teacher, attended the Novogrudok pedagogical school, while Zinaida Suvorova, a mother of two young children, was working as an administrator at the theater in Orsha. Litman Mor, who hailed from David-Gorodok in Polesia, was studying chemistry at Vilnius University, while Lev Ovsishcher was finishing his training as an aeronautical navigator in Chkalov (today's Orenburg), on the Ural river. Of the eight individuals, it was Zofia Brzozowska whose family had suffered the greatest violent disruption under Soviet rule. Part of the landed Polish gentry in the Novogrudok region, her family was evicted from its small estate in 1940. Her father, grandfather, and uncle were arrested by the NKVD; their fates are unknown.[21]

To varying degrees, each of these eight individuals had seen their personal lives affected by the Soviet state—some, like Brzozowska, only in violent ways; others also in more positive ways. As different as their experiences and their relationship to Soviet rule were, June 22, 1941, marked a deep rupture in all of their lives. Three years of Nazi occupation turned the Belarusian lands into infernos of death and devastation. While some worlds were completely eradicated, first and foremost the world of East European Jewry, others underwent fundamental change. When German rule ended in the summer of 1944, and ultimately the war in May 1945, it brought relief and joy but also uneasiness and trepidations about the future, combined with an immeasurable grief. As Chasia Bornstein-Bielicka, the sole survivor of her family, recalled from the months she spent in Grodno after liberation, she and the other few survivors lived "detached from the surrounding world . . . in a steadily expanding bubble of pain."[22] Like Litman Mor, who returned to David-Gorodok after the war only to have confirmed that his entire family had been killed in the Holocaust, Bornstein-Bielicka had no intention of staying in a place where every corner reminded her of her loss. While Litman Mor, like Zofia Brzozowska, left the Soviet Union under the conditions of the Polish-Soviet population exchange, Bornstein-Bielicka was smuggled by an acquaintance across the Polish-Belarusian border in the summer of 1945.[23]

Yet even after the most extreme and traumatic violence, even when individuals are subjected to the most repressive political regimes, social life continues in some form—something that, as Veena Das and Arthur Kleinman have written, is both the source of possibilities and of very deep perplexities.[24] For many people who lived through war and Nazi occupation, family and close friends became their most important source of strength. Zinaida Suvorova, who, except for her two small children, had lost her entire family, remarried quickly after the war. Her new husband had lost his wife and children; together, they moved to Vilnius, where they built a new family.[25] What gave Chasia Bornstein-Bielicka the strength to continue living was a mission she took up in March 1946 in Łódź. She became the head of a children's home, set up under the auspices of Hashomer Hatzair, whose goal it was to bring orphaned Jewish children from Poland to Palestine. For the next one and a half years, Bornstein-Bielicka stayed with the children, along a journey that took them through various camps in Germany, France, and Cyprus until they arrived in August 1947 in Palestine.[26] For someone like Vladimir Khartanovich, it was the rebuilding of Soviet Belarus that filled him with a deep sense of purpose. Unlike Chasia Bornstein-Bielicka, Khartanovich, who lost two brothers at the front during the war, still had remnants of his prewar life and village community to return to. Demobilized from the Red Army, he returned to his home village of Achukevichi in 1946. Shortly thereafter, he was assigned a post in the district executive committee and tasked with the rebuilding of roads across the district. When the Soviet authorities began to collectivize western Belarus's agriculture in the late 1940s, Khartanovich took the lead in transforming Achukevichi into a collective farm, an endeavor that he took much pride in.[27]

Yet while Khartanovich was able to find meaning in the task, he turned a blind eye to the coercion and violence that was an integral part of the process. Throughout his life, Khartanovich, whose war years in the Red Army had solidified his belief in communism, remained a dedicated communist and admirer of Stalin. Others like Lev Ovsishcher, whose postwar career as an officer in the Red Army took him to Moscow and Georgia before returning to Belarus, and Ol'ga Bembel'-Dedok, who continued to live in Minsk after the war, developed a more ambivalent relationship with the Soviet state.[28] Even more critical of the Soviet Union was Vasil' Bykaŭ. Bykaŭ was first demobilized from the army, but shortly thereafter again called up for service, which took him all the way east to Vladivostok and the Kuril Islands. Finally demobilized in 1955, he settled in Grodno and began to work at the local newspaper. At the end of the decade, his first novellas were published. The Second World War was the main topic of his writings, yet in ways that deviated from the official canon. With his personal, literary explorations of the complexity of human behavior, he increasingly began to subvert official narratives of heroism. Throughout the later decades of the Soviet Union, he occupied somewhat of a middle ground—not part of the Soviet literary mainstream but not entirely outside its institutions either.[29] Although Ol'ga Bembel'-Dedok, Zofia Brzozowska, Chasia Bornstein-Bielicka, Vladimir Khartanovich, Litman Mor, Lev Ovsishcher, and Zinaida Suvorova did not leave a literary oeuvre like Bykaŭ, memoirs like those by Ol'ga Bembel-Dedok show well just how much she used personal writings to try to make sense of her wartime experiences. Indeed, as much as these eight individuals differed in their reflections of the war years, their memoirs and recollections attest to the centrality that the Second World War and the years of Nazi occupation had in their personal lives. Forever dividing them into a prewar and a postwar life, the war radically transformed their lives and the places they called, or used to call, home. For these eight individuals, as for countless others, the Second World War never became history but remained ever present.

Note on Wartime Losses

In the scholarly literature, significant disagreement exists about Belarus's wartime losses, in both absolute and proportionate numbers. Some historians write that one-fifth of the population of Belarus died during the war, others speak of one-fourth, yet others of one-third.[1] How can these discrepancies be explained? Here I examine the available source basis, its shortcomings, and its inherent problems and I provide my own calculations.

To begin with, it is important to note that both Belarus and Ukraine are counting their dead within their post-1945 borders, which include most of the parts of eastern Poland that were annexed to the Soviet Union in 1939. Poland, in contrast, counts its war dead within the pre-1939 Polish borders, as a result of which a double count of about two million people occurs. Scholarly assessments of Belarus's wartime losses always refer to the republic in its post-1945 borders. However, some of these are based on inaccurate population size estimates. Some scholars have mistakenly conflated the pre-1941 and post-1945 borders of Belarus—which were not identical, given that the territory of pre-1941 Belarus was larger than the territory of post-1945 Belarus. In consequence, these scholars have based their calculations on an incorrect prewar population size (by which is meant the size of the population on the eve of the German invasion). Establishing the correct population size in the summer of 1941 for the territories that would form post-1945 Belarus is important because it otherwise leads to inaccurate calculations of the republic's proportionate wartime losses (the number of war dead in relation to the overall population size). Moreover, some scholars have determined the 1941 population size of Soviet Belarus on the basis of the 1939 Soviet census, but they have overlooked the fact that the Soviet regime manipulated the 1939 census in an effort to cover up the population losses that resulted from the collectivization of agriculture and the Great Terror.[2] The 1937 Soviet census provided a more accurate picture. It registered 5.19 million people living in Belarus at the time. Population growth in the years 1937–1940 probably offset the population losses that resulted from the Great Terror.[3] After the annexation of eastern Poland, the population size of Belarus increased to 9.92 million people.[4] Factoring in population growth in the subsequent two years, on the eve of the German occupation, the population size of Belarus was close to ten million people.[5] In 1945, the Soviet Union handed seventeen of the twenty-three districts of Belostok (Białystok) oblast and three districts of Brest oblast back to Poland. An estimated one million people lived in these regions before 1941.[6] If we subtract this number from the 1941 population size of Belarus, we arrive at the number of nine million people who on the eve of the German occupation resided on the territory that would constitute post-1945 Belarus. This nine million is the number on which calculations of Soviet Belarus's wartime losses should be based.

In addition to confusion surrounding Belarus's population size in 1941, the scholarly disagreement on wartime losses is connected to problems inherent in the available primary sources. Calculations of wartime losses are based on two main sets of sources: German wartime documents and Soviet postwar investigations. The former group encompasses thousands of individual reports on the murder of Jews, on death rates in the prisoner-of-war camps, and on the killings of civilians in the course of antipartisan operations. Based on these German sources as well as Soviet postwar witness testimonies, Christian Gerlach, in his authoritative study on the topic, has concluded that the German forces murdered 945,000–995,000 civilians. Of these, 500,000–550,000 were Jews, and 345,000 were victims of so-called antipartisan operations. Another (estimated) 100,000 civilians were killed for a variety of different reasons. Moreover, 700,000 prisoners of war died in German captivity on territory that would constitute post-1945 Belarus.[7] Writing specifically on the Holocaust, other researchers have concluded that the number of Jews killed on Belarusian territory (in its post-1945 borders, not including the Białystok region) was higher, up to 671,000 people, almost the entire Jewish population of the republic.[8]

The Soviet sources on which calculations of wartime losses are based mainly consist of reports by the Extraordinary State Commission (ChGK), the Soviet commission that was created in 1942 to investigate and establish German crimes in the occupied territories and to determine the extent of material destruction. The numbers provided by the ChGK are higher than the numbers based on German sources. According to a provisional report compiled in July 1945 by the Extraordinary State Commission of Belarus, 1,387,166 civilians (*grazhdanskoe naselenie*, also called *mirnoe naselenie*) and 790,596 Soviet prisoners of war—in total, 2,177,762 people—were killed during the war on the territory that would constitute post-1945 Belarus.[9] The final ChGK report gives a slightly higher number: 2,219,316 people, including 1,409,225 civilians and 810,091 prisoners of war, were killed during the war on the territory that would constitute post-1945 Belarus.[10] It is important to note that the ChGK's findings do not mean that all of the victims were prewar residents of Belarus. The civilians that the German forces killed in Belarus were, with the exception of an estimated fifty thousand Jews from Central Europe, all local residents. It remains unclear, though, how many of the Red Army soldiers who died in German captivity on the territory of Belarus were pre-1941 residents of the republic.

While the German and Soviet numbers on the prisoners of war who died in German captivity are quite close to each other, the discrepancy between the two sets of sources pertaining to civilian deaths is significant (up to 500,000 individuals). How can the difference between the lower German numbers and the higher Soviet numbers be explained? According to Christian Gerlach, the higher Soviet numbers probably resulted from the double counting of victims and from the way in which Soviet investigators calculated the number of victims in mass graves.[11] The ChGK's work included the excavation of graves, yet because the bodies were already decayed and the German authorities had tried to erase traces of their crimes by burning corpses and razing death camps to the ground, Soviet investigators had to establish the number of dead found in a mass grave by calculating the average body size in relation to the volume of the grave. It is arguable how precise this method could be; in any case, a margin of error was unavoidable. The same, however, applies to German sources. The Nazis did not document all killing operations and even if they did, not all of these materials were preserved.[12] As with wartime losses in general, full accuracy is impossible; the discrepancy between the German and the Soviet sources cannot be resolved.

Another reason for the scholarly disagreement on Belarus's wartime losses is connected to the lack of sources for one particular group: soldiers.

According to an authoritative report issued by the Russian Ministry of Defense and authored by a group of historians headed by Grigorii Krivosheev, the Soviet armed forces, including its state security organs, lost 8,668,400 soldiers in the Second World War. Breakdowns for the individual republics, however, do not exist.[13] To reach a rough estimate for each republic, one can calculate the ratio of a republic's population to the overall population of the Soviet Union, then apply this ratio to the overall number of people who served in the Soviet armed forces. Since Belarus's pre-1941 population (in the republic's 1941 borders, including Białystok region) accounted for about 5 percent of the overall Soviet population, this would mean that of the Soviet soldiers who died in the war, 5 percent, about 433,400 people, were residents of Belarus (in its pre-1941 borders).[14] That number, though, seems too low. According to Aleksei Litvin, more than 500,000 men from Belarus were mobilized into the Red Army in 1941. Considering the high mortality rates in the first months of the war and the mass death of soldiers in German captivity, it is unlikely that many of the men drafted in 1941 survived.[15] When the Red Army reconquered Belarus in the summer of 1944, it carried out a draft among the local population, as a result of which around 750,000 men were mobilized.[16] It is unknown how many of them died in the last months of the war. Overall, it seems plausible that at least 700,000 men (and women) died as Red Army soldiers (either at the front, in hospitals in the rear, or in German captivity). In addition, according to the Belarusian Staff of the Partisan Movement, 37,378 people died fighting with the partisans in Belarus or went missing, but their actual number may have been higher, too.[17] To the number of combatants killed needs to be added an estimated few thousand men who, as former citizens of Poland and prewar residents of western Belarus, died fighting with the Polish Anders army. In short, a conservative estimate of 750,000 residents of prewar Belarus (living in the territories that would constitute post-1945 Belarus) who died as combatants during the war seems plausible.

Finally, it is unknown how many civilians who were taken to Germany as forced laborers died during the war. What also cannot be established with certainty is the number of civilians who were killed in occupied territory as a result of German-Soviet partisan warfare. The German side routinely overreported the number of partisans killed and underreported the number of civilians they murdered during the antipartisan operations. Similarly, the partisans overreported the number of German soldiers killed. They also underreported the number of civilians that they killed or disguised them as the killings of Germans or those deemed traitors. Christian Gerlach calculated that the German forces killed about 345,000 people during their antipartisan operations in Belarus (in its post-1945 borders), the overwhelming majority of them civilians.[18] In turn, according to the Belarusian Staff of the Partisan Movement, between June 1941 and January 1944, the partisans in Belarus killed 17,431 local policemen and others who were deemed traitors, probably village heads, translators, and anyone else sought to have collaborated with the Germans.[19] Most of them will have been prewar residents of Belarus. Yet the actual numbers must have been higher, given that the numbers for the second half of 1944 are missing. The number of civilians (family members of policemen or village heads but other civilians, too) who died at the hands of partisans is unknown, but the historical evidence, discussed in chapter 2, suggests that several hundred, perhaps a few thousand, civilian victims of partisan violence seem like a reasonable estimate.

Putting the different pieces together, I have thus reached the following numbers pertaining to the population that by 1941 lived in the territories that would constitute post-1945 Soviet Belarus:

- *945,000–1,116,000 civilian deaths, killed by the German forces in occupied territory*—this included almost the entire Jewish population of the republic, an estimated 500,000–671,000 Jews (thus reflecting both the lower and the higher estimates put forth by researchers); 345,000 civilians, most of them rural residents, who were killed by German forces during the antipartisan operations; and an additional 100,000 civilians who were killed for a variety of different reasons.
- *750,000 combatant deaths*—including at least 700,000 men (and women) who died as Red Army soldiers either at the front, in hospitals in the rear, or in German captivity; 37,378 people who died fighting with the partisans, in the majority residents of Belarus; and an estimated few thousand men who, as former citizens of Poland and prewar residents of western Belarus, died fighting with the Polish Anders army.
- Additionally, the Soviet partisans killed at least 17,431 people, most of these in all likelihood residents of Belarus, who served in the German-organized local police forces or else were deemed traitors. The partisans probably also killed several hundred, perhaps a few thousand, more civilians (family members of policemen or village heads but also other civilians). In total, an estimate of *twenty thousand victims of partisan retributive violence*—that is, residents of Belarus who were killed by the partisans—seems like a reasonable number.

Adding up these numbers, one reaches a total of 1,715,000–1,886,000 people who on the eve of the German occupation lived in the territories that would constitute post-1945 Soviet Belarus and who were killed as a direct result of the war. If one applies the higher number of civilian deaths provided by the Extraordinary State Commission (1,359,225 civilian deaths, not including the estimated 50,000 Jewish victims from Central Europe), then the overall number of war dead would have to be higher: 2,129,225 people (including the victims of partisan violence, whom it is unlikely that the ChGK included in their overall tally).

Taking both the lowest and the highest absolute numbers (1,715,000–2,129,225) of war deaths and applying this numerical range to the 1941 population size of the territories that would constitute post-1945 Belarus, one arrives at the following proportionate wartime losses: 19–22 percent of the population that on the eve of the German occupation lived in the territories that would constitute post-1945 Belarus were killed or died as a direct result of the war. These numbers are lower than those that are taught in schools and universities throughout Belarus today, according to which every third resident of the republic died in the war. According to the National Archive of Belarus, which also represents the government's position, "between 2.5 to 3 million and more" residents of Belarus (*zhiteli Belarusi*) died in the war, "no less than every third."[20] Yet those who cite these numbers (including Aleksandr Lukashenko, the authoritarian ruler of Belarus) overlook the fact that the National Archive of Belarus by now includes in its estimates not just the direct losses of the war (as a result of violence or deliberate killing policies), but indirect losses (*kosvennye poteri*), too.[21] Indirect losses are usually understood to mean deaths as a result of malnourishment, disease, or general wartime deprivation. Unfortunately, it is unclear how the National Archive of Belarus defines indirect losses. Neither is it clear on what sources the estimates are based nor what the ratio of direct to indirect losses was.

Another method that is commonly used by demographers—contrasting prewar and postwar population sizes—can be employed to test the plausibility of these estimates. However, in light of the massive population movement into and out of Belarus that took place in the first post-Nazi occupation years, it needs to be kept in mind that relying on postwar population statistics before 1948 would yield distorted results.[22] Beginning in 1948, war-related population movement declined significantly. If that year's (1948) population size (7.43 million people) is subtracted from the population size of 1941 (9 million in the territories that would form post-1945 Belarus), one finds that 1.57 million, or 17.4 percent fewer people were living in the republic.[23] This number by and large corresponds to the proportionate wartime losses that I have proposed above. There is, of course, a margin of error in this method. Comprehensive data on the number of prewar inhabitants of other Soviet republics who after 1944 moved to Belarus do not exist. Neither do data on the number of prewar inhabitants of Belarus who survived the war but settled outside Soviet Belarus, although it is possible that these numbers by and large offset one another. Still, the comparison of population sizes is meant to complement the calculations that I have reached on the basis of German and Soviet documents, combined with informed estimates.

To conclude, 1.7–2.1 million people, or 19–22 percent of the population that by June 1941 lived in the territories that would constitute post-1945 Soviet Belarus, were killed or died as a direct result of the war. This means that every fifth inhabitant, or if we want to allow for as broad a margin of error as possible, every fourth inhabitant of the republic (in its post-1945 borders) was killed or died as a direct result of the Second World War.

Notes

Introduction

1. Quoted from Ol'ga Bembel'-Dedok, *Vospominaniia* (Minsk: Propilei, 2006), 147.

2. Timothy Snyder, *Bloodlands: Europe between Hitler and Stalin* (New York: Basic Books, 2010), 165–66; Stephen Kotkin, *Stalin*, vol. 2: *Waiting for Hitler, 1929–1941* (London: Penguin, 2017), 897.

3. Christian Gerlach, *Kalkulierte Morde: Die deutsche Wirtschafts- und Vernichtungspolitik in Weißrußland 1941 bis 1944* (Hamburg: Hamburger Edition, 1999), 128–33.

4. Quoted from Neomi Izhar, *Chasia Bornstein-Bielicka: One of the Few. A Resistance Fighter and Educator, 1939–1947* (Jerusalem: Yad Vashem, 2009), 99.

5. Quoted from Zofia Brzozowska, "Wspomnienia z lat 1939–1945 przeżytych na Kresach Wschodnich." Recollections. Ośrodek Karta, Archiwum Wschodnie (hereafter AW) II/1252/2K, l. 5.

6. Vasil' Bykov, *Dolgaia doroga domoi: Kniga vospominanii* (Moscow: Ast, 2005); Litman Mor, *The War for Life* (Tel Aviv: n.p., 2007).

7. The title of my book is intellectually indebted to Heonik Kwon's seminal study on the memory of the Vietnam War (*Ghosts of War in Vietnam* [Cambridge: Cambridge University Press, 2008]). In contrast to Kwon, who studies the memory of tragic war death through popular imaginaries of ghosts, I use "ghosts of war" in a more metaphorical sense to mean specifically the choices that people made and that they were forced to make under Nazi occupation, and the ways in which these haunted postwar state and society, communities, and individuals alike. I have also found the following two books, with their brilliant combination of narrative and analysis, extremely inspiring: Mary Fulbrook, *A Small Town near Auschwitz: Ordinary Nazis and the Holocaust* (New York: Oxford University Press, 2012); and Marci Shore, *Caviar and Ashes: A Warsaw's Generation's Life and Death in Marxism, 1918–1968* (New Haven: Yale University Press, 2006).

8. The key works on transitional justice are Priscilla Hayner, *Unspeakable Truth: Transitional Justice and the Challenge of Truth Commissions*, 2nd ed. (Routledge: New York, 2011); Martha Minow, *Between Vengeance and Forgiveness: Facing History after Genocide and Mass Violence* (Boston: Beacon, 1998); Ruti G. Teitel, *Transitional Justice* (Oxford: Oxford University Press, 2000); and Ruti G. Teitel, *Globalizing Transitional Justice: Contemporary Essays* (Oxford: Oxford University Press, 2014). For a critical assessment of what criminal prosecution can achieve, see Laurel E. Fletcher and Harvey M. Weinstein, "Violence and Social Repair: Rethinking the Contribution of Justice to Reconciliation," *Human Rights Quarterly* 24 (2002): 573–639; and Eric Stover and Harvey M. Weinstein, eds., *My Neighbor, My Enemy: Justice and Community in the Aftermath of Mass Atrocity* (Cambridge: Cambridge University Press, 2004). For a

critique of the "liberal-legalist narrative" underlying the field of transitional justice, see Dustin N. Sharp, *Rethinking Transitional Justice for the Twenty-First Century: Beyond the End of History* (Cambridge: Cambridge University Press, 2018), viii–ix.

9. There were sixteen Soviet republics from August 1940 on and fifteen republics from July 1956 on.

10. On the emergence of Soviet Belarusian statehood and the interwar years, see Per Anders Rudling, *The Rise and Fall of Belarusian Nationalism, 1906–1931* (Pittsburgh: University of Pittsburgh Press, 2015).

11. Seventeen of the twenty-three districts of the pre-1941 Białystok region (called Belostok oblast between 1939 and 1941) including the city of Białystok and three districts of Brest oblast were handed back to Poland in 1945. See Anatol' F. Vialiki, *Belarus' u savetska-pol'skikh mizhdziarzhaŭnykh adnosinakh, 1944–1959 hh. XX st.* (Minsk: BDPU, 2010), 11–34.

12. To speak of the republic's "prewar population" would be incorrect, given that the pre-1941 territory of Belarus was larger than its post-1945 territory. It is important to note that both Belarus and Ukraine are counting their dead within their post-1945 borders, which include most of the parts of eastern Poland that were annexed to the Soviet Union in 1939, whereas Poland counts its dead within the pre-1939 Polish borders—as a result of which a double count of about two million people occurs. Nevertheless, Belarus would still be among the European countries with the highest proportionate human wartime losses even if one were only to calculate the number of dead for pre-1939 Belarus—that is, the territory that after 1939 came to be eastern Belarus.

13. These are my own calculations. In the scholarly literature, much disagreement exists on Belarus's wartime losses. For a detailed discussion of the available sources, their inherent problems, and how I have arrived at this number, see my Note on Wartime Losses.

14. John Sweets has described this dilemma for the population of Vichy France (*Choices in Vichy France: The French under Nazi Occupation* [New York: Oxford University Press, 1994], 169).

15. "Soviet citizens" included the inhabitants of the regions annexed in 1939–1940, regardless of whether they self-identified as such. The literature on the German occupation of the Soviet Union is extensive. For studies that examine its impact on the local populations, see Omer Bartov, *Anatomy of a Genocide: The Life and Death of a Town Called Buczacz* (New York: Simon & Schuster, 2018); Karel C. Berkhoff, *Harvest of Despair: Life and Death in Ukraine under Nazi Rule* (Cambridge, MA: Belknap, 2004); Alexander Brakel, *Unter Rotem Stern und Hakenkreuz: Baranowicze 1939 bis 1944. Das westliche Weißrussland unter sowjetischer und deutscher Besatzung* (Paderborn: Schöningh, 2009); Bernhard Chiari, *Alltag hinter der Front: Besatzung, Kollaboration und Widerstand in Weißrussland 1941–1944* (Düsseldorf: Droste, 1998); Laurie R. Cohen, *Smolensk under the Nazis: Everyday Life in Occupied Russia* (Rochester: University of Rochester Press, 2013); Martin Dean, *Collaboration in the Holocaust: Crimes of the Local Police in Belorussia and Ukraine* (Houndmills: Palgrave, 2000); Johannes Due Enstad, *Soviet Russians under Nazi Occupation: Fragile Loyalties in World War II* (Cambridge: Cambridge University Press, 2018); Tanja Penter, *Kohle für Stalin und Hitler: Arbeiten und Leben im Donbass, 1929–1953* (Essen: Klartext, 2010); Dieter Pohl, *Die Herrschaft der Wehrmacht: Deutsche Militärbesatzung und einheimische Bevölkerung in*

der Sowjetunion 1941–1944 (Munich: Oldenbourg, 2008); and Leonid Rein, *The Kings and the Pawns: Collaboration in Byelorussia during World War II* (New York: Berghahn Books, 2011).

16. For discussions on what constituted collaboration, cooperation, or accommodation, see, for example, Timothy Brook, *Collaboration: Japanese Agents and Local Elites in Wartime China* (Cambridge, MA: Harvard University Press, 2005), 1–13; Philippe Burrin, *France under the Germans: Collaboration and Compromise* (New York: New Press, 1998), 1–4, 459–67; Christoph Dieckmann, Babette Quinkert, and Tatjana Tönsmeyer, "Editorial," in *Kooperation und Verbrechen: Formen der "Kollaboration" im östlichen Europa 1939–1945*, ed. Christoph Dieckmann, Babette Quinkert, and Tatjana Tönsmeyer (Göttingen: Wallstein, 2003), 9–21; and Rein, *Kings and the Pawns*, 11–55.

17. Quoted from Jan T. Gross, "Themes for a Social History of War Experience and Collaboration," in *The Politics of Retribution in Europe: World War II and Its Aftermath*, ed. István Deák, Jan T. Gross, and Tony Judt (Princeton: Princeton University Press, 2000), 15–35, here 24 (first quotation), 26 (second quotation).

18. Kai Struve, "Anti-Jewish Violence in the Summer of 1941 in Eastern Galicia and Beyond," in *Romania and the Holocaust: Events—Contexts—Aftermath*, ed. Simon Geissbühler (Stuttgart: ibidem, 2016), 89–113. The book that sparked scholarly and public debates on local anti-Jewish violence was Jan T. Gross, *Neighbors: The Destruction of the Jewish Community in Jedwabne, Poland* (Princeton: Princeton University Press, 2001). For additional literature, see chapter 2.

19. On double occupation: Snyder, *Bloodlands*, 190. On stereotypical perceptions of Jews as supporters of communism: Gross, *Neighbors*, 46–53, 111–17, 152–56; Joanna Michlic, "The Soviet Occupation of Poland, 1939–1941, and the Stereotype of the Anti-Polish and Pro-Soviet Jew," *Jewish Social Studies* 13, no. 3 (2007): 135–76.

20. Jeffrey S. Kopstein and Jason Wittenberg, *Intimate Violence: Anti-Jewish Pogroms on the Eve of the Holocaust* (Ithaca: Cornell University Press, 2018), 14–16, 129. The book studies local anti-Jewish violence in six of the eight former Polish provinces that constituted eastern Poland before 1939, with a main focus on the Białystok region and eastern Galicia. For lack of local census data crucial to their research design, Kopstein and Wittenberg could not include Wilno and Nowogródek voivodships, which comprised large parts of the regions that constituted western Belarus in 1941.

21. On the radical Polish Right: Sara Bender, "Not Only in Jedwabne: Accounts of the Annihilation of the Jewish Shtetlach in Northeastern Poland in the Summer of 1941," *Holocaust Studies* 19, no. 1 (2013): 1–38, here 8, 28. On radical nationalist groups: Struve, "Anti-Jewish Violence," 103–13.

22. Diana Dumitru, *The State, Antisemitism, and Collaboration in the Holocaust: The Borderlands of Romania and the Soviet Union* (Cambridge: Cambridge University Press, 2016), 5–7.

23. For an older example of this exceptionalism argument in the Anglo-American literature, see Nicholas Vakar, *Belorussia: The Making of a Nation* (Cambridge, MA: Harvard University Press, 1956), 187. A more recent example is Barbara Epstein, *The Minsk Ghetto, 1941–1943: Jewish Resistance and Soviet Internationalism* (Berkeley: University of California Press, 2008), 43–46, 57–60. For one of many examples from Belarusian historiography, see Viktor Balakirev et al., eds., *Spasennaia zhizn': Zhizn' i*

vyzhivanie v Minskom getto (Minsk: Limarius, 2010), 10–12. Rein makes a similar observation about the exceptionalism argument (*Kings and the Pawns*, 259).

24. Writing on the extensive communal violence that engulfed the Kulen Vakuf region in Bosnia-Herzegovina in the summer of 1941, Max Bergholz has cautioned against static, generalizing interpretations of interethnic violence. Instead, he has drawn attention to the highly varied behavior of micro-level actors in multiethnic regions, which explains why continued escalation of violence on the ground can vary greatly according to time and place (*Violence as a Generative Force: Identity, Nationalism, and Memory in a Balkan Community* [Ithaca: Cornell University Press, 2016], 310–12).

25. On the war behind the front: Brakel, *Unter Rotem Stern und Hakenkreuz*, 279–379; Masha Cerovic, *Les enfants de Staline: La guerre des partisans soviétiques (1941–1944)* (Paris: Seuil, 2018), 231–62; Alexander V. Prusin, *The Lands Between: Conflict in the East European Borderlands, 1870–1992* (Oxford: Oxford University Press, 2010), 177–90; Kenneth Slepyan, *Stalin's Guerrillas: Soviet Partisans in World War II* (Lawrence: University Press of Kansas, 2006), 79–84.

26. Lawrence L. Langer coined this term with regard to the choices faced by Jewish ghetto and camp inmates, where "critical decisions did not reflect options between life and death, but between one form of 'abnormal' response and another, both imposed by a situation that was in no way of the victim's own choosing" ("The Dilemma of Choice in the Deathcamps," *Centerpoint* 4, no. 1 [1980]: 224).

27. Quoted from Stathis N. Kalyvas, *The Logic of Violence in Civil War* (Cambridge: Cambridge University Press, 2006), 389.

28. Dumitru, *State, Antisemitism, and Collaboration*, 1–9, 235 (quotation).

29. The Białystok region, where local violence against Jews was high during the summer of 1941, possibly continued to be the exception (meaning that the non-Jewish population continued to be more antagonistic toward Jews than in other parts of western Belarus, thus resembling the situation in Bessarabia).

30. Joseph Stalin, *On the Great Patriotic War of the Soviet Union: Speeches, Orders of the Day, and Answers to Foreign Press Correspondents* (Moscow: Foreign Languages Publishing House, 1944), 12–14.

31. Quoted from Rossiiskii gosudarstvennyi arkhiv sotsial'no-politicheskoi istorii (hereafter RGASPI) f. 625, op. 1, d. 44, l. 238.

32. Between 1944 and 1947, the Chinese Nationalist government prosecuted 30,185 Chinese nationals (deemed *hanjian*, literally "traitors to the Han Chinese") for collaboration with the Japanese wartime occupation regime. Of these, 14,932 were convicted. These statistics are incomplete, though, and thus estimates. It is unknown how many Chinese nationals were tried by the Chinese communists. Given the magnitude of the war in East Asia and the intensity of the Chinese Civil War (1946–1949), the actual numbers were perhaps closer to those of the Soviet Union. See Barak Kushner, *Men to Devils, Devils to Men: Japanese War Crimes and Chinese Justice* (Cambridge, MA: Harvard University Press, 2015), 120; and Yun Xia, *Down with Traitors: Justice and Nationalism in Wartime China* (Seattle: University of Washington Press, 2018), 6–8.

33. This is a revised and more conservative estimate than previously given in Franziska Exeler, "The Ambivalent State: Determining Guilt in the Post-World War II Soviet Union," *Slavic Review* 75, no. 3 (2016): 607. It is based on the statistics

(by year) provided in Oleg Mozokhin, *Pravo na repressii: Vnesudebnye polnomochiia organov gosudarstvennoi bezopasnosti. Statisticheskie svedeniia o deiatel'nosti VChK-OGPU-NKVD-MGB SSSR (1918–1953)* (Moscow: Kuchkovo pole, 2006), 481–626. There are no statistics available from 1954 on. See the discussion on numbers in Mark Edele, *Stalin's Defectors: How Red Army Soldiers Became Hitler's Collaborators, 1941–1945* (Oxford: Oxford University Press, 2017), 140–41.

34. Norwegian courts, for example, tried 3 percent (more than 168,000 people) of the country's population for collaboration with the Germans, about four times more than Belgium and six times more than France. The picture changes, though, if conviction and acquittal rates as well as type and length of sentence are factored in. In Belgium, 60 percent of all defendants received prison sentences, whereas in Norway, only about 18 percent did. France sentenced ten times more defendants to death than Czech courts but carried out only about one-tenth of the sentences. Czech courts, in contrast, carried out almost all death sentences. See Tony Judt, *Postwar: A History of Europe since 1945* (New York: Penguin, 2005), 45–50; Martin Conway, "Justice in Postwar Belgium: Popular Responses and Political Realities," in *Politics of Retribution in Europe*, 134; Luc Huyse, "The Criminal Justice System as a Political Actor in Regime Transitions: The Case of Belgium, 1944–50," in *Politics of Retribution in Europe*, 161; and Benjamin Frommer, *National Cleansing: Retribution against Nazi Collaborators in Postwar Czechoslovakia* (Cambridge: Cambridge University Press, 2005), 2–3, 90–91, 321.

35. Amir Weiner, *Making Sense of War: The Second World War and the Fate of the Bolshevik Revolution* (Princeton: Princeton University Press, 2001), 136–37. In developing his argument, Weiner provides examples of policemen, village heads, and Ukrainian nationalists, yet he also applies the term to anyone accused of having helped the Germans: "The irreversibility of any form of collaboration was further underlined by the absolute denial of political or social rehabilitation, even in the face of a dire need for experienced personnel" (183).

36. Jeffrey Jones, *Everyday Life and the "Reconstruction" of Soviet Russia during and after the Great Patriotic War, 1943–1948* (Bloomington: Indiana University Press, 2008); Olaf Mertelsmann and Aigi Rahi-Tamm, "Cleansing and Compromise: The Estonian SSR in 1944–1945," *Cahiers du monde russe* 49, no. 2 (2008): 319–40; Tanja Penter, "Local Collaborators on Trial: Soviet War Crimes Trials under Stalin (1943–1953)," *Cahiers du monde russe* 49, no. 2 (2008): 341–64; Vanessa Voisin, *L'URSS contre ses traîtres: L'épuration soviétique, 1941–1955* (Paris: Publications de la Sorbonne, 2015), 427–30.

37. Of the 360 civilians who in May and June 1944 were tried under the treason article 58-1a (or 63-1), for example, 9 percent received the death penalty, while the rest were sentenced to forced labor camp, most of them to ten years and more. Of the 134 people tried under the April 1943 decree, all received forced labor sentences. See the report on the NKVD military tribunals in Belarus for the second quarter of 1944 (National'nyi arkhiv Respubliki Belarus' [hereafter NARB] f. 4p, op. 29, d. 22, l. 35).

38. Between 1943 and 1945, around 5 percent of the defendants received the death sentence (Penter, "Local Collaborators," 356).

39. In the sources, "all people's war" is used synonymously with "all people's struggle" (*vsenarodnaia bor'ba*), and "all people's partisan war" with "all people's partisan struggle" (*vsenarodnaia partizanskaia bor'ba*).

40. Bykov, *Dolgaia doroga domoi*, 135.

41. Bembel'-Dedok, *Vospominaniia*, 182.

42. Quoted from Mor, *War for Life*, 221.

43. Quoted from Mor, *War for Life*, 220.

44. Stephen Kotkin, *Magnetic Mountain: Stalinism as a Civilization* (Berkeley: University of California Press, 1995).

45. On the partisan-civilian relationship: Slepyan, *Stalin's Guerrillas*, 157–62; Kenneth Slepyan, "Partisans, Civilians, and the Soviet State: An Overview," in *War in a Twilight World: Partisan and Anti-Partisan Warfare in Eastern Europe, 1939–45*, ed. Ben Shepherd and Juliette Pattinson (Basingstoke: Palgrave MacMillan, 2010), 35–57.

46. On silence and its historical variations: Efrat Ben-Ze'ev, Ruth Ginio, and Jay Winter, eds., *Shadows of War: A Social History of Silence in the Twentieth Century* (Cambridge: Cambridge University Press, 2010). On trying to reconcile individual memories of violent mass death with existing public and domestic commemorative orders: Heonik Kwon, *After the Massacre: Commemoration and Consolation in Ha My and My Lai* (Berkeley: University of California Press, 2006). On the interplay between official and private memory: Polly Jones, *Myth, Memory, Trauma: Rethinking the Stalinist Past in the Soviet Union, 1953–1970* (New Haven: Yale University Press, 2016); Lisa Kirschenbaum, *The Legacy of the Siege of Leningrad, 1941–1995: Myth, Memories, and Monuments* (Cambridge: Cambridge University Press, 2006).

47. On more present-day discourses on the "Partisan Republic" in Belarus: Alexandra Goujon, "Memorial Narratives of WWII Partisans and Genocide in Belarus," *East European Politics and Societies* 24, no. 1 (2010): 6–25; Simon Lewis, *Belarus—Alternative Visions: Nation, Memory and Cosmopolitanism* (Abingdon: Routledge, 2019), 53–80; David Marples, *"Our Glorious Past": Lukashenka's Belarus and the Great Patriotic War* (Stuttgart: ibidem, 2014), 103–37; Aleksandr Smolenchuk (Ales' Smalianchuk), "Pamiat' na pogranich'e (na primere pamiati o Vtoroi mirovoi voine)," in *Belorusy: Natsiia pogranich'ia*, ed. Aleksandr Kravtsevich, Aleksandr Smolenchuk, and Sergei Tokt' (Vilnius: EGU, 2011), 159–206.

48. On the Sovietization of the regions annexed in 1939 and 1940: Felix Ackermann, *Palimpsest Grodno: Nationalisierung, Nivellierung und Sowjetisierung einer mitteleuropäischen Stadt 1919–1991* (Wiesbaden: Harrassowitz, 2010); Tarik Cyril Amar, *The Paradox of Ukrainian Lviv: A Borderland City between Stalinists, Nazis, and Nationalists* (Ithaca: Cornell University Press, 2015); Kate Brown, *A Biography of No Place: From Ethnic Borderland to Soviet Heartland* (Cambridge, MA: Harvard University Press, 2005); Svetlana Frunchak, "Commemorating the Future in Post-War Chernivtsi," *East European Politics and Societies* 24, no. 3 (2010): 435–63; Iryna Kashtalian, *The Repressive Factors of the USSR's Internal Policy and Everyday Life of the Belarusian Society (1944–1953)* (Wiesbaden: Harrassowitz, 2016); Małgorzata Ruchniewicz, *Wieś zachodniobiałoruska 1944–1953: Wybrane aspekty* (Wrocław: Wydawnistwo Uniwersytet Wrocławskiego, 2010); Jan Szumski, *Sowietyzacja Zachodniej Białorusi 1944–1953: Propaganda i edukacja w służbie ideologii* (Cracow: Arcana, 2010); Elena Zubkova, *Pribaltika i Kreml' 1940–1953* (Moscow: ROSSPEN, 2008).

49. The best-known case of gendered retribution and sexual punishment is that of France. See Fabrice Virgili, *Shorn Women: Gender and Punishment in Liberation France* (Oxford: Berg, 2002). In the eyes of Soviet state security officers, women accused of

collaboration with the Germans were "socially harmful elements" (Voisin, *L'URSS contre ses traîtres*, 275–85).

50. The commission conducted interviews during the war and immediately after liberation from Nazi occupation. On the commission and its interviews: Oleg Budnitskii, "A Harvard Project in Reverse: Materials of the Commission of the USSR Academy of Sciences on the History of the Great Patriotic War—Publications and Interpretations," *Kritika: Explorations in Russian and Eurasian History* 19, no. 1 (2018): 175–202.

51. Judt, *Postwar*, 803–31; Peter Novick, *The Holocaust in American Life* (Boston: Houghton Mifflin, 1999), 1–11.

52. The scholarship on memory and history is tremendous. Within that literature, "memory" refers to many different phenomena, from cognitive and neural processes of remembering to autobiographical narratives and acts of public commemoration, to name just a few. For an overview, see Joan Tumblety, "Introduction: Working with Memory as Source and Subject," in *Memory and History: Understanding Memory as Source and Subject*, ed. Joan Tumblety (Abingdon: Routledge, 2013), 1–16.

53. According to official data compiled by the Belarusian Staff of the Partisan Movement on January 1, 1946, in total, the partisan movement in Belarus comprised 360,491 individuals from the summer of 1941 to its disbandment in the summer of 1944. This included 79,484 partisans who guarded family camps or fulfilled supporting functions, but for whom no further information exists. For the remaining 281,007 individuals (16 percent of them women), additional information on their gender, ethnicity, social background, prewar profession, and year as well as circumstances under which they joined are available. The numbers appear to refer to the partisan movement within the pre-1941 borders of the republic (including Belostok/Białystok oblast). See the data compiled by the Belarusian Staff of the Partisan Movement, January 1, 1946, NARB f. 4p, op. 33a, d. 634, ll. 1–10.

1. Contested Space

1. On the notion of borderlands: Jeremy Adelman and Stephen Aron, "From Borderlands to Borders: Empires, Nation-States, and the Peoples in Between in North American History," *American Historical Review* 104, no. 3 (1999): 816; Omer Bartov and Eric D. Weitz, "Introduction: Coexistence and Violence in the German, Habsburg, Russian, and Ottoman Borderlands," in *Shatterzones of Empires: Coexistence and Violence in the German, Habsburg, Russian, and Ottoman Borderlands*, ed. Omer Bartov and Eric D. Weitz (Bloomington: Indiana University Press, 2013), 1–20.

2. Eric Hobsbawm, *The Age of Extremes: The Short Twentieth Century, 1914–1991* (London: Michael Joseph, 1995).

3. Bembel'-Dedok, *Vospominaniia*, 21.

4. On the region's geography and economy in the late nineteenth century: Vakar, *Belorussia*, 30–36; Steven L. Guthier, "The Belorussians: National Identification and Assimilation, 1897–1970," *Soviet Studies* 29, 1 (1977), 37–61, here 43. Until the early nineteenth century, most peasants belonged to the Uniate Church, a mixture of Eastern Orthodoxy and Roman Catholicism. After the government in St. Petersburg abolished it in 1839, the bulk of the peasantry converted to Russian Orthodoxy (Andrew Savchenko, *Belarus—a Perpetual Borderland* [Leiden: Brill, 2009], 39–42).

5. The number of Belarusian-speakers was highest for Mogilev province, where the census recorded that 82 percent of the population spoke Belarusian as their first language, followed (in order) by speakers of Yiddish, Russian, and other languages. The lowest number of Belarusian-speakers (44 percent) was recorded for Grodno province, although they still constituted the largest language group here, followed by speakers of Ukrainian, Yiddish, Polish, and other languages. See *Pervaia vseobshchaia perepis' naseleniia Rossiiskoi imperii 1897 g.* (St. Petersburg: Izdanie Tsentral'nago statisticheskago komiteta Ministerstva vnutrennikh del, 1900–1904), 64–75, 80–83, 96–99, 102–3.

6. On the censuses: Piotr Eberhardt, *Przemiany narodowościowe na Białorusi* (Warsaw: Editions Spotkania, 1994), 19–20, 77–79; Vakar, *Belorussia*, 121. On the Russian empire's anti-Polish measures: Theodore Weeks, *Nation and State in Late Imperial Russia: Nationalism and Russification on the Western Frontier, 1863–1914* (DeKalb: Northern Illinois University Press, 1996), 12–14, 54–59, 99–102.

7. At the close of the nineteenth century, Jews constituted 14 percent of the population in the five imperial provinces of Minsk, Mogilev, Vitebsk, Vil'na, and Grodno (Vakar, *Belorussia*, 94; Guthier, "Belorussians," 44–45).

8. Weeks, *Nation and State*, 88.

9. Guthier, "Belorussians," 45. Whereas it must have been difficult to draw neat distinctions among the region's Slavic vernaculars, this was not the case with Yiddish, which is distinct from Slavic. One can thus assume that the 1897 census data on Yiddish was quite accurate.

10. Theodore Weeks, *Vilnius between Nations, 1795–2000* (DeKalb: Northern Illinois University Press, 2015), 59–61.

11. Belarusian (in its regional variations) was the language of the market and as such known by many who otherwise spoke Polish, Russian, or Yiddish at home. Yet peasants could also know some Yiddish that they had learned in interaction with Jewish artisans or traders, and older people knew Russian from the time of the tsarist empire.

12. Eberhardt, *Przemiany narodowościowe*, 20; Rudling, *Rise and Fall*, 3. On national indifference: Tara Zahra, "Imagined Noncommunities: National Indifference as a Category of Analysis," *Slavic Review* 69, no. 1 (2010): 93–119. This is also how the 1897 census takers saw it. Instead of asking people directly about their nationality, imperial ethnographers and statisticians used information on religion, native language, and estate (*soslovie*) to determine a person's nationality (*narodnost'*). They did so because they did not trust that the concept of nationality held much meaning for their respondents. See Juliette Cadiot, "Searching for Nationality: Statistics and National Categories at the End of the Russian Empire (1897–1917)," *Russian Review* 64, no. 3 (2005): 444.

13. Joshua Sanborn, *Imperial Apocalypse: The Great War and the Destruction of the Russian Empire* (Oxford: Oxford University Press, 2015), 239–62.

14. Khartanovich, *Gody nashei molodosti*, 14.

15. Bembel'-Dedok, *Vospominaniia*, 22.

16. Eric Lohr, *Nationalizing the Russian Empire: The Campaign against Enemy Aliens during World War I* (Cambridge, MA: Harvard University Press, 2003), 139–40, 144; Eric Lohr, "The Russian Army and the Jews: Mass Deportation, Hostages, and Violence during World War I," *Russian Review* 60, no. 3 (2001): 404–19; S. Pivovarchik,

"Tragedii pervoi mirovoi voiny: 'Evreishpiony.' Po materialam Natsional'nogo istoricheskogo archiva Belarusi v Grodno," in *Mirovoi krizis 1914–1920 godov i sud'ba vostochnoevropeiskogo evreistva*, ed. Oleg Budnitskii (Moscow: ROSSPEN, 2005), 82.

17. By the second year of the war, an estimated 3.3–6 million subjects of the Russian empire had become refugees (Peter Gatrell, *A Whole Empire Walking: Refugees in Russia during World War I* [Bloomington: Indiana University Press, 1999], 3, 31).

18. Testimony of Zinaida Suvorova, Yad Vashem Archives (hereafter YV) O.3/11082, l. 2.

19. Vejas Gabriel Liulevicius, *War Land on the Eastern Front: Culture, National Identity, and German Occupation in World War I* (Cambridge: Cambridge University Press, 2000), 7–8, 21, 29, 60, 71–75, 106, 125–27.

20. Lohr, "Russian Army," 414–15; Rudling, *Rise and Fall*, 70–75.

21. Quoted from Sulia Wolozhinski Rubin, *Against the Tide: The Story of an Unknown Partisan* (Jerusalem: Posner and Sons, 1980), 55–56.

22. Ben-Chion Pinchuk, *Shtetl Jews under Soviet Rule: Eastern Poland on the Eve of the Holocaust* (Oxford: Basil Blackwell, 1990), 119.

23. Lev Ovsishcher, *Vozvrashchenie* (Jerusalem: Kakhol'-Lavan, 1988), 9.

24. For a detailed assessment, see Rudling, *Rise and Fall*, 66–122.

25. Perhaps as many as 150,000 Jews were murdered across the lands of the former Russian empire, and countless women and girls raped. See Elissa Bemporad, *Legacy of Blood: Jews, Pogroms, and Ritual Murder in the Lands of the Soviets* (New York: Oxford University Press, 2019), 7; Elissa Bemporad, *Becoming Soviet Jews: The Bolshevik Experiment in Minsk* (Bloomington: Indiana University Press, 2013), 27–30; Oleg Budnitskii, *Russian Jews between the Reds and the Whites, 1917–1920*, trans. Timothy J. Portice (Philadelphia: University of Pennsylvania Press, 2012), 216–74; L. B. Miliakova, ed., *Kniga pogromov: Pogromy na Ukraine, v Belorussii i evropeiskoi chasti Rossii v period grazhdanskoi voiny 1918–1922 gg. Sbornik dokumentov* (Moscow: ROSSPEN, 2007), 609–49; and Rudling, *Rise and Fall*, 114–18.

26. Timothy Snyder, *The Reconstruction of Nations: Poland, Ukraine, Lithuania, Belarus, 1569–1999* (New Haven: Yale University Press, 2003), 60–65.

27. Francine Hirsch, *Empire of Nations: Ethnographic Knowledge and the Making of the Soviet Union* (Ithaca: Cornell University Press, 2005), 67, 149–50; Rudling, *Rise and Fall*, 124–29, 163.

28. Hirsch, *Empire of Nations*, 149–55.

29. Zina Gimpelevich, *Vasil Bykaŭ: His Life and Works* (Montreal: McGill-Queen's University Press, 2005), 14.

30. Hirsch, *Empire of Nations*, 148–55.

31. Vladimir Khartanovich, *Gody nashei molodosti: Vospominaniia. Poslevoennyi mirnyi trud: Vospominaniia* (Slonim: Slonimskaia tipografiia, 2006), 13–14.

32. AW II/1252/2K, l. 1. On Czombrów, see also "Czombrów: Pierwowzór Soplicowa wczoraj i dziś," *Echa Polesia: Kwartalnik Polaków na Polesiu*, October 29, 2015, http://polesie.org/4429/czombrow-pierwowzor-soplicowa-wczoraj-i-dzis/.

33. Izhar, *Chasia Bornstein-Bielicka*, 18–19.

34. AW II/1252/2K, l. 1.

35. Mor, *War for Life*, 11–15; Joice M. Nankivell and Sydney Loch, *The River of a Hundred Ways: Life in the War-Devastated Areas of Eastern Poland* (London: Allen and Unwin, 1924), 56–63.

36. Savchenko, *Belarus*, 100–104; Werner Benecke, *Die Ostgebiete der Zweiten Polnischen Republik: Staatsmacht und öffentliche Ordnung in einer Minderheitenregion 1918–1939* (Cologne: Böhlau, 1999), 81–137.

37. Khartanovich, *Gody nashei molodosti*, 15.

38. As recalled by Maria Gedymin, born in Nowogródek in 1929 (AW II/1285/2K, l. 4).

39. The interwar Polish state conducted two censuses, one in 1921 and another in 1931, but like the 1897 Russian imperial census, these were informed by politics. Aiming to increase the official number of Polish-speakers in the eastern regions, they recorded people of Roman Catholic faith as Poles, even if their first language was Belarusian, and categorized more than 700,000 locals in Polesia as speakers of *tutejszy*, the local language, and not as Belarusian speakers (Eberhardt, *Przemiany narodowościowe*, 77–79; Vakar, *Belorussia*, 121).

40. Benecke, *Ostgebiete*, 317–21; Kathryn Ciancia, *On Civilization's Edge: A Polish Borderland in the Interwar World* (Oxford: Oxford University Press, 2021), 57–58.

41. Ezra Mendelsohn, *The Jews of East Central Europe between the Two World Wars* (Bloomington: Indiana University Press, 1983), 68–83. On Vilnius: Mor, *War for Life*, 42–43. On Grodno: Izhar, *Chasia Bornstein-Bielicka*, 49.

42. For differing assessments of the repressive nature of the Polish state toward its Belarusian minority, compare Rudling, *Rise and Fall*, 164–70, 243–74; and Savchenko, *Belarus*, 104–13.

43. Ciancia, *On Civilization's Edge*, 3–4, 9–15, 19–46.

44. Khartanovich, *Gody nashei molodosti*, 13–32.

45. Khartanovich, *Gody nashei molodosti*, 24–25, 45–46, 63.

46. Quoted from Khartanovich, *Gody nashei molodosti*, 20.

47. Khartanovich, *Gody nashei molodosti*, 21, quotation on 48.

48. Khartanovich, *Gody nashei molodosti*, 120–27.

49. Kotkin, *Magnetic Mountain*, 2, 23, 358–59; Stephen Kotkin, "Modern Times: The Soviet Union and the Interwar Conjuncture," *Kritika: Explorations in Russian and Eurasian History* 2, no. 1 (2001): 111–64. Elissa Bemporad has argued that the civil war pogroms led Jewish communities to see the Bolsheviks as the least bad of all options and thus influenced the process of Jewish integration and acculturation into the Soviet system (*Legacy of Blood*, 20–34).

50. Bemporad, *Becoming Soviet Jews*, 202–10; Joanna Michlic-Coren, "Anti-Jewish Violence in Poland, 1918–1939 and 1945–1947," *Polin: Studies in Polish Jewry* 13 (2000): 34–61.

51. Ovsishcher, *Vozvrashchenie*, 14–16, quotation on 14.

52. On Soviet nationality policy: Hirsch, *Empire of Nations*, 1–18; Terry Martin, *The Affirmative Action Empire: Nations and Nationalism in the Soviet Union, 1923–1939* (Ithaca: Cornell University Press, 2001), 1–27. Specifically on Belarus: Bemporad, *Becoming Soviet Jews*, 81–111; Rudling, *Rise and Fall*, 123–63.

53. Peter Holquist, *Making War, Forging Revolution: Russia's Continuum of Crisis, 1914–1921* (Cambridge, MA: Harvard University Press, 2002), 285–86.

54. Bemporad, *Becoming Soviet Jews*, 31.

55. Golfo Alexopoulos, *Stalin's Outcasts: Aliens, Citizens, and the Soviet State, 1926–1936* (Ithaca: Cornell University Press, 2003), 2–6.

56. Lynne Viola, *Peasant Rebels under Stalin: Collectivization and the Culture of Peasant Resistance* (Oxford: Oxford University Press, 1996), 21–24.

57. Quoted from Gimpelevich, *Vasil Bykaŭ*, 16 (first quotation), 18 (second quotation).

58. Gimpelevich, *Vasil Bykaŭ*, 19–20.

59. Viola, *Peasant Rebels*, vii.

60. Viola, *Peasant Rebels*, 38–55, 89–91, 99, 235, 238–40.

61. Only in 1974 did peasants receive internal passports. See Gijs Kessler, "The Passport System and State Control over Population Flows in the Soviet Union, 1932–1940," *Cahiers du monde russe* 42, no. 2–4 (2001): 477–504; and David Shearer, *Policing Stalin's Socialism: Repression and Social Order in the Soviet Union, 1924–1953* (New Haven: Yale University Press, 2009), 243–84.

62. Viola, *Peasant Rebels*, 209.

63. Diana Siebert, *Bäuerliche Alltagsstrategien in der Belarussischen SSR (1921–1941): Die Zerstörung patriarchalischer Familienwirtschaft* (Stuttgart: Frank Steiner, 1998), 150–57.

64. Since collectivization continued throughout the second half of the 1930s, although at a slower pace, the total number of people deported from Belarus must have been a few thousand higher (Uladzimir Adamushka, *Palitychnyia represii 20–50-ykh hadoŭ na Belarusi* [Minsk: Belarus', 1994], 10; Siebert, *Bäuerliche Alltagsstrategien*, 159–60; Snyder, *Bloodlands*, 27). In the special settlements in the Northern Region, the mortality rate was estimated to be 15 percent by July 1931, and much higher among children (Lynne Viola, V. P. Danilov, N. A. Ivnitskii, and Denis Kozlov, eds., *The War Against the Peasantry, 1927–1930: The Tragedy of the Soviet Countryside* [New Haven: Yale University Press, 2005], 275).

65. Ovsishcher, *Vozvrashchenie*, 25.

66. Pavel Polian, *Against Their Will: The History and Geography of Forced Migrations in the USSR* (Budapest: Central European University Press, 2004), 69, 93; Martin, *Affirmative Action Empire*, 322–23.

67. The first public show trial was the 1922 trial of Socialist Revolutionaries. See Marc Jansen, *A Show Trial under Lenin: The Trial of the Socialist Revolutionaries, Moscow 1922* (The Hague: Martinus Nijhoff, 1982), 27, 50; and Julie A. Cassiday, "Marble Columns and Jupiter Lights: Theatrical and Cinematic Modeling of Soviet Show Trials in the 1920s," *Slavic and East European Journal* 42, no. 4 (1998): 640–60.

68. *Ugolovnyi kodeks RSFSR: Redaktsii 1926 goda s izmeneniiami i dopolneniiami do 1 iiulia 1927 goda* (Moscow: Iuridicheskoe izdatel'stvo NKIu RSFSR., 1927), 24–30.

69. *Ugolovnyi kodeks* (Moscow: Iuridicheskoe izdatel'stvo NKIu SSSR, 1940), 26–27.

70. Wladislaw Hedeler, *Chronik der Moskauer Schauprozesse 1936, 1937 und 1938: Planung, Inszenierung, und Wirkung* (Berlin: Akademie, 2003); William Chase, "Stalin as Producer: The Moscow Show Trials and the Construction of Mortal Threats," in *Stalin: A New History*, ed. Sarah Davies and James Harris (Cambridge: Cambridge University Press, 2005), 234.

71. Sheila Fitzpatrick, "How the Mice Buried the Cat: Scenes from the Great Purges of 1937 in the Russian Provinces," *Russian Review* 52, no. 3 (1993): 299–320. On Belarus: Iryna Ramanava, "The 'Lepel Case' and Regional Show Trials in the Belarusian Soviet

Socialist Republic (BSSR) in 1937," in *Political and Transitional Justice in Germany, Poland, and the Soviet Union from the 1930s to the 1950s*, ed. Magnus Brechtken, Władisław Bułhak and Jürgen Zarusky (Göttingen: Wallstein, 2019), 54–73.

72. V. N. Khaustov, V. P. Naumov, and N. S. Plotnikova, eds., *Lubianka: Stalin i Glavnoe upravlenie gosbezopasnosti NKVD 1937–1938* (Moscow: Mezhdunarodnyi fond "Demokratiia," 2004), 6.

73. Emanuil Ioffe, *Ot Miasnikova do Malofeeva: Kto rukovodil BSSR* (Minsk: Belarus', 2008), 73–98.

74. On Volkov and Berman's role during the Great Terror: Emanuil Ioffe, *Panteleimon Ponomarenko: "Zheleznyi" stalinist* (Minsk: Kharvest, 2015), 33–40.

75. On Ponomarenko: Ioffe, *Panteleimon Ponomarenko*, 5. On Tsanava: Emanuil Ioffe, *Lavrentii Tsanava: Ego nazyvali "Belorusskii Beriia"* (Minsk: Adukatsyia i vykhavanne, 2016), 6–11.

76. By late 1939, for example, the five most important positions on the Mogilev obkom had recently been filled anew (Gosudarstvennyi arkhiv obshchestvennykh ob"edinenii Mogilevskoi oblasti [hereafter GAOOMO] f. 9, op. 1a, d. 131, ll. 9–10).

77. On Malenkov: Oleg Khlevniuk, *Master of the House: Stalin and His Inner Circle* (New Haven: Yale University Press, 2009), 226–27. On Beriia and Tsanava: Amy Knight, *Beria—Stalin's First Lieutenant* (Princeton: Princeton University Press, 1993), 91, 122. On Malenkov and Ponomarenko, see the memoir by Afanasii Kovalev, until his 1939 arrest a high-ranking official in Belarus (*Kolokol moi—Pravda* [Minsk: Belarus', 1989], 139).

78. Bemporad, *Becoming Soviet Jews*, 189–95; Tat'iana Prot'ko, *Stanovlenie sovetskoi totalitarnoi sistemy v Belarusi (1917–1941 gg.)* (Minsk: Tesei, 2002), 131–35; Rudling, *Rise and Fall*, 294–97.

79. On Belarus: V. P. Danilov, Roberta Thompson Manning, and Lynne Viola, eds., *Tragediia sovetskoi derevni: Kollektivizatsiia i raskulachivanie. Dokumenty i materialy*, vol. 5: *1937–1939*, bk. 2: *1938–1939* (Moscow: Rossiiskaia politicheskaia entsiklopediia, 2006), 156. On the Kulak Operation in the Soviet Union at large: Snyder, *Bloodlands*, 78–86.

80. On the Koren'shchina: Viacheslav Nosevich, *Traditsionnaia belorusskaia derevnia v evropeiskoi perspektive* (Minsk: Tekhnalohiia, 2004), 18–22, 310, 326–28 (table 65).

81. Nikita V. Petrov and Arsenii B. Roginskii, "Pol'skaia operatsiia NKVD 1937–1938 gg.," in *Repressii protiv poliakov i pol'skikh grazhdan*, ed. Aleksandr E. Gur'ianov (Moscow: Zven'ia, 1997), 41, table 2. According to Tat'iana Prot'ko, the number of victims was higher: 21,407 people in total (*Stanovlenie*, 336). On "spies": Iryna Ramanava, "Zhytstse va ŭmovakh savetskaha pahranichcha: Belaruskae pahranichcha pa savetski bok dziarzhaŭnai miazhy ŭ 1930-ia hh.," in *Pograniczna Białorusi w perspektywie interdyscyplinarnej—Pamezhzhy Belarusi ŭ mizhdystsyplinarnai perspektyve*, ed. Elżbieta Smułkowa and Anna Engelking (Warsaw: DiG, 2007), 77–79. On the Polish Operation in the Soviet Union at large: Snyder, *Bloodlands*, 89–104.

82. Snyder, *Bloodlands*, 80–82.

83. Ioffe, *Panteleimon Ponomarenko*, 59.

84. According to NKVD sources, 51,794 people were arrested in Belarus from October 1, 1936, to July 1, 1938, most of them as part of the Kulak Operation and the Polish Operation. See source 66 in Danilov, Manning, and Viola, *Tragediia sovetskoi*

derevni, 5, bk. 2:161. However, the total number of deaths must have been higher by at least a couple of thousand, as Stalin called a halt to the mass killings only in November 1938. The total number of people killed in Belarus during the Great Terror is my own estimate. It is unknown how many people were killed during the Kulak Operation, but it is known that almost 90 percent of those who were arrested during the Polish Operation were killed. In the Soviet Union at large, the percentage of death sentences to Gulag sentences during the Great Terror was roughly equal. Applying this ratio to Belarus, an estimate of at least thirty thousand people who were killed by the NKVD from October 1936 to July 1938 seems reasonable. This corresponds with the numbers provided by Iryna Ramanava, who writes that from the spring of 1937 to November 1938, the NKVD arrested almost fifty-five thousand people in Belarus, of whom more than twenty-seven thousand were executed ("'Lepel Case' and Regional Show Trials," 73).

85. Khartanovich, *Gody nashei molodosti*, 53.

86. David Marples, "Kuropaty: The Investigation of a Stalinist Historical Controversy," *Slavic Review* 53, no. 2 (1994): 517.

87. Ovsishcher, *Vozvrashchenie*, 17. On Kublichi and Bychki: Bykov, *Dolgaia doroga domoi*, 35; Gimpelevich, *Vasil Bykaŭ*, 24–25.

88. Quoted from: Bembel'-Dedok, *Vospominaniia*, 144–45.

89. Adamushka, *Palitychnyia represii*, 9. Significantly higher numbers (up to 1.5 million victims from 1917 to 1953) also circulate in the scholarly literature, but these are implausible.

90. For the January 1937 census data that registered 5.19 million people living in Soviet Belarus at that time, see table 6 in N. A. Aralovets, V. B. Zhiromskaia, and I. N. Kiselev, eds., *Vsesoiuznaia perepis' naseleniia 1937 g.: Kratkie itogi* (Moscow: Institut istorii SSSR AN SSSR, 1991), 59. In contrast to the 1939 census, which the government falsified to cover up the number of victims of state violence, scholars agree that the 1937 census is more or less accurate: A. G. Volkov, "Perepis' naseleniia 1937 goda: Vymysly i pravda," *Ekspress-informatsiia: Seriia "Istoriia statistiki"* 3–5, pt. 2 (1990), 6–63; Catherine Merridale, "The 1937 Census and the Limits of Stalinist Rule," *Historical Journal* 39, no. 1 (1996): 235.

91. It also granted the city of Wilno to still-independent Lithuania, which the Soviet Union then annexed in the summer of 1940 (Snyder, *Bloodlands*, 116–17, 142).

92. Belostok (Białystok) oblast had an estimated 1.35 million inhabitants. See V. S. Kozhurin, "O chislennosti naseleniia SSSR nakanune Velikoi Otechestvennoi voiny (neizvestnye dokumenty)," *Voenno-istoricheskii zhurnal* no. 2 (1991): 25–26.

93. Jan T. Gross, *Revolution from Abroad: The Soviet Conquest of Poland's Western Ukraine and Western Belorussia*, exp. ed. (Princeton: Princeton University Press, 2002), 263–64; Panteleimon Ponomarenko, *Tridtsat' let sovetskoi vlasti v Belorussii* (Minsk: Gosudarstvennoe izdatel'stvo BSSR, 1947), 33.

94. Quoted from "Druzhba i bratstvo narodov SSSR," *Sovetskaia Belorussiia*, September 23, 1939.

95. Bembel'-Dedok, *Vospominaniia*, 141.

96. Khartanovich, *Gody nashei molodosti*, 65–67.

97. Quoted from Henryk Bułhak's recollections (AW I/70, l. 29). The author was born in Wilno in 1930.

98. Izhar, *Chasia Bornstein-Bielicka*, 72.

99. On the different accounts and interpretation of what happened in September 1939 in Grodno: Ackermann, *Palimpsest Grodno*, 93–98.

100. Izhar, *Chasia Bornstein-Bielicka*, 74–80.

101. Gross, *Revolution from Abroad*, 35–45.

102. Quoted from AW II/1252/2K, l. 2.

103. Quoted from AW II/1252/2K, l. 2.

104. Ackermann, *Palimpsest Grodno*, 100, 104; Wolozhinski Rubin, *Against the Tide*, 121–23.

105. Pinchuk, *Shtetl Jews under Soviet Rule*, 136.

106. Ackermann, *Palimpsest Grodno*, 100, 104, 112; Brakel, *Unter Rotem Stern und Hakenkreuz*, 63–64, 74–75; Gross, *Revolution from Abroad*, 126–29, 267.

107. Izhar, *Chasia Bornstein-Bielicka*, 71–98.

108. Michlic-Coren, "Anti-Jewish Violence in Poland," 37. Specifically on Grodno: Ackermann, *Palimpsest Grodno*, 59–60.

109. Izhar, *Chasia Bornstein-Bielicka*, 61, 80.

110. Ruchniewicz, *Wieś zachodniobiałoruska*, 90–117, 475.

111. For the total number of arrests, see Grzegorz Hryciuk, "Victims 1939–1941: The Soviet Repressions in Eastern Poland," in *Shared History—Divided Memory: Jews and Others in Soviet-Occupied Poland, 1939–1941*, ed. Elazar Barkan, Elizabeth A. Cole, and Kai Struve (Leipzig: Leipziger Universitätsverlag, 2007), 182–84. The numbers for Belarus are my own calculations based on Piotr Eberhardt, *Political Migrations on Polish Territories (1939–1950)* (Warsaw: IGiPZ PAN, 2011), 60, table III.4; O. A. Gorlanov and Arsenii B. Roginskii, "Ob arestakh v zapadnykh oblastiakh Belorussii i Ukrainy v 1939–1941 gg.," in Gur'ianov, *Repressii protiv poliakov*, 88; and U. I. Adamushka et al., eds., *"Ty z zakhodniai, ia z uskhodniai nashai Belarusi . . ." Verasen' 1939 h.–1956 h. Dakumenty i materyialy*, 2 vols. (Minsk: NARB, 2009), 1:250. To this have to be added an unknown number of people arrested between March and June 19, 1941, which is why the overall number of forty-three thousand arrested seems highly plausible.

112. Ioffe, *Panteleimon Ponomarenko*, 71–76.

113. For the total number of deportees: Hryciuk, "Victims 1939–1941," 195. The number of deportees from western Belarus is derived as follows. According to NKVD sources, 101,726 plus an unknown number of people that made up an additional train load (echelon) were deported from western Belarus in the three deportations in 1940. Since on average, one echelon encompassed 1,000 people, one reaches 102,726 people in total. To that one needs to add 22,353 people who were deported from western Belarus on the night of June 19–20, 1940, which adds up to 125,079 deportees. See Aleksandr E. Gur'ianov, "Pol'skie spetspereselentsy v SSSR v 1940–1941 gg.," in Gur'ianov, *Repressii protiv poliakov*, 119; and Adamushka et al., *"Ty z zakhodniai"*, 1:250.

114. Quoted from AW II/1252/2K, l. 3.

115. AW II/1252/2K, ll. 3–4.

116. Aleksandr Gur'ianov, "Die sowjetische Repressionspolitik in den besetzten polnischen Ostgebieten 1939–1941," in *Polen unter deutscher und sowjetischer Besatzung 1939–1945*, ed. Jacek Andrzej Młynarczyk (Osnabrück: Fibre, 2009), 220, table 1. Hryciuk arrives at a higher number: according to him, the Soviet occupation of eastern Poland resulted in the "death or departure" of 720,000 people from this region, but he

includes prisoners of war who were released from Soviet confinement, civilians who were forcibly recruited for work in the Soviet Union, and about 150,000 men who were drafted into the Red Army in 1940 and 1941 ("Victims 1939–1941," 199–200).

117. Considering territorial proportions, it is plausible to assume that of the thirty-nine thousand Polish prisoners of war kept in Soviet confinement by December 1939, about ten thousand came from western Belarus (Hryciuk, "Victims 1939–1941," 179–81).

118. That percentage is derived on the basis of statistics issued in December 1941 by the Polish government in exile in London. According to this source, by the fall of 1939, 4.73 million people lived in the territories (including Białystok voivodeship) that the Soviets annexed to Belarus. Of these (according to the government data), 43.9 percent were adherents of Roman Catholicism, 46.5 percent of Christian Orthodoxy (*prawosławne*), and 9.3 percent of Judaism. See *Mały rocznik statystyczny Polski: Wrzesień 1939–czerwiec 1941*, published by the Polish Ministry of Information (Warsaw: Zakład Wydawnictw Statystycznych, 1990), 5, table 11, and 10, table 17. Not included in these calculations are refugees (mostly Jewish) from German-occupied western Poland.

119. On individual agency: Kotkin, *Magnetic Mountain*, 154–55, 215–37.

120. Benecke, *Ostgebiete*, 133; Guthier, "Belorussians," 60.

121. Bemporad, *Becoming Soviet Jews*, 4–7, 112–44, 211.

122. Ovsishcher, *Vozvrashchenie*, 9–27.

123. Arkadii Zel'tser, *Evrei sovetskoi provintsii: Vitebsk i mestechki 1917–1941* (Moscow: ROSSPEN, 2006), 317–28.

124. Quoted from Ovsishcher, *Vozvrashchenie*, 14.

125. Quoted from Bembel'-Dedok, *Vospominaniia*, 67.

126. AW II/1252/2K, ll. 1–2.

127. Khartanovich, *Gody nashei molodosti*, 16–18.

128. Izhar, *Chasia Bornstein-Bielicka*, 61–63.

129. On generational differences within Jewish communities: Anika Walke, *Pioneers and Partisans: An Oral History of Nazi Genocide in Belorussia* (Oxford: Oxford University Press, 2015), 5, 37–66.

130. Zel'tser, *Evrei sovetskoi provintsii*, 418–19.

131. Leonid Smilovitsky, "A Demographic Profile of the Jews in Belorussia from the Pre-War Time to the Post-War Time," *Journal of Genocide Research* 5, no. 1 (2003): 117, 121.

132. Quoted from YV O.3/11082, l. 5.

133. YV O.3/11082, ll. 5–6. For similar life stories, see Walke, *Pioneers and Partisans*, 37–66.

134. On distance between the Slavic villages and the Jewish urban population in interwar Belarus: Daniel Romanovsky, "The Holocaust in the Eyes of Homo Sovieticus: A Survey Based on Northeastern Belorussia and Northwestern Russia," *Holocaust and Genocide Studies* 13, no. 3 (1999): 375.

2. At the Heart of Darkness

1. YV O.3/11082, ll. 6–7, quotation l. 7.

2. YV O.3/11082, ll. 5–8.

3. Martin Dean and Mel Hecker, eds., *The United States Holocaust Memorial Museum Encyclopedia of Camps and Ghettos, 1933–1945*, vol. 2: *Ghettos in German-Occupied Eastern Europe*, pt. A (Bloomington: Indiana University Press, 2012), 1709–12.

4. YV O.3/11082, ll. 8–25.

5. Wolozhinski Rubin, *Against the Tide*, 63–65; AW II/1252/2K, l. 5; V. I. Adamushko et al., eds., *Belarus' v pervye mesiatsy Velikoi Otechestvennoi voiny (22 iiunia–avgust 1941 g.): Dokumenty i materialy* (Minsk: NARB, 2006), 112.

6. Gerlach, *Kalkulierte Morde*, 129, 791.

7. Quoted from Kaplan's letter in RGASPI f. 83, op. 1, d. 13, ll. 20, 21.

8. Quoted from RGASPI f. 83, op. 1, d. 13, ll. 20, 22.

9. Rebecca Manley, *To the Tashkent Station: Evacuation and Survival in the Soviet Union at War* (Ithaca: Cornell University Press, 2009), 66–76.

10. Quoted from RGASPI f. 17, op. 88, d. 480, l. 74.

11. "Front" in Russian means "Army Group."

12. On their travel route (with slight variations): V. I. Adamushko et al., eds., *Belorusy v sovetskom tylu, iiul' 1941 g.–1944 g.: Sbornik dokumentov i materialov*, 2 vols. (Minsk: NARB, 2010), 1:82–88; Adamushko et al., *Belarus' v pervye mesiatsy*, 32–47. On Ponomarenko, see also Ioffe, *Panteleimon Ponomarenko*, 93–102.

13. Adamushko et al., *Belorusy v sovetskom tylu*, 1:14–15.

14. Ioffe, *Panteleimon Ponomarenko*, 112.

15. See Ponomarenko's report to Molotov, August 18, 1941, in Adamushko et al., *Belorusy v sovetskom tylu*, 1:184–209. On the archives, see NARB, f. 4p, op. 29, d. 603, l. 401.

16. Manley, *To the Tashkent Station*, 32–47.

17. This was the case with Dania Berzin's family from Gomel' (Dania Berzin, *Vospominaniia o nashem detstve* [Rishon le-Tsiyon: MeDial, 2009], 6–33).

18. Manley, *To the Tashkent Station*, 52.

19. Albert Kaganovitch, *The Long Life and Swift Death of Jewish Rechitsa: A Community in Belarus, 1625–2000* (Madison: University of Wisconsin Press, 2013), 259–60.

20. Ovsishcher, *Vosvrashchenie*, 51–54.

21. Adamushko et al., *Belorusy v sovetskom tylu*, 1:145. Other estimates range from 300,000 to 1,000,000 people (evacuees and refugees). See the discussion in Ioffe, *Panteleimon Ponomarenko*, 127–31.

22. On Ukraine and the Baltic republics: Alexander Statiev, *The Soviet Counterinsurgency in the Western Borderlands* (Cambridge: Cambridge University Press, 2010), 54–55.

23. On Cherven': Anna Kaminski, ed., *Mestsy pamiatsi akhviaraŭ kamunizmu ŭ Belarusi* (Berlin: Bundesstiftung Aufarbeitung, 2011), 219–30.

24. Quoted from his report to the Central Committee of Belarus, August 5, 1941 (RGASPI f. 17, op. 88, d. 480, l. 132). On the Grodno prison breakout: Ackermann, *Palimpsest Grodno*, 129. On executions of prison inmates in Pinsk, Oshmiany, Vileika, Glubokoe, and Shumilinskii district in Vitebsk oblast: Kaminski, *Mestsy pamiatsi*, 140, 150–52, 232–33, 245–47; Iryna Kashtalian, "Belarus' pad uplyvam palitychnykh represii savetskaha chasu (1917–1953 hh.)," in Kaminski, *Mestsy pamiatsi*, 17. On similar incidents in Ukraine and Lithuania: Gross, *Revolution from Abroad*, 178–81.

25. Estimates regarding the total number of prison inmates shot by the NKVD in the western regions of the Soviet Union vary. According to their own sources, members of the NKVD killed 11,319 prisoners (Statiev, *Soviet Counterinsurgency*, 55). Kai Struve provides a slightly lower number, 7,500 to 10,000 victims (*Deutsche Herrschaft, ukrainischer Nationalismus, antijüdische Gewalt: Der Sommer 1941 in der Westukraine* [Berlin: De Gruyter Oldenbourg, 2015], 216). That number may be too low, as it does not include the number of inmates in corrective labor colonies. In addition to the prisons proper, only two corrective labor colonies in Belarus were evacuated. The majority of those imprisoned in twenty-three other colonies were shot during the first days of the war. By December 1941, the NKVD in Moscow was still not able to determine what had happened to another forty-nine corrective labor colonies located on Belarusian territory (Aleksandr Kokurin et al., eds., *Prikazano pristupit': Evakuatsiia zakliuchennykh iz Belarusi v 1941 godu. Sbornik dokumentov* [Minsk: NARB, 2005], 54–56).

26. Quoted from his report, December 2, 1941 (NARB f. 4p, op. 33a, d. 63, l. 83). On looting in Bobruisk, see also Kaplan's report (RGASPI f. 83, op. 1, d. 13, l. 22).

27. On Kublichi: Dean and Hecker, *United States Holocaust Memorial Museum Encyclopedia of Camps and Ghettos*, 1694–95. On Antonovo, see Arsen Vanitskii's recollections: Arsen Vanitskii, "Voina i derevnia," *Nioman*, no. 4 (2000): 215.

28. Quoted from her recollections: Regina Bakunovich, "Okkupirovannoe detstvo: Vospominanie-monolog," *Nioman*, no. 9 (1998): 192.

29. Quoted from Shalom Cholawsky, *The Jews of Bielorussia during World War II* (Amsterdam: Harwood Academic Publishers, 1998), 271.

30. On Brest, see Ioffe's report, probably written between July 8 and October 11, 1941 (RGASPI f. 17, op. 88, d. 480, l. 140). On Grodno: RGASPI f. 17, op. 88, d. 480, l. 132.

31. Quoted from the report by A. Minchenko, secretary of the Pinsk obkom, probably written between July 8 and October 11, 1941 (RGASPI f. 17, op. 88, d. 480, l. 108).

32. Quoted from his report, July 13, 1941 (RGASPI f. 17, op. 88, d. 480, l. 10).

33. In July 1943, Army Group Center Rear Area came under the command of General Ludwig Kübler of the Wehrmacht (Gerlach, *Kalkulierte Morde*, 135).

34. Gerlach, *Kalkulierte Morde*, 134–42, 156–68, 173–76, 180, 196–200.

35. Gerlach, *Kalkulierte Morde*, 180–96, quotation 182.

36. In the Nazi racial hierarchy, Balts ranked higher than Slavs, which is why the German occupation of the three Baltic states was to some extent less harsh than that of the other western regions of the Soviet Union (Mark Mazower, *Hitler's Empire: Nazi Rule in Occupied Europe* [London: Penguin, 2009], 154–55).

37. Berkhoff, *Harvest of Despair*, 1, 44; Gerlach, *Kalkulierte Morde*, 46–59; Rein, *Kings and the Pawns*, 88–93.

38. Gerlach, *Kalkulierte Morde*, 1126–30. Berlin did use starvation whenever it deemed that tactic useful, such as during the 1941–1944 blockade of Leningrad, when more than one million inhabitants died of hunger (Snyder, *Bloodlands*, 160–63, 172–73).

39. Gerlach, *Kalkulierte Morde*, 456–79.

40. Gerd Ueberschär and Wolfram Wette, eds., *"Unternehmen Barbarossa": Der deutsche Überfall auf die Sowjetunion 1941. Berichte, Analysen, Dokumente* (Paderborn: Schöningh, 1984), 312–14.

41. Quoted from Klaus-Michael Mallmann, Andrej Angrick, Jürgen Matthäus, and Martin Cüppers, eds., *Die "Ereignismeldungen UdSSR" 1941: Dokumente der Einsatzgruppen in der Sowjetunion*, vol. 1 (Darmstadt: Wissenschaftliche Buchgesellschaft, 2011), 21. Until mid-July 1941, Einsatzgruppe B was called Einsatzgruppe C (Gerlach, *Kalkulierte Morde*, 185).

42. Mallmann et al.,*"Ereignismeldungen UdSSR,"* 547–48; Gerlach, *Kalkulierte Morde*, 503–9.

43. Snyder, *Bloodlands*, 175–84. Christian Streit, *Keine Kameraden: Die Wehrmacht und die sowjetischen Kriegsgefangenen 1941–1945*, 2nd ed. (Bonn: Dietz, 1991), 24, 187–89, writes of 2.5–3.3 million killed. On Belarus: Gerlach, *Kalkulierte Morde*, 778–834; NARB f. 845, op. 1, d. 146, l. 10.

44. Michaela Kipp, *"Grossreinemachen im Osten": Feindbilder in deutschen Feldpostbriefen im Zweiten Weltkrieg* (Frankfurt am Main: Campus, 2014), 19, 50–56, 119–25, 152, 460.

45. See the report by a man named Iazykovich, secretary of the Poles'e obkom, no date but must have been between July and October 1941 (RGASPI f. 17, op. 88, d. 480, ll. 91, 95).

46. Wendy Jo Gertjejanssen, "Victims, Heroes, Survivors: Sexual Violence on the Eastern Front during World War II" (PhD diss., University of Minnesota, 2004), 154–225, 253–317; Regina Mühlhäuser, *Eroberungen: Sexuelle Gewalttaten und intime Beziehungen deutscher Soldaten in der Sowjetunion, 1941–1945* (Hamburg: Hamburger Edition, 2010), 85–100, 214–39.

47. Interview with Iurii Taits, August 28, 1944, conducted by the Commission for the History of the Great Patriotic War, Institut rossiskoi istorii RAN (hereafter IRI RAN) f. 2, razdel II, op. 4, d. 117, ll. 7–8.

48. Dean, *Collaboration*, 105–6; Markus Eikel and Valentina Sivaieva, "City Mayors, Raion Chiefs and Village Elders in Ukraine, 1941–4: How Local Administrators Co-Operated with the German Occupation Authorities," *Contemporary European History* 23, no. 3 (2014): 408, 411–13; Gerlach, *Kalkulierte Morde*, 196–202; Rein, *Kings and the Pawns*, 100–107.

49. Dean, *Collaboration*, 60; Gerlach, *Kalkulierte Morde*, 202–9. District Białystok was primarily staffed with personnel from adjacent East Prussia, but even here, the mayors of smaller towns were usually locals, as were village heads, police forces, and administrative staff.

50. Gerlach, *Kalkulierte Morde*, 199n428, 202, 204–5.

51. Dean, *Collaboration*, 60; Rein, *Kings and the Pawns*, 325–28, 364–77. For the population size under German rule, see Babette Quinkert, "Einleitung," in *Deutsche Besatzung in der Sowjetunion 1941–1944: Vernichtungskrieg, Reaktionen, Erinnerung*, ed. Babette Quinkert and Jörg Morré (Paderborn: Schöningh, 2014), 11.

52. Gerlach, *Kalkulierte Morde*, 209.

53. Waitman Wade Beorn, *Marching into Darkness: The Wehrmacht and the Holocaust in Belarus* (Cambridge, MA: Harvard University Press, 2014); Hannes Heer, "Killing Fields: The Wehrmacht and the Holocaust in Belorussia, 1941–1942," *Holocaust and Genocide Studies* 11, no. 1 (1997): 79–101.

54. Petra Rentrop, *Tatorte der "Endlösung": Das Ghetto Minsk und die Vernichtungsstätte von Maly Trostinez* (Berlin: Metropol, 2011).

55. Izhar, *Chasia Bornstein-Bielicka*, 151–52.

56. Dean and Hecker, *United States Holocaust Memorial Museum Encyclopedia*, xxxi–xxxv.

57. Sara Bender, *The Jews of Białystok during World War II and the Holocaust* (Waltham: Brandeis University Press, 2008), 90–97.

58. Dean and Hecker, *United States Holocaust Memorial Museum Encyclopedia*, xxxiii–xxxv.

59. Ovsishcher, *Vozvrashchenie*, 51–54. On Bogushevsk: Dean and Hecker, *United States Holocaust Memorial Museum Encyclopedia*, 1725–26.

60. Dean, *Collaboration*, 78. This also pertains to District Białystok, with the exception that the liquidation of provincial ghettos in November 1942 went hand in hand with the establishment of five regional transit camps, in which Jews were concentrated before being sent to extermination camps in German-occupied Poland (Dean and Hecker, *United States Holocaust Memorial Museum Encyclopedia*, 858–62).

61. Dean and Hecker, *United States Holocaust Memorial Museum Encyclopedia*, 1247–51.

62. Quoted from Wolozhinski Rubin, *Against the Tide*, 73.

63. Quoted from Wolozhinski Rubin, *Against the Tide*, 73.

64. Wolozhinski Rubin, *Against the Tide*, 82–149; Dean and Hecker, *United States Holocaust Memorial Museum Encyclopedia*, 1248–51; Jack Kagan and Dov Cohen, *Surviving the Holocaust with the Russian Jewish Partisans* (London: Vallentine Mitchell, 1998), 77–84.

65. Dean and Hecker, *United States Holocaust Memorial Museum Encyclopedia*, 866–70, 1233–37.

66. These numbers are based on different estimates taken from Gerlach, *Kalkulierte Morde*, 1158; Leonid Smilovitskii, *Katastrofa evreev v Belorussii, 1941–1944 gg.* (Tel Aviv: Biblioteka Matveia Chernogo, 2000), 27–28; and Gennadii Vinnitsa, *Kholokost na okkupirovannoi territorii Vostochnoi Belarusi v 1941–1944 gg.* (Minsk: Kovcheg, 2011), 193. If we include the Białystok region, the number of Jews living in pre-1941 Belarus probably amounted to 1,000,000, and the number of victims up to 831,000, perhaps even higher. On different estimates of the size of the Białystok region's Jewish population: Dean and Hecker, *United States Holocaust Memorial Museum Encyclopedia*, 858–62.

67. Dean, *Collaboration*, 78–99; Gerlach, *Kalkulierte Morde*, 612–13, 625; Rein, *Kings and the Pawns*, 268–69.

68. Wolozhinski Rubin, *Against the Tide*, 149.

69. Rein, *Kings and the Pawns*, 266–67.

70. Dean, *Collaboration*, 105–6. On Borisov: Aleksei Litvin, "Mestnaia vspomogatel'naia politsiia na territorrii Belarusi (iiul' 1941–iiul' 1944 gg.)," in *Belarus' u XX stahoddzi*, vol. 2, ed. Igor' Kuznetsov and Iakov Basin (Minsk: no publisher, 2003), http://jewishfreedom.org/page647.html.

71. Wolozhinski Rubin, *Against the Tide*, 46–70, 137, quotation on 69.

72. Quoted from the testimony of Sofiia Khabai (YV O.3/4212, l. 3).

73. Eberhardt, *Przemiany narodowościowe*, 68, table 14; *Davyd-Haradok Memorial Book = Memorial Book of David-Horodok*, trans. from the Yiddish and part of the 1981 Hebrew original (New York: New York Public Library, 2003), 4–9. The memorial book is also available at https://www.jewishgen.org/Yizkor/Davyd-Haradok/Davyd-Haradok.html#TOC.

74. Quoted from Miriam Bragman's testimony in *Davyd-Haradok Memorial Book*, 109.

75. Quoted from Meier Hershl Korman's testimony in *Davyd-Haradok Memorial Book*, 98.

76. Rein, *Kings and the Pawns*, 273–77.

77. Dean, *Collaboration*, 9; Aleksandr Litin and Ida Shenderovich, eds., *Istoriia mogilevskogo evreistva: Dokumenty i liudi. Nauchno-populiarnye ocherki i zhizneopisaniia*, vol. 2, pt. 2 (Mogilev: Ameliia Print, 2009), 264.

78. Quoted from his report (NARB f. 4p, op. 33a, d. 63, l. 83).

79. See the recollections by Zalman Uri Gurevitz, translated from the Hebrew Memorial Book on Kurenits, http://eilatgordinlevitan.com/kurenets/k_pages/stories_gurevitz.html.

80. Leonid Smilovitsky, "Righteous Gentiles, the Partisans, and Jewish Survival in Belorussia, 1941–1944," *Holocaust and Genocide Studies* 11, no. 3 (1997): 305. For more examples, see the entries on Berezino and Klimovichi in Dean and Hecker, *United States Holocaust Memorial Museum Encyclopedia*, 1646–47, 1682–83.

81. Bembel'-Dedok, *Vospominaniia*, 172–87.

82. Izhar, *Chasia Bornstein-Bielicka*, 197–99, quotation on 198, also 199–201 on non-Jewish neighbors denouncing Jews in hiding.

83. Quoted from his recollections, probably written in 1958, in Belorusskii gosudarstvennyi arkhiv-muzei literatury i iskusstva (hereafter BGAMLI) f. 353, op. 1. d. 253, l. 2.

84. Gerlach, *Kalkulierte Morde*, 143.

85. Quoted from Anastasiia Voskabovich's witness statement, given to the prosecutor of Pukhovichskii district on September 27, 1944, in Bundesarchiv Lichterfelde (hereafter BArch) B 162/7537, l. 124.

86. Quoted from the report by the NKVD officer A. Ostretsov, December 10, 1941, and the report by the NKVD officer Murzinov, December 8, 1941, in NARB f. 4p, op. 33a, d. 63, ll. 49, 75; also ll. 187–96 (December 17, 1941, report by NKVD officer Nikolai Bogdanov).

87. Quoted from Shapovalov's report, no date, probably written in 1941 (RGASPI f. 17, op. 88, d. 480, l. 137).

88. Quoted from Zaitsev's report, November 21, 1941 (NARB f. 4p, op. 33a, d. 63, l. 277).

89. Interview with I. S. Shurman, September 8, 1942 (IRI RAN f. 2, razdel II, op. 4, d. 4, l. 4).

90. "Ereignismeldung UdSSR No. 43," August 3, 1941 (BArch R58/217, l. 166); "Ereignismeldung UdSSR No. 97," September 28, 1941 (BArch R58/217, ll. 418–20); "Meldungen aus den besetzten Ostgebieten Nr. 11" (BArch R58/698, ll. 33–35). On the conflict: Brakel, *Unter Rotem Stern und Hakenkreuz*, 119–39; Chiari, *Alltag hinter der Front*, 272–80.

91. Kazimierz Krajewski, "Der Bezirk Nowogródek der Heimatarmee: Nationalitätenkonflikte und politische Verhältnisse 1939–1945," in *Die polnische Heimatarmee: Geschichte und Mythos der Armia Krajowa seit dem Zweiten Weltkrieg*, ed. Bernhard Chiari (Munich: Oldenbourg, 2003), 575.

92. Rein, *Kings and the Pawns*, 166–79.

93. For Eva S., though, who had family members deported to Siberia during the collectivization of agriculture in eastern Belarus in the 1930s, it was important to stress that her family never helped the Germans but instead was loyal to the Soviet Union: "We loved Stalin, we loved our country." Author's interview with Eva S., June 16, 2011, Grodno, Belarus.

94. David Myshanka (Kolpenitskii), *Komu zhit' i komu umeret'* . . . (Tel Aviv: M+, 2002), 37; Dean, *Collaboration*, 66–68, 76–77.

95. On local policemen visiting German brothels in Minsk: interview with Iurii Taits (IRI RAN f. 2, razdel II, op. 4, d. 117, l. 8). On Jewish property being a major incentive for locals to join the police, as recalled by Jewish survivors: Romanovsky, "Holocaust in the Eyes of Homo Sovieticus," 371.

96. BArch B 162/7537, l. 124; Romanovsky, "Holocaust in the Eyes of Homo Sovieticus," 359.

97. Wolozhinski Rubin, *Against the Tide*, 46–70.

98. See the report by NKVD officer Korzhov, December 8, 1941 (NARB f. 4p, op. 33a, d. 63, l. 166).

99. On psychological and physical pressure, see chapter 4.

100. See, for example, Diana Dumitru, "An Analysis of Soviet Postwar Investigation and Trial Documents and Their Relevance for Holocaust Studies," in *The Holocaust in the East: Local Perpetrators and Soviet Responses*, ed. Michael David-Fox, Peter Holquist, and Alexander Martin (Pittsburgh: University of Pittsburgh Press, 2014), 142–57; Diana Dumitru, "Listening to Silence: What Soviet Postwar Trial Materials Resist Revealing about the Holocaust," *S.I.M.O.N. Shoah: Intervention. Methods. Documentation* 7, no. 1 (2020): 4–12; and Edele, *Stalin's Defectors*, 12–15.

101. Dean, *Collaboration*, 64–65.

102. Dean, *Collaboration*, 65–67.

103. Quoted from Lidiia Kozlova, "Moia zhizn' i moia voina," *Nioman*, no. 5 (2008): 142.

104. Quoted from IRI RAN f. 2, razdel II, op. 4, d. 4, l. 12.

105. Anna Adamovich, "I tak bylo kazhdyi den'," *Nioman*, no. 10 (1999): 155.

106. The city administration of Mogilev, for instance, put empty Jewish houses up for sale in the spring of 1942. See Archives of the United States Holocaust Memorial Museum (hereafter USHMM) RG-53.006M, Mogilev Oblast Archive Records, 1941–1945, Reel 2: City Administration of Mogilev, 1941–1944, f. 260, op. 1, d. 29, ll. 76, 78; d. 45, ll. 30, 41. On the local administration and its responsibilities: Brakel, *Unter Rotem Stern und Hakenkreuz*, 183–87.

107. As also shown by Rein, *Kings and the Pawns*, 263–72.

108. Struve, *Deutsche Herrschaft*, 36.

109. Bender, "Not Only in Jedwabne," 12–26.

110. Bender, "Not Only in Jedwabne," 23–25.

111. Gross, *Neighbors*, 72–89.

112. Quoted from Lichtenberg's testimony, quoted in Andrzej Żbikowski, "Pogroms in Northeastern Poland—Spontaneous Reactions and German Instigations," in *Shared History—Divided Memory*, 336n69.

113. Quoted from Shalom Yoran, *The Defiant: A True Story* (Lewes: Book Guild, 1996), 52.

114. It is unclear whether Ioffe was personally present in Gorodishche or whether he heard about this incident from someone else on his flight east. Quoted from his report (RGASPI f. 17, op. 88, d. 480, l. 144).

115. Martin Small and Vic Shayne, *Remember Us: From My Shtetl through the Holocaust* (New York: iUniverse, 2008), 106–11.

116. Dean and Hecker, *United States Holocaust Memorial Museum Encyclopedia,* 1212–14 (Korelichi), 1228–30 (Deliatichi), 1146–48 (Vidzy); Shammai Tokel, "The Liquidation of the Stolin Jewish Community," trans. Meir Razy, in *Stolin: A Memorial to the Jewish Communities of Stolin and Vicinity*, ed. A. Avatichi and Y. Ben-Zakkai (Tel Aviv, 1952), 216–22. Partial English translation of the Hebrew original, available at JewishGen, https://www.jewishgen.org/yizkor/stolin/sto208.html#Page216; Yoran, *Defiant*, 55 (Kurenits).

117. Bender, "Not Only in Jedwabne," 27.

118. Quoted from Tokel, "The Liquidation of the Stolin Jewish Community," 217; Small and Shayne, *Remember Us*, 104–9; Żbikowski, "Pogroms in Northeastern Poland," 336n69.

119. On pogroms in Sarny, Berezhnytsia, and Serniki (Sernyky), the latter then part of Soviet Belarus, today part of Ukraine: Dean and Hecker, *United States Holocaust Memorial Museum Encyclopedia*, 1334–35, 1463–66.

120. See the entry by Jared McBride and Alexander Kruglov on Olevs'k in Dean and Hecker, *United States Holocaust Memorial Museum Encyclopedia*, 1553–55. On differences between new and old Soviet territories: Wendy Lower, "Pogroms, Mob Violence, and Genocide in Western Ukraine, Summer 1941: Varied Histories, Explanations, and Comparisons," *Journal of Genocide Research* 13, no. 3 (2011): 228–29.

121. Snyder, *Bloodlands*, 190.

122. Berkhoff, *Harvest of Despair*, 64–88; Cohen, *Smolensk under the Nazis*, 103; Weiner, *Making Sense of War*, 280. For a first, if brief regional comparison, see Yitzhak Arad, "The Local Population in the German-Occupied Territories of the Soviet Union and Its Attitude toward the Murder of the Jews," in *Nazi Europe and the Final Solution*, ed. David Bankier and Israel Gutman (Jerusalem: Yad Vashem, 2003), 233–48.

123. On the comparison: Struve, *Deutsche Herrschaft*, 681–91; Struve, "Anti-Jewish Violence," 103–13. On individual regions and towns: John-Paul Himka, "The Lviv Pogrom of 1941: The Germans, Ukrainian Nationalists, and the Carnival Crowd," *Canadian Slavonic Papers/Revue canadienne des slavistes* 53, no. 2–4 (2011): 209–43; Lower, "Pogroms, Mob Violence, and Genocide in Western Ukraine"; Jared McBride, "'A Sea of Blood and Tears': Ethnic Diversity and Mass Violence in Nazi-Occupied Volhynia, Ukraine, 1941–1944" (PhD diss., University of California, Los Angeles, 2014), 122–49; Grzegorz Rossoliński-Liebe, "Der Verlauf und die Täter des Lemberger Pogroms vom Sommer 1941: Zum aktuellen Stand der Forschung," *Jahrbuch für Antisemitismusforschung* 22 (2013): 207–43; Vladimir Solonari, "Patterns of Violence: The Local Population and the Mass Murder of Jews in Bessarabia and Northern Bukovina, July–August 1941," *Kritika: Explorations in Russian and Eurasian History* 8, no. 4 (2007): 749–87; Żbikowski, "Pogroms in Northeastern Poland," 315–54.

124. Kopstein and Wittenberg, *Intimate Violence*, 14–16, 129. The book's two detailed case studies focus on the Białystok region and eastern Galicia, leaving it unclear whether their argument could also apply to the towns in Pinsk oblast that experienced pogroms (in interwar Poland, part of Polesie voivodship).

125. Struve, *Deutsche Herrschaft*, 681–91; Struve, "Anti-Jewish Violence," 103–13.

126. Bender, "Not Only in Jedwabne," 8, 28.

127. Rein, *Kings and the Pawns*, 93–98, 230–33.

128. As argued by Gross, *Neighbors*, xxi.

129. Ackermann, *Palimpsest Grodno*, 59–60, 143–50.

130. *Davyd-Haradok Memorial Book*, 4–9.

131. Jared McBride has made a similar argument for Volhynia ("Sea of Blood and Tears," 130–31, 147–48).

132. Dumitru, *State, Antisemitism, and Collaboration*, 235.

133. Izhar, *Chasia Bornstein-Bielicka*, 126–267.

134. Izhar, *Chasia Bornstein-Bielicka*, 221–22.

135. Izhar, *Chasia Bornstein-Bielicka*, 155–56.

136. Izhar, *Chasia Bornstein-Bielicka*, 229–30.

137. Izhar, *Chasia Bornstein-Bielicka*, 232–64.

138. Quoted from YV O.3/11082, l. 24.

139. Quoted from YV O.3/11082, l. 4.

140. YV O.3/11082, ll. 1–45.

141. Quoted from Izhar, *Chasia Bornstein-Bielicka*, 7.

142. For a detailed and nuanced discussion of the motivations for rescue in the Volhynian context, see McBride, "'Sea of Blood and Tears,'" 392.

143. Dumitru, *State, Antisemitism, and Collaboration*, 1–9, 235 (quotation).

144. Quoted from the interview with Iurii Taits (IRI RAN f. 2, razdel II, op. 4, d. 117, l. 16).

145. Epstein, *Minsk Ghetto*, 12–17.

146. The Białystok region possibly continued to be the exception, meaning that the local civilian population here continued to be more antagonistic toward the Jewish population than in other parts of western Belarus.

147. Quoted in Slepyan, *Stalin's Guerrillas*, 15.

148. Report by S. N. Strom, secretary of the Kirov raikom, and S. R. Podol'tsev, secretary of the Bykhov raikom, August 5, 1941 (RGASPI f. 17, op. 88, d. 480, l. 127).

149. Report by Nikolai Ermakovich, September 11, 1941 (RGASPI f. 17, op. 88, d. 480, l. 172).

150. Report by a man named Kol'shkin, secretary of the Minsk obkom, on the activity of NKVD officers in Minsk, Borisov, and Slutsk, no date, but probably summer of 1941 (RGASPI f. 17, op. 88, d. 480, ll. 114–17).

151. Quoted from the interview with Mikhail D'iachkov, September 19, 1942 (IRI RAN f. 2, razdel II, op. 4, d. 10, l. 3).

152. Quoted from IRI RAN f. 2, razdel II, op. 4, d. 10, l. 2.

153. See, for example, the interview with the partisan Aleksandr Sakevich, who was active in Minsk oblast, August 12, 1944 (IRI RAN f. 2, razdel II, op. 4, d. 10, l. 2); and Slepyan, *Stalin's Guerrillas*, 25.

154. Quoted from the report by Shapovalov, secretary of the Pinsk obkom, no date, but must have been in 1941 (RGASPI f. 17, op. 88, d. 480, l. 138).

155. This, for example, happened to D'iachkov's unit (IRI RAN f. 2, razdel II, op. 4, d. 10, ll. 2–8). See also Slepyan, *Stalin's Guerrillas*, 26–40, 79–84, 122–23.

156. Quoted from the interview with Stepan Shupeniia, December 2, 1944 (IRI RAN f. 2, razdel II, op. 4, d. 166, l. 6).

157. Quoted from IRI RAN f. 2, razdel II, op. 4, d. 166, l. 6.

158. Cerovic, *Les enfants de Staline*, 46–48; Christoph Dieckmann, *Deutsche Besatzungspolitik in Litauen, 1941–1944* (Göttingen: Wallstein, 2011), 1428–61; McBride, "'Sea of Blood and Tears,'" 438–43; Bogdan Musial, *Sowjetische Partisanen 1941–1944: Mythos und Wirklichkeit* (Paderborn: Schöningh, 2009), 117–21; Slepyan, *Stalin's Guerrillas*, 28–29; Statiev, *Soviet Counterinsurgency*, 73–75.

159. Musial, *Sowjetische Partisanen 1941–1944*, 125–42.

160. Musial, *Sowjetische Partisanen 1941–1944*, 147–68; Slepyan, *Stalin's Guerrillas*, 122–28.

161. Musial, *Sowjetische Partisanen 1941–1944*, 178–80.

162. Izhar, *Chasia Bornstein-Bielicka*, 244–57.

163. Slepyan, *Stalin's Guerrillas*, 42–43.

164. Gerlach, *Kalkulierte Morde*, 877–84.

165. Interview with Mikhail Peregudovyi, December 7, 1944 (IRI RAN f. 2, razdel II, op. 4, d. 153, l. 2). On the German orders and their effect: Musial, *Sowjetische Partisanen 1941–1944*, 122–25.

166. In total, an estimated 30,000–50,000 Jews fled to the Belarusian forests (Gerlach, *Kalkulierte Morde*, 744). On the Bielski partisans, see Nechama Tec, *Defiance: The True Story of the Bielski Partisans* (Oxford: Oxford University Press, 1993).

167. On fear of encountering non-Jewish partisans: interview with Iurii Taits (IRI RAN f. 2, razdel II, op. 4, d. 117, l. 15); Wolozhinski Rubin, *Against the Tide*, 133; Leonid Smilovitsky, "Antisemitism in the Soviet Partisan Movement, 1941–1944: The Case of Belorussia," *Holocaust and Genocide Studies* 20, no. 2 (2006): 207–34.

168. Jörn Hasenclever, *Wehrmacht und Besatzungspolitik in der Sowjetunion: Die Befehlshaber der rückwärtigen Heeresgebiete 1941–1943* (Paderborn: Schöningh, 2010), 474–522, quote 503.

169. Gerlach, *Kalkulierte Morde*, 885–93.

170. Quoted from Ales' Adamovich, Ianka Bryl', and Vladimir Kolesnik, eds., *Ia iz ognennoi derevni . . .* (Moscow: Sovetskii pisatel', 1991), 43; Ales Adamovich, Yanka Bryl, and Vladimir Kolesnik, eds., *Out of the Fire* (Moscow: Progress Publishers, 1980), 51. Henceforth, I cite the English version.

171. Adamovich, Bryl, and Kolesnik, *Out of the Fire*, 31–34.

172. See Tsanava's report, May 18, 1943 (NARB f. 4p, op. 33a, d. 151, ll. 295–96).

173. Quoted from Adamovich, Bryl, and Kolesnik, *Out of the Fire*, 31–32.

174. This refers to the post-1945 territories. See E. M. Grinevich, N. A. Denisova, N. V. Kirillova, and V. D. Selemenev, eds., *Tragediia belorusskikh dereven', 1941–1944: Dokumenty i materialy* (Moscow: Fond "Istoricheskaia pamiat'," 2011), 8. It is unclear how many villages were annihilated, including all of their inhabitants.

175. Gerlach, *Kalkulierte Morde*, 1158.

176. Gerlach, *Kalkulierte Morde*, 899.

177. Per Anders Rudling, "The Khatyn Massacre in Belorussia: A Historical Controversy Revisited," *Holocaust and Genocide Studies* 26, no. 1 (2012): 29–58.

178. Quoted from Adamovich, Bryl, and Kolesnik, *Out of the Fire*, 50.

179. On the ubiquity of such rumors, see the interview with I. Shurman (IRI RAN f. 2, razdel II, op. 4, d. 4, l. 3). On defeatism among the Soviet population: Oleg Budnitskii, "The Great Patriotic War and Soviet Society: Defeatism, 1941–42," *Kritika: Explorations in Russian and Eurasian History* 15, no. 4 (2014): 767–97.

180. See Tsanava's report, dated January 2, 1943, and corresponding NKVD investigations (NARB f. 4p, op. 33a, d. 151, ll. 155–58, 163–66, quotation on 165).

181. Slepyan, *Stalin's Guerrillas*, 157–62.

182. YV O.3 / 11082, l. 37.

183. On the ubiquity of sexual harassment: Slepyan, *Stalin's Guerrillas*, 194–206. On memory, taboos, and silences relating to the issue: Walke, *Pioneers and Partisans*, 153–63.

184. Quoted from Wolozhinski Rubin, *Against the Tide*, 109.

185. NARB f. 4p, op. 33a, d. 634, ll. 1–10.

186. The percentage refers to the 281,007 individuals for whom this information is available (NARB f. 4p, op. 33a, d. 634, ll. 1–10).

187. Adamovich, Bryl, and Kolesnik, *Out of the Fire*, 60.

188. See his interview, October 23, 1942 (IRI RAN f. II, razdel II, op. 4, d. 19, l. 11).

189. Ivan Danilov, *Neudobnaia istoriia glazami zapadnogo belorusa* (Minsk: Izdatel'stvo Viktora Khursika, 2009), 224.

190. IRI RAN f. 2, razdel II, op. 4, d. 166, l. 8.

191. Musial, *Sowjetische Partisanen 1941–1944*, 181–82.

192. According to the postwar Soviet memoir literature, Soviet partisans and underground fighters killed almost 464,000 German military personnel and Germans working in the occupation regime on the territory that would constitute post-1945 Soviet Belarus. See, for example, the memoir by Panteleimon Ponomarenko, *Vsenarodnaia bor'ba v tylu nemetsko-fashistskikh zakhvatchikov 1941–1944* (Moscow: Nauka, 1986), 378n1. German wartime sources cannot corroborate these numbers. As human losses had to be reported to the responsible agencies and relatives, falsifications would have been uncovered. For a discussion: Gerlach, *Kalkulierte Morde*, 866; Musial, *Sowjetische Partisanen 1941–1944*, 290–92.

193. Quoted from Mor, *War for Life*, 166.

194. Cerovic, *Les Enfants de Staline*, 236–37, 252–62; Slepyan, *Stalin's Guerrillas*, 79–84; Alexander Statiev, "Soviet Partisan Violence against Soviet Civilians: Targeting Their Own," *Europe-Asia Studies* 66, no. 9 (2014): 1525–52.

195. IRI RAN f. 2, razdel II, op. 4, d. 10, ll. 10–11.

196. Musial, *Sowjetische Partisanen 1941–1944*, 261, 290–97.

197. Underreporting civilian deaths or claiming them to have been Germans is known, for example, from the village of Drazhno in Minsk oblast. The event was researched, using archival sources and oral history interviews, by Viktar Khursik, *Kroŭ i popel Drazhna: Historyia partyzanskaha zlachynstva* (Minsk: Vydavets Khursik, 2003), 48–49. Several hundred, perhaps a few thousand, civilian victims of partisan violence seem like a reasonable estimate. See Note on Wartime Losses.

198. See Itzak Nahmanovitch's testimony in *Davyd-Haradok Memorial Book*, 95. For more examples of Jews taking revenge, see Sara Bender, "Life Stories as Testament and Memorial: The Short Life of the Neqama Battalion, an Independent Jewish Partisan Unit Operating during the Second World War in the Narocz Forest, Belarus," *East European Jewish Affairs* 42, no. 1 (2012): 9; and Kagan and Cohen, *Surviving the Holocaust*, 89–90.

199. Quoted from Shurman's interview (IRI RAN f. 2, razdel II, op. 4, d. 4, l. 5).

200. Quoted from the interview with Varfolomei Lapenko, September 25, 1942 (IRI RAN f. 2, razdel II, op. 4, d. 7, l. 5).

201. IRI RAN f. 2, razdel II, op. 4, d. 7, l. 3.

202. Yoran, *Defiant*, 137.

203. Nikolai Obryn'ba, *Red Partisan: The Memoir of a Soviet Resistance Fighter on the Eastern Front* (Washington, DC: Potomac Books, 2007), 147–49.

204. Obryn'ba, *Red Partisan*, 178.

205. See the report from the local commander's office in Berezino, passed on by the field commander's office in Mogilev, September 10, 1942 (BArch R 20/11, l. 147). On collective punishment: Rein, *Kings and the Pawns*, 138–40; Slepyan, *Stalin's Guerrillas*, 81; Statiev, "Soviet Partisan Violence," 1542–47.

206. Khursik, *Kroŭ i popel Drazhna*, 8, 17, 26–27, 76, 79. For more examples of villages burned down by partisans: Cerovic, *Les Enfants de Staline*, 258; Musial, *Sowjetische Partisanen 1941–1944*, 359–67.

207. Quoted from Musial, *Sowjetische Partisanen 1941–1944*, 362.

208. Quoted from IRI RAN f. 2, razdel II, op. 4, d. 166, l. 14.

209. Quoted from Vladimir Rott, *Naperekor sud'be*, bk. 1: *Radosti pechalei: Garadna-Mishkol'ts-Bobruisk-Tomsk-Tol'iatti-Toronto* (Moscow: B.S.G.-Press, 2008), 103.

210. As recorded in Andrea Gotzes, *Krieg und Vernichtung 1941–1945: Sowjetische Zeitzeugen erinnern sich* (Darmstadt: Wissenschaftliche Buchgesellschaft, 2006), 83.

211. Brakel, *Unter Rotem Stern und Hakenkreuz*, 349–52, also sources no. 1–13 in Bogdan Musial, ed., *Sowjetische Partisanen in Weißrußland: Innenansichten aus dem Gebiet Baranoviči, 1941–1944. Eine Dokumentation* (Munich: De Gruyter, 2004), 156–81.

212. Gerlach, *Kalkulierte Morde*, 1040–52.

213. On the multidimensionality of the war behind the front, see Prusin, *Lands Between*, 177–90.

214. Krajewski, "Der Bezirk Nowogródek," 570–71.

215. See Ponomarenko's secret letter to the Belarusian Staff of the Partisan Movement and communist underground organizations in Białystok/Belostok, Brest, Baranovichi, Vileika, and Pinsk oblasts, August 2, 1943 (NARB f. 4p, op. 33a, d. 397, ll. 2–6).

216. Musial, *Sowjetische Partisanen 1941–1944*, 406–33. For more detail, see Zygmunt Boradyn, *Niemen rzeka niezgody: Polsko-sowiecka wojna partyzancka na Nowogródczyźnie 1943–1944* (Warsaw: Oficyna Wydawnicza Rytm, 1999).

217. AW II/1252/2K, ll. 5–7.

218. See, for example, Yoran, *Defiant*, 175–76.

219. Slepyan, *Stalin's Guerrillas*, 157–62.

220. Author's interview with Mariia L., November 22, 2010, Molodechno, Belarus. For a similar view from a partisan himself, see Mor, *War for Life*, 163.

221. Quoted from Langer, "Dilemma of Choice in the Deathcamps," 224.

222. For examples, see Chiari, *Alltag hinter der Front*, 151–59.

223. Quoted from Romanov's report (RGASPI f. 625, op. 1, d. 61, l. 821).

224. Quoted from Mor, *War for Life*, 163.

225. Quoted from Golovkin and Gutkin's report, December 21, 1941 (NARB f. 4p, op. 33a, d. 63, l. 116).

226. On rumors and fears in 1941, see IRI RAN f. 2, razdel II, op. 4, d. 4, l. 4. On peasants initially welcoming the Germans with bread and salt but then becoming fully loyal to the partisans: IRI RAN f. 2, razdel II, op. 4, d. 19, l. 10. On the popualtion in southeastern Belarus and western Russia initially being hostile toward partisans,

see the report by the NKVD officer Vasilii Zasukhin, December 3, 1941 (NARB f. 4p, op. 33a, d. 63, l. 27).

227. Quoted from Gusev's report (NARB f. 4p, op. 33a, d. 151, l. 152).

228. Quoted from Svetlana Alexievich, *The Unwomanly Face of War: An Oral History of Women in World War II*, exp. and rev. ed. of the 1985 Russian original (New York: Random House, 2018), 260.

229. Quoted from Yoran, *Defiant*, 141.

230. All quotes from Yoran, *Defiant*, 141–42.

231. Quoted from Yoran, *Defiant*, 136.

232. Quoted from IRI RAN f. 2, razdel II, op. 4, d. 19, l. 16.

233. For studies that explore commonalities and patterns in partisan and guerrilla wars: Kalyvas, *Logic of Violence in Civil War*; Shepherd and Pattison, *War in a Twilight World*.

3. Post-1944

1. David R. Stone, "Operations on the Eastern Front, 1941–1945," in *The Cambridge History of the Second World War*, vol. 1, ed. John Ferris and Evan Mawdsley (Cambridge: Cambridge University Press, 2015), 351–54.

2. Izhar, *Chasia Bornstein-Bielicka*, 161–266.

3. Quoted in Vakar, *Belorussia*, 209.

4. Specifically on Minsk and postwar migration, see Thomas Bohn, *Minsk–Musterstadt des Sozialismus: Stadtplanung und Urbanisierung in der Sowjetunion nach 1945* (Cologne: Böhlau, 2008), 154–55.

5. Petr Lebedev, "Vozvrashchenie," *Nioman*, no. 10 (1986): 135–54.

6. Quoted from Lebedev, "Vozvrashchenie," 136.

7. Quoted from her recollections in Alexievich, *Unwomanly Face of War*, 286.

8. On the military draft: V. I. Adamushko et al., eds., *Osvobozhdennaia Belarus': Dokumenty i materialy.* 2 vols. (Minsk: NARB, 2004), 2:11. On partisans who joined the Red Army after disbandment: NARB f. 4p, op, 33a, d. 634, l. 1. On demobilization: Mark Edele, *Soviet Veterans of the Second World War: A Popular Movement in an Authoritarian Society, 1941–1991* (Oxford: Oxford University Press, 2008), 22. The exact number of demobilized soldiers who returned to Belarus is unknown. This is my own estimate. On the experience and meaning of demobilization: Robert Dale, *Demobilized Veterans in Late Stalinist Leningrad: Soldiers to Civilians* (London: Bloomsbury Academic, 2015).

9. Gimpelevich, *Vasil Bykaŭ*, 33–44. In his memoirs, Bykaŭ tells the story of his demobilization slightly differently: while he was serving in Ukraine, he was granted leave from the army to visit his family. He returned to Ukraine only to be discharged from the army shortly afterward (Bykov, *Dolgaia doroga domoi*, 134–38).

10. See the report of July 18, 1945, to the Central Committee in Minsk (NARB f. 4p, op. 29, d. 311, ll. 10–15). On sexual violence: Seth Bernstein, "Ambiguous Homecoming: Retribution, Exploitation, and Social Tensions during Repatriation to the USSR, 1944–1946," *Past and Present* 242, no. 1 (2019): 211–15.

11. NARB 4p, op. 29, d. 311, ll. 1–9.

12. Overall, between 4.2 million (by March 1946) and 5.35 million Soviet citizens, civilians and former POWs, were repatriated to the Soviet Union. Compare the

different calculations: Bernstein, "Ambiguous Homecoming," 202; Ulrike Goeken-Haidl, *Der Weg zurück: Die Repatriierung sowjetischer Zwangsarbeiter und Kriegsgefangener während und nach dem Zweiten Weltkrieg* (Essen: Klartext, 2006), 545–50; Pavel Polian, *Deportiert nach Hause: Sowjetische Kriegsgefangene im "Dritten Reich" und ihre Repatriierung* (Munich: Oldenbourg, 2001), 166.

13. Quoted from Bykov, *Dolgaia doroga domoi*, 136.

14. These numbers pertain to Belarus in its post-1945 borders (Galina Knat'ko et al., eds., *Belorusskie ostarbaitery: Repatriatsiia. Dokumenty i materialy*, pt. 2 [Minsk: NARB, 1998], 501). It is unclear how many former prisoners of war were prewar residents of Belarus, but among all repatriated prisoners of war, there were 135,000 ethnic Belarusians. Considering that most of them might have been prewar residents of Belarus and adding to that a few thousand former prisoners of war, residents of Belarus but not ethnic Belarusians, one reaches the figure of 150,000 people (Polian, *Deportiert nach Hause*, 165).

15. Quoted from her recollections in E. I. Liul'kina, ed., *Voina i ukradennye gody: Zhivye svidetel'stva ostarbaiterov Belarusi* (Minsk: I. P. Logvinov, 2010), 117.

16. Since individual breakdowns by republic do not exist, these numbers have to remain estimates. I have arrived at these numbers based on E. M. Andreev, L. E. Darskii, and T. L. Khar'kova, "Liudskie poteri SSSR vo Vtoroi mirovoi voine: Metodika otsenki i rezul'taty," in *Liudskie poteri SSSR v Velikoi Otechestvennoi voine*, ed. R. B. Evdokimov (St. Petersburg: Blits, 1995), 37–42; Kozhurin, "O chislennosti naseleniia SSSR," 21–26; Grigorii Krivosheev, ed., *Soviet Casualties and Combat Losses in the Twentieth Century* (London: Greenhill, 1997), 84–85; and Aleksei Litvin, "K voprosu o kolichestve liudskikh poter' Belarusi v gody Velikoi Otechestvennoi voiny (1941–1945 gg.)," in *Belarus' u XX stahoddzi*, vol. 1, ed. Igor' Kuznetsov and Iakov Basin (Minsk: n.p., 2002), http://jewishfreedom.org/page611.html.

17. NARB f. 4p, op. 33a, d. 634, l. 1.

18. Musial, *Sowjetische Partisanen 1941–1944*, 261.

19. Bykov, *Dolgaia doroga domoi*, 136.

20. Quoted from her recollections (name unknown) in Alexievich, *Unwomanly Face of War*, 268.

21. Quoted from her recollections (name unknown) in Alexievich, *Unwomanly Face of War*, 268.

22. Quoted from Alexievich, *Unwomanly Face of War*, 268–69.

23. Adamovich, Bryl, and Kolesnik, *Out of the Fire*, 183–90, 224–25.

24. These numbers are based on different estimates taken from Gerlach, *Kalkulierte Morde*, 1158; Smilovitskii, *Katastrofa evreev v Belorussii*, 27–28; and Vinnitsa, *Kholokost na okkupirovannoi territorii*, 193.

25. Berzin, *Vospominaniia o nashem detstve*, 34–37; Ovsishcher, *Vozvrashchenie*, 118.

26. Quoted from Raisa Gorodinskaia, *O sebe, o rodnykh, o druz'iakh i tovarishchakh: Vospominaniia uznika getto, partizanki Gorodinskoi (Beshkinoi) Raisy Abramovny* (Tel Aviv: n.p., 2008), 55.

27. Gorodinskaia, *O sebe, o rodnykh*, 55.

28. Quoted from Izhar, *Chasia Bornstein-Bielicka*, 279.

29. Izhar, *Chasia Bornstein-Bielicka*, 279.

30. Quoted from Izhar, *Chasia Bornstein-Bielicka*, 280.

31. Gorodinskaia, *O sebe, o rodnykh*, 55–62, quotation on 62.

32. Gorodinskaia, *O sebe, o rodnykh*, 56; Izhar, *Chasia Bornstein-Bielicka*, 46–61, 125–39, 161–73, 181–83, 202–5, 232–38, 263–64, 284–91, 373–79.

33. Dean, *Collaboration in the Holocaust*, 148–59; Gerlach, *Kalkulierte Morde*, 501. Not all of them would have been prewar inhabitants of Belarus.

34. Of Schutzmannschaft Battalions 115 and 118, which consisted primarily of Ukrainians and which were deployed in Belarus until July 1944, 100–120 members were repatriated to the Soviet Union after the war, most of them by force. See Per Anders Rudling, "Terror and Local Collaboration in Occupied Belarus: The Case of the *Schutzmannschaft* Battalion 118. I. Background," in *Historical Yearbook* 8 (2011): 210.

35. Quoted from his report (name unknown), no earlier than July 24, 1944 (NARB f. 4p, op. 29, d. 311, l. 89).

36. See Shymanets's recollections in Aliaksandar Adzinets, *Pavaennaia emihratsyia: Skryzhavan'ni liosaŭ. Zbornik uspaminaŭ* (Minsk: Medisont, 2007), 585–90, quotation on 586.

37. See Barys Kit's recollections in Adzinets, *Pavaennaia emihratsyia*, 528–42, quotation on 538.

38. Rein, *Kings and the Pawns*, 173–75.

39. Adzinets, *Pavaennaia emihratsyia*, 528–42. The former student is quoted in Lidziia Savik, *Kosmas belarusa: Zhytstsiapis Barysa Uladzimiravicha Kita, asvetnika, vuchonaha, patryiota* (Minsk: Minskaia drukarskaia fabryka, 1996), 83.

40. Report by Stepanenko, head of the party's information sector, June 28, 1944 (NARB f. 4p, op. 29, d. 29, ll. 75–76).

41. Quoted from Paul Kohl, *"Ich wundere mich, daß ich noch lebe": Sowjetische Augenzeugen berichten* (Gütersloh: Mohn, 1990), 45.

42. Maria Epsztein, *Macierzyństwo za drutami: Wspomnienia, 1940–1980* (Montreal: Polish-Jewish Heritage Foundation of Canada, 2005), 119–20.

43. Quoted from Galadzhev's report, June 29, 1944 (NARB f. 4p, op. 29, d. 61, l. 53).

44. Quoted from NARB f. 4p, op. 29, d. 61, ll. 55–56.

45. Quoted from NARB f. 4p, op. 29, d. 61, ll. 57.

46. Quoted from his letter, excerpts of which the NKGB sent to Ponomarenko (NARB f. 4p, op. 29, d. 22, l. 41). Dislike of collective farms was universal among the Soviet peasantry (Elena Zubkova, *Poslevoennoe sovetskoe obshchestvo: Politika i povsednevnost' 1945–1953* [Moscow: ROSSPEN, 2000], 61–69).

47. AW II/1252/2K, ll. 1–9, typewritten version.

48. Wolozhinski Rubin, *Against the Tide*, 172–81.

49. Szumski, *Sowietyzacja Zachodniej Białorusi*, 40.

50. Specifically on Turovskii district, Poles'e oblast, fall 1944: NARB f. 4p, op. 29, d. 29, ll. 163–64. By the fall of 1944, an estimated 12,000–14,000 members of the OUN-UPA were active in southern Belarus (Igor' Valakhanovich, *Antisovetskoe podpol'e na territorii Belarusi v 1944–1953 gg.* [Minsk: BGU, 2002], 108).

51. Adamushko et al., *Belorusy v sovetskom tylu*, 1:82–88; Adamushko et al., *Belarus' v pervye mesiatsy*, 32–47.

52. Reconstructed based on Adamushko et al., *Belarus' v pervye mesiatsy*, 20–22; Adamushko et al., *Belorusy v sovetskom tylu*, 1:20–21, 54–58; Ioffe, *Ot Miasnikova do Malofeeva*, 99–113, 182–86, 260–62.

53. Ioffe, *Ot Miasnikova do Malofeeva*, 124–30; Ioffe, *Lavrentii Tsanava*, 444–60.

54. Compare the bibliographical sketches in V. I. Adamushko et al., eds., *Osvobozhdennaia Belarus': Dokumenty i materialy*. 2 vols. (Minsk: NARB, 2004), 1:310–70; Ioffe, *Lavrentii Tsanava*, 6–11; Ioffe, *Panteleimon Ponomarenko*, 8–25.

55. See the reports on cadres, July 1944–May 1945 (NARB f. 4p, op. 29, d. 184, ll. 77–88).

56. Adamushko et al., *Osvobozhdennaia Belarus'*, 1:38, 73, 76.

57. See Avkhimovich's report, not earlier than March 20, 1942, in Adamushko et al., *Belorusy v sovetskom tylu*, 1:54–58.

58. See Vetrov's report, June 22, 1943, in V. I. Adamushko et al., eds., *Belorusy v sovetskom tylu, iiul' 1941 g.–1944 g.: Sbornik dokumentov i materialov*, 2 vols. (Minsk: NARB, 2010), 2:81–82.

59. See the report by the Central Committee of Belarus to Moscow: Adamushko et al., *Osvobozhdennaia Belarus'*, 1:77; also specifically on Mogilev oblast, June 1944 (NARB f. 4p, op. 29, d. 29, ll. 75–76); and Poles'e oblast, August 1944 (RGASPI f. 17, op. 88, d. 268, l. 20).

60. Adamushko et al., *Osvobozhdennaia Belarus'*, 1:89, 329, 351–52. On the procuracy, see Vetrov's report, August 19, 1944 (NARB f. 4p, op. 29, d. 56, l. 3).

61. Adamushko et al., *Osvobozhdennaia Belarus'*, 1:38, 73, 76.

62. NARB f. 4p, op. 29, d. 32, ll. 3–5. For similar examples from Poles'e oblast, August 1944: RGASPI f. 17, op. 88, d. 268, l. 21.

63. Quoted from Aleksandr Feigel', *Zhizn' i sud'ba* (Israel, n.p., 2008), 229.

64. Quoted from Khartanovich, *Gody nashei molodosti*, 90.

65. Lebedev, "Vozvrashchenie," 136, 139, 141–45. On the collectivization of western Belarus, during which the Soviet authorities deported about five thousand people to special settlements or forced labor camps in Siberia: Ruchniewicz, *Wieś zachodniobiałoruska*, 326.

66. By October 1946, the MGB had about 5,500 employees. Due to the inaccessibility of the Belarusian KGB archive, it is unknown how many people worked for the MVD in Belarus. For biographical sketches of leading MVD officers in Belarus from 1945 to 1951: Ioffe, *Lavrentii Tsanava*, 290, 306–13.

67. Quoted from the resolution, January 1, 1944, printed in Adamushko et al., *Osvobozhdennaia Belarus'*, 1:34.

68. These remarks were reported by civilian informers to the NKGB. Quoted from NARB f. 4p, op. 33a, d. 400, l. 361.

69. NARB f. 4p, op. 29, d. 29, ll. 87–88.

70. Valakhanovich, *Antisovetskoe podpol'e*, 20–130.

71. Statiev, *Soviet Counterinsurgency*, 119.

72. For the text of the July 27, 1944, agreement: Adamushka et al., *"Ty z zakhodniai*, 1:13–14. Also in detail: Vialiki, *Belarus' u savetska-pol'skikh*, 11–34.

73. Vialiki, *Belarus' u savetska-pol'skikh*, 33–34; Catherine Gousseff, "Evacuation versus Repatriation: The Polish-Ukrainian Population Exchange, 1944–6," in *The Disentanglement of Populations: Migration, Expulsion and Displacement in Post-War Europe 1944–49*, ed. Jessica Reinisch and Elizabeth White (Basingstoke: Palgrave MacMillan, 2011), 91–111.

74. See the NKVD order on the population transfer, September 17, 1944: Adamushko et al., *Osvobozhdennaia Belarus'*, 1:184–86. Among those repatriated to Poland in the mid-1940s were inhabitants of western Belarus who had been deported from this

region during the Soviet occupation of 1939–1941. See, for example, the recollections by Henryk Bułhak (AW 1/70), and Irene Rożek (AW I/680).

75. Anatol' F. Vialiki, *Na razdarozhzhy: Belarusy i paliaki ŭ chas perasialennia (1944–1946 hh.)* (Minsk: BDPU, 2005), 220–23, 306–7.

76. Quoted from Brzozowska's recollections (AW II/1252/2K, l. 8).

77. His story was recorded by the journalist Beate Pawlak (Martin Pollack, ed., *Von Minsk nach Manhattan: Polnische Reportagen* [Vienna: Zsolnay, 2006], 77–84).

78. Vialiki, *Na razdarozhzhy*, 221. On the need to develop the right kind of national self-consciousness, see the internal party discussions about the resettlement of Poles from Brest oblast, April 30, 1945 (NARB f. 4p, op. 29, d. 311, ll. 178–80).

79. The situation in western Ukraine differed markedly due to the ethnic cleansing of Polish villages carried out by Ukrainian nationalists, which probably convinced the Soviet authorities that it was best for the rural Polish-speaking population to leave, too (Gousseff, "Evacuation versus Repatriation," 94). Seen in comparison, the Polish-Lithuanian population exchange occupied a middle ground between the Ukrainian and the Belarusian "models," with Lithuanian communists pushing for the ethnic homogenization of Vilnius but in rural areas prioritizing manpower over ethnicity (Dzmitry Halavach, "Reshaping Nations: Population Politics and Sovietization in the Polish-Soviet Borderlands, 1944–1948" [PhD diss., Princeton University, 2019], 340–46).

80. *Itogi vsesoiuznoi perepisi naseleniia 1959 goda. Belorusskaia SSR* (Moscow: Gosstatizdat Tsentral'nogo statisticheskogo upravleniia pri Sovete Ministrov SSSR, 1963), 124–25; on Grodno: Ackermann, *Palimpsest Grodno*, xvii.

81. Valakhanovich, *Antisovetskoe podpol'e*, 63–64.

82. Valakhanovich, *Antisovetskoe podpol'e*, 77, 108.

83. See the definition of bandits by the Main Directorate for NKVD Internal Troops, July 1, 1943: Rossiiskii gosudarstvennyi voennyi arkhiv (hereafter RGVA) f. 38656, op. 1, d. 10, l. 1. On the origins of the language on "banditry" in the civil war: Statiev, *Soviet Counterinsurgency*, 13–21.

84. Kalyvas, *Logic of Violence*, 17.

85. See the November 1944 report from Artimenkov, military prosecutor of the NKVD forces in Belarus, to Ponomarenko (NARB f. 4p, op. 29, d. 61, ll. 201–2).

86. According to Soviet sources, from 1944 to 1946, 130,295 people were killed in western Ukraine. Most of them were civilians, and most of them were victims of the Soviet forces. During that time, 21,142 people were killed in Lithuania, 2,674 people in Latvia, and 1,212 people in Estonia (Statiev, *Soviet Counterinsurgency*, 110, 125).

87. Quoted from the report (NARB f. 4p, op. 61, d. 360a, l. 29). Compare Statiev, *Soviet Counterinsurgency*, 110, 125; Valakhanovich, *Antisovetskoe podpol'e*, 88, 128–30.

88. Ivan Danilov, *Razmyshlenniia zapadnogo belorusa* (Minsk: Izdatel' V. Khursik, 2009), 9. On people from eastern Belarus traveling in 1946 to the western oblasts to buy food: GAMO f. 1p, op. 2, d. 143, ll. 136, 469. In letters that the NKVD intercepted in December 1945, peasants from Minsk oblast wrote about their terrible living conditions and the lack of payment from the collective farms (GAMO f. 1p, op. 2, d. 143, ll. 14, 17, 46–50).

89. Danilov, *Razmyshlenniia zapadnogo belorusa*, 227 (quotation), 249.

90. Mikhas' Charniaŭski, ed., *"Nia boitsesia akhviaraŭ i pakut!" Dakumenty i materyialy pra dzeinas'ts' miadzel'ska-smarhonskaha antykomunistychnaha padzem'ia (1948–1950 hh.)* (Vilnius: Nasha Buduchynia, 2006), 127–43.

91. On young people fleeing to the forests in Baranovichi oblast to avoid being sent to factories in the Donbas or Stalingrad or to attend schools for industrial training (FZO): NARB f. 4p, op. 41, d. 393, l. 211. For a few examples of many reports on "banditry," May–December 1944: NARB f. 4p, op. 29, d. 29, ll. 56, 60, 92–93, 142, 145–46, 158–60, 163–64, 172, 191–93.

92. See the NKVD report from Minsk oblast, December 1945: GAMO f. 1p, op. 2, d. 143, ll. 26–27.

93. Quoted from GAMO f. 1p, op. 2, d. 143, l. 83, February 1946; for another example, see l. 92, January 1945.

94. For several examples from January and February 1945, Minsk oblast: GAMO f. 1p, op. 2, d. 143, ll. 6–7, 80, 84, 90–91, 96, 105, 107 (quotation).

95. GAMO f. 1p, d. 2, op. 143, l. 5.

96. GAMO f. 1p, op. 2, d. 143, ll. 91–92 (quotation 92).

97. Quoted from his speech, June 20, 1944 (NARB f. 1440, op. 3, d. 523, ll. 72, 77).

98. Quoted from NARB f. 1440, op. 3, d. 523, ll. 73, 77.

99. Quoted from Ponomarenko's speech, March 29, 1945 (NARB f. 1440, op. 3, d. 523, l. 163).

100. Weiner, *Making Sense of War*, 136.

101. Quoted from Ponomarenko's February 25, 1946, speech, which was published a few days later in *Sovetskaia Belorussiia* (NARB f. 1440, op. 3, d. 523, l. 340).

102. First and second quotation from Ponamarenko's March 29, 1945, speech, third from his February 25, 1946, speech (NARB f. 1440, op. 3, d. 523, l. 340). Fourth to sixth quotations from his report on the work of the Central Committee in 1946 (NARB f. 4p, op. 61, d. 360a, l. 4).

103. Quoted from Rusak's interrogation, February 10, 1944 (NARB f. 4p, op. 33a, d. 614, l. 23).

104. NARB f. 4p, op. 33a, d. 614, ll. 1–35.

105. See, for example, a list with the names of 465 locals (mostly from Minsk oblast) accused of working for the Germans, May 8, 1943 (NARB f. 4p, op. 33a, d. 151, ll. 227–39, 247–70). Further lists can be found in NARB either among the Special Sector files of the Communist Party of Belarus—for instance, NARB f. 4p, op. 33a, d. 204; and NARB f. 4p, op. 33a, d. 704—or among the files of the Belarusian Staff of the Partisan Movement (most of the *dela* in NARB f. 1450, op. 21).

106. As reported by Tsanava to Ponomarenko, January 2, 1943 (NARB f. 4p, op. 33a, d. 151, ll. 176–80).

107. Musial, *Sowjetische Partisanen 1941–1944*, 314–15.

108. Quoted from NARB f. 4p, op. 29, d. 12, l. 149.

109. Musial, *Sowjetische Partisanen 1941–1944*, 315.

110. On the police: Paul Hagenloh, "'Chekist in Essence, Chekist in Spirit': Regular and Political Police in the 1930s," *Cahier du monde russe* 42, no. 2–4 (2001): 447–75. On the development of crime surveillance and passport and residence registration catalogues: Shearer, *Policing Stalin's Socialism*, 158–80.

111. GAMO f. 1p, op. 2, d. 54, ll. 3, 125.

112. Aleksandr Epifanov, *Otvetstvennost' za voennye prestupleniia, sovershennye na territorii SSSR v gody Velikoi Otechestvennoi voiny, 1941–1956 gg.* (Volgograd: MVD, 2005), 73.

113. Adamushko et al., *Belorusy v sovetskom tylu*, 1:14–15; Epifanov, *Otvetstvennost'*, 73. Also for Ukraine: Oleksandr Melnyk, "Historical Politics, Legitimacy Contests, and the (Re-)Construction of Political Communities in Ukraine during the Second World War" (PhD diss., University of Toronto, 2016), 107–26.

114. Quoted from the order (RGVA f. 38656, op. 1, d. 10, l. 20). On screening the material: Epifanov, *Otvetstvennost'*, 76. Specifically on such practices in the Baltics: Olaf Mertelsmann and Aigi Rahi-Tamm, "Cleansing and Compromise: The Estonian SSR in 1944–1945," *Cahiers du monde russe* 49, 2 (2008), 327; Amir Weiner and Aigi Rahi-Tamm, "Getting to Know You: The Soviet Surveillance System, 1939–57," *Kritika: Explorations in Russian and Eurasian History* 13, no. 1 (2012): 23–24.

115. See the letter from the archive director to the KGB in Mogilev oblast (USHMM, RG-53.006M, Reel 3: Cherikov District Administration [Mogilev Oblast], 1941–1942, f. 302, op. 1, d. 1, no page number.

116. For evidence on force during interrogations see chapter 4; for letters from Soviet citizens see chapter 5.

117. Author's interview with Petr K., June 13, 2011, Naguevichi, Belarus.

118. Aleksei Popov, *15 vstrech s generalom KGB Bel'chenko* (Moscow: OLMA-Press, 2002), 228–30. This is a book glorifying Bel'chenko's accounts, not a critical historical assessment.

119. See the report by NKGB officers Zalogin and Fomkin to Tsanava, no date, but must have been fall 1943 (NARB f. 4p, op. 33a, d. 400, ll. 356–62).

120. See Tsanava's report, November 13 or 15, 1944 (NARB f. 4p, op. 33a, d. 400, ll. 314–15).

121. That number included a small number of so-called residents and agents. See the report by MVD boss Sergei Bel'chenko, November 1947, in Andrzej Chmielarz et al., eds., *NKWD o polskim podziemiu 1944–1948: Konspiracja polska na Nowogródczyźnie i Grodzieńszczyźnie* (Warsaw: Instytut Studiów Politycznych PAN, 1997), 51.

122. Marina Sorokina, "People and Procedures: Toward a History of the Investigation of Nazi Crimes in the USSR," *Kritika: Explorations in Russian and Eurasian History* 6, no. 4 (2005): 801.

123. Sorokina, "People and Procedures," 824; Weiner and Rahi-Tamm, "Getting to Know You," 29–30.

124. Quoted from the copy of the original report (BArch B 162/7535, l. 42).

125. BArch B 162/7535, ll. 42–45.

4. Determining Guilt

1. Quoted from Vladimir Svetlov, "'Osvobozhdennyi' Minsk 1944 goda," in *Repressivnaia politika sovetskoi vlasti v Belarusi: Sbornik nauchnykh rabot*, ed. Igor' N. Kuznetsov and Iakov Basin (Minsk: Memorial, 2007), 2:333–45, here 335.

2. Quoted from Svetlov, "'Osvobozhdennyi' Minsk," 335.

3. Quoted from Svetlov, "'Osvobozhdennyi' Minsk," 341.

4. Svetlov, "'Osvobozhdennyi' Minsk," 343.

5. In the case of Belarus, these documents were sent to the first secretary of the Communist Party of Belarus. They are accessible, with limits, at the National Archive of Belarus.

6. Stalin, *On the Great Patriotic War*, 13–14, quotation on 14.

7. Karel C. Berkhoff, *Motherland in Danger: Soviet Propaganda during World War II* (Cambridge, MA: Harvard University Press, 2012), 234–40.

8. Stalin, *On the Great Patriotic War*, 12–13, quotation on 12.

9. Quoted from the leaflet (RGASPI f. 625, op. 1, d. 44, l. 238).

10. The numbers are based on the statistics (by year) provided in Mozokhin, *Pravo na repressii*, 481–626. Unfortunately, the available statistics are incomplete, contain overlapping categories, and due to restricted archival access also cannot be cross-checked.

11. "Treason" translates into Russian as both *predatel'stvo* and *izmena*. A "traitor" was therefore a *predatel'* or an *izmennik*. *Predatel'stvo* and *izmena* were used interchangeably in Soviet documents. The legal category for treason was *izmena rodine*, meaning regardless of whether someone was accused of *predatel'stvo* or *izmena*, he or she would formally always have been prosecuted for treason, *izmena rodine*. *Kollaboratsionist* (collaborator) and *kollaboratsionizm* (collaboration) are more recent additions to the Russian vocabulary.

12. On East Asia: Kushner, *Men to Devils*, 120; Konrad M. Lawson, "Wartime Atrocities and the Politics of Treason in the Ruins of the Japanese Empire, 1937–1953" (PhD diss., Harvard University, 2012); 1–9, 33–49. On Europe: Judt, *Postwar*, 44–50; Sergey Kudryashov and Vanessa Voisin, "The Early Stages of Legal Purges in Soviet Russia (1941–1945)," *Cahiers du monde russe* 49, no. 2 (2008): 268–69.

13. On the fusion of civil and military authority: Harold J. Berman and Miroslav Kerner, *Soviet Military Law and Administration* (Cambridge, MA: Harvard University Press, 1955), 64–65, 101–2, 109–10, 133–34.

14. Berman and Kerner, *Soviet Military Law*, 110–24, 163. The lowest court in the Red Army was the divisional military court; the next highest, the army group military court. The lowest court within the NKVD was the regional military court (for example, the military court of the NKVD of Minsk oblast), and the next level was the republican court of the NKVD (for example, the military court of the NKVD in Belarus). While the Red Army military courts were directly subordinated to the People's Commissariat of Defense, the NKVD military courts were subordinated to the People's Commissariat of Internal Affairs. Ultimately, both types of military courts were subordinated to the Military Division of the Supreme Court of the USSR, the highest court in the Soviet Union. In addition, the People's Commissariat of Justice and the Office of the Prosecutor-General of the USSR also exercised supervision over the military trials (Berman and Kerner, *Soviet Military Law*, 64–65, 101–3, 109–10, 123, 133–34).

15. Quoted from Aron Trainin, Vladimir Men'shagin, and Zinaida Vyshinskaia, *Ugolovnyi kodeks RSFSR: Kommentarii* (Moscow: Iuridicheskoe izdatel'stvo NKIu SSSR, 1944), 65.

16. Quoted from Trainin, Men'shagin, and Vyshinskaia, *Ugolovnyi kodeks RSFSR*, 64; *Ugolovnyi kodeks Belorusskoi SSR* (Moscow: Iuridicheskoe izdatel'stvo NKIu SSSR, 1944), 12. For the legal basis of postwar punishment, see Kudryashov and Voisin, "Early Stages."

17. See the respective penal codes (Trainin, Men'shagin, and Vyshinskaia, *Ugolovnyi kodeks RSFSR*, 64–77; *Ugolovnyi kodeks Belorusskoi SSR*, 12–14).

18. Trainin, Men'shagin, and Vyshinskaia, *Ugolovnyi kodeks RSFSR*, 64; *Ugolovnyi kodeks Belorusskoi SSR*, 12.

19. Trainin, Men'shagin, and Vyshinskaia, *Ugolovnyi kodeks RSFSR*, 67; *Ugolovnyi kodeks Belorusskoi SSR*, 20.

20. On the internal review process: NARB f. 4p, op. 29, d. 603, l. 175; Berman and Kerner, *Soviet Military Law*, 123. On the denial of a right of appeal: Kudryashov and Voisin, "Early Stages," 273.

21. Kudryashov and Voisin, "Early Stages," 283–84; Voisin, *L'URSS contre ses traîtres*, 155–67. On the prewar conflict: Gábor T. Rittersporn, "Terror and Soviet Legality: Police vs. Judiciary, 1933–1940," in *Anatomy of Terror: Political Violence under Stalin*, ed. James Harris (Oxford: Oxford University Press, 2013), 184–88.

22. Kudryashov and Voisin, "Early Stages," 272.

23. *Rabotali u nemtsev* can also be translated as "working for the Germans" or "working with the Germans."

24. For the text of the April 19, 1943, decree, see Politburo Protocol no. 40 (RGASPI f. 17, op. 3, d. 1047, ll. 34, 232–33). On its origin: Epifanov, *Otvetstvennost'*, 17–37; Andreas Hilger, Nikita Petrov, and Günther Wagenlehner, "Der 'Ukaz 43': Entstehung und Problematik des Dekrets des Präsidiums des Obersten Sowjets vom 19. April 1943," in *Sowjetische Militärtribunale*, vol. 1: *Die Verurteilung deutscher Kriegsgefangener 1941–1953*, ed. Andreas Hilger, Ute Schmidt, and Günther Wagenlehner (Cologne: Böhlau, 2001), 184–85; Manfred Zeidler, *Stalinjustiz contra NS-Verbrechen: Die Kriegsverbrecherprozesse gegen deutsche Kriegsgefangene in der UdSSR in den Jahren 1943–1952. Kenntnisstand und Forschungsprobleme* (Dresden: Hannah-Arendt-Institut für Totalitarismusforschung, 1996), 16–18.

25. Penter, "Local Collaborators on Trial," 349; G. S. Anashkin, *Otvetstvennost' za izmenu rodine i spionazh* (Moscow: Iuridicheskaia literatura, 1964), 43.

26. Penter, "Local Collaborators," 349–50; Anashkin, *Otvetstvennost'*, 43–44.

27. Quoted from Anashkin, *Otvetstvennost'*, 44.

28. NARB f. 4p, op. 29, d. 22, l. 35.

29. Penter, "Local Collaborators," 356.

30. NARB f. 4p, op. 29, d. 600, ll. 233–34.

31. Quoted from Irena Krajewska's recollections (AW I/396, l. 8). Torture applied to members of the student underground in Molodechno oblast, tried in 1950, included needles driven under nails and breaking ribs and teeth (Charniaŭski, *"Nia boitsesia"*, 131).

32. Quoted from the investigative report, January 7, 1947 (NARB f. 4p, op. 29, d. 600, l. 64). On lack of witnesses and torture acknowledged in reports by the state security organs, see d. 22, ll. 35–37; d. 600, ll. 227–32.

33. Jeffrey Burds, "Gender and Policing in Soviet West Ukraine, 1944–1948," *Cahiers du monde russe* 22, no. 2–4 (2001), 317–18; Marta Havryshko, "Women's Body as Battlefield: Sexual Violence during Soviet Counterinsurgency in Western Ukraine in the [sic] 1944–1953," *Euxeinos: Governance and Culture in the Black Sea Region* 9, no. 27 (2019), 97–101; Statiev, *Soviet Counterinsurgency*, 282–85.

34. On confessions as sufficient proof of guilt: Berman and Kerner, *Soviet Military Law*, 111–12.

35. For examples of such complaints, see the report by Military Prosecutor Artimenkov, no earlier than March 28, 1944 (NARB f. 4p, op. 29, d. 61, l. 24); and the report from Ivan Vetrov, chief prosecutor of the BSSR, August 20, 1944 (NARB f. 4p, op. 29, d. 56, l. 5).

36. See, for example, the report by the head of the MVD military tribunals of Belarus, I. Sakharov, on the tribunals' work in the fourth quarter of 1946 (NARB f. 4p, op. 29, d. 600, ll. 217, 223, 227–32).

37. Polian, *Against Their Will*, 140–53.

38. Statiev, *Soviet Counterinsurgency*, 110, table 4.4, and 125, table 4.10.

39. On the abolition of the death penalty: Berman and Kerner, *Soviet Military Law*, 89–90.

40. Galina Ivanova, *Istoriia GULAGa 1918–1958: Sotsial'no-ekonomicheskii i politiko-pravovoi aspekty* (Moscow: Nauka, 2006), 266–71.

41. Report by Lieutenant Colonel of Justice V. Chalikov, February 10, 1948 (NARB f. 4p, op. 29, d. 688, l. 189).

42. NARB f. 4p, op. 29, d. 688, l. 155.

43. For 1948, see NARB f. 4p, op. 62, d. 43, l. 395.

44. On Kliapino, see Tsanava's report, November 22, 1943 (NARB f. 4p, op. 33a, d. 400, ll. 376–84).

45. A. Kh. Valiev, *Zapiski voennogo prokurora (Velikaia Otechestvennaia voina 1941–1945 gg.)* (Kazan': Matbugar Iorty, 2000), 122–24.

46. Quoted from the decree (RGASPI f. 17, op. 3, d. 1047, l. 233).

47. Valiev, *Zapiski voennogo prokurora*, 122–24.

48. See the report by I. Sakharov, August 2, 1944 (NARB f. 4p, op. 29, d. 22, l. 34).

49. In the first half of 1946, probably two more trials, one in Dzerzhinskii district and one in Smolevichi, were open to the public. See the respective NKVD reports (GAMO f. 1p, op. 2, d. 143, ll. 167–74, 264–71).

50. See the February 25, 1946, NKVD report on the trial and the verdict (GAMO f. 1p, op. 2, d. 143, ll. 137–40, 143–53).

51. "Sud idze," *Stsiag komunizma*, February 21, 1946.

52. See, for example, "Sudebnyi protess po delu o zlodeianiiakh, sovershennykh nemetsko-fashistskimi prestupnikami v BSSR," *Sovetskaia Belorussiia*, January 16, 1946, and subsequent issues of January 17–30, 1946.

53. I surveyed the most important central newspapers (*Pravda, Izvestiia, Krasnaia zvezda*), the main newspapers of the republics where the trials took place (*Sovetskaia Belorussiia, Sovetskaia Latviia, Sovetskaia Litva, Sovetskaia Estoniia*, and *Sovetskaia Ukraina*; Soviet Russia did not have a separate republican newspaper), and some of the newspapers of the regions where the trials took place (for example *Rabochii put'* for Smolensk oblast and *Brianskii rabochii* for Briansk oblast). Media coverage included newsreel as well as newspaper articles in both German and English, issued by the Soviet authorities in East Germany and the Soviet government in London, respectively. On international press coverage: Zeidler, *Stalinjustiz contra NS-Verbrechen*, 30.

54. "Sudovy pratses," *Stsiag komunizma*, January 21, 1946; USHMM RG–06.025*03, War Crimes Investigations and Prosecutions, Minsk 1945–1946 (N-18763, tom 18), Bruno Franz Mittmann, Reel 599–604.

55. *Stsiag komunizma* covered the trial on February 21, 1946, and February 28, 1946. In the first postwar years, *Sovetskaia Belorussiia* served as both the republic's main newspaper and the newspaper of Minsk oblast. It was published in Russian. *Zviazda*, the republic's main Belarusian-language newspaper, also did not cover the trial.

56. Franziska Exeler, "Nazi Atrocities, International Criminal Law, and Soviet War Crimes Trials: The Soviet Union and the Global Moment of Post-Second World War Justice," in *The New Histories of International Criminal Law: Retrials,* ed. Immi Tallgren and Thomas Skouteris (Oxford: Oxford University Press, 2019), 200–205.

57. Fitzpatrick, "How the Mice Buried the Cat," 299.

58. Lukasz Hirszowicz, "The Holocaust in the Soviet Mirror," in *The Holocaust in the Soviet Union: Studies and Sources on the Destruction of the Jews in the Nazi-Occupied Territories of the USSR, 1941–1945*, ed. Lucjan Dobroszyski and Jeffrey Gurock (Armonk, NY: M. E. Sharpe, 1993), 39–46.

59. "Sud nad predateliami," *Pravda*, March 10, 1962; "Narod ne proshchaet," *Sovetskaia Belorussiia*, March 9, 1962, and subsequent issues (March 10, March 13, March 14, March 16, 1962); "Nel'ha zabyts', nel'ha daravats'!," *Zara*, March 10, 1962, and subsequent issues (March 13, March 14, March 16); "Nel'ha zabyts', nel'ha daravats'!," *Chyrvonaia zviazda*, March 10, 1962, and subsequent issues (March 13, March 15); "Nel'zia zabyt', nel'zia prostit'!," *Sovetskaia rodina*, March 14, 1962 and March 17, 1962.

60. Quoted from Artimenkov's report, September 8, 1949 (NARB f. 4p, op. 62, d. 43, l. 358).

61. Quoted from NARB f. 4p, op. 62, d. 43, l. 358.

62. Immo Rebitschek, "Feindbilder auf dem Prüfstand: Sowjetische Kollaborateure im Fokus der Revisionskommissionen, 1954 und 1955," *Jahrbücher für Geschichte Osteuropas* 65, no. 2 (2017): 266–78.

63. See the text of the amnesty decree in A. N. Artizov et al., eds., *Reabilitatsiia: Kak eto bylo. Dokumenty Prezidiuma TsK KPSS i drugie materialy*, 3 vols. (Moscow: Mezhdunarodnyi fond "Demokratiia," 2000), 1:259–60.

64. On the prosecution and repatriation of German prisoners of war: Andreas Hilger, *Deutsche Kriegsgefangene in der Sowjetunion, 1941–1956: Kriegsgefangenenpolitik, Lageralltag und Erinnerung* (Essen: Klartext, 2000), 255–82.

65. Amir Weiner, "The Empires Pay a Visit: Gulag Returnees, East European Rebellions, and Soviet Frontier Politics," *Journal of Modern History* 78, no. 2 (2006): 364.

66. This assessment is based on my study of trial documents (copies of KGB archive files) available at the United States Holocaust Memorial Museum, to be found in RG-31.018M (Postwar War Crimes Trials Related to the Holocaust, 1945–1970), with material from Ukraine, and RG 26.004M (War Crimes Investigation and Trial Records from the Former Lithuanian KGB Archives, 1944–1992). For a similar assessment, see Alexander Prusin, "The 'Second Wave' of Soviet Justice: The 1960s War Crimes Trials," in *Rethinking Holocaust Justice: Essays across Disciplines,* ed. Norman J. W. Goda (New York: Berghahn Books, 2018), 130.

67. Iryna Sklokina, "Trials of Nazi Collaborators in the Context of Soviet Propaganda, Nationality Policy and the Cold War (1960–80s)," in *Collaboration in Eastern Europe during the Second World War and the Holocaust*, ed. Peter Black, Béla Rásky, and Marianne Windsperger (Vienna: VWI, 2019), 67–86.

68. Prusin, "'Second Wave' of Soviet Justice," 132–35.

69. "Narod ne proshchaet," *Sovetskaia Belorussiia*, March 9, 1962.

70. Gerlach, *Kalkulierte Morde*, 917, 1107.

71. Alexander Prusin has identified twenty trials with about 130 defendants that took place between 1959 and 1970 ("'Second Wave" of Soviet Justice," 130–31).

72. Exeler, "Nazi Atrocities," 213.

73. Joshua Rubenstein and Ilya Altman, eds., *The Unknown Black Book: The Holocaust in the German-Occupied Soviet Territories* (Bloomington: Indiana University Press, 2008), xxxvi. I thank Ilya Kukulin for bringing this to my attention.

74. The town is given by its previous name, Koidanovo, in the report. Quoted from Krysanov's report, March 5, 1946 (GAMO f. 1p, d. 2, op. 143, l. 174).

75. GAMO f. 1p, op. 2, d. 143, ll. 137–40, 143–53. An additional fifty-two people had asked to be heard, but their wishes could not be accommodated.

76. GAMO f. 1p, op. 2, d. 143, ll. 137–40, 143–53.

77. Quoted from Mikhodievskii's letter (Gosudarstvennyi arkhiv Rossiiskoi Federatsii [hereafter GARF] f. 7523, op. 31, d. 160, l. 57).

78. Quoted from GARF f. 7523, op. 31, d. 160, l. 57.

79. Quoted from Khves'ko's letter (GARF f. 7523, op. 31, d. 594, l. 162).

80. Quoted from GARF f. 7523, op. 31, d. 594, l. 162.

81. The reports can be found in NARB f. 4p, op. 29, dd. 22, 61, 62, 63, 126, 128, 600, 603, 688; op. 62, dd. 43, 148.

82. On Ponomarenko's role, see Slepyan, *Stalin's Guerrillas,* 43–44, 47, 225–27.

83. Musial, *Sowjetische Partisanen 1941–1944*, 265–66. On NKVD informers' efforts in Gomel' and Poles'e oblasts who prepared the defection of policemen to the Soviet side in August 1943, and on policemen and soldiers of the Russian Liberation Army who joined the partisans in Mogilev oblast in September 1943, see NARB f. 4p, op. 33a, d. 400, ll. 98–99, 154.

84. Quoted in Slepyan, *Stalin's Guerrillas,* 221.

85. Quoted from NARB f. 4p, op. 33a, d. 400, ll. 151–52. On death sentences, see Musial, *Sowjetische Partisanen 1941–1944*, 268–69.

86. See Mazur's report of April 7, 1944, on these events, which appear to have taken place in the summer of 1943 (NARB f. 4p, op. 29, d. 7, l. 26).

87. Quoted from NARB f. 4p, op. 33a, d. 400, l. 202.

88. NARB f. 4p, op. 33a, d. 634, ll. 1–10.

89. Quoted from NARB f. 4p, op. 33a, d. 634, ll. 1–10.

90. See Ivan Nizov's letter, May 16, 1945 (NARB f. 4p, op. 29, d. 472, ll. 211–19). The Radionov Brigade also goes by the name Rodionov, Gil'-Radionov, or Radionov-Gil.

91. Quoted from NARB f. 4p, op. 29, d. 472, l. 217.

92. Alexander Dallin and Ralph S. Mavrogordato, "Rodionov: A Case-Study in Wartime Redefection," *American Slavic and East European Review* 18, no. 1 (1959): 27–28; Musial, *Sowjetische Partisanen 1941–1944*, 195–207.

93. Quoted from Nizov's letter (NARB f. 4p, op. 29, d. 472, l. 213). The burning of Azartsy probably took place on August 12, 1943, six days before the Radionov brigade defected to the Soviet side. The information comes from the unpublished memoirs of Władysław Wielki, whose relatives died in that operation (André Wielki, email correspondence with author, January 28, 2019).

94. See the report by I. Sakharov, January 26, 1946 (NARB f. 4p, op. 62, d. 43, l. 38). For similar cases: NARB f. 4p, op. 62, d. 43, ll. 275, 396.

95. Quoted from Sakharov's report, October 6, 1949 (NARB f. 4p, op. 62, d. 43, l. 396).

96. Joseph Stalin, *Problems of Leninism* (Moscow: Foreign Languages Publishing House, 1947), 318.

97. Quoted from NARB f. 1440, op. 3, d. 522, l. 154.

98. Quoted from Ponamarenko's February 25, 1946, speech (NARB f. 1440, op. 3, d. 523, l. 340); also his speeches of June 20, 1944 (ll. 73, 77), and March 29, 1945 (l. 163).

99. As argued by Slepyan, *Stalin's Guerrillas*, 43–44, 47.

100. See the report, June 20, 1946 (GAMO f. 1p, op. 9, d. 35, l. 16).

101. See the report by Minister of Education P. Saevich, probably January 1948 (NARB f. 4p, op. 17, d. 103, ll. 8 [quotation], 12).

102. Quoted from NARB f. 4p, op. 17, d. 103, l. 12.

103. See Note on Wartime Losses.

104. See the police report, December 7, 1944 (GAMO f. 1p, op. 2, d. 54, l. 125).

105. See the report by K. Korshuk, head of the Minsk oblispolkom, and P. Benenson, head of the school department, July 20, 1951 (GAMO f. 1p, op. 9, d. 118, l. 11).

106. See the statistics in NARB f. 4p, op. 17, d. 103, l. 42.

107. See Maksimenko's report, 22 June 1946 (GAMO f. 1p, op. 2, d. 143, l. 570).

108. Quoted from GAMO f. 1p, op. 2, d. 143, ll. 561–62.

109. Quoted from GAMO f. 1p, op. 2, d. 143, l. 560.

110. Quoted from his report, March 31, 1948 (NARB f. 4p, op. 29, d. 688, l. 390).

111. Quoted from his letter, name unknown, July 3, 1951, in Aleksiandr Huzhaloŭski, ed., "... *Milastsi Vashai prosim", al'bo Adzin hod u naveishai historyi Belarusi, adliustravany ŭ listakh, zaiavakh, skarhakh i inshykh formakh zvarotu hramadzian* (Minsk: n.p., 2006), 79.

112. Karel C. Berkhoff locates this suspicion at the highest level, in and around Stalin's inner circle (*Motherland in Danger*, 223, 242).

113. Quoted from the *anketa* of F. V. Prutnikov, January 7, 1947 (NARB f. 4p, op. 29, d. 729, l. 392).

114. Quoted from Dolzhenko's letter, June 7, 1946 (GARF f. 7523, op. 32, d. 443, l. 2).

115. Author's interview with Liubov' I., May 18, 2011, Minsk, Belarus.

116. See his letter, May 31, 1951, in Huzhaloŭski, ed., "... *Milastsi Vashai prosim*," 216–17.

117. Quoted from Mor, *War for Life*, 189.

118. Quoted from her letter, December 20, 1945 (GAMO f. 1p, op. 2, d. 143, ll. 76–77).

119. Slepyan, *Stalin's Guerrillas*, 277.

120. Quoted from: Feigel', *Zhizn' i sud'ba*, 274.

121. Quoted from Aleksei Litvin and E. A. Kasperovich, "Trudnaia pamiat' voiny," *Nioman*, no. 7 (1994): 153.

5. Loss, Grief, and Reckonings

1. Mor, *War for Life*.

2. Eberhardt, *Przemiany narodowościowe*, 68, table 14; *Davyd-Haradok Memorial Book*, 4–9.

3. Quoted from Mor, *War for Life*, 192.

4. Quoted from Mor, *War for Life*, 194.

5. Quoted from Mor, *War for Life*, 194, 196.

6. Quoted from Mor, *War for Life*, 197–98.

7. All quotes from Mor, *War for Life*, 198.

8. Quoted from Mor, *War for Life*, 198.

9. Quoted from Mor, *War for Life*, 199.

10. Mor, *War for Life*, 199–205.

11. Bykov, *Dolgaia doroga domoi*, 135.

12. Quoted from Ivan Lipai, "Eto gor'koe slovo 'svoboda' . . .," *Nioman*, no. 3 (1996): 206.

13. Author's interview with Sofiia Brudner, September 19, 2010, Rekhovot, Israel.

14. Wolozhinski Rubin, *Against the Tide*, 171–72, caption image 5.

15. Quoted from: Bembel'-Dedok, *Vospominaniia*, 182.

16. Bembel'-Dedok, *Vospominaniia*, 181–82.

17. Quoted from Bembel'-Dedok, *Vospominaniia*, 182.

18. Quoted from Bembel'-Dedok, *Vospominaniia*, 182.

19. Quoted from Bembel'-Dedok, *Vospominaniia*, 182–83.

20. Quoted from Bembel'-Dedok, *Vospominaniia*, 183.

21. Quoted from Bembel'-Dedok, *Vospominaniia*, 181.

22. Quoted from his letter, June 12, 1951, in Huzhaloŭski, ". . . *Milastsi Vashai prosim*," 247.

23. Quoted from his letter, July 15, 1951, in Huzhaloŭski, ". . . *Milastsi Vashai prosim*," 217–18.

24. Danilov, *Neudobnaia istoriia*, 223–28, quotation on 228.

25. See the testimonies in *Davyd-Haradok Memorial Book*, 92–110.

26. Quoted from Mor, *War for Life*, 207.

27. Quoted from Mor, *War for Life*, 221.

28. Quoted from Mor, *War for Life*, 220.

29. Mor, *War for Life*, 212–53.

30. Smilovitsky, "Demographic Profile," 122.

31. Ovsishcher, *Vozvrashchenie*, 54, 114–15.

32. Izhar, *Chasia Bornstein-Bielicka*, 284–91; Wolozhinski Rubin, *Against the Tide*, 178–84.

33. On the widespread urge for retribution and postwar trials in both Western and Eastern Europe, see the essays in Deák, Gross, and Judt, *Politics of Retribution in Europe*; for a good overview also Judt, *Post-War*, 44–50.

34. See the report, October 16, 1945 (NARB f. 4p, op. 29, d. 311, ll. 128–31).

35. Quoted from the report, October 16, 1945 (NARB f. 4p, op. 29, d. 311, ll. 128 [quotation], 129).

36. Quoted from the report, October 24, 1945 (RGASPI f. 17, op. 88, d. 382, l. 48).

37. Quoted from the report to Ponomarenko, no earlier than November 4, 1944 (NARB f. 4p, op. 29, d. 29, l. 191).

38. See the report by Naroenko, deputy to the prosecutor of Belarus, September 30, 1944 (NARB f. 4p, op. 29, d. 56, l. 42).

39. See the KGB report to the Central Committee in Moscow, no earlier than August 1956 (Rossiiskii gosudarstvennyi arkhiv noveishei istorii [hereafter RGANI] f. 5, op. 33, d. 21, ll. 17–18).

40. Judt, *Post-War*, 42–43; Lawson, "Wartime Atrocities and the Politics of Treason," 4, 339–40.

41. For example, in Czechoslovakia: Frommer, *National Cleansing*, 33–62.

42. Quoted from Adamovich, Bryl, and Kolesnik, *Out of the Fire*, 60–61.

43. On the (by and large) destruction of antinationalist resistance in Belarus by the end of 1946, see Ponomarenko's report for 1946 (NARB f. 4p, op. 61, d. 360a, l. 29). On the western borderlands: Statiev, *Soviet Counterinsurgency*, 105–37; Prusin, *Lands Between*, 205.

44. See the definition of bandits by the Main Directorate for NKVD Internal Troops, July 1, 1943 (RGVA f. 38656, op. 1, d. 10, l. 1).

45. By July 1, 1946, 35 percent of Soviet officials who worked in these positions in Baranovichi, Minsk, Bobruisk, and Mogilev oblasts were former partisans. The situation was similar in the remaining eight oblasts. See the individual data compiled by the Sovnarkom/Council of Ministers' cadre department (NARB f. 7, op. 3, d. 1628, l. 2; d. 1633, ll. 9, 18, 50, 72, 79).

46. Report to Ponomarenko, August 8, 1944 (NARB f. 4p, op. 29, d. 29, l. 106).

47. Report by Ivan Vetrov, September 26, 1944 (NARB f. 4p, op. 29, d. 56, l. 23).

48. Sorokina, "People and Procedures," 825–26; Svetlov, "'Osvobozhdennyi' Minsk," 343.

49. GAMO f. 1p, op. 2, d. 143, l. 139.

50. Quoted from GAMO f. 1p, op. 2, d. 143, l. 139.

51. GAMO f. 1p, op. 2, d. 143, ll. 139, 152–53.

52. Aharon Moravtchik, "My Small Revenge for the Heinous Crime (A Chapter from My Memoirs)," in *Davyd-Haradok Memorial Book*, 119–29.

53. See the testimony of Sofiia Khabai (YV O.3/4212, ll. 1–14).

54. Quoted from YV O.3/4212, l. 11.

55. Quoted from YV O.3/4212, l. 11.

56. YV O.3/4212, 1. 11.

57. Both quotations from YV O.3/4212, l. 11.

58. YV O.3/4212, l. 3.

59. Both quotations from YV O.3/4212, l. 11.

60. Both quotations from YV O.3/4212, l. 11–12.

61. Quoted from YV O.3/4212, ll. 11–12.

62. Jeffrey Burds, "Agentura: Soviet Informants' Networks and the Ukrainian Underground in Galicia, 1944–48," *East European Politics and Societies* 11, no. 1 (1997): 115–19.

63. Golfo Alexopoulos, "Exposing Illegality and Oneself: Complaint and Risk in Stalin's Russia," in *Reforming Justice in Russia, 1864–1996: Power, Culture, and the Limits of Legal Order*, ed. Peter H. Solomon (Armonk: M. E. Sharpe, 1997), 169–70; A. Ia. Livshin, I. B. Orlov and O. V. Khlevniuk, eds., *Pis'ma vo vlast', 1928–1939: Zaiavleniia, zhaloby, donosy, pis'ma v gosudarstvennye struktury i sovetskim vozhdiam* (Moscow: ROSSPEN, 2002), 5–12.

64. Quoted from his letter, December 26, 1944 (NARB f. 4p, op. 29, d. 462, l. 437).

65. Quoted from his letter, April 1946 (GARF f. 7523, op. 31, d. 586, l. 131).

66. Quoted from GARF f. 7523, op. 31, d. 586, ll. 131–32.

67. All quotations from GARF f. 7523, op. 31, d. 586, ll. 132–33.

68. Sheila Fitzpatrick, "Signals from Below: Soviet Letters of Denunciation of the 1930s," *Journal of Modern History* 68, no. 4 (1996): 837.

69. RGASPI f. 83, op. 1, d. 13, ll. 20, 22; Bakunovich, "Okkupirovannoe detstvo," 192; Rott, *Naperekor sud'be*, 92.

70. Dean, *Collaboration*, 97. On Ushachi: Romanovsky, "Holocaust in the Eyes of Homo Sovieticus," 372.

71. See chapter 2.

72. Quoted from Bembel'-Dedok, *Vospominaniia*, 159.

73. USHMM RG-53.006M, Reel 2: City Administration of Mogilev, 1941–1944, f. 260, op. 1, d. 29, ll. 76, 78; d. 45, ll. 30, 41.

74. Author's interview with Sofiia Brudner, September 19, 2010, Rekhovot, Israel.

75. Leonid Smilovitsky, "The Struggle of Belorussian Jews for the Restitution of Possessions and Housing in the First Postwar Decade," *East European Jewish Affairs* 30, no. 2 (2000): 63–64.

76. Mor, *War for Life*, 221.

77. Examples: letter from the procuracy of Belarus about Red Army soldier Fridburg, September 13, 1945 (NARB f. 4p, op. 29, d. 188, l. 77); letter by Red Army officer I. G. Gol'man, no earlier than June 1946 (NARB f. 4p, op. 29, d. 472, l. 41); letter by Ch. S. Iashchina and follow-up correspondence, July 19, 1946 (NARB f. 4p, op. 29, d. 508, ll. 309–10, 314, 316); Mogilev gorkom report on Red Army soldier Ioffe, February 20, 1946 (NARB f. 4p, op. 29, d. 508, l. 586). On Jews seeking property restitution in postwar Ukraine: Elena Jakel, "'Ukraine without Jews'? Nationality and Belonging in Soviet Ukraine, 1943–48" (PhD diss., University of Illinois, Urbana-Champaign, 2014), 39–51.

78. Mark B. Smith, *Property of Communists: The Urban Housing Program from Stalin to Khrushchev* (DeKalb: Northern Illinois University Press, 2010), 3–18, 143–44.

79. On confusion within the state apparatus over how to apply existing legislation and the struggle of evacuees to reclaim apartments: Manley, *To the Tashkent Station*, 256–64.

80. VY O.3/11082, l. 41.

81. Quoted from his letter, no later than September 25, 1946 (NARB f. 4p, op. 29, d. 516, ll. 40, 46).

82. On these practices in 1945 and 1946, see the reports by the Bobruisk obkom, March 25, 1946 (NARB f. 4p, op. 29, d. 508, l. 358); and December 27, 1946 (NARB f. 4p, op. 29, d. 516, l. 132).

83. Quoted from the Molodechno obkom report, September 18, 1945 (NARB f. 4p, op. 29, d. 469, l. 163).

84. See the reports by Ivan Vetrov, chief prosecutor of Belarus, August 20, 1944 (NARB f. 4p, op. 29, d. 56, ll. 5–11) and December 30, 1944 (ll. 79–81).

85. Quoted from his report, December 30, 1944 (NARB f. 4p, op. 29, d. 56, l. 81).

86. Quoted from his report, August 20, 1944 (NARB f. 4p, op. 29, d. 56, ll. 7–8).

87. See, for example, the letter from the demobilized soldier Shimanovich, who was unable to evict a Soviet official from the house he previously lived in, and follow-up correspondence in April–August 1946 (NARB f. 4p, op. 29, d. 510, ll. 650, 653–55, 657–58).

88. Compare the different assessments in Smilovitsky, "Struggle of Belarusian Jews," 62–68, and Manley, *To the Tashkent Station*, 262–64.

89. For a successful example, see Berzin, *Vospominaniia*, 35.

90. See the party's correspondence with Borisevich, May 31, 1945 (NARB f. 4p, op. 29, d. 472, ll. 668–69). For similar cases in Minsk, Vitebsk, and Pinsk oblasts in 1945–1946, see NARB f. 4p, op. 29, d. 472, ll. 97, 580, 587, 618–19; d. 469, l. 283; and d. 510, l. 738.

91. For examples of such cases as cited in MVD reports, see NARB f. 4p, op. 29, d. 600, l. 42 (January 17, 1947); and NARB f. 4p, op. 62, d. 148, ll. 134 (January 16, 1950).

92. Author's interview with Vitalii A., June 13, 2011, Slonim, Belarus.

93. Both quotations from Vasil'ev's letter, April 1946 (NARB f. 4p, op. 29, d. 510, l. 380).

94. Report from the Orsha raikom, May 11, 1946 (NARB f. 4p, op. 29, d. 510, ll. 383–85).

95. See the report by V. Chalikov, head of the MVD military tribunals in Belarus, January 16, 1950 (NARB f. 4p, op. 62, d. 148, ll. 13–14).

96. Quoted from Bakunovich, "Okkupirovannoe detstvo," 192.

97. Quoted from Bakunovich, "Okkupirovannoe detstvo," 207.

98. Author's interview with Asia L. and Ernst L., October 6, 2010, Munich, Germany.

6. Belarus, the Partisan Republic

1. Petr Kalinin, *Partizanskaia respublika* (Moscow: Voenizdat, 1964).

2. Quoted from Petr Kalinin, *Partizanskaia respublika*, 2nd ed. (Minsk: Belarus', 1968), 193.

3. Quoted from Kalinin, *Partizanskaia respublika* (1968), 377.

4. Quoted from Kalinin, *Partizanskaia respublika* (1968), 377.

5. Quoted from "Torzhestvo belorusskogo naroda," *Sovetskaia Belorussiia*, May 10, 1945.

6. Quoted from "Torzhestvo belorusskogo naroda," *Sovetskaia Belorussiia*, May 10, 1945.

7. For the view that Stalin erased ordinary Soviet citizens from the narrative, see Jeffrey Brooks, *Thank You, Comrade Stalin! Soviet Public Culture from Revolution to Cold War* (Princeton: Princeton University Press, 2000), 193–98.

8. This is based on my analysis of the republic's two main newspapers *Sovetskaia Belorussiia* (in Russian) and *Zviazda* (in Belarusian); select regional newspapers in either Belarusian or Russian such as *Bol'shevik Palessia* (Poles'e oblast), *Homel'skaia praŭda* (Gomel' oblast), *Grodnenskaia pravda* (Grodno oblast), *Polesskaia pravda* (Pinsk oblast), and *Za radzimu* (Mogilev oblast); and select district newspapers like *Stsiag komunizma* (Pukhovichskii district), *Sovetskaia rodina* (Gorodishchenskii district), and *Vol'naia pratsa* (Slonimskii district).

9. Quoted from "Vossoedinenie belorusskogo naroda v edinom Belorusskom sovetskom gosudarstve," *Sovetskaia Belorussiia*, September 16, 1945.

10. Quoted from "Oni borolis' za schast'e Rodiny," *Grodnenskaia pravda*, September 17, 1945.

11. Quoted from "Slavnyi iubilei Sovetskoi Belorussii," *Pravda*, January 2, 1949.

12. Quoted from Lavrentii Tsanava, *Vsenarodnaia partizanskaia voina v Belorussii protiv fashistskikh zakhvatchikov*, pt. 1: *Zarozhdenie i razvitie partizanskogo dvizheniia* (Minsk: Gosizdat BSSR, 1949), 20.

13. Quoted from Tsanava, *Vsenarodnaia partizanskaia voina*, 21.

14. Lisa Kirschenbaum, "Nothing Is Forgotten: Individual Memory and the Myth of the Great Patriotic War," in *Histories of the Aftermath: The Legacies of World War II in Comparative European Perspective*, ed. Robert Moeller and Frank Biess (New York: Berghahn Books, 2010), 70–72; Yan Mann, "Contested Memory: Writing the Great Patriotic War's Official History during Khrushchev's Thaw" (PhD diss., Arizona State University, 2016), 132–62.

15. "Narod pomnit," *Sovetskaia Belorussiia*, August 28, 1960.

16. "Narod pomnit," *Sovetskaia Belorussiia*, December 1, 1960; "Narod pomnit," *Sovetskaia Belorussiia*, December 4, 1960; "Narod pomnit," *Sovetskaia Belorussiia*, May 24, 1961.

17. On the proliferation of war memoirs: Nina Tumarkin, *The Living and the Dead: The Rise and Fall of the Cult of World War II in Russia* (New York: BasicBooks, 1994), 99–110; Slepyan, *Stalin's Guerrillas*, 280–87.

18. Quoted from "Razgoraetsia plamia partizanskoi voiny v Belorussii," *Pravda*, July 22, 1941.

19. Quoted from his speech, March 29, 1945 (NARB f. 1440, op. 3, d. 523, l. 169).

20. NARB f. 4p, op. 33a, d. 634, ll. 1–10.

21. On the omission of Jews from the partisan war narrative: Per Anders Rudling, "'For a Heroic Belarus!' The Great Patriotic War as Identity Marker in the Lukashenka and Soviet Belarusian Discourses," *Nationalities Affairs (Sprawy Narodowościowe)* 32 (2008), 47–50.

22. For a few examples: "Partizany Belorussii v boiakh za Rodinu," *Sovetskaia Belorussiia*, June 28, 1947; "Povest' o partizanskoi voine," *Sovetskaia Belorussiia*, November 3, 1948; "Kniga o partizanskom dvizhenii v Belorussii," *Sovetskaia Belorussiia*, April 23, 1950.

23. "V musee istorii Velikoi Otechestvennoi voiny," *Sovetskaia Belorussiia*, October 24, 1944.

24. Quoted from "Belorussiia voretsia," *Krasnaia zvezda*, May 17, 1942.

25. Quoted from "Belorussiia voretsia," *Krasnaia zvezda*, May 17, 1942.

26. Quoted from "Belorussiia voretsia," *Krasnaia zvezda*, May 17, 1942.

27. For the dates of the mass execution of Jews in the towns cited by Ponomarenko, see Gerlach, *Kalkulierte Morde*, 586 (Bykhov in September 1941), 595–97 (Vitebsk in October 1941), 599–600 (Shklov and Bobruisk in October 1941), 600–601 (Orsha in September–December 1941), 601, 684 (Polotsk in December 1941 and February 1942), 601 (Surazh in late 1941), 607 (El'sk in October 1941), 608 (Lel'chitsy in September 1941), 612 (Slutsk in October 1941), 684 (Liozno and Beshenkovichi in February 1942), and 684 (Cherven' in late January/early February 1942). The murder of the Jews of Minsk was carried out in several stages from 1941 to the final liquidation of the ghetto in October 1943. Petrikovo is probably the town Petrikov in southeastern Belarus. On mass executions in Petrikov in September 1941: Gerlach, *Kalkulierte Morde*, 607. On Glusk in December 1941: Dean and Hecker, *United States Holocaust Memorial Museum Encyclopedia*, 1670–72.

28. Several such references can be found in the individual reports filed in RGASPI f. 17, op. 88, d. 480, ll. 56–62, 90–96, 123–24, 140–45; NARB f. 4p, op. 33a, d. 63, ll. 73–102, 144–47, 170–74, 179–83, 187–96, 199–232, 267–94, 300–14.

29. Quoted from Zasukhin's report, December 3, 1941 (NARB f. 4p, op. 33a. d. 63, l. 26).

30. Quoted from Ponomarenko's report to Stalin, August 19, 1941 (RGASPI f. 17, op. 88, d. 480, l. 156).

31. Karel C. Berkhoff, "'Total Annihilation of the Jewish Population': The Holocaust in the Soviet Media, 1941–45," *Kritika: Explorations in Russian and Eurasian History* 10, no. 1 (2009): 61–105.

32. Berkhoff, "'Total Annihilation,'" 100–104.

33. Girsh Smoliar, "'Teplaia' vstrecha evreev-partizan v osvobozhdennom Minske," *Vozrozhdenie*, no. 4–5 (1975): 184–85.

34. Quoted from Evgenij Rosenblat, "Belarus: Specific Features of the Region's Jewish Collaboration and Resistance," in *Collaboration and Resistance during the Holocaust: Belarus, Estonia, Latvia, Lithuania*, ed. David Gaunt, Paul A. Levine, and Laura Palosuo (Bern: Peter Lang, 2004), 281.

35. "Ne zabudem, ne prostim," *Sovetskaia Belorussiia*, May 8, 1945.

36. "Uzhasy getto," *Sovetskaia Belorussiia*, May 8, 1945.

37. For a detailed analysis of the exhibition and discussion of the curators' agency: Anne Hasselmann, "Zwischen Dokumentation und Zeitzeugenschaft: Die Museen in Moskau, Minsk und Tscheljabinsk 1941–1956" (PhD diss., University of Basel, 2019), 179–95.

38. Arkadi Zeltser, *Unwelcome Memory: Holocaust Monuments in the Soviet Union* (Jerusalem: Yad Vashem Publications, 2018), 122–36.

39. Hersh Smolar, *Fun Minsker geto* (Minsk: Der Emes, 1946), was translated into Russian as *Mstiteli getto* (Moscow: Der Emes, 1947). The book was published in English as *Resistance in Minsk* (Oakland: Magnes Memorial Museum, 1966). After his immigration to Israel, Smolar published a revised, this time uncensored memoir on the Minsk underground: Hersh Smolar, *Sovietishe Yidn hinter geto-tsoymen* (Tel Aviv: Y. L. Perets, 1985), translated into English as *The Minsk Ghetto: Soviet-Jewish Partisans against the Nazis* (New York: Holocaust Library, 1989).

40. Hasselmann, "Zwischen Dokumentation," 197–202.

41. Quoted from Nachum Alpert, *The Destruction of Slonim Jewry: The Story of the Jews of Slonim during the Holocaust* (New York: Holocaust Library, 1989), xii.

42. Smilovitsky, "Antisemitism," 207.

43. Quoted from Kalinin, *Partizanskaia respublika* (1968), 372.

44. According to the numbers compiled in January 1946 by the Belarusian Staff of the Partisan Movement, of the 281,007 partisans for whom detailed information exists, 2.14 percent (6,014 individuals) were Jewish (NARB f. 4p, op. 33a, d. 634, ll. 1–10). For higher estimates (up to fifteen thousand, including underground fighters), see Smilovitsky, "Antisemitism," 217.

45. Kalinin, *Partizanskaia respublika* (1968), 372.

46. Ponomarenko, *Vsenarodnaia bor'ba*, 128.

47. Quoted from the excerpt from his letter, compiled August 18, 1944 (GAMO f. 1p, op. 2, d. 54, l. 20).

48. Quoted from the excerpt from his letter, compiled September 1, 1944 (GAMO f. 1p, op. 2, d. 54, l. 54).

49. Quoted from the excerpt from his letter, compiled August 18, 1944 (GAMO f. 1p, op. 2, d. 54, l. 18).

50. Both quotations from the excerpt from M. M. Birilo's letter (GAMO f. 1p, op. 2, d. 54, l. 18).

51. Smolenchuk, "Pamiat' na Pogranich'e," 160–72.

52. On the official image of the partisan war in independent Belarus, see also Goujon, "Memorial Narratives," 9–12; and Marples, *"Our Glorious Past,"* 103–37.

53. Quoted from Aleksandr Kovaleniia et al., eds., *Belarus' v gody Velikoi Otechestvennoi voiny 1941–1945* (Minsk: BELTA, 2005), 8.

54. Quoted from Alexievich, *Unwomanly Face of War*, 251.

55. Smolenchuk, "Pamiat' na Pogranich'e," 183–93.

56. Smolenchuk, "Pamiat' na Pogranich'e," 186–91.

57. Volia Shamalava, "Tseni vainy: Politseiskiia i partyzany ŭ pamiatsi nasel'nitstva belaruskaŭ veski," *Homo Historicus: Hadavik antrapalahichnai historyi* (2008): 384–89.

58. Quoted from IRI RAN f. 2, razdel II, op. 4, d. 117, l. 10.

59. As suggested by Andrew Wilson, *Belarus: The Last European Dictatorship* (New Haven: Yale University Press, 2011), 114.

60. Ioffe, *Lavrentii Tsanava*, 444–60; Adamushko et al., *Osvobozhdennaia Belarus'*, 1:315, 352–53, 364–66.

61. Adamushko et al., *Osvobozhdennaia Belarus'*, 1:330.

62. Panteleimon Ponomarenko, "Sobytiia moei zhizni," part 2, *Nioman*, no. 4 (1992): 136.

63. Ioffe, *Ot Miasnikova do Malofeeva*, 119–30.

64. Ioffe, *Ot Miasnikova do Malofeeva*, 131–43.

65. Michael Urban, *An Algebra of Soviet Power: Elite Circulation in the Belorussian Republic, 1966–86* (Cambridge: Cambridge University Press, 1989), 116–17, 130, 132.

66. See the report by Levitskii, secretary of Poles'e obkom, August 20, 1944 (RGASPI f. 17, op. 88, d. 268, l. 21).

67. See the party report, December 13, 1944 (Gosudarstvennyi arkhiv obshchestvennykh ob"edinenii Grodnenskoi oblasti [hereafter GAOOGO] f. 2191, op. 1, d. 2, l. 3).

68. See the statistics provided by the Sovnarkom/Council of Ministers' Cadres Department (NARB f. 7, op. 3, d. 1628, l. 51).

69. NARB f. 7, op. 3, d. 1633, l. 9. By April 1948, the number was down to 33 percent (NARB f. 7, op. 3, d. 1641, ll. 25–32).

70. NARB f. 7, op. 3, d. 1644, ll. 1–14.

71. NARB f. 4p, op. 33a, d. 634, l. 1.

72. Quoted from the report by the Gomel' obkom, July 25, 1946 (NARB f. 4p, op. 29, d. 130, l. 102).

73. Quoted from the report, February 7, 1945 (NARB f. 4p, op. 29, d. 184, ll. 53–54).

74. This refers to the 280,007 partisans for whom such data exist (NARB f. 4p, op. 33a, d. 634, ll. 1–10).

75. On suspicion toward partisans: Slepyan, *Stalin's Guerrillas*, 277.

76. On the career of these men: Ioffe, *Ot Miasnikova do Malofeeva*, 99–113, 120–43; Adamushko et al., *Osvobozhdennaia Belarus'*, 1:315, 330, 352–53, 364–66.

77. Quoted from the letter to Khrushcheev, October 17, 1959 (RGANI f. 5, op. 31, d. 147, l. 2).

78. Quoted from RGANI f. 5, op. 31, d. 147, l. 2.

79. Quoted from RGANI f. 5, op. 31, d. 147, l. 3.

80. Quoted from RGANI f. 5, op. 31, d. 147, ll. 3, 7.

81. E. I. Baranovskii, "Nekotorye osobennosti raboty spetsial'nykh komissii po dopolnitel'nomu izucheniiu otdel'nykh voprosov istorii Minskogo antifashistskogo podpolia i roli v nem I. K. Kovaleva," in *Belarus' i Hermaniia: Historyia i suchasnasts'. Materyialy mizhnarodnai navukovai kanferentsyi*, vol. 8, ed. S.Ia. Novikaŭ et al. (Minsk: MDLU, 2010), 5–6; Epstein, *Minsk Ghetto*, 253–56.

82. On the place of the Minsk ghetto underground within the Minsk city-wide underground, see Epstein, *Minsk Ghetto*, 110–38.

83. Epstein, *Minsk Ghetto*, 231–39.

84. Report from special agent Zhukovich, October 24, 1942 (NARB f. 4p, op. 33a, d. 644, ll. 13–15).

85. Report from a man called Krysanov, head of the NKVD operational-chekist group of Minsk oblast, April 17, 1943 (NARB f. 4p, op. 33a, d. 151, ll. 244–46).

86. Panteleimon Ponomarenko, "Sobytiia moei zhizni," part 1, *Nioman*, no. 3 (1992): 163–64; Panteleimon Ponomarenko, "Dnevnik," *Nioman*, no. 8 (2008): 174.

87. Quoted from Kalinovskii's recollections, no date, but probably 1958 (BGAMLI f. 353, op. 1, d. 253, l. 2).

88. See Smolar's report, no date, but no later than December 1948 (NARB f. 4p, op. 33a, d. 662, ll. 1–29).

89. Epstein, *Minsk Ghetto*, 231–34, 251.

90. Quoted from RGANI f. 5, op. 31, d. 147, l. 4.

91. Baranovskii, "Nekotorye osobennosti raboty," 6–7. On Kozlov, see also Epstein, *Minsk Ghetto*, 253–56.

92. Epstein, *Minsk Ghetto*, 256–57.

93. "Besstrashnye," *Pravda*, June 3, 1960; "Besstrashnye," *Sovetskaia Belorussiia*, June 5, 1960. In July 1960, *Sovetskaia Belorussiia* also published a several issues-long article on the Minsk underground: "O partiinom podpol'e v Minske v gody VOV," *Sovetskaia Belorussiia*, July 2, July 4, July 7, July 15, 1960.

94. Ivan Novikov, *O partiinom podpol'e v Minske v gody Velikoi Otechestvennoi voiny (iiun' 1941—iiul' 1944 gg.)* (Minsk: Gosizdat, 1961); Ivan Novikov, *Bessmertie Minska* (Minsk: Belarus', 1977); Ivan Novikov, *Minsk—gorod geroi* (Moscow: Voenizdat, 1986). Novikov's correspondence with the underground members and their recollections are kept in BGAMLI f. 3535.

95. Baranovskii, "Nekotorye osobennosti raboty," 13–15; A. F. Khatskevich, "Probivaetsia pravda polveka: Novaia stranitsa istorii Minskogo antifashistskogo podpolia," *Nioman*, no. 4 (1992): 121–30.

96. Quoted from Baranovskii, "Nekotorye osobennosti raboty," 10.

97. Ioffe, *Ot Miasnikova do Malofeeva*, 122; Ioffe, *Lavrentii Tsanava*, 444–60.

98. Quoted from RGANI f. 5, op. 31, d. 147, ll. 4–5.

99. On the border dispute: Ponomarenko, "Sobytiia moei zhizni," 1:156–58; on the rivalry with Khrushchev, see Ponomarenko's interview with the historian Georgii Kumanev (*Riadom so Stalinym: Otkrovennye svidetel'stva. Vstrechi, besedy, interv'iu, dokumenty* [Moscow: Bylina, 1999], 96–109, quotation 99).

100. From June 1941 to May 1945, Khrushchev met forty-five times with Stalin in his office, while Ponomarenko met twenty-four times with him. See A. A. Chernobaev et al., eds., *Na prieme u Stalina: Tetradi (zhurnaly) zapisei lits, priniatykh I. V. Stalinym (1924–1953gg.)* (Moscow: Novyi khronograf, 2008), 337–453.

101. Elena Zubkova, "The Rivalry with Malenkov," in *Nikita Khrushchev*, ed. William Taubman, Sergei Khrushchev, and Abbott Gleason (New Haven: Yale University Press, 2000), 67–84.

102. Quoted from RGANI f. 5, op. 31, d. 147, l. 3.

103. Weiner, *Making Sense of War*, 208–9.

104. In this respect, official discourse in present-day Belarus displays many similarities to Ponomarenko's version of civilian suffering during the war. According to the government of Aleksandr Lukashenko, in wartime Belarus, the Germans pursued a "genocide of the Belarusian people" (*genotsid belorusskogo naroda*). *Narod* is understood here in an ethnic sense, meaning ethnic Belarusians only. Apart from the question of whether this narrative is factually correct, of equal importance is what it marginalizes or, depending on the context, omits entirely—namely, the genocide of Belarus's Jewish communities. See, for example, Lukashenko's speech at the Khatyn memorial on March 23, 2021: "Vystuplenie Prezidenta Belarusi Aleksandra Lukashenko na respublikanskom mitinge-rekvieme 'Lampada pamiati,' priurochennom k 78-i godovshchine khatynskoi tragedii," *Belta*, https://www.belta.by/video_official/getRecord/7113/. The historiographical mainstream in Belarus reflects the official line. While most authors do not ignore the murder of Belarus's Jewish communities entirely, it is mentioned selectively, and the suffering of the Slavic population is typically covered in greater detail. See, for example, Kovaleniia et al., *Belarus' v gody Velikoi Otechestvennoi voiny*, 148–67. On memory discourses and selective remembering in present-day Belarus, see Magdalena Waligórska, "Remembering the Holocaust on the Fault Lines of East and West-European Memorial Cultures: The New Memorial Complex in Trastsianets, Belarus," *Holocaust Studies* 24, no. 4 (2017): 1–25.

105. Kumanev, *Riadom so Stalinym*, 93–144, in particular 97–98.

Afterword

1. In defining what made this moment global, I draw inspiration from Sebastian Conrad, *What Is Global History?* (Princeton: Princeton University Press, 2016), 64–72; Erez Manela, *The Wilsonian Moment: Self-Determination and the International Origins of Anticolonial Nationalism* (Oxford: Oxford University Press, 2007), 5–13; and Margherita Zanasi, "Globalizing Hanjian: The Suzhou Trials and the Post-World War II Discourse on Collaboration," *American Historical Review* 113, no. 3 (2008): 731–51.

2. Francine Hirsch, *Soviet Judgment at Nuremberg: A New History of the International Military Tribunal after World War II* (Oxford: Oxford University Press, 2020).

3. Between 1943 and 1956, when prosecutions were ended, about 34,000 members of the German military and 2,883 members of the Japanese military were prosecuted, as were probably a few hundred, maybe thousands of other European Axis soldiers. See Hilger, *Deutsche Kriegsgefangene*, 314–31, 353–67; and V. A. Gavrilov and E. L. Katasonova, eds., *Iaponskie voennoplennye v SSSR, 1945–1956* (Moscow: Mezhdunarodnyi fond "Demokratiia," 2013), 17, 1387.

4. For a more detailed discussion, see Exeler, "Nazi Atrocities," 213–16.

5. The dichotomy can be found, for example, in Judith N. Shklar, *Legalism: Law, Morals, and Political Trials*, 2nd ed. (Cambridge, MA: Harvard University Press, 1986), 145–48, 209–10. Gerry Simpson writes that show trials share some striking resemblances with war crimes trials—in particular, procedural deficiencies—but ultimately upholds the distinction (*Law, War, and Crime: War Crimes Trials and the Reinvention of International Law* [Cambridge: Polity, 2007], 105–31).

6. Gary Jonathan Bass, *Stay the Hand of Vengeance: The Politics of War Crimes Tribunals* (Princeton: Princeton University Press, 2000), 8, 12, 16, 35, 285, 310. Bass writes here of international war crimes trials, but some of the examples that he cites should more accurately be described as hybrid trials, given that they applied a mixture of international and domestic law.

7. Bass, *Stay the Hand*, 27–28; Shklar, *Legalism*, 201–7; Simpson, *Law, War, and Crime*, 108–10.

8. István Deák, *Europe on Trial: The Story of Collaboration, Resistance, and Retribution during World War II* (Boulder: Westview, 2015), 197–208; also the essays in Deák, Gross, and Judt, *Politics of Retribution in Europe.*

9. On procedural shortcomings of Western Allies' trials in Europe and Asia: Hilary Earl, *The Nuremberg SS-Einsatzgruppen Trial, 1945–1958: Atrocity, Law, and History* (Cambridge: Cambridge University Press, 2009), 297–301; Yuma Totani, *Justice in Asia and the Pacific Region, 1945–1952: Allied War Crimes Prosecution* (Cambridge: Cambridge University Press, 2015), 12–20.

10. Tomaz Jardim, *The Mauthausen Trial: American Military Justice in Germany* (Cambridge, MA: Harvard University Press, 2012), 6, 202–6, 213.

11. This included the 1945–1946 British trial of members of the Indian National Army, who had fought alongside the Japanese army against the British forces on the Burmese front. The defendants were charged not with having committed war crimes but with murder and treason, meaning betrayal of the country that had colonized India. Their prosecution sparked much public outrage in India, with protest against it forming part of the larger anticolonial struggle (Lawson, "Wartime Atrocities," 46–94, 148–64).

12. In one case, it is known that the Soviet prosecution fabricated a charge: at the December 1945–January 1946 trial of German military personnel at Leningrad, two witnesses testified that in 1941, SS units had killed Polish officers in the forest of Katyn. Although the murder had in fact been committed by the NKVD in the spring of 1940, one of the defendants, Arno Dürre, admitted to having taken part in these killings. See Alexander Victor Prusin, "'Fascist Criminals to the Gallows!' The Holocaust and Soviet War Crimes Trials, December 1945–February 1946," *Holocaust and Genocide Studies* 17, no. 1 (2003): 15.

13. See the report by the MGB officer Antishin, October 25, 1947, in Haluzevyi derzhavnyi arkhiv Sluzhby bezpeky Ukrainy (HDA SBU) f. 60, papka 1288, tom 1, ll. 19–21.

14. Quoted from the report on the trial by the NKGB officer Martynov, January 11, 1946 (HDA SBU f. 7, op. 9, delo 11, l. 154).

15. Quoted from Martynov's reports (HDA SBU f. 7, op. 9, delo 11, l. 155 [January 11, 1946], l. 162 [January 12, 1946]).

16. Quoted from Fedorov's report, November 18, 1947 (HDA SBU f. 60, papka 1288, tom 1, l. 80).

17. Edwin L. James, "Red Propaganda Coup Seen in Atrocity Trial," *New York Times*, December 19, 1943.

18. Quoted from Edmund Stevens, *Russia Is No Riddle* (New York: Greenberg Publishers, 1945), 111.

19. Stevens, *Russia Is No Riddle*, 114.

20. "The atmosphere of the Kharkov trial room was distinctly reminiscent of the famous Treason Trials of 1936–38." Quoted from Stevens, *Russia Is No Riddle*, 111.

21. AW II/1252/2K, ll. 1–4; YV O.3/11082, ll. 4–5; Bembel'-Dedok, *Vospominaniia*, 102–3; Bykov, *Dolgaia doroga domoi*, 36–41; Izhar, *Chasia Bornstein-Bielicka*, 84–86; Khartanovich, *Gody nashei molodosti*, 70–76; Mor, *War for Life*, 53–60; Ovsishcher, *Vozvrashchenie*, 38.

22. Quoted from Izhar, *Chasia Bornstein-Bielicka*, 269.

23. AW II/1252/2K, l. 8; Izhar, *Chasia Bornstein-Bielicka*, 269; Mor, *War for Life*, 212–32.

24. Veena Das and Arthur Kleinman, "Introduction," in *Remaking a World: Violence, Social Suffering, and Recovery*, ed. Veena Das et al. (Berkeley: University of California Press, 2001), 24.

25. YV O.3/11082, ll. 42–43.

26. Izhar, *Chasia Bornstein-Bielicka*, 310–80.

27. Khartanovich, *Gody nashei molodosti*, 87–188.

28. Bembel'-Dedok, *Vospominaniia*, 183; Khartanovich, *Gody nashei molodosti*, 87–188; Ovsishcher, *Vozvrashchenie*, 117–225.

29. Bykov, *Dolgaia doroga domoi*, 173–91; Gimpelevich, *Vasil' Bykaŭ*, 3–7, 44–53; Lewis, *Belarus*, 83–111.

Note on Wartime Losses

1. For a few examples, see Snyder, *Bloodlands*, 404 (20 percent of the "prewar population of the Belarusian territories"); Litvin, "K voprosu o kolichestve" (25 percent of the "prewar population"); Gimpelevich, *Vasil' Bykaŭ*, 33 ("a third of the Belarusian population was dead by the time of the Soviet victory in May 1945").

2. See, for example, Gerlach, *Kalkulierte Morde*, 1159 (10.6 million); Kozhurin, "O chislennosti naseleniia SSSR," 26 (10.42 million). This refers to the population size within the pre-1941 borders of the republic.

3. Aralovets, Zhiromskaia, and Kiselev, *Vsesoiuznaia perepis' naseleniia 1937g.*, 59. On the falsifications in the 1939 census and a discussion of the 1937 census: Volkov, "Perepis' naseleniia 1937 goda," 6–63; Merridale, "1937 Census," 235.

4. The population size of western Belarus (including the Białystok region) is based on statistics issued in December 1941 by the Polish government-in-exile in London. By the fall of 1939, 4.73 million people lived in the territories (including Białystok voivodeship) that the Soviet Union annexed to Belarus. Not included in these calculations are refugees (mostly Jewish) from German-occupied western Poland. *Mały rocznik statystyczny Polski*, 5, table 11, and 10, table 17.

5. A small stretch of land in the northwest of Belarus was transferred to Lithuania in 1940. It is unknown how many people lived there but as this was a rural and sparsely populated area, probably not more than a few thousand.

6. The figure of one million people is my estimate. According to Soviet population statistics, by January 1, 1940, 1.348 million people lived in Belostok (Białystok) oblast, which probably did not include refugees from western Poland. The city of Grodno, which by 1939 had a population of 49,200 people and belonged to Belostok oblast in 1939–1941, remained in Belarus after 1945, and thus has to be subtracted from this number. See Document 1: "Chislennost' naseleniia SSSR na 1 ianvaria 1940 goda (predvaritel'noe ischislenie)," printed in Kozhurin, "O chislennosti naseleniia SSSR," 25; *Itogi vsesoiuznoi perepisi naseleniia 1959 goda*, 13, table 6.

7. Gerlach, *Kalkulierte Morde*, 1158.

8. Smilovitskii, *Katastrofa evreev v Belorussii*, 27–28; Vinnitsa, *Kholokost na okkupirovannoi territorii*, 193.

9. Of these, 1.34 million people were shot and tortured to death (*zamucheno*), 38,087 civilians were burned to death, 886 were hanged, and 2,771 died as a result of aerial bombardment. See the July 1945 report by the Extraordinary State Commission of Belarus (NARB f. 845, op. 1, d. 146, l. 10).

10. See the final, undated report (no later than September 1945) (NARB f. 845, op. 1, d. 146, l. 9).

11. Gerlach, *Kalkulierte Morde*, 1158n82.

12. Gerlach, *Kalkulierte Morde*, 24–34.

13. Krivosheev, *Soviet Casualties*, 84–85.

14. The Soviet Union had an estimated population of 196.7 million by mid-1941 (Andreev, Darskii, and Khar'kova, "Liudskie poteri SSSR," 40).

15. Litvin, "K voprosu o kolichestve."

16. Adamushko et al., *Osvobozhdennaia Belarus'*, 1:9.

17. NARB f. 4p, op. 33a, d. 634, l. 1.

18. Gerlach, *Kalkulierte Morde*, 1158.

19. Musial, *Sowjetische Partisanen*, 261.

20. "Posledstviia Velikoi Otechestvennoi voiny dlia Belarusi," National Archives of Belarus, accessed April 2, 2021, http://archives.gov.by/home/tematicheskie-razrabotki-arhivnyh-dokumentov-i-bazy-dannyh/istoricheskie-sobytiya/velikaya-otechestvennaya-vojna-belarus/istoriya-vojny-obzor-sobytij/posledstviya-velikoj-otechestvennoj-vojny-dlya-belarusi.

21. See, for example, Lukashenko's speech on Victory Day, May 9, 2020: "Vystuplenie Prezidenta Belarusi na voennom parade v oznamenovanie 75-i godovshchiny Velikoi Pobedy," *Belta*, accessed April 6, 2021, https://www.belta.by/president/view/vystuplenie-prezidenta-belarusi-na-voennom-parade-v-oznamenovanie-75-j-godovschiny-velikoj-pobedy-390276-2020/; Goujon, "Memorial Narratives," 15.

22. Using the population size of 1945 or 1946 thus leads to inaccurate conclusions, as reached, for example, in Adamushko et al., *Osvobozhdennaia Belarus'*, 1:7.

23. See the population statistics compiled by Gosplan, April 1, 1948 (NARB f. 30, f. 5, d. 1693, l. 204).

Bibliography

Archives

Belarus

Belorusskii gosudarstvennyi arkhiv-muzei literatury i iskusstva (BGAMLI), Minsk
Fond 353 Ivan Grigorevich Novikov (Novikaŭ)
Opis' 1 [*no title*]

Gosudarstvennyi arkhiv Minskoi oblasti (GAMO), Minsk
Fond 1p Minskii oblastnoi komitet KP(b) Belorussii
Opis' 2 Osobyi sektor 1944–1948 gg.
Opis' 9 Otdel propaganda i agitatsii za 1944–1968 goda

Gosudarstvennyi arkhiv obshchestvennykh ob"edinenii Grodnenskoi oblasti (GAOOGO), Grodno
Fond 2191 Novogrudskii raikom partii
Opis' 1 1944–1948 gg.

Gosudarstvennyi arkhiv obshchestvennykh ob"edinenii Mogilevskoi oblasti (GAOOMO), Mogilev
Fond 9 Mogilevskii oblastnoi komitet KP(b)B
Opis' 1a Osobyi sektor 1938–1941 gg.

Natsional'nyi arkhiv Respubliki Belarus' (NARB), Minsk
Fond 4p Tsentral'nyi komitet Kommunisticheskaia partiia Belorussii (TsK KPB)
Opis' 17 Otdel shkol i nauki 1934–1959 gg.
Opis' 29 Osobyi sektor 1941–1958 gg.
Opis' 33a Osobyi sektor (materialy perioda Velikoi Otechestvennoi voiny) 1941–1984 gg.
Opis' 61 Biuro TsK KP(b)B (protokoly) 1944–1947 gg.
Opis' 62 Osobyi sektor 1949–1963/78 gg.

Fond 7 Sovet narodnykh komissarov/Sovet ministrov BSSR
Opis' 3 1942–1950 gg.

Fond 30 Tsentral'noe statisticheskoe upravlenie TsSU BSSR
Opis' 5 1943–1951 gg.

Fond 845 Belorusskaia respublikanskaia komissiia sodeistviia Chrezvychainoi gosudarstvennoi komissii (ChGK)
Opis' 1 7.5.1943–9.1945

Fond 1440 Institut istorii partii pri TsK KPB
Opis' 3 Sektor istorii partii 1883–1950 gg.

Fond 1450 Belorusskii shtab partizanskogo dvizheniia (BShPD)
Opis' 2 Dokumentov grazhdan-uchastnikov partizanskogo dvizheniia, iz nagrazhdeniia rozyska partizan i ikh semei, pogibshikh partizan 1941–1946 gg.
Opis' 21 Materialy osobykh otdelov—materialy na izmennikov Rodine, lichnye dela, sledstvennye, udostovereniia lichnosti, ugolovnye dela 1941–1945 gg.

Germany

Bundesarchiv Lichterfelde (BArch), Berlin
R 20 Truppen und Schulen der Ordnungspolizei, Chef der Bandenkampfverbände
R 58 Reichssicherheitshauptamt

Bundesarchiv Ludwigsburg/Zentrale Stelle der Landesjustizverwaltungen zur Aufklärung nationalsozialistischer Verbrechen (BArch), Ludwigsburg
B 126 Ermittlungsakten

Israel

Yad Vashem Archives (YV), Jerusalem
Testimonies O.3

Poland

Ośrodek Karta, Archiwum Wschodnie (AW), Warsaw
Relacje AW I, AW II

Russia

Gosudarstvennyi arkhiv Rossiiskoi Federatsii (GARF), Moscow
Fond 7523 Verkhovnyi Sovet SSSR
Opis' 31 Priemnaia predsedatelia prezidiuma Verkhovnogo Soveta SSSR 1946 g.

Institut rossiskoi istorii RAN (IRI RAN), Moscow
Fond 2 Komissiia istorii Velikoi Otechestvennoi voiny
Razdel II Istoriia partizanskogo dvizheniia
Opis' 4 Materialy o partizanskom dvizhenii v Belorussii

Rossiiskii gosudarstvennyi arkhiv noveishei istorii (RGANI), Moscow
Fond 5 Apparat TsK KPSS 1952–1984 gg.
Opis' 31 Otdel partiinykh organov TsK KPSS po soiuznym respublikam 1954–1962 gg.
Opis' 33 Otdel propagandy i agitatsii TsK KPSS po soiuznym respublikam 1956–1962 gg.

Rossiiskii gosudarstvennii arkhiv sotsial'no-politicheskoi istorii (RGASPI), Moscow
Fond 17 Tsentral'nyi komitet VKP(b)-KPSS
Opis' 3 Politbiuro TsK VKP(b) 1919–1952 gg.
Opis' 88 Sektor informatsii organizatsionno-instruktorskogo otdela TsK VKP(b) 1938–1955 gg.

Fond 82 Lichnyi fond: Molotov Viacheslav Mikhailovich
Opis' 2 1907–1986 gg.

Fond 83 Lichnyi fond: Malenkov Georgii Maksimilianovich
Opis' 1 [*no title*]

Fond 625 Lichnoe delo: Ponomarenko Panteleimon Kondrat'evich
Opis' 1 [*no title*]

Rossiiskii gosudarstvennyi voennyi arkhiv (RGVA), Moscow
Fond 38656 Upravlenie vnutrennikh voisk NKVD belorusskogo okruga g. Gomel', g. Minsk 6.4.1944–18.6.1946
Opis' 1 [*no title*]

Ukraine

Haluzevyi derzhavnyi arkhiv Sluzhby bezpeky Ukrainy (HDA SBU), Kiev
Fond 7 [*no title*]
Fond 60 [*no title*]

United States

Archives of the United States Holocaust Memorial Museum (USHMM), Washington DC

RG-26.004M War Crimes Investigation and Trial Records from the Former Lithuanian KGB Archives, 1944–1992

RG-31.018M Postwar War Crimes Trials Related to the Holocaust, 1945–1970

RG-53.006M Mogilev Oblast Archive Records, 1941–1945

RG-06.025 War Crimes Investigations and Prosecutions

Oral History Interviews

Vitalii A., June 13, 2011, Slonim, Belarus
Sofiia B., September 19, 2010, Rekhovot, Israel
Liubov' I., May 18, 2011, Minsk, Belarus
Petr K., June 13, 2011, Naguevichi, Belarus
Asia L. and Ernst L., October 6, 2010, Munich, Germany
Mariia L., November 22, 2010, Molodechno, Belarus
Eva S., June 16, 2011, Grodno, Belarus

Newspapers and Periodicals

Bol'shevik Palessia
Brianskii rabochii
Chyrvonaia zviazda
Echa Polesia: Kwartalnik polaków na Polesiu
Grodnenskaia pravda
Homel'skaia praŭda
Izvestiia
Kalhasnaia pratsa
Krasnaia zvezda
New York Times
Polesskaia pravda
Pravda
Rabochii put'
Sovetskaia Belorussiia
Sovetskaia Estoniia
Sovetskaia Latviia
Sovetskaia Litva
Sovetskaia rodina

Sovetskaia Ukraina
Stsiag komunizma
Vol'naia pratsa
Zara
Za radzimu
Zviazda

Printed Sources

Ackermann, Felix. *Palimpsest Grodno: Nationalisierung, Nivellierung und Sowjetisierung einer mitteleuropäischen Stadt 1919–1991*. Wiesbaden: Harrassowitz, 2010.

Adamovich, Ales', Ianka Bryl', and Vladimir Kolesnik, eds. *Ia iz ognennoi derevni . . .* Moscow: Sovetskii pisatel', 1991.

Adamovich, Ales, Yanka Bryl, and Vladimir Kolesnik, eds. *Out of the Fire*. Moscow: Progress Publishers, 1980.

Adamovich, Anna. "I tak bylo kazhdyi den'." *Nioman*, no. 10 (1999): 143–74.

Adamushka, U. I., et al., eds. *"Ty z zakhodniai, ia z uskhodniai nashai Belarusi . . .": Verasen' 1939 h.–1956 h. Dakumenty i materyialy*, 2 vols. Minsk: NARB, 2009.

Adamushka, Uladzimir. *Palitychnyia represii 20–50-ykh hadoŭ na Belarusi*. Minsk: Belarus', 1994.

Adamushko, V. I., et al., eds. *Belarus' v pervye mesiatsy Velikoi Otechestvennoi voiny (22 iiunia–avgust 1941 g.): Dokumenty i materialy*. Minsk: NARB, 2006.

Adamushko, V. I., et al., eds. *Belorusy v sovetskom tylu, iiul' 1941g.–1944 g.: Sbornik dokumentov i materialov*, 2 vols. Minsk: NARB, 2010.

Adamushko, V. I., et al., eds. *Osvobozhdennaia Belarus': Dokumenty i materialy*, 2 vols. Minsk: NARB, 2004.

Adelman, Jeremy, and Stephen Aron. "From Borderlands to Borders: Empires, Nation-States, and the Peoples in between in North American History." *American Historical Review* 104, no. 3 (1999): 814–41.

Adzinets, Aliaksandar. *Pavaennaia emihratsyia: Skryzhavan'ni liosaŭ. Zbornik uspaminaŭ*. Minsk: Medisont, 2007.

Alexievich, Svetlana. *The Unwomanly Face of War: An Oral History of Women in World War II*. Exp. and rev. ed. of 1985 Russian original. New York: Random House, 2018.

Alexopoulos, Golfo. "Exposing Illegality and Oneself: Complaint and Risk in Stalin's Russia." In *Reforming Justice in Russia, 1864–1996: Power, Culture, and the Limits of Legal Order*, edited by Peter H. Solomon, 168–89. Armonk: M. E. Sharpe, 1997.

Alexopoulos, Golfo. *Stalin's Outcasts: Aliens, Citizens, and the Soviet State, 1926–1936*. Ithaca: Cornell University Press, 2003.

Alpert, Nachum. *The Destruction of Slonim Jewry: The Story of the Jews of Slonim during the Holocaust*. New York: Holocaust Library, 1989.

Amar, Tarik Cyril. *The Paradox of Ukrainian Lviv: A Borderland City between Stalinists, Nazis, and Nationalists*. Ithaca: Cornell University Press, 2015.

Anashkin, G. S. *Otvetstvennost' za izmenu rodine i spionazh*. Moscow: Iuridicheskaia literatura, 1964.

Andreev, E. M., L. E. Darskii, and T. L. Khar'kova. "Liudskie poteri SSSR vo Vtoroi mirovoi voine: Metodika otsenki i rezul'taty." In *Liudskie poteri SSSR v Velikoi Otechestvennoi voine*, edited by R. B. Evdokimov, 37–42. St. Petersburg: Blits, 1995.

Arad, Yitzhak. "The Local Population in the German-Occupied Territories of the Soviet Union and Its Attitude toward the Murder of the Jews." In *Nazi Europe and the Final Solution*, edited by David Bankier and Israel Gutman, 233–48. Jerusalem: Yad Vashem, 2003.

Aralovets, N. A., V. B. Zhiromskaia, and I. N. Kiselev, eds. *Vsesoiuznaia perepis' naseleniia 1937g.: Kratkie itogi*. Moscow: Institut istorii SSSR AN SSSR, 1991.

Artizov, A. N., et al. *Reabilitatsiia: Kak eto bylo. Dokumenty Prezidiuma TsK KPSS i drugie materialy*. 3 vols. Moscow: Mezhdunarodnyi fond "Demokratiia," 2000.

Bakunovich, Regina. "Okkupirovannoe detstvo: Vospominanie-monolog." *Nioman*, no. 9 (1998): 189–215.

Balakirev, Viktor, et al., eds. *Spasennaia zhizn': Zhizn' i vyzhivanie v Minskom getto*. Minsk: Limarius, 2010.

Baranovskii, E. I. "Nekotorye osobennosti raboty spetsial'nykh komissii po dopolnitel'nomu izucheniiu otdel'nykh voprosov istorii Minskogo antifashistskogo podpolia i roli v nem I. K. Kovaleva." In *Belarus' i Hermaniia: Historyia i suchasnasts'. Materyialy mizhnarodnai navukovai kanferentsyi*, vol. 8, edited by S. Ia. Novikaŭ et al., 5–16. Minsk: MDLU, 2010.

Bartov, Omer. *Anatomy of a Genocide: The Life and Death of a Town Called Buczacz*. New York: Simon and Schuster, 2018.

Bartov, Omer, and Eric D. Weitz. "Introduction: Coexistence and Violence in the German, Habsburg, Russian, and Ottoman Borderlands." In *Shatterzones of Empires: Coexistence and Violence in the German, Habsburg, Russian, and Ottoman Borderlands*, edited by Omer Bartov and Eric D. Weitz, 1–20. Bloomington: Indiana University Press, 2013.

Bass, Gary. *Stay the Hand of Vengeance: The Politics of War Crimes Tribunals*. Princeton: Princeton University Press, 2002.

Bembel'-Dedok, Ol'ga. *Vospominaniia*, Minsk: Propilei, 2006.

Bemporad, Elissa. *Becoming Soviet Jews: The Bolshevik Experiment in Minsk*. Bloomington: Indiana University Press, 2013.

Bemporad, Elissa. *Legacy of Blood: Jews, Pogroms, and Ritual Murder in the Lands of the Soviets*. New York: Oxford University Press, 2019.

Bender, Sara. *The Jews of Białystok during World War II and the Holocaust*. Waltham: Brandeis University Press, 2008.

Bender, Sara. "Life Stories as Testament and Memorial: The Short Life of the Neqama Battalion, an Independent Jewish Partisan Unit Operating during the Second World War in the Narocz Forest, Belarus." *East European Jewish Affairs* 42, no. 1 (2012): 1–24.

Bender, Sara. "Not Only in Jedwabne: Accounts of the Annihilation of the Jewish Shtetlach in Northeastern Poland in the Summer of 1941." *Holocaust Studies* 19, no. 1 (2013): 1–38.

Benecke, Werner. *Die Ostgebiete der Zweiten Polnischen Republik: Staatsmacht und öffentliche Ordnung in einer Minderheitenregion 1918–1939*. Cologne: Böhlau, 1999.

Ben-Ze'ev, Efrat, Ruth Ginio, and Jay Winter, eds. *Shadows of War: A Social History of Silence in the Twentieth Century*. Cambridge: Cambridge University Press, 2010.

Beorn, Waitman Wade. *Marching into Darkness: The Wehrmacht and the Holocaust in Belarus*. Cambridge, MA: Harvard University Press, 2014.

Berkhoff, Karel C. *Harvest of Despair: Life and Death in Ukraine under Nazi Rule*. Cambridge, MA: Belknap, 2004.

Berkhoff, Karel C. *Motherland in Danger: Soviet Propaganda during World War II*. Cambridge, MA: Harvard University Press, 2012.

Berkhoff, Karel C. "'Total Annihilation of the Jewish Population': The Holocaust in the Soviet Media, 1941–45." *Kritika: Explorations in Russian and Eurasian History* 10, no. 1 (2009): 61–105.

Bergholz, Max. *Violence as a Generative Force: Identity, Nationalism, and Memory in a Balkan Community*. Ithaca: Cornell University Press, 2016.

Berman, Harold J., and Miroslav Kerner. *Soviet Military Law and Administration*. Cambridge, MA: Harvard University Press, 1955.

Bernstein, Seth. "Ambiguous Homecoming: Retribution, Exploitation, and Social Tensions during Repatriation to the USSR, 1944–1946." *Past and Present* 242, no. 1 (2019): 193–226.

Berzin, Dania. *Vospominaniia o nashem detstve*. Rishon le-Tsiyon: MeDial, 2009.

Bohn, Thomas. *Minsk–Musterstadt des Sozialismus: Stadtplanung und Urbanisierung in der Sowjetunion nach 1945*. Cologne: Böhlau, 2008.

Boradyn, Zygmunt. *Niemen rzeka niezgody: Polsko-sowiecka wojna partyzancka na Nowogródczyźnie 1943–1944*. Warsaw: Oficyna Wydawnicza Rytm, 1999.

Brakel, Alexander. *Unter Rotem Stern und Hakenkreuz: Baranowicze 1939 bis 1944. Das westliche Weißrussland unter sowjetischer und deutscher Besatzung*. Paderborn: Schöningh, 2009.

Brook, Timothy. *Collaboration: Japanese Agents and Local Elites in Wartime China*. Cambridge, MA: Harvard University Press, 2005.

Brooks, Jeffrey. *Thank You, Comrade Stalin! Soviet Public Culture from Revolution to Cold War*. Princeton: Princeton University Press, 2000.

Brown, Kate. *A Biography of No Place: From Ethnic Borderland to Soviet Heartland*. Cambridge, MA: Harvard University Press, 2005.

Budnitskii, Oleg. "The Great Patriotic War and Soviet Society: Defeatism, 1941–42." *Kritika: Explorations in Russian and Eurasian History* 15, no. 4 (2014): 767–97.

Budnitskii, Oleg. "A Harvard Project in Reverse: Materials of the Commission of the USSR Academy of Sciences on the History of the Great Patriotic War—Publications and Interpretations." *Kritika: Explorations in Russian and Eurasian History* 19, no. 1 (2018): 175–202.

Budnitskii, Oleg. *Russian Jews between the Reds and the Whites, 1917–1920*. Translated by Timothy J. Portice. Philadelphia: University of Pennsylvania Press, 2012.

Burds, Jeffrey. "Agentura: Soviet Informants' Networks and the Ukrainian Underground in Galicia, 1944–48." *East European Politics and Societies* 11, no. 1 (1997): 89–130.

Burds, Jeffrey. "Gender and Policing in Soviet West Ukraine, 1944–1948." *Cahiers du monde russe* 22, no. 2–4 (2001): 279–320.

Burrin, Philippe. *France under the Germans: Collaboration and Compromise*. New York: New Press, 1998.

Bykov, Vasil'. *Dolgaia doroga domoi: Kniga vospominanii.* Moscow: AST, 2005.

Cadiot, Juliette. "Searching for Nationality: Statistics and National Categories at the End of the Russian Empire (1897–1917)." *Russian Review* 64, no. 3 (2005): 440–55.

Cassiday, Julie A. "Marble Columns and Jupiter Lights: Theatrical and Cinematic Modeling of Soviet Show Trials in the 1920s." *Slavic and East European Journal* 42, no. 4 (1998): 640–60.

Cerovic, Masha. *Les enfants de Staline: La guerre des partisans soviétiques (1941–1944).* Paris: Seuil, 2018.

Charniaŭski, Mikhas', ed. *"Nia boitsesia akhviaraŭ i pakut!" Dakumenty i materyialy pra dzeinas'ts' miadzel'ska-smarhonskaha antykomunistychnaha padzem'ia (1948–1950 hh.).* Vilnius: Nasha buduchynia, 2006.

Chase, William. "Stalin as Producer: The Moscow Show Trials and the Construction of Mortal Threats." In *Stalin: A New History,* edited by Sarah Davies and James Harris, 226–48. Cambridge: Cambridge University Press, 2005.

Chernobaev, A. A., et al., eds. *Na prieme u Stalina: Tetradi (zhurnaly) zapisei lits, priniatykh I. V. Stalinym (1924–1953 gg.).* Moscow: Novyi khronograf, 2008.

Chiari, Bernhard. *Alltag hinter der Front: Besatzung, Kollaboration und Widerstand in Weißrussland 1941–1944.* Düsseldorf: Droste, 1998.

Chmielarz, Andrzej, et al., eds. *NKWD o polskim podziemiu 1944–1948: Konspiracja polska na Nowogródczyźnie i Grodzieńszczyźnie.* Warsaw: Instytut Studiów Politycznych PAN, 1997.

Ciancia, Kathryn. *On Civilization's Edge: A Polish Borderland in the Interwar World.* Oxford: Oxford University Press, 2021.

Cholawsky, Shalom. *The Jews of Bielorussia during World War II.* Amsterdam: Harwood Academic Publishers, 1998.

Cohen, Laurie R. *Smolensk under the Nazis: Everyday Life in Occupied Russia.* Rochester: University of Rochester Press, 2013.

Conrad, Sebastian. *What Is Global History?* Princeton: Princeton University Press, 2016.

Conway, Martin. "Justice in Postwar Belgium: Popular Responses and Political Realities." In *The Politics of Retribution in Europe: World War II and Its Aftermath,* edited by István Deák, Jan T. Gross, and Tony Judt, 133–56. Princeton: Princeton University Press, 2000.

Dale, Robert. *Demobilized Veterans in Late Stalinist Leningrad: Soldiers to Civilians.* London: Bloomsbury Academic, 2015.

Dallin, Alexander, and Ralph S. Mavrogordato. "Rodionov: A Case-Study in Wartime Redefection." *American Slavic and East European Review* 18, no. 1 (1959): 25–33.

Danilov, Ivan. *Neudobnaia istoriia glazami zapadnogo belorusa.* Minsk: Izdatel'stvo Viktora Khursika, 2009.

Danilov, Ivan. *Razmyshleniia zapadnogo belorusa.* Minsk: Izdatel' V. Khursik, 2009.

Danilov, V. P., Roberta Thompson Manning, and Lynne Viola, eds. *Tragediia sovetskoi derevni: Kollektivizatsiia i raskulachivanie. Dokumenty i materialy.* Vol. 5: *1937–1939,* bk. 2: *1938–1939.* Moscow: Rossiiskaia politicheskaia entsiklopediia, 2006.

Deák, István. *Europe on Trial: The Story of Collaboration, Resistance, and Retribution during World War II*. Boulder: Westview, 2015.

Das, Veena, and Arthur Kleinman, "Introduction." In *Remaking a World: Violence, Social Suffering, and Recovery*, edited by Veena Das, Arthur Kleinman, Margaret Lock, Mamphela Ramphele, and Pamela Reynolds, 1–30. Berkeley: University of California Press, 2001.

Davyd-Haradok Memorial Book = Memorial Book of David-Horodok. Translated from the Yiddish and part of the 1981 Hebrew original. New York: New York Public Library, 2003.

Dean, Martin. *Collaboration in the Holocaust: Crimes of the Local Police in Belorussia and Ukraine*. Houndmills: Palgrave, 2000.

Dean, Martin, and Mel Hecker, eds. *The United States Holocaust Memorial Museum Encyclopedia of Camps and Ghettos, 1933–1945*. Vol. 2: *Ghettos in German-Occupied Eastern Europe*. Part A. Bloomington: Indiana University Press, 2012.

Dieckmann, Christoph. *Deutsche Besatzungspolitik in Litauen, 1941–1944*. Göttingen: Wallstein, 2011.

Dieckmann, Christoph, Babette Quinkert, and Tatjana Tönsmeyer, "Editorial." In *Kooperation und Verbrechen: Formen der "Kollaboration" im östlichen Europa 1939–1945*, edited by Christoph Dieckmann, Babette Quinkert, and Tatjana Tönsmeyer, 9–21. Göttingen: Wallstein, 2003.

Dumitru, Diana. "An Analysis of Soviet Postwar Investigation and Trial Documents and Their Relevance for Holocaust Studies." In *The Holocaust in the East: Local Perpetrators and Soviet Responses*, edited by Michael David-Fox, Peter Holquist, and Alexander Martin, 142–57. Pittsburgh: University of Pittsburgh Press, 2014.

Dumitru, Diana. "Listening to Silence: What Soviet Postwar Trial Materials Resist Revealing about the Holocaust." *S.I.M.O.N. Shoah: Intervention. Methods. Documentation* 7, no. 1 (2020): 4–12.

Dumitru, Diana. *The State, Antisemitism, and Collaboration in the Holocaust: The Borderlands of Romania and the Soviet Union*. Cambridge: Cambridge University Press, 2016.

Earl, Hilary. *The Nuremberg SS-Einsatzgruppen Trial, 1945–1958: Atrocity, Law and History*. Cambridge: Cambridge University Press, 2009.

Eberhardt, Piotr. *Political Migrations on Polish Territories (1939–1950)*. Warsaw: IGiPZ PAN, 2011.

Eberhardt, Piotr. *Przemiany narodowościowe na Białorusi*. Warsaw: Editions Spotkania, 1994.

Edele, Mark. *Soviet Veterans of the Second World War: A Popular Movement in an Authoritarian Society, 1941–1991*. Oxford: Oxford University Press, 2008.

Edele, Mark. *Stalin's Defectors: How Red Army Soldiers Became Hitler's Collaborators, 1941–1945*. Oxford: Oxford University Press, 2017.

Eikel, Markus, and Valentina Sivaieva. "City Mayors, Raion Chiefs, and Village Elders in Ukraine, 1941–4: How Local Administrators Co-Operated with the German Occupation Authorities." *Contemporary European History* 23, no. 3 (2014): 405–28.

Enstad, Johannes Due. *Soviet Russians under Nazi Occupation: Fragile Loyalties in World War II*. Cambridge: Cambridge University Press, 2018.

Epifanov, Aleksandr. *Otvetstvennost' za voennye prestupleniia, sovershennye na territorii SSSR v gody Velikoi Otechestvennoi voiny, 1941–1956 gg.* Volgograd: MVD, 2005.

Epifanov, Aleksandr. "Strafverfolgung von Kriegsverbrechern aus den Reihen der Wehrmacht in der UdSSR." In *Der Vernichtungskrieg im Osten: Verbrechen der Wehrmacht in der Sowjetunion—aus Sicht russischer Historiker,* edited by Gabriele Gorzka and Knut Stang, 111–30. Kassel: University of Kassel Press, 1999.

Epstein, Barbara. *The Minsk Ghetto, 1941–1943: Jewish Resistance and Soviet Internationalism.* Berkeley: University of California Press, 2008.

Epsztein, Maria. *Macierzyństwo za drutami: Wspomnienia, 1940–1980.* Montreal: Polish-Jewish Heritage Foundation of Canada, 2005.

Exeler, Franziska. "The Ambivalent State: Determining Guilt in the Post-World War II Soviet Union." *Slavic Review* 75, no. 3 (2016): 606–29.

Exeler, Franziska. "Nazi Atrocities, International Criminal Law, and Soviet War Crimes Trials: The Soviet Union and the Global Moment of Post-Second World War Justice." In *The New Histories of International Criminal Law: Retrials,* edited by Immi Tallgren and Thomas Skouteris, 189–219. Oxford: Oxford University Press, 2019.

Exeler, Franziska. "What Did You Do during the War? Personal Responses to the Aftermath of Nazi Occupation." *Kritika: Explorations in Russian and Eurasian History* 17, no. 4 (2016): 805–35.

Feigel', Aleksandr. *Zhizn' i sud'ba.* Israel: n.p., 2008.

Fitzpatrick, Sheila. "How the Mice Buried the Cat: Scenes from the Great Purges of 1937 in the Russian Provinces." *Russian Review* 52, no. 3 (1993): 299–320.

Fitzpatrick, Sheila. "Signals from Below: Soviet Letters of Denunciation of the 1930s." *Journal of Modern History* 68, no. 4 (1996): 831–66.

Fletcher, Laurel E., and Harvey M. Weinstein. "Violence and Social Repair: Rethinking the Contribution of Justice to Reconciliation." *Human Rights Quarterly* 24 (2002): 573–639.

Frommer, Benjamin. *National Cleansing: Retribution against Nazi Collaborators in Postwar Czechoslovakia.* Cambridge: Cambridge University Press, 2005.

Frunchak, Svetlana. "Commemorating the Future in Post-War Chernivtsi." *East European Politics and Societies* 24, no. 3 (2010): 435–63.

Fulbrook, Mary. *A Small Town near Auschwitz: Ordinary Nazis and the Holocaust.* New York: Oxford University Press, 2012.

Gatrell, Peter. *A Whole Empire Walking: Refugees in Russia during World War I.* Bloomington: Indiana University Press, 1999.

Gavrilov, V. A., and E. L. Katasonova, eds. *Iaponskie voennoplennye v SSSR: 1945–1956.* Moscow: Mezhdunarodnyi fond "Demokratiia," 2013.

Gerlach, Christian. *Kalkulierte Morde: Die deutsche Wirtschafts- und Vernichtungspolitik in Weißrußland 1941 bis 1944.* Hamburg: Hamburger Edition, 1999.

Gertjejanssen, Wendy Jo. "Victims, Heroes, Survivors: Sexual Violence on the Eastern Front during World War II." PhD diss., University of Minnesota, 2004.

Gimpelevich, Zina. *Vasil Bykaŭ: His Life and Works.* Montreal: McGill-Queen's University Press, 2005.

Goeken-Haidl, Ulrike. *Der Weg zurück: Die Repatriierung sowjetischer Zwangsarbeiter und Kriegsgefangener während und nach dem Zweiten Weltkrieg.* Essen: Klartext, 2006.

Gorlanov, O. A., and Arsenii B. Roginskii. "Ob arestakh v zapadnykh oblastiakh Belorussii i Ukrainy v 1939–1941 gg." In *Repressii protiv poliakov i pol'skikh grazhdan*, edited by Aleksandr E. Gur'ianov, 77–113. Moscow: Zven'ia, 1997.

Gorodinskaia, Raisa. *O sebe, o rodnykh, o druz'iakh i tovarishchakh: Vospominaniia uznika getto, partizanki Gorodinskoi (Beshkinoi) Raisy Abramovny*. Tel Aviv: n.p., 2008.

Gotzes, Andrea. *Krieg und Vernichtung 1941–1945: Sowjetische Zeitzeugen erinnern sich*. Darmstadt: Wissenschaftliche Buchgesellschaft, 2006.

Goujon, Alexandra. "Memorial Narratives of WWII Partisans and Genocide in Belarus." *East European Politics and Societies* 24, no. 1 (2010): 6–25.

Gousseff, Catherine. "Evacuation versus Repatriation: The Polish-Ukrainian Population Exchange, 1944–6." In *The Disentanglement of Populations: Migration, Expulsion, and Displacement in Post-War Europe 1944–49*, edited by Jessica Reinisch and Elizabeth White, 91–111. Basingstoke: Palgrave MacMillan, 2011.

Grinevich, E. M., N. A. Denisova, N. V. Kirillova, and V. D. Selemenev, eds. *Tragediia belorusskikh dereven', 1941–1944: Dokumenty i materialy*. Moscow: Fond "Istoricheskaia pamiat'," 2011.

Gross, Jan T. *Neighbors: The Destruction of the Jewish Community in Jedwabne, Poland*. Princeton: Princeton University Press, 2001.

Gross, Jan T. *Revolution from Abroad: The Soviet Conquest of Poland's Western Ukraine and Western Belorussia*. Exp. ed. Princeton: Princeton University Press, 2002.

Gross, Jan T. "Themes for a Social History of War Experience and Collaboration." In *The Politics of Retribution in Europe: World War II and Its Aftermath*, edited by István Deák, Jan T. Gross, and Tony Judt, 15–35. Princeton: Princeton University Press, 2000.

Gurevitz, Zalman Uri. "Recollections." Translated from the Hebrew Memorial Book on Kurenits. Accessed August 10, 2019. http://eilatgordinlevitan.com/kurenets/k_pages/stories_gurevitz.html.

Gur'ianov, Aleksandr E. "Pol'skie spetspereselentsy v SSSR v 1940–1941 gg." In *Repressii protiv poliakov i pol'skikh grazhdan*, edited by Aleksandr E. Gur'ianov, 114–36. Moscow: Zven'ia, 1997.

Gur'ianov, Aleksandr E. "Die sowjetische Repressionspolitik in den besetzten polnischen Ostgebieten 1939–1941." In *Polen unter deutscher und sowjetischer Besatzung 1939–1945*, edited by Jacek Andrzej Młynarczyk, 217–32. Osnabrück: Fibre, 2009.

Guthier, Steven L. "The Belorussians: National Identification and Assimilation, 1897–1970." *Soviet Studies* 29, no. 1 (1977): 37–61.

Hagenloh, Paul. "'Chekist in Essence, Chekist in Spirit': Regular and Political Police in the 1930s." *Cahier du monde russe* 42, no. 2–4 (2001): 447–75.

Halavach, Dzmitry. "Reshaping Nations: Population Politics and Sovietization in the Polish-Soviet Borderlands, 1944–1948." PhD diss., Princeton University, 2019.

Hasenclever, Jörn. *Wehrmacht und Besatzungspolitik in der Sowjetunion: Die Befehlshaber der rückwärtigen Heeresgebiete 1941–1943*. Paderborn: Schöningh, 2010.

Hasselmann, Anne. "Zwischen Dokumentation und Zeitzeugenschaft: Die Museen in Moskau, Minsk und Tscheljabinsk 1941–1956." PhD diss., University of Basel, 2019.

Havryshko, Marta. "Women's Body as Battlefield: Sexual Violence during Soviet Counterinsurgency in Western Ukraine in the [sic] 1944–1953." *Euxeinos: Governance and Culture in the Black Sea Region* 9, no. 27 (2019): 85–113.

Hayner, Pricilla. *Unspeakable Truth: Transitional Justice and the Challenge of Truth Commissions*. 2nd ed. New York: Routledge, 2011.

Hedeler, Wladislaw. *Chronik der Moskauer Schauprozesse 1936, 1937 und 1938: Planung, Inszenierung, und Wirkung*. Berlin: Akademie, 2003.

Heer, Hannes. "Killing Fields: The Wehrmacht and the Holocaust in Belorussia, 1941–1942." *Holocaust and Genocide Studies* 11, no. 1 (1997): 79–101.

Hilger, Andreas. *Deutsche Kriegsgefangene in der Sowjetunion, 1941–1956: Kriegsgefangenenpolitik, Lageralltag und Erinnerung*. Essen: Klartext, 2000.

Hilger, Andreas, Nikita Petrov, and Günther Wagenlehner. "Der 'Ukaz 43': Entstehung und Problematik des Dekrets des Präsidiums des Obersten Sowjets vom 19. April 1943." In *Sowjetische Militärtribunale*. Vol. 1: *Die Verurteilung deutscher Kriegsgefangener 1941–1953*, edited by Andreas Hilger, Ute Schmidt, and Günther Wagenlehner, 177–209. Cologne: Böhlau 2001.

Himka, John-Paul. "The Lviv Pogrom of 1941: The Germans, Ukrainian Nationalists, and the Carnival Crowd." *Canadian Slavonic Papers/Revue canadienne des slavistes* 53, no. 2–4 (2011): 209–43.

Hirsch, Francine. *Empire of Nations: Ethnographic Knowledge and the Making of the Soviet Union*. Ithaca: Cornell University Press, 2005.

Hirsch, Francine. *Soviet Judgment at Nuremberg: A New History of the International Military Tribunal after World War II*. Oxford: Oxford University Press, 2020.

Hirszowicz, Lukasz. "The Holocaust in the Soviet Mirror." In *The Holocaust in the Soviet Union: Studies and Sources on the Destruction of the Jews in the Nazi-Occupied Territories of the USSR, 1941–1945*, edited by Lucjan Dobroszyski and Jeffrey Gurock, 39–46. Armonk: M. E. Sharpe, 1993.

Hobsbawm, Eric. *The Age of Extremes: The Short Twentieth Century, 1914–1991*. London: Michael Joseph, 1995.

Holquist, Peter. *Making War, Forging Revolution: Russia's Continuum of Crisis, 1914–1921*. Cambridge, MA: Harvard University Press, 2002.

Hryciuk, Grzegorz. "Victims 1939–1941: The Soviet Repressions in Eastern Poland." In *Shared History—Divided Memory: Jews and Others in Soviet-Occupied Poland, 1939–1941*, edited by Elazar Barkan, Elizabeth A. Cole, and Kai Struve, 173–200. Leipzig: Leipziger Universitätsverlag, 2007.

Huyse, Luc. "The Criminal Justice System as a Political Actor in Regime Transitions: The Case of Belgium, 1944–50." In *The Politics of Retribution in Europe: World War II and Its Aftermath*, edited by István Deák, Jan T. Gross, and Tony Judt, 157–72. Princeton: Princeton University Press, 2000.

Huzhaloŭski, Aleksiandr, ed. *". . . Milastsi Vashai prosim", al'bo Adzin hod u naveishai historyi Belarusi, adliustravany ŭ listakh, zaiavakh, skarhakh i inshykh formakh zvarotu hramadzian*. Minsk: n.p., 2006.

Ioffe, Emanuil. *Lavrentii Tsanava: Ego nazyvali "Belorusskii Beriia."* Minsk: Adukatsyia i vykhavanne, 2016.

Ioffe, Emanuil. *Ot Miasnikova do Malofeeva: Kto rukovodil BSSR*. Minsk: Belarus', 2008.

Ioffe, Emanuil. *Panteleimon Ponomarenko: "Zheleznyi" stalinist*. Minsk: Kharvest, 2015.

Itogi vsesoiuznoi perepisi naseleniia 1959 goda: Belorusskaia SSR. Moscow: Gosstatizdat Tsentral'nogo statisticheskogo upravleniia pri Sovete Ministrov SSSR, 1963.

Ivanova, Galina. *Istoriia GULAGa 1918–1958: Sotsial'no-ekonomicheskii i politiko-pravovoi aspekty*. Moscow: Nauka, 2006.

Izhar, Neomi. *Chasia Bornstein-Bielicka: One of the Few. A Resistance Fighter and Educator, 1939–1947*. Jerusalem: Yad Vashem, 2009.

Jakel, Elena. "'Ukraine without Jews'? Nationality and Belonging in Soviet Ukraine, 1943–48." PhD diss., University of Illinois, Urbana-Champaign, 2014.

Jansen, Marc. *A Show Trial under Lenin: The Trial of the Socialist Revolutionaries, Moscow 1922*. The Hague: Martinus Nijhoff, 1982.

Jardim, Tomaz. *The Mauthausen Trial: American Military Justice in Germany*. Cambridge, MA: Harvard University Press, 2012.

Jones, Jeffrey. *Everyday Life and the "Reconstruction" of Soviet Russia during and after the Great Patriotic War, 1943–1948*. Bloomington: Indiana University Press, 2008.

Jones, Polly. *Myth, Memory, Trauma: Rethinking the Stalinist Past in the Soviet Union, 1953–1970*. New Haven: Yale University Press, 2016.

Judt, Tony. *Postwar: A History of Europe since 1945*. London: Penguin, 2005.

Kagan, Jack, and Dov Cohen. *Surviving the Holocaust with the Russian Jewish Partisans*. London: Vallentine Mitchell, 1998.

Kaganovitch, Albert. *The Long Life and Swift Death of Jewish Rechitsa: A Community in Belarus, 1625–2000*. Madison: University of Wisconsin Press, 2013.

Kalinin, Petr. *Partizanskaia respublika*. Moscow: Voenizdat, 1964. 2nd ed. Minsk: Belarus', 1968.

Kalyvas, Stathis N. *The Logic of Violence in Civil War*. Cambridge: Cambridge University Press, 2006.

Kashtalian, Iryna. "Belarus' pad uplyvam palitychnykh represii savetskaha chasu (1917–1953 hh.)." In *Mestsy pamiatsi akhviaraŭ kamunizmu ŭ Belarusi*, edited by Anna Kaminski, 9–20. Berlin: Bundesstiftung Aufarbeitung, 2011.

Kashtalian, Iryna. *The Repressive Factors of the USSR's Internal Policy and Everyday Life of the Belarusian Society (1944–1953)*. Wiesbaden: Harrassowitz, 2016.

Kaminski, Anna, ed. *Mestsy pamiatsi akhviaraŭ kamunizmu ŭ Belarusi*. Berlin: Bundesstiftung Aufarbeitung, 2011.

Kessler, Gijs. "The Passport System and State Control over Population Flows in the Soviet Union, 1932–1940." *Cahiers du monde russe* 42, no. 2–4 (2001): 477–504.

Khartanovich, Vladimir. *Gody nashei molodosti: Vospominaniia. Poslevoennyi mirnyi trud: Vospominaniia*. Slonim: Slonimskaia tipografiia, 2006.

Khatskevich, A. F. "Probivaetsia pravda polveka: Novaia stranitsa istorii Minskogo antifashistskogo podpolia." *Nioman*, no. 4 (1992): 121–30.

Khaustov, V. N., V. P. Naumov, and N. S. Plotnikova, eds. *Lubianka: Stalin i glavnoe upravlenie gosbezopasnosti NKVD 1937–1938*. Moscow: Mezhdunarodnyi fond "Demokratiia," 2004.

Khursik, Viktar. *Kroŭ i popel Drazhna: Historyia partyzanskaha zlachynstva*. Minsk: Vydavets Khursik, 2003.

Kipp, Michaela. *"Grossreinemachen im Osten": Feindbilder in deutschen Feldpostbriefen im Zweiten Weltkrieg*. Frankfurt am Main: Campus, 2014.

Kirschenbaum, Lisa. *The Legacy of the Siege of Leningrad, 1941–1995: Myth, Memories, and Monuments*. Cambridge: Cambridge University Press, 2006.

Kirschenbaum, Lisa. "Nothing Is Forgotten: Individual Memory and the Myth of the Great Patriotic War." In *Histories of the Aftermath: The Legacies of World War II in Comparative European Perspective*, edited by Robert Moeller and Frank Biess, 67–82. New York: Berghahn Books, 2010.

Knat'ko, Galina, et al., eds. *Belorusskie ostarbaitery: Repatriatsiia. Dokumenty i materialy*. Part 2. Minsk: NARB, 1998.

Knight, Amy. *Beria—Stalin's First Lieutenant*. Princeton: Princeton University Press, 1993.

Kohl, Paul. *"Ich wundere mich, daß ich noch lebe": Sowjetische Augenzeugen berichten*. Gütersloh: Mohn, 1990.

Kokurin, Aleksandr, et al., eds. *Prikazano pristupit': Evakuatsiia zakliuchennykh iz Belarusi v 1941 godu. Sbornik dokumentov*. Minsk: NARB, 2005.

Khlevniuk, Oleg. *Master of the House: Stalin and His Inner Circle*. New Haven: Yale University Press, 2009.

Kopstein, Jeffrey S., and Jason Wittenberg. *Intimate Violence: Anti-Jewish Pogroms on the Eve of the Holocaust*. Ithaca: Cornell University Press, 2018.

Kotkin, Stephen. *Magnetic Mountain: Stalinism as a Civilization*. Berkeley: University of California Press, 1995.

Kotkin, Stephen. "Modern Times: The Soviet Union and the Interwar Conjuncture." *Kritika: Explorations in Russian and Eurasian History* 2, no. 1 (2001): 111–64.

Kotkin, Stephen. *Stalin*. Vol. 2: *Waiting for Hitler, 1929–1941*. London: Penguin, 2017.

Kovaleniia, Aleksandr, et al., eds. *Belarus' v gody Velikoi Otechestvennoi voiny 1941–1945*. Minsk: BELTA, 2005.

Kovalev, Afanasii. *Kolokol moi—Pravda*. Minsk: Belarus', 1989.

Kozhurin, V. S. "O chislennosti naseleniia SSSR nakanune Velikoi Otechestvennoi voiny (neizvestnye dokumenty)." *Voenno-istoricheskii zhurnal*, no. 2 (1991): 21–26.

Kozlova, Lidiia. "Moia zhizn' i moia voina." *Nioman*, no. 5 (2008): 140–56.

Krajewski, Kazimierz. "Der Bezirk Nowogródek der Heimatarmee: Nationalitätenkonflikte und politische Verhältnisse 1939–1945." In *Die polnische Heimatarmee: Geschichte und Mythos der Armia Krajowa seit dem Zweiten Weltkrieg*, edited by Bernhard Chiari, 563–85. Munich: Oldenbourg, 2003.

Krivosheev, Grigorii, ed. *Soviet Casualties and Combat Losses in the Twentieth Century*. London: Greenhill, 1997.

Kudryashov, Sergey, and Vanessa Voisin. "The Early Stages of Legal Purges in Soviet Russia (1941–1945)." *Cahiers du monde russe* 49, no. 2 (2008): 263–95.

Kumanev, Georgii. *Riadom so Stalinym: Otkrovennye svidetel'stva. Vstrechi, besedy, interv'iu, dokumenty*. Moscow: Bylina, 1999.

Kushner, Barak. *Men to Devils, Devils to Men: Japanese War Crimes and Chinese Justice*. Cambridge, MA: Harvard University Press, 2015.

Kwon, Heonik. *After the Massacre: Commemoration and Consolation in Ha My and My Lai*. Berkeley: University of California Press, 2006.

Kwon, Heonik. *Ghosts of War in Vietnam*. Cambridge: Cambridge University Press, 2008.

Langer, Lawrence L. "The Dilemma of Choice in the Deathcamps." *Centerpoint* 4, no. 1 (1980): 222–32.

Lawson, Konrad M. "Wartime Atrocities and the Politics of Treason in the Ruins of the Japanese Empire, 1937–1953." PhD diss., Harvard University, 2012.

Lebedev, Petr. "Vozvrashchenie." *Nioman*, no. 10 (1986): 135–54.

Lewis, Simon. *Belarus—Alternative Visions: Nation, Memory, and Cosmopolitanism*. Abingdon: Routledge, 2019.

Lin'kov, Grigorii. *Voina v tylu vraga.* Moscow: Sovetskii pisatel', 1947.

Lipai, Ivan. "Eto gor'koe slovo 'svoboda' . . ." *Nioman,* no. 3 (1996): 150–209.

Litin, Aleksandr, and Ida Shenderovich, eds. *Istoriia mogilevskogo evreistva: Dokumenty i liudi. Nauchno-populiarnye ocherki i zhizneopisaniia.* Book 2, part 2. Mogilev: Ameliia Print, 2009.

Litvin, Aleksei. "K voprosu o kolichestve liudskikh poter' Belarusi v gody Velikoi Otechestvennoi voiny (1941–1945 gg.)." In *Belarus' u XX stahoddzi,* vol. 1, edited by Igor' Kuznetsov and Iakov Basin. Minsk: n.p., 2002. http://jewishfreedom.org/page611.html.

Litvin, Aleksei. "Mestnaia vspomogatel'naia politsiia na territorrii Belarusi (iiul' 1941–iiul' 1944 gg.)." In *Belarus' u XX stahoddzi,* vol. 2, edited by Igor' Kuznetsov and Iakov Basin. Minsk: n.p., 2003. http://jewishfreedom.org/page647.html.

Litvin, Aleksei, and E. A. Kasperovich. "Trudnaia pamiat' voiny." *Nioman,* no. 7 (1994): 152–56.

Liulevicius, Vejas Gabriel. *War Land on the Eastern Front: Culture, National Identity, and German Occupation in World War I.* Cambridge: Cambridge University Press, 2000.

Liul'kina, E. I., ed. *Voina i ukradennye gody: Zhivye svidetel'stva ostarbaiterov Belarusi.* Minsk: I. P. Logvinov, 2010.

Livshin, A. Ia., I. B. Orlov, and O. V. Khlevniuk, eds. *Pis'ma vo vlast', 1928–1939: Zaiavleniia, zhaloby, donosy, pis'ma v gosudarstvennye struktury i sovetskim vozhdiam.* Moscow: ROSSPEN, 2002.

Lohr, Eric. *Nationalizing the Russian Empire: The Campaign against Enemy Aliens during World War I.* Cambridge, MA: Harvard University Press, 2003.

Lohr, Eric. "The Russian Army and the Jews: Mass Deportation, Hostages, and Violence during World War I." *Russian Review* 60, no. 3 (2001): 404–19.

Lower, Wendy. "Pogroms, Mob Violence, and Genocide in Western Ukraine, Summer 1941: Varied Histories, Explanations, and Comparisons." *Journal of Genocide Research* 13, no. 3 (2011): 217–46.

Mallmann, Klaus-Michael, Andrej Angrick, Jürgen Matthäus, and Martin Cüppers, eds. *Die "Ereignismeldungen UdSSR" 1941: Dokumente der Einsatzgruppen in der Sowjetunion.* Vol. 1. Darmstadt: Wissenschaftliche Buchgesellschaft, 2011.

Mały rocznik statystyczny Polski: Wrzesień 1939–czerwiec 1941. Warsaw: Zakład Wydawnictw Statystycznych, 1990.

Manela, Erez. *The Wilsonian Moment: Self-Determination and the International Origins of Anticolonial Nationalism.* Oxford: Oxford University Press, 2007.

Manley, Rebecca. *To the Tashkent Station: Evacuation and Survival in the Soviet Union at War.* Ithaca: Cornell University Press, 2009.

Mann, Yan. "Contested Memory: Writing the Great Patriotic War's Official History during Khrushchev's Thaw." PhD diss., Arizona State University, 2016.

Marples, David. "Kuropaty: The Investigation of a Stalinist Historical Controversy." *Slavic Review* 53, no. 2 (1994): 513–23.

Marples, David. *"Our Glorious Past": Lukashenka's Belarus and the Great Patriotic War.* Stuttgart: ibidem, 2014.

Martin, Terry. *The Affirmative Action Empire: Nations and Nationalism in the Soviet Union, 1923–1939.* Ithaca: Cornell University Press, 2001.

Mazower, Mark. *Hitler's Empire: Nazi Rule in Occupied Europe.* London: Penguin, 2009.

McBride, Jared. "'A Sea of Blood and Tears': Ethnic Diversity and Mass Violence in Nazi-Occupied Volhynia, Ukraine, 1941–1944." PhD diss., University of California, Los Angeles, 2014.

Melnyk, Oleksandr. "Historical Politics, Legitimacy Contests, and the (Re-)Construction of Political Communities in Ukraine during the Second World War." PhD diss., University of Toronto, 2016.

Mendelsohn, Ezra. *The Jews of East Central Europe between the Two World Wars.* Bloomington: Indiana University Press, 1983.

Merridale, Catherine. "The 1937 Census and the Limits of Stalinist Rule." *Historical Journal* 39, no. 1 (1996): 225–40.

Mertelsmann, Olaf, and Aigi Rahi-Tamm. "Cleansing and Compromise: The Estonian SSR in 1944–1945." *Cahiers du monde russe* 49, 2 (2008): 319–40.

Michlic, Joanna. "The Soviet Occupation of Poland, 1939–1941, and the Stereotype of the Anti-Polish and Pro-Soviet Jew." *Jewish Social Studies* 13, no. 3 (2007): 135–76.

Michlic-Coren, Joanna. "Anti-Jewish Violence in Poland, 1918–1939 and 1945–1947." *Polin: Studies in Polish Jewry* 13 (2000): 34–61.

Miliakova, L. B., ed. *Kniga pogromov: Pogromy na Ukraine, v Belorussii i evropeiskoi chasti Rossii v period grazhdanskoi voiny 1918–1922 gg. Sbornik dokumentov.* Moscow: ROSSPEN, 2007.

Minow, Martha. *Between Vengeance and Forgiveness: Facing History after Genocide and Mass Violence.* Boston: Beacon, 1998.

Mor, Litman. *The War for Life.* Tel Aviv: n.p., 2007.

Mozokhin, Oleg. *Pravo na repressii: Vnesudebnye polnomochiia organov gosudarstvennoi bezopasnosti. Statisticheskie svedeniia o deiatel'nosti VChK-OGPU-NKVD-MGB SSSR (1918–1953).* Moscow: Kuchkovo pole, 2006.

Mühlhäuser, Regina. *Eroberungen: Sexuelle Gewalttaten und intime Beziehungen deutscher Soldaten in der Sowjetunion, 1941–1945.* Hamburg: Hamburger Edition, 2010.

Musial, Bogdan. *Sowjetische Partisanen 1941–1944: Mythos und Wirklichkeit.* Paderborn: Schöningh, 2009.

Musial, Bogdan, ed. *Sowjetische Partisanen in Weißrußland: Innenansichten aus dem Gebiet Baranoviči, 1941–1944. Eine Dokumentation.* Munich: De Gruyter, 2004.

Myshanka (Kolpenitskii), David. *Komu zhit' i komu umeret'* . . . Tel Aviv: M+, 2002.

Nankivell, Joice M., and Sydney Loch. *The River of a Hundred Ways: Life in the War-Devastated Areas of Eastern Poland.* London: Allen and Unwin, 1924.

Nosevich, Viacheslav. *Traditsionnaia belorusskaia derevnia v evropeiskoi perspektive.* Minsk: Tekhnalohiia, 2004.

Novick, Peter. *The Holocaust in American Life.* Boston: Houghton Mifflin, 1999.

Novikov, Ivan. *Bessmertie Minska.* Minsk: Belarus', 1977.

Novikov, Ivan. *Minsk—gorod geroi.* Moscow: Voenizdat, 1986.

Novikov, Ivan. *O partiinom podpol'e v Minske v gody Velikoi Otechestvennoi voiny (iiun' 1941–iiul' 1944 gg.).* Minsk: Gosizdat, 1961.

Obryn'ba, Nikolai. *Red Partisan: The Memoir of a Soviet Resistance Fighter on the Eastern Front.* Washington, DC: Potomac Books, 2007.

Ovsishcher, Lev. *Vozvrashchenie.* Jerusalem: Kakhol'-Lavan, 1988.

Penter, Tanja. *Kohle für Stalin und Hitler: Arbeiten und Leben im Donbass, 1929–1953*. Essen: Klartext, 2010.

Penter, Tanja. "Local Collaborators on Trial: Soviet War Crimes Trials under Stalin (1943–1953)." *Cahiers du monde russe* 49, no. 2 (2008): 341–64.

Pervaia vseobshchaia perepis' naseleniia Rossiiskoi imperii 1897 g. St. Petersburg: Izdanie Tsentral'nago statisticheskago komiteta ministerstva vnutrennikh del, 1900–1904.

Petrov, Nikita V., and Arsenii B. Roginskii, "'Pol'skaia operatsiia' NKVD 1937–1938 gg." In *Repressii protiv poliakov i pol'skikh grazhdan*, edited by Aleksandr E. Gur'ianov, 22–43. Moscow: Zven'ia, 1997.

Pinchuk, Ben-Chion. *Shtetl Jews under Soviet Rule: Eastern Poland on the Eve of the Holocaust*. Oxford: Basil Blackwell, 1990.

Pivovarchik, S. "Tragedii pervoi mirovoi voiny: 'Evreishpiony.' Po materialam Natsional'nogo istoricheskogo archiva Belarusi v Grodno." In *Mirovoi krizis 1914–1920 godov i sud'ba vostochnoevropeiskogo evreistva*, edited by Oleg Budnitskii, 70–83. Moscow: ROSSPEN, 2005.

Pohl, Dieter. *Die Herrschaft der Wehrmacht: Deutsche Militärbesatzung und einheimische Bevölkerung in der Sowjetunion 1941–1944*. Munich: Oldenbourg, 2008.

Polian, Pavel. *Against Their Will: The History and Geography of Forced Migrations in the USSR*. Budapest: Central European University Press, 2004.

Polian, Pavel. *Deportiert nach Hause: Sowjetische Kriegsgefangene im "Dritten Reich" und ihre Repatriierung*. Munich: Oldenbourg, 2001.

Pollack, Martin, ed. *Von Minsk nach Manhattan: Polnische Reportagen*. Vienna: Zsolnay, 2006.

Ponomarenko, Panteleimon. "Dnevnik." *Nioman*, no. 8 (2008): 173–83.

Ponomarenko, Panteleimon. "Sobytiia moei zhizni." Part 1. *Nioman*, no. 3 (1992): 150–77. Part 2. *Nioman*, no. 4 (1992): 132–58.

Ponomarenko, Panteleimon. *Tridtsat' let sovetskoi vlasti v Belorussii*. Minsk: Gosudarstvennoe izdatel'stvo BSSR, 1947.

Ponomarenko, Panteleimon. *Vsenarodnaia bor'ba v tylu nemetsko-fashistskikh zakhvatchikov 1941–1944*. Moscow: Nauka, 1986.

Popov, Aleksei. *15 vstrech s generalom KGB Bel'chenko*. Moscow: OLMA-Press, 2002.

Prot'ko, Tat'iana. *Stanovlenie sovetskoi totalitarnoi sistemy v Belarusi (1917–1941 gg.)*. Minsk: Tesei, 2002.

Prusin, Alexander V. "'Fascist Criminals to the Gallows!' The Holocaust and Soviet War Crimes Trials, December 1945–February 1946." *Holocaust and Genocide Studies* 17, no. 1 (2003): 1–30.

Prusin, Alexander V. *The Lands Between: Conflict in the East European Borderlands, 1870–1992*. Oxford: Oxford University Press, 2010.

Prusin, Alexander V. "The 'Second Wave' of Soviet Justice: The 1960s War Crimes Trials." In *Rethinking Holocaust Justice: Essays across Disciplines*, edited by Norman J. W. Goda, 129–37. New York: Berghahn Books, 2018.

Quinkert, Babette. "Einleitung." In *Deutsche Besatzung in der Sowjetunion 1941–1944: Vernichtungskrieg, Reaktionen, Erinnerung*, edited by Babette Quinkert and Jörg Morré, 11–23. Paderborn: Schöningh, 2014.

Ramanava, Iryna. "The 'Lepel Case" and Regional Show Trials in the Belarusian Soviet Socialist Republic (BSSR) in 1937." In *Political and Transitional Justice in Germany, Poland and the Soviet Union from the 1930s to the 1950s*, edited by Magnus Brechtken, Władisław Bułhak, and Jürgen Zarusky, 54–73. Göttingen: Wallstein, 2019.

Ramanava, Iryna. "Zhytstse va ŭmovakh savetskaha pahranichcha: Belaruskae pahranichcha pa savetski bok dziarzhaŭnai miazhy ŭ 1930-ia hh." In *Pograniczna Białorusi w perspektywie interdyscyplinarnej—Pamezhzhy Belarusi ŭ mizhdystsyplinarnai perspektyve*, edited by Elżbieta Smułkowa and Anna Engelking, 73–101. Warsaw: DiG, 2007.

Rebitschek, Immo. "Feindbilder auf dem Prüfstand: Sowjetische Kollaborateure im Fokus der Revisionskommissionen, 1954 und 1955." *Jahrbücher für Geschichte Osteuropas* 65, no. 2 (2017): 262–81.

Rein, Leonid. *The Kings and the Pawns: Collaboration in Byelorussia during World War II*. New York: Berghahn Books, 2011.

Rentrop, Petra. *Tatorte der "Endlösung": Das Ghetto Minsk und die Vernichtungsstätte von Maly Trostinez*. Berlin: Metropol, 2011.

Rittersporn, Gabor T. "Terror and Soviet Legality: Police vs. Judiciary, 1933–1940." In *Anatomy of Terror: Political Violence under Stalin*, edited by James Harris, 176–91. Oxford: Oxford University Press, 2013.

Romanovsky, Daniel. "The Holocaust in the Eyes of Homo Sovieticus: A Survey Based on Northeastern Belorussia and Northwestern Russia." *Holocaust and Genocide Studies* 13, no. 3 (1999): 355–82.

Rosenblat, Evgenij. "Belarus: Specific Features of the Region's Jewish Collaboration and Resistance." In *Collaboration and Resistance during the Holocaust: Belarus, Estonia, Latvia, Lithuania*, edited by David Gaunt, Paul A. Levine, and Laura Palosuo, 261–82. Bern: Peter Lang, 2004.

Rossoliński-Liebe, Grzegorz. "Der Verlauf und die Täter des Lemberger Pogroms vom Sommer 1941: Zum aktuellen Stand der Forschung." *Jahrbuch für Antisemitismusforschung* 22 (2013): 207–43.

Rott, Vladimir. *Naperekor sud'be*. Book 1: *Radosti pechalei: Garadna-Mishkol'ts-Bobruisk-Tomsk-Tol'iatti-Toronto*. Moscow: B.S.G.-Press, 2008.

Rubenstein, Joshua, and Ilya Altman, eds. *The Unknown Black Book: The Holocaust in the German-Occupied Soviet Territories*. Bloomington: Indiana University Press, 2008.

Ruchniewicz, Małgorzata. *Wieś zachodniobiałoruska 1944–1953: Wybrane aspekty*. Wrocław: Wydawnistwo Uniwersytet Wrocławskiego, 2010.

Rudling, Per Anders. "'For a Heroic Belarus!' The Great Patriotic War as Identity Marker in the Lukashenka and Soviet Belarusian Discourses." *Nationalities Affairs (Sprawy Narodowościowe)* 32 (2008): 43–62.

Rudling, Per Anders. "The Khatyn Massacre in Belorussia: A Historical Controversy Revisited." *Holocaust and Genocide Studies* 26, no. 1 (2012): 29–58.

Rudling, Per Anders. *The Rise and Fall of Belarusian Nationalism, 1906–1931*. Pittsburgh: University of Pittsburgh Press, 2015.

Rudling, Per Anders. "Terror and Local Collaboration in Occupied Belarus: The Case of the *Schutzmannschaft* Battalion 118. I. Background." *Historical Yearbook* 8 (2011): 195–214.

Sanborn, Joshua. *Imperial Apocalypse: The Great War and the Destruction of the Russian Empire*. Oxford: Oxford University Press, 2015.

Savchenko, Andrew. *Belarus—a Perpetual Borderland*. Leiden: Brill, 2009.

Savik, Lidziia. *Kosmas belarusa: Zhytstsiapis Barysa Uladzimiravicha Kita, asvetnika, vuchonaha, patryiota*. Minsk: Minskaia drukarskaia fabryka, 1996.

Shamalava, Volia. "Tseni vainy: Politseiskiia i partyzany ŭ pamiatsi nasel'nitstva belaruskaŭ veski." *Homo Historicus: Hadavik antrapalahichnai historyi* (2008): 384–89.

Sharp, Dustin N. *Rethinking Transitional Justice for the Twenty-First Century: Beyond the End of History*. Cambridge: Cambridge University Press, 2018.

Shearer, David. *Policing Stalin's Socialism: Repression and Social Order in the Soviet Union, 1924–1953*. New Haven: Yale University Press, 2009.

Shklar, Judith N. *Legalism: Law, Morals, and Political Trials*. 2nd ed. Cambridge, MA: Harvard University Press, 1986.

Shore, Marci. *Caviar and Ashes: A Warsaw's Generation's Life and Death in Marxism, 1918–1968*. New Haven: Yale University Press, 2006.

Siebert, Diana. *Bäuerliche Alltagsstrategien in der Belarussischen SSR (1921–1941): Die Zerstörung patriarchalischer Familienwirtschaft*. Stuttgart: Frank Steiner, 1998.

Simpson, Gerry. *Law, War and Crime: War Crimes Trials and the Reinvention of International Law*. Cambridge: Polity, 2007.

Sklokina, Iryna. "Trials of Nazi Collaborators in the Context of Soviet Propaganda, Nationality Policy, and the Cold War (1960–80s)." In *Collaboration in Eastern Europe during the Second World War and the Holocaust*, edited by Peter Black, Béla Rásky, and Marianne Windsperger, 67–86. Vienna: VWI, 2019.

Slepyan, Kenneth. "Partisans, Civilians, and the Soviet State: An Overview." In *War in a Twilight World: Partisan and Anti-Partisan Warfare in Eastern Europe, 1939–45*, edited by Ben Shepherd and Juliette Pattinson, 35–57. Basingstoke: Palgrave MacMillan, 2010.

Slepyan, Kenneth. *Stalin's Guerrillas: Soviet Partisans in World War II*. Lawrence: University Press of Kansas, 2006.

Small, Martin, and Vic Shayne. *Remember Us: From My Shtetl through the Holocaust*. New York: iUniverse, 2008.

Smilovitskii, Leonid. *Katastrofa evreev v Belorussii, 1941–1944 gg.* Tel Aviv: Biblioteka Matveia Chernogo, 2000.

Smilovitsky, Leonid. "Antisemitism in the Soviet Partisan Movement, 1941–1944: The Case of Belorussia." *Holocaust and Genocide Studies* 20, no. 2 (2006): 207–34.

Smilovitsky, Leonid. "A Demographic Profile of the Jews in Belorussia from the Pre-War Time to the Post-War Time." *Journal of Genocide Research* 5, no. 1 (2003): 117–29.

Smilovitsky, Leonid. "Righteous Gentiles, the Partisans, and Jewish Survival in Belorussia, 1941–1944." *Holocaust and Genocide Studies* 11, no. 3 (1997): 301–29.

Smilovitsky, Leonid. "The Struggle of Belorussian Jews for the Restitution of Possessions and Housing in the First Postwar Decade." *East European Jewish Affairs* 30, no. 2 (2000): 53–70.

Smith, Mark B. *Property of Communists: The Urban Housing Program from Stalin to Khrushchev*. DeKalb: Northern Illinois University Press, 2010.

Smolar, Hersh. *Fun Minsker geto*. Minsk: Der Emes, 1946.

Smolar, Hersh. *The Minsk Ghetto: Soviet-Jewish Partisans against the Nazis*. New York: Holocaust Library, 1989.

Smolar, Hersh. *Mstiteli getto*. Moscow: Der Emes, 1947.

Smolar, Hersh. *Resistance in Minsk*. Oakland: Magnes Memorial Museum, 1966.

Smolar, Hersh. *Sovietishe Yidn hinter geto-tsoymen*. Tel Aviv: Y. L. Perets, 1985.

Smolenchuk, Aleksandr (Ales' Smalianchuk). "Pamiat' na pogranich'e (na primere pamiati o Vtoroi mirovoi voine)." In *Belorusy: Natsiia pogranich'ia*, edited by Aleksandr Kravtsevich, Aleksandr Smolenchuk, and Sergei Tokt', 159–206. Vilnius: EGU, 2011.

Smoliar, Girsh. "'Teplaia' vstrecha evreev-partizan v osvobozhdennom Minske." *Vozrozhdenie*, no. 4–5 (1975): 178–85.

Snyder, Timothy. *Bloodlands: Europe between Hitler and Stalin*. New York: Basic Books, 2010.

Snyder, Timothy. *The Reconstruction of Nations: Poland, Ukraine, Lithuania, Belarus, 1569–1999*. New Haven: Yale University Press, 2003.

Solonari, Vladimir. "Patterns of Violence: The Local Population and the Mass Murder of Jews in Bessarabia and Northern Bukovina, July–August 1941." *Kritika: Explorations in Russian and Eurasian History* 8, no. 4 (2007): 749–87.

Sorokina, Marina. "People and Procedures: Toward a History of the Investigation of Nazi Crimes in the USSR." *Kritika: Explorations in Russian and Eurasian History* 6, no. 4 (2005): 797–831.

Stalin, Joseph. *On the Great Patriotic War of the Soviet Union: Speeches, Orders of the Day, and Answers to Foreign Press Correspondents*. Moscow: Foreign Languages Publishing House, 1944.

Stalin, Joseph. *Problems of Leninism*. Moscow: Foreign Languages Publishing House, 1947.

Stevens, Edmund. *Russia Is No Riddle*. New York: Greenberg Publishers, 1945.

Statiev, Alexander. *The Soviet Counterinsurgency in the Western Borderlands*. Cambridge: Cambridge University Press, 2010.

Statiev, Alexander. "Soviet Partisan Violence against Soviet Civilians: Targeting their Own." *Europe-Asia Studies* 66, no. 9 (2014): 1525–52.

Stone, David R. "Operations on the Eastern Front, 1941–1945," in *The Cambridge History of the Second World War*, vol. 1, edited by John Ferris and Evan Mawdsley, 331–57. Cambridge: Cambridge University Press, 2015.

Stover, Eric, and Harvey M. Weinstein, eds. *My Neighbor, My Enemy: Justice and Community in the Aftermath of Mass Atrocity*. Cambridge: Cambridge University Press, 2004.

Streit, Christian. *Keine Kameraden: Die Wehrmacht und die sowjetischen Kriegsgefangenen 1941–1945*. 2nd ed. Bonn: Dietz, 1991.

Struve, Kai. "Anti-Jewish Violence in the Summer of 1941 in Eastern Galicia and Beyond." In *Romania and the Holocaust: Events—Contexts—Aftermath*, edited by Simon Geissbühler, 89–113. Stuttgart: ibidem, 2016.

Struve, Kai. *Deutsche Herrschaft, ukrainischer Nationalismus, antijüdische Gewalt: Der Sommer 1941 in der Westukraine*. Berlin: De Gruyter Oldenbourg, 2015.

Svetlov, Vladimir. "'Osvobozhdennyi' Minsk 1944 goda." In *Repressivnaia politika sovetskoi vlasti v Belarusi: Sbornik nauchnykh rabot*, edited by Igor' N. Kuznetsov and Iakov Basin, 2:333–45. Minsk: Memorial, 2007.

Sweets, John. *Choices in Vichy France: The French under Nazi Occupation*. New York: Oxford University Press, 1994.

Szumski, Jan. *Sowietyzacja Zachodniej Białorusi 1944–1953: Propaganda i edukacja w służbie ideologii*. Cracow: Arcana, 2010.

Tec, Nechama. *Defiance: The True Story of the Bielski Partisans*. Oxford: Oxford University Press, 1993.

Teitel, Ruti G. *Globalizing Transitional Justice: Contemporary Essays*. Oxford: Oxford University Press, 2014.

Teitel, Ruti G. *Transitional Justice*. Oxford: Oxford University Press, 2000.

Tokel, Shammai. "The Liquidation of the Stolin Jewish Community." Translated by Meir Razy. In *Stolin: A Memorial to the Jewish Communities of Stolin and Vicinity*, edited by A. Avatichi and Y. Ben-Zakkai, 216–22. Tel Aviv, 1952. Partial English translation of Hebrew original. https://www.jewishgen.org/yizkor/stolin/sto208.html#Page216.

Totani, Yuma. *Justice in Asia and the Pacific Region, 1945–1952: Allied War Crimes Prosecution*. Cambridge: Cambridge University Press, 2015.

Trainin, Aron, Vladimir Men'shagin, and Zinaida Vyshinskaia. *Ugolovnyi kodeks RSFSR: Kommentarii*. Moscow: Iuridicheskoe izdatel'stvo NKIu SSSR, 1944.

Tsanava, Lavrentii. *Vsenarodnaia partizanskaia voina v Belorussii protiv fashistskikh zakhvatchikov.* Part 1: *Zarozhdenie i razvitie partizanskogo dvizheniia*. Minsk: Gosizdat BSSR, 1949.

Tumarkin, Nina. *The Living and the Dead: The Rise and Fall of the Cult of World War II in Russia*. New York: Basic Books, 1994.

Tumblety, Joan. "Introduction: Working with Memory as Source and Subject." In *Memory and History: Understanding Memory as Source and Subject*, edited by Joan Tumblety, 1–16. Abingdon: Routledge, 2013.

Ueberschär, Gerd, and Wolfram Wette, eds. *"Unternehmen Barbarossa": Der deutsche Überfall auf die Sowjetunion 1941. Berichte, Analysen, Dokumente*. Paderborn: Schöningh, 1984.

Ugolovnyi kodeks. Moscow: Iuridicheskoe izdatel'stvo NKIu SSSR, 1940.

Ugolovnyi kodeks Belorusskoi SSR. Moscow: Iuridicheskoe izdatel'stvo NKIu SSSR, 1944.

Ugolovnyi kodeks RSFSR: Redaktsii 1926 goda s izmeneniiami i dopolneniiami do 1 iiulia 1927 goda. Moscow: Iuridicheskoe izdatel'stvo NKIu RSFSR, 1927.

Urban, Michael. *An Algebra of Soviet Power: Elite Circulation in the Belorussian Republic 1966–86*. Cambridge: Cambridge University Press, 1989.

Vakar, Nicholas. *Belorussia: The Making of a Nation*. Cambridge, MA: Harvard University Press, 1956.

Valakhanovich, Igor'. *Antisovetskoe podpol'e na territorii Belarusi v 1944–1953 gg.* Minsk: BGU, 2002.

Valiev, A. Kh. *Zapiski voennogo prokurora (Velikaia Otechestvennaia voina 1941–1945 gg.)*. Kazan': Matbugar Iorty, 2000.

Vanitskii, Arsen. "Voina i derevnia." *Nioman*, no. 4 (2000): 211–25.

Vialiki, Anatol' F. *Belarus' u savetska-pol'skikh mizhdziarzhaŭnykh adnosinakh, 1944–1959 hh. XX st.* Minsk: BDPU, 2010.

Vialiki, Anatol' F. *Na razdarozhzhy: Belarusy i paliaki ŭ chas perasialennia (1944–1946 hh.)*. Minsk: BDPU, 2005.

Vinnitsa, Gennadii. *Kholokost na okkupirovannoi territorii Vostochnoi Belarusi v 1941–1944 gg.* Minsk: Kovcheg, 2011.

Viola, Lynne. *Peasant Rebels under Stalin: Collectivization and the Culture of Peasant Resistance*. Oxford: Oxford University Press, 1996.

Viola, Lynne, V. P. Danilov, N. A. Ivnitskii, and Denis Kozlov, eds. *The War against the Peasantry, 1927–1930: The Tragedy of the Soviet Countryside*. New Haven: Yale University Press, 2005.

Virgili, Fabrice. *Shorn Women: Gender and Punishment in Liberation France*. Oxford: Berg, 2002.

Voisin, Vanessa. *L'URSS contre ses traîtres: L'Épuration soviétique, 1941–1955*. Paris: Publications de la Sorbonne, 2015.

Volkov, A. G. "Perepis' naseleniia 1937 goda: Vymysly i pravda." *Ekspress-informatsiia: Seriia "Istoriia statistiki"* 3–5, part 2 (1990): 6–63.

Waligórska, Magdalena. "Remembering the Holocaust on the Fault Lines of East and West-European Memorial Cultures: The New Memorial Complex in Trastsianets, Belarus." *Holocaust Studies* 24, no. 4 (2017): 1–25.

Walke, Anika. *Pioneers and Partisans: An Oral History of Nazi Genocide in Belorussia*. Oxford: Oxford University Press, 2015.

Weeks, Theodore. *Nation and State in Late Imperial Russia: Nationalism and Russification on the Western Frontier, 1863–1914*. DeKalb: Northern Illinois University Press, 1996.

Weeks, Theodore. *Vilnius between Nations, 1795–2000*. DeKalb: Northern Illinois University Press, 2015.

Weiner, Amir. "The Empires Pay a Visit: Gulag Returnees, East European Rebellions, and Soviet Frontier Politics." *Journal of Modern History* 78, no. 2 (2006): 333–76.

Weiner, Amir. *Making Sense of War: The Second World War and the Fate of the Bolshevik Revolution*. Princeton: Princeton University Press, 2001.

Weiner, Amir, and Aigi Rahi-Tamm. "Getting to Know You: The Soviet Surveillance System, 1939–57." *Kritika: Explorations in Russian and Eurasian History* 13, no. 1 (2012): 5–54.

Wilson, Andrew. *Belarus: The Last European Dictatorship*. New Haven: Yale University Press, 2011.

Wolozhinski Rubin, Sulia. *Against the Tide: The Story of an Unknown Partisan*. Jerusalem: Posner and Sons, 1980.

Xia, Yun. *Down with Traitors: Justice and Nationalism in Wartime China*. Seattle: University of Washington Press, 2018.

Yoran, Shalom. *The Defiant: A True Story*. Lewes: Book Guild, 1996.

Zahra, Tara. "Imagined Noncommunities: National Indifference as a Category of Analysis." *Slavic Review* 69, no. 1 (2010): 93–119.

Zanasi, Margherita. "Globalizing Hanjian: The Suzhou Trials and the Post–World War II Discourse on Collaboration." *American Historical Review* 113, no. 3 (2008): 731–51.

Żbikowski, Andrzej. "Pogroms in Northeastern Poland—Spontaneous Reactions and German Instigations." In *Shared History—Divided Memory: Jews and Others in Soviet-Occupied Poland, 1939–1941*, edited by Elazar Barkan, Elizabeth A. Cole, and Kai Struve, 315–54. Leipzig: Leipziger Universitätsverlag, 2007.

Zeidler, Manfred. *Stalinjustiz contra NS-Verbrechen: Die Kriegsverbrecherprozesse gegen deutsche Kriegsgefangene in der UdSSR in den Jahren 1943–1952. Kenntnisstand und*

Forschungsprobleme. Dresden: Hannah-Arendt-Institut für Totalitarismusforschung, 1996.

Zeltser, Arkadi. *Unwelcome Memory: Holocaust Monuments in the Soviet Union*. Jerusalem: Yad Vashem Publications, 2018.

Zel'tser, Arkadii. *Evrei sovetskoi provintsii: Vitebsk i mestechki 1917–1941*. Moscow: ROSSPEN, 2006.

Zubkova, Elena. *Poslevoennoe sovetskoe obshchestvo: Politika i povsednevnost' 1945–1953*. Moscow: ROSSPEN, 2000.

Zubkova, Elena. *Pribaltika i Kreml' 1940–1953*. Moscow: ROSSPEN, 2008.

Zubkova, Elena. "The Rivalry with Malenkov." In *Nikita Khrushchev*, edited by William Taubman, Sergei Khrushchev, and Abbott Gleason, 67–84. New Haven: Yale University Press, 2000.

Index

Page numbers in *italics* indicate illustrations.